WITHDRAWN

THE
OXFORD BOOK OF
SCHOOLDAYS

WITHDRAWN

The Oxford Book of
SCHOOLDAYS

EDITED BY

Patricia Craig

OXFORD UNIVERSITY PRESS

1994

Oxford University Press, Walton Street, Oxford OX2 6DP

Oxford New York Toronto
Delhi Bombay Calcutta Madras Karachi
Kuala Lumpur Singapore Hong Kong Tokyo
Nairobi Dar es Salaam Cape Town
Melbourne Auckland Madrid
and associated companies in
Berlin Ibadan

Oxford is a trade mark of Oxford University Press

Introduction and selection © Patricia Craig 1994

First published 1994

British Library Cataloguing in Publication Data
Data available

Library of Congress Cataloging in Publication Data
The Oxford book of schooldays / edited by Patricia Craig.
p. cm.
1. Schools—Great Britain—Literary collections.
2. Education—Great Britain—Literary collections.
3. School children—Great Britain—Literary collections.
4. English literature. I. Craig, Patricia.
PR1111.E38094 1994 820.8'0355—dc20 93–22686
ISBN 0–19–214203–8

1 3 5 7 9 10 8 6 4 2

Typeset by Best-set Typesetter Ltd., Hong Kong
Printed in Great Britain
on acid-free paper by
Bookcraft (Bath) Ltd.
Midsomer Norton, Avon

CONTENTS

INTRODUCTION

The boys, as they talked to the girls from the Marcia Blaine school, stood on the far side of their bicycles holding the handlebars, which established a protective fence of bicycle between the sexes, and the impression that at any moment the boys were likely to be away.

So opens one of the most famous school stories of the twentieth century, Muriel Spark's *The Prime of Miss Jean Brodie*, with its Edinburgh boldness and sharp definition. The point about this novel is the way in which the school setting is used to encapsulate intrigues and anomalies in the world at large—and, at the same time, since it *is* a novel and not a memoir, the author is at liberty to impose a pattern as highly wrought as she can make it over certain remembered events of her childhood. The reason for doing this, of course, is to extract the fullest flavour from the experience of having gone to school at that particular time—the 1930s—and in that place.

The Oxford Book of Schooldays aims to put together a collection of such expressive extracts, and to arrange these in such a way that an overall picture of education in Britain will emerge. If, however, the book adds up to a historical overview (as I hope it does), it's not by any means a linear or a straightforward one. Information—about conditions, attitudes to schooling, and so forth—is scattered throughout this anthology (along with plenty of diversion), but it's almost incidental to the stimulating or entertaining properties of the pieces selected. No receptive reader will fail to pick up facts about the systems prevailing at one period or another; but, more than this, it's the reactions of individuals that provide the sharpest illumination, and make the surest means of establishing an atmosphere.

Where and how are these expressed? Well, novelists like Muriel Spark get at certain truths and essences by way of invention, but it isn't only the fiction writers who have pungent material at their fingertips when it comes to the topic of education. Most people have vivid memories of their schooldays, whether liking or loathing sets the tone; and between these two comes a whole range of responses. It's a matter of luck, indeed, whether or not your temperament is at odds with the kind of schooling you're subjected to; and some of the most pointed criticisms of one educational system or another have come from those exposed to it, and unsubdued by it, at an impressionable age. 'I must digress to say that I think the manner of learning children in village schools very erroneous' (John Clare); 'it must strike the impartial, that blacking shoes, and running on errands, are rather redundant parts of a liberal education' (George Colman the Younger). As far as the latter is concerned—the issues of fagging and flogging in the public schools were debated fiercely throughout the eighteenth and nineteenth centuries, with even the young Queen Victoria and her adviser, Lord Melbourne, at one point addressing the pros and cons of resorting to the birch. The figure of the flogging schoolmaster, with gown awry and arm upraised, had become embedded in the popular imagination long before it reached its final (comic) embodiment in Dr Birchemall of the *Magnet* (a spoof within an imitation). It remains as an egregious element in the traditional public-school education, running back through celebrated floggers like Dr Keate and Dr Busby, to Roger Ascham's announcement at the beginning of *The Scholemaster*, that 'Divers Scholers of Eaton be runne awaie from the Schole for feare of beating'.

As the public schools, and their pupils, became more sophisticated, 'feare of beating' gave way in many cases to a kind of bravado about the matter: the thing was to take such punishments in one's stride. Hardihood was the first requirement of the public schoolboy ('Great schools suit best the sturdy and the rough', as Cowper has it), especially during the more rip-roaring phase in public-school history, before Dr Arnold came along to redirect the moral tone— though by all accounts carrying on in a manner no less high-handed than high-minded. 'Would you your son should be a sot or dunce' (William Cowper again), 'lascivious, headstrong or all these at once': then by all means pack him off to a school at which such excesses flourish, where no distinction is made between an assembly of boys and a bear-garden. Even as late as the 1820s, one schoolboy writing home to his mother recalls drunken Eton seniors staggering about between 'the side of the water' and their tutor's; the same boy (James Milnes Gaskell) also recounts a fight to the death between a bully and one of his victims, the cause of death apparently being the half-pint of brandy swallowed by the latter in an effort to keep his strength up. And in the mid-1840s, at Harrow—according to Augustus Hare—small boys (fags) were sent off in the evening by sixth-formers 'to bring back porter under their greatcoats'.

Drunkenness, bullying, fagging, and fisticuffs: critics of the system, indeed, had plenty to get their teeth into. Parson Adams—in Henry Fielding's *Joseph Andrews* (1742)—gave them a catchphrase, even if his famous utterance had to be reiterated seriously, and not with the playfulness intended by the novelist, to make it fit the bill: 'Public Schools are the Nurseries of all Vice and Immorality.' That was as it may be—but even so, to many observers, the public-school system still seemed the best available: 'a public school is what is necessary & is that which will add to his happiness hereafter & be a source of great satisfaction to yourself', wrote Lord William Russell to a friend about the proposed education of his son. All the other forms of schooling—through the grammar schools, free schools, charity schools, dissenting schools, parish schools, dame schools, or whatever—showed comparable defects, right down to the school set up as 'a last resource' (according to Oliver Goldsmith, writing in 1759), by the failed butcher or barber, who truly didn't have a great deal to offer in the way of sustained scholarship.

The history of education from the earliest times is tied up with politics and social history: even if, as educational historians have pointed out, the three-tier system (i.e. primary, secondary, and university education) existed in a rudimentary form from the medieval period on, it nevertheless excluded from its benefits the vast majority of the population, whose social position didn't entitle them to instruction in any branch of learning. The first English schools, the grammar schools (for the teaching of Latin) and song schools (specializing in church music) were attached to monasteries and cathedrals, and catered almost entirely for those intending to make a career in the Church. However, with the broadening of curricula, and pupils' exposure to the ideas of 'pagan' philosophers, it became inevitable that a secularizing element should enter into the business of teaching; and by the end of the fifteenth century, with the foundation of independent colleges such as Winchester and Eton, education had received the impetus it needed to expand and diversify. New grammar schools, too, tended to be state-controlled rather than church-controlled. Some provision was made at all these institutions for 'poor scholars' whose intellects were up to it, but in practice education remained largely in the hands of the upper and middle classes of English society, and things didn't change very much in this respect over the next few centuries. A Committee appointed to enquire into 'the Education of the Lower Orders' in 1816, came up with the following information: 'that a very large number of poor children are wholly without the means of Instruction, although their Parents appear to be very desirous of obtaining that advantage for them'.

Indeed. The Victorian educationalist George Griffith (an associate of Forster's) lost no opportunity to deplore—in verse or prose— the falling away from the original high standard of egalitarianism that had overtaken the so-called free schools, like the one at Kidderminster, or the Charter House school in London—'A time there was,' he says, 'when our free school was FREE, / When all were taught regardless of a fee.' The poorest children of all, in early Victorian England, had literally to be gathered up off the streets and marshalled in 'Ragged schools'—and we can't help feeling that the anonymous author of *The Philosophy of Ragged Schools* (Caroline F. Cornwallis), writing in 1851, is being a sight too sanguine when she claims that this very haphazard scheme of education had almost brought an end to juvenile crime in Aberdeen (to take that particular city). The important thing, one feels, was to bring these vagrant children under some kind of discipline—and it wasn't a recent concern, even then. Education, pronounced Charles Hoole in 1660, was the best deterrent to 'all loose kinde of behaviour . . . as it is too commonly to be seen, especially with the poorer sort, taken from the Schole and permitted to run wildeing up and down without any control'. This social commentator was at one with Dr Arnold in his view of boyhood as a state 'riotous, insolent and annoying to others, like the gaiety of a drunken man'.

During the seventeenth and eighteenth centuries, innumerable efforts to provide educational facilities for the lower-middle and working classes—according to Raymond Williams in his social study *The Long Revolution* (1961)—resulted in a 'bewildering variety of forms' of primary school, 'ranging from instruction by priests to private adventure schools' (of the sort held up to ridicule by Goldsmith, above)—village schools, hedge schools, one-room schools, church schools of various denominations, Sunday schools (in which education was equated with 'moral rescue'), and all the rest of it; and only the most exceptional among the poorer pupils stood a chance of rising within the system. Burke's 'a dreadful schism in the British nation' has a particular relevance here. And even after the Education Act of 1871, 'the poor got their elementary schooling, but the caste system in English education remained' (Cole and Postgate, *The Common People*, 1938). H. G. Wells brought his pragmatist's shrewdness to bear on this topic: the Act, he says, 'was not an Act for common universal education, it was an Act to educate the lower classes for employment on lower-class lines'. Clearly, the time had not yet come for 'the filthy, sturdy, unkillable infants of the very poor' (in Ezra Pound's words) to inherit the earth. (One recent publication—Pamela Horn's *The Victorian and Edwardian Schoolchild*, 1989—contains disturbing images of boys got up in their sisters' cast-off dresses: poverty and social embarrassment at their most extreme.)

Education for all: but how did girls come into the picture? Obscurely and in a very limited way, at least before the establishment of schools such as Queen's College and Cheltenham Ladies' College (1848 and 1854 respectively). For all practical purposes, females were lumped together with that other vast, underprivileged section of British society; though it took a pioneer like Frances Buss to spot the connection. 'I say it is unwise and unjust to fix any arbitrary limit to the education the poor are to get. . . . So with the female sex, I say, let us throw open the gates through which the temple of knowledge is to be entered', she wrote in 1865, echoing Tennyson's line: 'Fling our doors wide! All, all, not one, but all!' Many first-hand accounts of girls' education are prefaced by complaints—'When I was young, education for girls of the leisured class was decidedly indifferent,' writes Louisa, Lady Antrim (referring to the 1860s). And if you go back to Crabbe's 'The Borough' (1810), you get the 'Ladies' School' as a place of confinement: there the wretched pupils sit, on the other side of high windows, looking out resentfully on 'all the envied tumult of the town'. But this isn't the place to go into this important topic—or even to consider the development of that colourful fictional genre, the school story, in the wake of Thomas Hughes. It's worth noting, though, that first of all the growth of democracy and its effect on education, and then the world encompassed by *Tom Brown's Schooldays* and its successors, have between them fixed in most people's minds a strong sense of the ethos of school as it's built into the fabric of British society; in other words, it's only in the last 150-odd years that school, as we know it, has taken on its distinctive character.

Or perhaps 140 years would be nearer the mark: the 1840s was probably the last decade in which (as Raymond Williams has it, writing about popular literature) 'schools, almost without exception [were] shown as terrible; not only are they places of temptation and wickedness, mean, cruel and educationally ridiculous, but also they are inferior to the home and family, as a way of bringing up children'. This was the age of Lowood, Dotheboys Hall, and so forth, when children—and especially charity children—were sent to school to suffer. Though the idea of school as a kind of prison or institution lingered on—you get it in Edwin Muir's powerful vignette concerning an accumulation of childhood misery, or in the account by Herbert Read of a milk-and-dry-bread regime—it was countered on all sides by a more positive approach to the business of school attendance, whether in the decorous recollections of someone like L. E. Jones (*A Victorian Boyhood*), or Angela Brazil revelling in schoolgirlishness from about 1910 on (and gloriously laying herself open to the attentions of mockers and parodists, with her 'sixteen jolly faces . . . grinning under sixteen school hats', and all the rest).

And of course there were those with an unbounded capacity for education, who were in their element with the unsparing teacher ('Evelyn began to feel stimulated, then; to taste the same cold sparkling joy that came to her when her mind got to grips with a chemistry problem', as Josephine Elder expressed it in her children's novel of 1929, *Evelyn Finds Herself*)—which brings us on to the foremost victory for social progress in the early part of the century, the opening up of grammar and other secondary schools to intelligent children from the working class.

Scholarship pupils didn't come into their own *en masse* until after the 1944 Education Act (when inferiority was transferred to the eleven-plus failures, and away from those whose parents couldn't afford school fees—creating a new area of inequity that had to be tackled in due course); but the whole drift in educational policy, after 1900, was towards providing the best facilities for the cleverest children, wherever they were found. The process was gradual, though, and never straightforward. 'Always the pride that prevailed in this working-class school was that it succeeded in turning out [fewer] recruits for the working class than any other of its kind in the district': this wry observation from Jack Common (born in Newcastle-upon-Tyne in 1903) points up a certain irony in the situation; and the psychological problems facing children plucked out of the back streets of British cities and enrolled as pupils at their most venerable institutions, have been well documented by Richard Hoggart and others. But for all that, it was a logical, unstoppable, and democratic drift.

The Oxford Book of Schooldays is an anthology, not a history of education (though one might hope that a fair amount of history would be absorbed by any conscientious reader). It is organized in eleven sections, under various headings: 'Concerning Education', 'Schools and Schoolmasters', and so on. Within each of these sections, the extracts are assembled in a roughly chronological way, but this isn't consistent: the first aim of an anthology of this kind should be to create a rich and effective pattern out of the material selected, and this means allowing for unexpected inclusions and juxtapositions—in other words, juggling with the material until it falls into the best (that is, the most compelling) configuration. It's a subjective business of course, and probably no two readers will find themselves in agreement over the extent to which it has succeeded; but this is a built-in hazard for the anthologist. A more serious problem, with a collection like this, concerns selection: given that *every* autobiographer (to take that example) has received an education of one kind or another, where on earth do you draw the line? Well, as far as I am concerned, at dullness, perfunctoriness, a failure to be alive to the experience in some vital respect—but again, this entails continuous subjective judgement, about which I make no apology. I am sorry if some obvious or very apposite accounts of schooling have been overlooked—and given the nature of the undertaking, this is bound to have happened—but I have tried to include as wide a range of views and reviews as possible, drawing on memoirs, autobiographies, fiction, poetry, social commentaries, letters, history, essays, tracts for the times, and anything else I've been able to lay my hand on. Another aim of any anthology is to achieve a proper balance—between extracts that run on too long and an over-abundance of snippets, between the representative and the singular, between the first things that everyone thinks of in relation to a particular subject, and the enthralling discoveries that come with closer scrutiny—and I have borne this in mind, as well, while arranging the material.

With the fiction-writers, on the whole, I have found it more salutary to stick to those who were writing out of their own experience, or at least about their own time; this cuts out a lot of school stories set in the past, and other exercises in re-creation (however successful). My main concern is with the impact of the experience on the individual, and with authenticity; and over and beyond these, to trace the playing fields, assembly halls, classrooms, studies, blackboards, inkwells, entrances marked 'Boys' and 'Girls', back through history, and through their incarnation in various kinds of writing. Liveliness and cogency: these are the first qualities I've looked for, along with a facility in evocation. In some cases, it has seemed more satisfactory to include a comment on a famous work, rather than a fragment of the work itself—you get the flavour of Ernest Raymond's *Tell England*, for example, from Arthur Marshall's cheerful review of it: and as a bonus, an astringency and humour quite outside the scope of that terrible novel.

Arthur Marshall is one commentator who is resolutely unsusceptible to the allure of Greyfriars; another is George Orwell, whose famous essay, 'Boys' Weeklies', casts a critical eye on the whole pseudo-public-school ethos as filtered through the imagination of 'Frank Richards' (Charles Hamilton). Hamilton's school stories, however (in the weekly *Gem* and *Magnet*) gained an extraordinary hold, especially among young working- and lower-middle-class readers between 1908 and 1940 (when the papers ceased publication). And Bunter himself—the fatuous fatty—is an outstanding figment of popular literature, and not to be excluded from an anthology such as this. I have, though, on the whole, kept, children's stories to a minimum. Angela Brazil and one or two others are in, to boost the element of frivolity; there's a piece from *Eric* before the thing turns turgid; and *Tom Brown* of course—as a seminal narrative—is well represented. As for the rest—some scenes and episodes really suggest themselves, and aren't to be resisted: Becky Sharpe shaking the dust of her Chiswick academy off her feet at the start of *Vanity Fair*, Jane Eyre acquiring fortitude at Lowood, the young Winston Churchill making a hash of his Latin, David Blaize with his thighs soaked with rain and sweat after a game of squash, very nearly undoing the purity of the captain of games. Interspersed with these are a number of interesting peculiarities—Henry Cooke, for example, in the wilds of Northern Ireland, going to school on a pair of stilts to keep his feet out of the wet; or Hugh Miller in Scotland grappling with his teacher—the pair of them lurching about the classroom until the boy trips over a form and puts an end to the combat. Incidentally, this is an anthology mainly of *English* schooldays (just to keep it within reasonable bounds); but other parts of Great Britain and Ireland get a showing, in the interests of presenting a fuller picture.

You will encounter some striking verdicts on education in these pages—Augustus Hare, for example, roundly declaring, 'I may truly say that I never learnt anything useful at Harrow'; H. E. Bates judging the whole school process 'absurd and useless'; and, of course, the famous Auden analogy: 'the best reason I have for opposing Fascism is that at school I lived in a Fascist state'. Some incidents will provoke laughter—for example, the alarming arrival of James Lees-Milne at his prep school, or (turning to fiction) any one of the contretemps devised by H. F. Ellis for his hero A. J. Wentworth, to show us exactly what an accident-prone prep schoolmaster with an innocent approach to teaching is up against ('I understand, Wentworth,' [said the headmaster], 'that you were seen sitting in a basket in the boot-room this morning at a time when you should have been supervising one of the mathematical sets?'). Others should have more to offer in the way of dissent, impiety, relish, or whatever—or should simply fill the reader with an onrush of nostalgia, or an appalled sense of recognition. Like all anthologies, this one is garnered from source-material of the past (in this case stretching back quite a long way); it makes no attempt to predict what is likely to happen to education in the future, or even to get to grips very strenuously with recent changes of policy and their effects. What it does instead (or should do, at any rate) is to put us in touch with a few of the splendours, pleasures, absurdities, defects, injustices, horrors, and other enormities connected in any way with what can be summed up as the idiosyncratic English education.

Many people have helped with comments, suggestions, and advice while this anthology was in the course of being compiled. Thanks are due, in particular, to Jeffrey Morgan, Gerry Keenan, and Nigel May for continuous encouragement and interest in the project; and to the following for help of various kinds: Nora T. Craig, June Benn, Jenny Joseph, Robert Johnstone, Tom Paulin, Catherine Aird, James Young, Jeremy Lewis, Judith Luna, Araminta Whitley, and Bernard Hills.

P.C.

London
1993

The Oxford Book of
SCHOOLDAYS

CONCERNING EDUCATION

'When I was a boy,' said the Provost *ex cathedra*, 'they ground me at grammar but did not quite break me. That is how our middle class public schools proceed. Mine [Dulwich] was one of the lesser middle class schools, and so all the more insistent on painful tasks and conventions. Although I have remained very attached to it (for some days were happy there) I have never forgiven it for the grinding I got. It was as though they were saying, "Just because you are reading ancient literature and not some grimy subject like chemistry, just because you are preparing for Cambridge and not for an apprenticeship in accountancy or a stool in a bank, *you need not think that your studies are to yield you pleasure.* They could do—we know that. But we are determined that they should not. Nor do we want any signs from you of temperament, originality (another word for irregularity), emotion, or enthusiasm for strange byways. We shall keep you to the routine 'Hammer, Hammer, Hammer on the hard high road': no 'hunting in the hills' for you." '

Simon Raven, The Old School, 1986

MR MACQUEDY. I confess, sir, this is excellent; but I cannot see why it should be better than a Tweed salmon at Kelso.

THE REVD DR FOLLIOTT. Sir, I will take a glass of Hock with you.

MR MACQUEDY. With all my heart, sir. There are several varieties of the salmon genus: but the common salmon the *salmo salar*, is only one species, one and the same everywhere, just like the human mind. Locality and education make all the difference.

THE REVD DR FOLLIOTT. Education! Well, sir, I have no doubt

schools for all are just as fit for the species *salmo salar* as for the genus *homo*. But you must allow, that the specimen before us has finished his education in a manner that does honour to his college. However, I doubt that the *salmo salar* is only one species, that is to say, precisely alike in all localities. I hold that every river has its own breed, with essential differences; in flavour especially. And as for the human mind, I deny that it is the same in all men. I hold that there is every variety of natural capacity from the idiot to Newton and Shakespeare; the mass of mankind, midway between these extremes, being blockheads of different degrees; education leaving them pretty nearly as it found them, with this single difference, that it gives a fixed direction to their stupidity, a sort of incurable wry neck to the thing they call their under-standing. So one nose points always east, and another always west, and each is ready to swear that it points due north. . . .

MR MACQUEDY. Well, sir . . . I cannot let slip the question we started just now. I say, cutting off idiots, who have no minds at all, all minds are by nature alike. Education (which begins from their birth) makes them what they are.

THE REVD DR FOLLIOTT. No, sir, it makes their tendencies, not their power. Caesar would have been the first wrestler on the village common. Education might have made him a Nadir Shah, it might also have made him a Washington; it could not have made him a merry-andrew, for our newspapers to extol as a model of eloquence.

MR MACQUEDY. Now, sir, I think education would have made him just anything, and fit for any station, from the throne to the stocks; saint or sinner, aristocrat or democrat, judge, counsel, or prisoner at the bar.

THOMAS LOVE PEACOCK, *Crotchet Castle*, 1831

The principal difficulty about the world in my head was that there seemed to be no connection at all between the idea of education I formed from the boys' weeklies and education as it was practised in the schools I knew. There was the boys' school at St Luke's, for example, where the headmaster was called Downey, a fierce, red, sweaty bull of a man with a white moustache, a bald head he was for ever wiping with a huge white handkerchief, and a long cane that he flourished joyously. The boys had a song about him that was probably first sung about an Elizabethan schoolmaster, but it fitted him perfectly:

> Tommy is a holy man,
>   He goes to Mass on Sunday,
> He prays to God to give him strength
>   To slap the boys on Monday.

This was probably true, because he combined the sanctimoniousness of a reformed pirate with the brutality of a half-witted drill sergeant. With him the cane was never a mere weapon; it was a real extension of his personality, like a musician's instrument or a ventriloquist's dummy—something you could imagine his bringing home with him and reaching out for in the middle of the night as a man reaches out for his wife or his bottle. . . .

Frequently, I carried a boys' paper in my satchel as a sort of promise of better things, and Downey watched me closely because he knew my weakness for glancing at it under my desk, as a man in mortal agony will glance at a crucifix. Once, he caught me with a paper called *The Scout* and held it up before the class with a roar of glee. 'Ho! ho! ho!' he chortled. 'Look who we have here! Look at our young scout! We'll soon knock the scouting out of him. . . . Hold out your hand, you little puppy!' I think he took more delight in catching us out than in beating us, because his stupidity was even greater than his brutality, if that was possible, and he seemed to regard all small boys as criminals with minds of extraordinary complexity and cunning, and greeted each new discovery of a plot with a sort of *Te Deum* of 'Ho! ho! ho's,' like a dictator who has just cracked a fresh liberal conspiracy.

Frank O'Connor, An Only Child, 1961

Another Hindrance to good Education, and I think the greatest of any, is that pernicious Custom in rich and noble Families, of entertaining French Tutors in their Houses. These wretched Pedagogues are enjoyned by the Father, to take special Care that the Boy shall be perfect in his French; by the Mother, that Master must not walk till he is hot, nor be suffered to play with other Boys, nor be wet in his Feet, nor daub his Cloaths, and to see that Dancing-master attends constantly, and does his Duty, she further insists, that the Child be not kept too long poring on his Book, because he is subject to sore eyes, and of a weakly Constitution.

By these Methods, the young Gentleman is in every Article as fully accomplished at eight Years old as at eight and twenty, Age adding only to the Growth of his Person and his Vice; so that if you should look at him in his Boy-hood thro' the magnifying End of a Perspective, and in his Manhood through the other, it would be impossible to spy any Difference; the same Airs, the same Strutt, the same Cock of his Hat, and Posture of his Sword (as far as the Change of Fashions will allow) the same Understanding, the same Compass of Knowledge, with the very same Absurdity, Impudence and Impertinence of Tongue.

He is taught from the Nursery, that he must inherit a great Estate, and hath no need to mind his Book, which is a Lesson he never forgets to the End of his Life. His chief Solace is to steal down, and play at Span-farthing with the Page, or young Black-a-moor, or little favourite Foot-boy, one of which is his principal Confident and Bosom-Friend.

There is one young Lord in this Town, who, by an unexampled Piece of good Fortune, was miraculously snatched out of the Gulph of Ignorance, confined to a publick School for a due Term of Years, well whipped when he deserved it, clad no better than his Comrades, and always their Play-fellow on the same Foot, had no Precedence in the School, but what was given him by his Merit, and lost it whenever he was negligent. It is well known how many Mutinies were bred at this unprecedented Treatment, what Complaints among his Relations, and other Great Ones of both Sexes; that his Stockings with silver Clocks were ravish'd from him; that he wore his own Hair; that his Dress was undistinguished; that he was not fit to appear at a Ball or Assembly, nor suffered to go to either: And it was with the utmost Difficulty, that he became qualified for his present Removal, where he may probably be farther persecuted, and possibly with Success, if the Firmness of a very worthy Governor, and his own good Dispositions will not preserve him. I confess, I cannot but wish he may go on in the Way he began, because I have a Curiosity to know by so singular an Experiment, whether Truth, Honour, Justice, Temperance, Courage, and good Sense, acquired by a School and College Education, may not produce a very tolerable Lad, although he should happen to fail in one or two of those Accomplishments, which in the general Vogue are held so important to the finishing of a Gentleman.

Swift, 'An Essay on Modern Education', 1728

They had not gone far, before *Adams* calling to *Joseph*, asked him if he had attended to the Gentleman's Story; he answered, 'to all the former Part.' 'And don't you think,' says he, 'he was a very unhappy Man in his Youth?' 'A very unhappy Man indeed,' answered the other. '*Joseph*,' cries *Adams*, screwing up his Mouth, 'I have found it; I have discovered the Cause of all the Misfortunes which befel him. A public School, *Joseph*, was the Cause of all the Calamities which he afterwards suffered. Public Schools are the Nurseries of all Vice and Immorality. All the wicked Fellows whom I remember at the University were bred at them.—Ah Lord! I can remember as well as if it was but yesterday, a Knot of them; they called them King's Scholars, I forget why—very wicked Fellows! *Joseph*, you may thank the Lord you were not bred at a public School, you would never have preserved your Virtue as you have. The first Care I always take, is of a Boy's Morals, I had rather he should be a Blockhead than an Atheist or a Presbyterian. What is all the Learning of the World compared to his immortal Soul? What shall a Man take in exchange for his Soul? But the Masters of great Schools trouble themselves about no such thing. I have known a

Lad of eighteen at the University, who hath not been able to say his Catechism; but for my own part, I always scourged a Lad sooner for missing that than any other Lesson. Believe me, Child, all that Gentleman's Misfortunes arose from his being educated at a public School.'

'It doth not become me,' answer'd *Joseph*, 'to dispute any thing, Sir, with you, especially a matter of this kind; for to be sure you must be allowed by all the World to be the best Teacher of a School in all our County.' 'Yes, that,' says *Adams*, 'I believe, is granted me; that I may without much Vanity pretend to—nay I believe I may go to the next County too—but *gloriari non est meum.*'—'However, Sir, as you are pleased to bid me speak,' says *Joseph*, 'you know, my late Master, Sir *Thomas Booby*, was bred at a public School, and he was the finest Gentleman in all the Neighbourhood. And I have often heard him say, if he had a hundred Boys he would breed them all at the same Place. It was his Opinion, and I have often heard him deliver it, that a Boy taken from a public School, and carried into the World, will learn more in one Year there, than one of a private Education will in five. He used to say, the School itself initiated him a great way, (I remember that was his very Expression) for great Schools are little Societies, where a Boy of any Observation may see in Epitome what he will afterwards find in the World at large.' '*Hinc illæ lachrymæ*; for that very Reason,' quoth *Adams*, 'I prefer a private School, where Boys may be kept in Innocence and Ignorance: for, according to that fine Passage in the Play of *Cato*, the only *English* Tragedy I ever read,

> If Knowledge of the World must make Men Villains,
> May *Juba* ever live in Ignorance.

Who would not rather preserve the Purity of his Child, than wish him to attain the whole Circle of Arts and Sciences; which, by the bye, he may learn in the Classes of a private School? for I would not be vain, but I esteem myself to be second to none, *nulli secundum*, in teaching these things; so that a Lad may have as much Learning in a private as in a public Education.' 'And with Submission,' answered *Joseph*, 'he may get as much Vice, witness several

Country Gentlemen, who were educated within five Miles of their own Houses, and are as wicked as if they had known the World from their Infancy. I remember when I was in the Stable, if a young Horse was vicious in his Nature, no Correction would make him otherwise; I take it to be equally the same among Men: if a Boy be of a mischievous wicked Inclination, no School, tho' ever so private, will ever make him good; on the contrary, if he be of a righteous Temper, you may trust him to *London*, or wherever else you please, he will be in no danger of being corrupted. Besides, I have often heard my Master say, that the Discipline practised in public Schools was much better than that in private.'—'You talk like a Jackanapes,' says *Adams*, 'and so did your Master. Discipline indeed! because one Man scourges twenty or thirty Boys more in a Morning than another, is he therefore a better Disciplinarian? I do presume to confer in this Point with all who have taught from *Chiron*'s time to this Day; and, if I was Master of six Boys only, I would preserve as good Discipline amongst them as the Master of the greatest School in the World. I say nothing, young Man; remember, I say nothing; but if Sir *Thomas* himself had been educated nearer home, and under the Tuition of somebody, remember, I name nobody, it might have been better for him—but his Father must institute him in the Knowledge of the World. *Nemo mortalium omnibus horis sapit.*' *Joseph* seeing him run on in this manner asked pardon many times, assuring him he had no Intention to offend. 'I believe you had not, Child,' said he, 'and I am not angry with you: but for maintaining good Discipline in a School; for this,——' And then he ran on as before, named all the Masters who are recorded in old Books, and preferred himself to them all. Indeed if this good Man had an Enthusiasm, or what the Vulgar call a Blind-side, it was this: He thought a Schoolmaster the greatest Character in the World, and himself the greatest of all Schoolmasters, neither of which Points he would have given up to *Alexander the Great* at the Head of his Army.

HENRY FIELDING, *Joseph Andrews*, 1742

When lo! a spectre rose, whose index-hand
Held forth the virtue of the dreadful wand;
His beaver'd brow a birchen garland wears,
Dropping with infants' blood, and mothers' tears.
O'er every vein a shuddering horror runs;
Eton and Winton shake through all their sons.
All flesh is humbled, Westminster's bold race
Shrink, and confess the genius of the place:
The pale boy-senator yet tingling stands,
And holds his breeches close with both his hands.
  Then thus. Since man from beast by words is known,
Words are man's province, words we teach alone,
When reason doubtful, like the Samian letter,
Points him two ways, the narrower is the better.
Placed at the door of Learning, youth to guide,
We never suffer it to stand too wide.

POPE, *The Dunciad*, 1728, Book IV

In a conversation with Dr Burney, in the year 1775, Johnson said, 'There is now less flogging in our great schools than formerly, but then less is learned there; so that what the boys get at one end they lose at the other.'

BOSWELL, *Life of Johnson*, 1791

I have not an opportunity to follow my French so closely as it requires, however tho' I get the less, yet I hope it will make it easier to me when I come to read it at Cambridge. The Seat yt I am in is the first in the School and has been so ever since Easter. Two or three have gone out of it above a year since to Cambridge, one of which got a Scholarship, so yt I find by those that stay yt I might have passed tolerably well with. Here, however, since I have had the Fortune to light of so good a Master I hope my time so far is not mispent. As to the leaving off my School-Authors at College I hope

8

I shall be very well qualified to do yt by Christmas for I have already read through most of Latin Virgil, and with moderate study I shall goe through Horace before Christmas. Terence I have at my finger Ends, so that after I have finished Horace and Virgil I shall have got all that I can at Sedbergh. Very few of our Class expect to come after Xmas; however they all goe at the beginning of the spring at the latest. The longer I stay after Xmas I will be so much the more behind hand in the profession yt I am like to get my living by. My Companion's parents live at Penrith. He was examined by a Fellow of Queen's College in Oxford. The Fellow said yt he had lost his time for he might have passed very well last Easter. I was generally reckoned his equal. I hope I have fully answered this Article.

We go to bed constantly at 9 and rise at 6; as for our Diversion, we take it any Afternoon. We both thrive very well and have never had anything like the Itch. Bob has grown the best yt ever was known in so little a time. I am affraid if he goes on the House will never hold him. I am affraid we must not trouble the Usher with his reading for he's held very throng at present so yt he has seldom a leisure hour to himself. I am in hopes that he is much improved. Mr Saunders gives him a mighty character for a good Scholar. I believe the Peak would be very acceptable, tho' Miss does not wear 'em at present, yet she designs it next spring. As to the Gold, Mr Saunders is so very careful of us that it cannot be mispent. We are both as well and easy as we can wish to be. We are very sorry to hear that my Aunt's eyes are so ill. . . . We are very well served as to our Diet. I hope Bob continues perfectly well disposed and may very safely be trusted with himself at Sedbergh after my departure to Cambridge. I am sure that he makes a very considerable progress in his Learning.

WILLIAM COTESWORTH to his father, 1716, in E. Hughes, North Country Life in the Eighteenth Century, 1952

Another thing very ordinary in the vulgar Method of Grammar-Schools there is, of which I see no Use at all, unless it be to baulk young Lads in the Way to learning Languages, which, in my

Opinion, should be made as easy and pleasant as may be; and that which was painful in it, as much as possible quite removed. That which I mean, and here complain of, is, their being forced to learn by heart, great Parcels of the Authors which are taught them; wherein I can discover no Advantage at all, especially to the Business they are upon. Languages are to be learned only by Reading and Talking, and not by Scraps of Authors got by heart; which when a Man's Head is stuffed with, he has got the just Furniture of a Pedant, and 'tis the ready Way to make him one; than which there is nothing less becoming a Gentleman. For what can be more ridiculous, than to mix the rich and handsome Thoughts and Sayings of others with a deal of poor Stuff of his own; which is thereby the more exposed, and has no other Grace in it, nor will otherwise recommend the Speaker, than a thread-bare Russet Coat would, that was set off with large Patches of Scarlet and glittering Brocade. Indeed, where a Passage comes in the way, whose Matter is worth Remembrance, and the Expression of it very close and excellent, (as there are many such in the antient Authors) it may not be amiss to lodge it in the Mind of young Scholars, and with such admirable Strokes of those great Masters sometimes exercise the Memories of School-Boys. But their learning of their Lessons by Heart, as they happen to fall out in their Books, without Choice or Distinction, I know not what it serves for, but to mispend their Time and Pains, and give them a Disgust and Aversion to their Books, wherein they find nothing but useless Trouble.

JOHN LOCKE, 'Some Thoughts Concerning Education', 1693

I think the manner of learning children in village schools very erroneous; that is, soon as they learn their letters, to task them with lessons from the Bible, and testament, and keeping them dinging at them without any change till they leave it. A dull boy never turns with pleasure to his schooldays, when he has often been beat 4 times for bad readings in 5 verses of Scripture, no more than a man in renew'd prosperity to the time when he was a debtor in a jail. Other books, as they grow up, become a novelty, and their task book at school, the Bible, loses its relish; the painful task of learning wearied the memory; irksome inconvenience never prompts recollection. The Bible, is laid by on its peacful shelf, and by 9 cottages out of 10 never disturb'd or turn'd to further than the minute's reference for reciting the text on a Sunday,—a task which most Christians nowadays think a sufficient duty, at least in the lower orders. I cannot speak with assurance, only where experience informs me; so much for village schools.

About now, all my stock of learning was gleaned from the six-penny Romances, of 'Cinderella', 'Little Red Riding Hood', 'Jack and the Beanstalk', 'Zig Zag', 'Prince Cherry', &c., &c., &c., and great was the pleasure, pain, or surprise, increased by allowing them authenticity, for I firmly believed every page I read, and considered I possessed in these the chief learning and literature of the country. But as it is common in villages to pass judgment on a lover of books as a sure indication of laziness, I was drove to the narrow necessity of stinted opportunitys to hide in woods and dingles of thorns in the fields on Sundays, to read these things which every sixpence, tho' the indefatigable savings of a penny and half penny, when collected, was willingly thrown away for, as opportunity offered, when hawkers offered them for sale at the door.

JOHN CLARE (b. 1793), *Autobiography*, first published in 1931

At nine or ten the masculine energies of the character are beginning to develop themselves; or, if not, no discipline will better aid in their development than the bracing intercourse of a great English classical school. Even the selfish are *there* forced into accommodating themselves to a public standard of generosity; and the effeminate into conforming to a rule of manliness. I was myself at two public schools, and I think with gratitude of the benefits which I reaped from both; as also I think with gratitude of that guardian in whose quiet household I learned Latin so effectually. But the small private schools, of which I had opportunities for gathering some brief experience—schools containing thirty to forty boys—were models of ignoble manners as regarded part of the juniors, and of favouritism as regarded the masters. Nowhere is the sublimity of public justice so broadly exemplified as in an English public school on the old Edward the Sixth or Elizabeth foundation. There is not in the universe such an Areopagus for fair play, and abhorrence of all crooked ways, as an English mob, or one of the time-honoured English 'foundation' schools.

Thomas De Quincey, *Confessions of an English Opium-Eater*, 1821

Many satisfy themselves with the assertion, that public education is the least troublesome; that a boy once sent to school is settled for several years of life, and will require only short returns of parental care twice a year at the holidays. It is hardly to be supposed, that those who think in this manner should have paid any anxious, or at least any judicious attention to the education of their children, previously to sending them to school. It is not likely that they should be very solicitous about the commencement of an education which they never meant to finish: they would think that what could be done during the first few years of life is of little consequence; that children from four to seven years old are too young to be taught; and that a school would speedily supply all deficiencies, and correct all those faults which begin at that age to be troublesome at home. Thus, to a public school, as to a general infirmary for mental disease, all desperate subjects are sent, as the last resource. They take with them the contagion of their vices, which quickly runs through the whole tribe of their companions, especially amongst those who happen to be nearly of their own age, whose sympathy peculiarly exposes them to the danger of infection. We are often told, that as young people have the strongest sympathy with each other, they will learn most effectually from each other's example. They do learn quickly from example, and this is one of the dangers of a public school: a danger which is not necessary, but incidental; a danger against which no school-master can possibly guard, but which

parents can, by the previous education of the pupils, prevent. Boys
are led, driven, or carried to school; and in a school-room they first
meet with those who are to be their fellow prisoners.

MARIA and R. L. EDGEWORTH, *Essays on Practical Education,*
new edn. 1822

Would you your son should be a sot or dunce,
Lascivious, headstrong, or all these at once;
That in good time the stripling's finish'd taste
For loose expense, and fashionable waste,
Should prove your ruin, and his own at last;
Train him in public with a mob of boys,
Childish in mischief only and in noise,
Else of a mannish growth, and five in ten
In infidelity and lewdness men.
There shall he learn, ere sixteen winters old,
That authors are most useful pawn'd or sold;
That pedantry is all that schools impart,
But taverns teach the knowledge of the heart;
There waiter Dick, with Bacchanalian lays,
Shall win his heart, and have his drunken praise,
His counsellor and bosom-friend shall prove,
And some street-pacing harlot his first love.
Schools, unless discipline were doubly strong,
Detain their adolescent charge too long;
The management of tiroes of eighteen
Is difficult, their punishment obscene.
The stout tall captain, whose superior size
The minor heroes view with envious eyes,
Becomes their pattern, upon whom they fix
Their whole attention, and ape all his tricks.
His pride, that scorns t' obey or to submit,
With them is courage; his effront'ry wit.

His wild excursions, window-breaking feats,
Robb'ry of gardens, quarrels in the streets,
His hairbreadth 'scapes, and all his daring schemes;
Transport them, and are made their fav'rite themes.

WILLIAM COWPER (1731–1800), 'Tirocinium; or, A Review
of Schools'

Before he had been a full year at Winchester, he had signalised himself in so many achievements in defiance to the laws and regulations of the place, that he was looked upon with admiration, and actually chosen *Dux*, or leader, by a large body of his co-temporaries. It was not long before his fame reached the ears of his master, who sent for Mr Jolter, communicated to him the informations he had received, and desired him to check the vivacity of his charge, and redouble his vigilance in time to come, else he should be obliged to make a public example of his pupil for the benefit of the school. . . .

As for Tom Pipes, he was not so properly the attendant of Peregrine, as master of the revels to the whole school. He mingled in all their parties, and superintended their diversions, deciding between boy and boy, as if he acted by commission under the great seal. He regulated their motions by his whistle, instructed the young boys in the games of hustle-cap, leap-frog, and chuck-farthing; imparted to those of a more advanced age the sciences of cribbage and all-fours, together with the method of storming the castle, acting the comedy of Prince Arthur, and other pantomimes, as they are commonly exhibited at sea; and instructed the seniors, who were distinguished by the appellation of bloods, in cudgel-playing, dancing the St Giles's hornpipe, drinking flip, and smoking tobacco. These qualifications had rendered him so necessary and acceptable to the scholars, that, exclusive of Perry's concern in the affair, his dismission, in all probability, would have produced some dangerous convulsion in the community.

TOBIAS SMOLLETT, *Peregrine Pickle*, 1751

Concerning Education

It may be guessed that Ernest was not the chosen friend of the more
sedate and well-conducted youths then studying at Roughborough.
Some of the less desirable boys used to go to public-houses and drink
more beer than was good for them; Ernest's inner self can hardly
have told him to ally himself to these young gentlemen, but he did
so at an early age, and was sometimes made pitiably sick by an
amount of beer which would have produced no effect upon a
stronger boy. Ernest's inner self must have interposed at this point
and told him that there was not much fun in this, for he dropped the
habit ere it had taken firm hold of him, and never resumed it; but he
contracted another at the disgracefully early age of between thirteen
and fourteen which he did not relinquish, though to the present day
his conscious self keeps dinging it into him that the less he smokes
the better.

And so matters went on till my hero was nearly fourteen years old.
If by that time he was not actually a young blackguard, he belonged
to a debatable class between the sub-reputable and the upper disreputable, with perhaps rather more leaning to the latter except so far
as vices of meanness were concerned, from which he was fairly free.
I gather this partly from what Ernest has told me, and partly from his
school bills, which I remember Theobald showed me with much
complaining. There was an institution at Roughborough called the
monthly merit money; the maximum sum which a boy of Ernest's
age could get was four shillings and sixpence; several boys got four
shillings and few less than sixpence, but Ernest never got more than
half-a-crown and seldom more than eighteen pence; his average
would, I should think, be about one and nine pence, which was just
too much for him to rank among the downright bad boys, but too
little to put him among the good ones.

Samuel Butler, The Way of All Flesh, 1903

Proceed, great days! till Learning fly the shore,
Till Birch shall blush with noble blood no more,
Till Thames see Eton's sons for ever play,

Till Westminster's whole year be holiday,
Till Isis' elders reel, their pupils sport,
And Alma Mater lie dissolv'd in port!

POPE, The Dunciad, 1728, Book III

Westminster School is such old ground, that little or nothing new can be said of it;—so I wish I could *skip school* altogether;—but it is too material a thread in a man's autobiographical web to be omitted.—Well then, Westminster School was founded by Queen Elizabeth, a Blue-Stocking, who, if history tell truth, must have spoken much better Greek and Latin than one in five thousand of her *foundees*;—and Doctor Busby, like other Doctors before and after him, flogg'd in it;—and geniuses and boobies have been brought up in it, who would have been geniuses and boobies had they been brought up anywhere else;—and Doctor Smith was head-master, in my time; and a very dull and good-natured head-master he was;—and Doctor Vincent was under-master, a man of νοῦς and learning, and plaguily severe;—his severity, indeed, might be incidental to his position, and arise from his having to do with the *young fry* of the school; for there is no *ratiocinating* with urchins of very tender years; you cannot make the same impression upon them as upon older lads, by expostulating, by shaming them, or by rousing their pride; and when there is no maintaining order by an appeal to their heads, nothing is left for it but an application to their tails;— and this last was Vincent's way of disciplining his infantry;—but he lost his temper, and struck and pinch'd the boys, in sudden bursts of anger, which was unwarrantable: a pedagogue is privileged to make his pupil red, in the proper place, with birch, but he has no right to squeeze him black and blue with his fingers;—and so I would have told Vincent, (who is now no more,) had I encounter'd him in my riper years;—but he subsided, I have heard, into the usual mildness of a head-master, when he succeeded to that situation, which was after I had quitted school.

GEORGE COLMAN the Younger (b. 1762), Random Records, 1830

Looking back to the short days of that Winter Half, I find that passages obsess my memory. Passages, narrow and wainscoted, down which we raced to the call of 'Lower boy!'; passages where we lingered and gossiped in front of notice-boards; passages sweating with moisture after a game of passage-football; the complicated passages of other Houses, through which one had to find a way, when Praepostor, to the Dame's room. For even a new boy had his week of office as Praepostor, when it was his business to mark in the Praepostor's Book the names of boys absent from Division or from Chapel, and to collect an 'excuse' for them from their Dame. The massive new Houses had not then been built, and we lived, for the most part, in intricate rabbit-warrens. When an epidemic of measles or mumps broke out, a dozen boys might be absent at one time, and a small Praepostor, wandering to 'W.D.'s' down Judy's passage, and thence to Donaldson's at the far end of Cow Lane, had sometimes to skip his breakfast. It was a bad system, now long abolished, but I loved my week of office. It was the sort of thing that could be tolerated at Eton, and only at Eton. And is there, perhaps, a taint of Original Jack-in-Office in all of us? May only the French enjoy being functionaries? I suspect, from the satisfaction I felt as I made my rounds with my long, narrow book, that I had the makings, never yet given a chance to develop, of a successful small-town Mayor.

My brother and I duly caught the measles, an event not worth recording had it not marked a definite step in the process of moulding us to a common pattern. For measles ended in sick leave, and to go on sick leave, to my grandmother at Camberley, we had to put on our 'change-clothes'. We had arrived at Eton in tails and Eton jacket respectively, and until the morning of going on sick leave no boy in the house knew, or could have suspected, the dreadful truth that our 'change-clothes', lying hid at the bottom of our ottomans, included knickerbockers. When we suddenly appeared, cheerful and unafraid, in our home-spun knickerbockers, the shock to Lowry's House was great. We, who had been amiable freaks, were in real danger of becoming 'touts', not merely eccentric but socially 'not quite, quite'. We were, in the event, forgiven, but we had had a fright, and I was thenceforward closely concerned with conformity to accepted standards. The measles thus left their mark, not on our bodies, but upon our souls. My brother explained, in the holidays, that knickerbockers were not the thing, and my mother saw to it that my father told us each to order a pair of trousers that should match, as near as might be, our coats and waistcoats. That they did not really match was of course spotted, and the cause of adverse comment. I can remember thinking that happiness—true peace of mind—could be mine if only my change-trousers could match my change-coat. I had to wait some years for that blessed marriage of twin-tweeds, and for the inward repose it brought me.

L. E. JONES, *A Victorian Boyhood*, 1955

The manner in which our youth of London are at present educated is, some in free-schools in the city, but the far greater number in boarding-schools about town. The parent justly consults the health of his child, and finds an education in the country tends to promote this much more than a continuance in town. Thus far he is right: if there were a possibility of having even our free-schools kept a little out of town, it would certainly conduce to the health and vigour of perhaps the mind as well as the body. It may be thought whimsical, but it is truth,—I have found by experience, that they who have spent all their lives in cities, contract not only an effeminacy of habit, but even of thinking.

But when I have said, that the boarding-schools are preferable to free-schools, as being in the country, this is certainly the only advantage I can allow them; otherwise it is impossible to conceive the ignorance of those who take upon them the important trust of education. Is any man unfit for any of the professions, he finds his last resource in setting up a school. Do any become bankrupts in trade, they still set up a boarding-school, and drive a trade this way, when all others fail: nay, I have been told of butchers and barbers, who have turned schoolmasters; and, more surprising still, made fortunes in their new profession.

OLIVER GOLDSMITH, 'The Bee: No. VI', 1759

I was a hypochondriac lad, and the sight of a boy in fetters upon the day of my first putting on the blue clothes was not exactly fitted to assuage the natural terrors of initiation. I was of tender years, barely turned of seven, and had only read of such things in books or seen them but in dreams. I was told he had *run away.* This was the punishment for the first offence. As a novice, I was soon after taken to see the dungeons. These were little, square Bedlam cells, where a boy could just lie at his length upon straw and a blanket—a mattress, I think, was afterwards substituted—with a peep of light let in askance from a prison orifice at top, barely enough to read by. Here the poor boy was locked in by himself all day, without sight of any but the porter who brought him his bread and water— who *might not speak to him*—or of the beadle, who came twice a week to call him out to receive his periodical chastisement, which was almost welcome, because it separated him for a brief interval from solitude:—and here he was shut up by himself *of nights* out of the reach of any sound, to suffer whatever horrors the weak nerves and superstition incident to his time of life might subject him to. This was the penalty for the second offence. Wouldst thou like, reader, to see what became of him in the next degree?

The culprit who had been a third time an offender, and whose expulsion was at this time deemed irreversible, was brought forth, as at some solemn *auto da fé*, arrayed in uncouth and most appalling attire. All trace of his late 'watchet weeds' carefully effaced, he was exposed in a jacket resembling those which London lamplighters formerly delighted in, with a cap of the same. The effect of this divestiture was such as the ingenious devisers of it could have anticipated. With his pale and frighted features, it was as if some of those disfigurements in Dante had seized upon him. In this disguisement he was brought into the hall, where awaited him the whole number of his school-fellows, whose joint lessons and sports he was thenceforth to share no more; the awful presence of the steward, to be seen for the last time; of the executioner beadle, clad in his state robe for the occasion; and of two faces more, of direr import, because never but in these extremities visible. These were governors, two of whom, by choice or charter, were always accustomed to officiate at the *ultima supplicia*; not to mitigate (so at least we understood it), but to enforce the uttermost stripe. Old Bamber Gascoigne and Peter Aubert, I remember, were colleagues on one occasion, when the beadle turning rather pale, a glass of brandy was ordered to prepare him for the mysteries. The scourging was, after the old Roman fashion, long and stately. The lictor accompanied the criminal quite round the hall. We were generally too faint with attending to the previous disgusting circumstances to make accurate report with our eyes of the degree of corporal suffering inflicted. Report, of course, gave out the back knotty and livid. After scourging, he was made over, in his *san benito*, to his friends, if he had any (but commonly such poor runagates were friendless), or to his parish officer, who, to enhance the effect of the scene, had his station allotted to him on the outside of the hall gate.

CHARLES LAMB, *Essays of Elia*, 1824

Eton,
May 10, 1824.

My dearest Mother,

As tomorrow's business is particularly difficult and as I am afraid I shall not be able to write a long letter, I take the present opportunity of beginning. I believe that some of the boys are in their disposition good natured, but when you hear the vulgarest, coarsest, and indeed I may say, the most brutal species of swearing in existence, the use of that language cannot but be shocking and offensive in the highest degree. Yesterday several of the boys followed me about, crying out; 'What! do you never swear?' Upon answering in the negative on the ground that it was decidedly wrong, they said: 'What a sap!' and for this reason I was assailed with hisses on entering the school room today, before the arrival of Dr Keate to give advice, and to read a kind of prayer in which he repeatedly put us in mind of the vanities of the world and the uncertainty of everything around us.

Notwithstanding all the care which it was possible for me to use, they have been in my room, seized one of my knives and snuffers, and I despair of ever recovering them. When I had gone to bed, Trench came into my room, swearing and pulled me about in every sort of way he could think of. One of them has also broken about 5 panes of glass in my window, and this is chiefly to be attributed to my not swearing with them. The more cold and quiet I am, the more am I hooted about the school. I indeed earnestly wish that I could fasten my door, but if I did, it would immediately be broken down. I have now finished dinner. Today I went into school, showed up my Map, but I had not done it in a superfine way, since I had not the implements of map making. If you make a mistake in giving the names of places accurately, you are flogged. Tomorrow is a whole holiday; and we have nothing to do except go to church twice, and to attend absence.

JAMES MILNES GASKELL, *An Eton Boy 1820–30*,
ed. Charles Milnes Gaskell, 1939

'As my old friend the Canon says of the Westminster students, "They're all so pious." It's all Arnold's doing; he spoilt the public schools.'

'My dear uncle,' said I, 'how can so venerable a sexagenarian utter so juvenile a paradox? How often have I not heard you lament the idleness and listlessness, the boorishness and vulgar tyranny, the brutish manners alike, and minds—'

'Ah,' said my uncle, 'I may have fallen in occasionally with the talk of the day; but at seventy one begins to see clearer into the bottom of one's mind. In middle life one says so many things in the way of business. Not that I mean that the old schools were perfect, any more than we old boys that were there. But whatever else they were or did, they certainly were in harmony with the world, and they certainly did not disqualify the country's youth for after-life and the country's service.'

'But, my dear sir, this bringing the schools of the country into harmony with public opinion is exactly—'

'Don't interrupt me with public opinion, my dear nephew; you'll quote me a leading article next. "Young men must be young men," as the worthy head of your college said to me touching a case of rustication. "My dear sir," said I, "I only wish to heaven they would be; but as for my own nephews, they seem to me a sort of hobbadi-hoy cherub, too big to be innocent, and too simple for anything else. They're full of the notion of the world being so wicked, and of their taking a higher line, as they call it. I only fear they'll never take any line at all." What is the true purpose of education? Simply to make plain to the young understanding the laws of the life they will have to enter. For example—that lying won't do, thieving still less; that idleness will get punished; that if they are cowards, the whole world will be against them; that if they will have their own way, they must fight for it. As for the conscience, mamma, I take it—such as mammas are now-a-days, at any rate— has probably set that agoing fast enough already. What a blessing to see her good little child come back a brave young devil-may-care!'

'Exactly, my dear sir. As if at twelve or fourteen a roundabout boy, with his three meals a day inside him, is likely to be over-troubled with scruples.'

'Put him through a strong course of confirmation and sacraments, backed up with sermons and private admonitions, and what is much the same as auricular confession, and really, my dear nephew, I can't answer for it but he mayn't turn out as great a goose as you—pardon me—*were* about the age of eighteen or nineteen.'

'But to have passed *through* that, my dear sir! surely that can be no harm.'

'I don't know. Your constitutions don't seem to recover it, quite. We did without these foolish measles well enough in my time.'

'Westminster had its Cowper, my dear sir; and other schools had theirs also, mute and inglorious, but surely not few.'

'Ah, ah! the beginning of troubles.'—

'You see, my dear sir, you must not refer it to Arnold, at all at all. Anything that Arnold did in this direction—'

'Why, my dear boy, how often have I not heard from you, how he used to attack offences, not as offences—the right view against discipline, but as sin, heinous guilt, I don't know what beside! Why didn't he flog them and hold his tongue? Flog them he did, but why preach?'

'If he did err in this way, sir, which I hardly think, I ascribe it to the spirit of the time. The real cause of the evil you complain of, which to a certain extent I admit, was, I take it, the religious movement of the last century, beginning with Wesleyanism, and culminating at last in Puseyism. This over-excitation of the religious sense, resulting in this irrational, almost animal irritability of conscience, was, in many ways, as foreign to Arnold as it is proper to—'

'Well, well, my dear nephew, if you like to make a theory of it, pray write it out for yourself nicely in full; but your poor old uncle does not like theories, and is moreover sadly sleepy.'

'Good night, dear uncle, good night. Only let me say you six more verses.'

ARTHUR HUGH CLOUGH, *Poems*, 1874; from *Epilogue to Dipsychus*

The public schools of those days were still virgin forests, untouched by the hand of reform. Keate was still reigning at Eton; and we possess, in the records of his pupils, a picture of the public school education of the early nineteenth century, in its most characteristic state. It was a system of anarchy tempered by despotism. Hundreds of boys, herded together in miscellaneous boarding-houses, or in that grim 'Long Chamber' at whose name in after years aged statesmen and warriors would turn pale, lived, badgered and over-awed by the furious incursions of an irascible little old man carrying a bundle of birch-twigs, a life in which licensed barbarism was mingled with the daily and hourly study of the niceties of Ovidian verse. It was a life of freedom and terror, of prosody and rebellion, of interminable floggings and appalling practical jokes. Keate ruled, unaided—for the under-masters were few and of no account—by sheer force of character. But there were times when even that indomitable will was overwhelmed by the flood of lawlessness. Every Sunday afternoon he attempted to read sermons to the whole school assembled; and every Sunday afternoon the whole school assembled shouted him down. The scenes in Chapel were far from edifying: while some antique Fellow doddered in the pulpit, rats would be let loose to scurry among the legs of the exploding boys. But next morning the hand of discipline would re-assert itself; and the savage ritual of the whipping-block would remind a batch of whimpering children that, though sins against man and God might be forgiven them, a false quantity could only be expiated in tears and blood.

Lytton Strachey, Eminent Victorians, 1918

As a child I was a muff and a milksop of the least endearing type, over-sensitive, hopeless at games, and a bit of a prig; doomed, in fact—or so one might have supposed—to be perpetually miserable at almost any British upper-middle-class boarding-school. I hated my prep school, to which I was sent because it catered—in an unofficial and rather hole-and-corner way—for Christian Scientists (Denton Welch followed me there a few years later, and seems to have loathed it as much as I did). From St Michael's I went to King's School, Canterbury, chosen by my father because it was near our home, and also because he happened to have known the headmaster at Oxford. His choice could hardly have been more unfortunate, for King's School, at that period, was notoriously tough, and a system of organized bullying prevailed which must, even for those days (the early Twenties), have been exceptional. After a week of appalling misery I ran away, only to be sent back, ignominiously, the same night. At the end of another week I ran away again, and this time my parents, in despair, decided to send me to Bedales. (I am told, by the way, that since those days King's School has been radically reformed, and is nowadays, from all accounts, a most happy and civilized establishment.)

At Bedales, for the first time in my life, I realized that it was possible to be happy at school. I had arrived in mid-term, frightened, guilty and on the defensive, and was at once made to feel completely at ease; my feelings, I suppose, must have been analogous to those of a refugee from some totalitarian State arriving in one of the Western democracies.

Jocelyn Brooke, in Brian Inglis (ed.), *John Bull's Schooldays*, 1961

The old dame schools had frequently been bad, but they were also sometimes good, though always unpretentious. But the systems of Bell and Lancaster, which their imbecile propounders said were 'with great propriety' called 'the STEAM ENGINE OF THE MORAL WORLD', annihilated any possibility of education. The device merely consisted of teaching blocks of information, generally in the form of answers to a series of questions, to a group of 'monitors', who then taught them to another group of children, and so forth. So knowledge was 'multiplied'; if an ill-disposed examiner asked the questions in the wrong order, the sham was disastrously exposed. Fortunately this rarely happened.

It is a notable example of the gullibility of the historian that this probably retrograde step is still frequently referred to as an advance. Mr and Mrs Hammond have disinterred specimens of the catechisms inflicted upon the children. One must suffice:

Monitor: You read in the lesson *The enamel is disposed in crescent-shaped ridges*. What is the enamel?
Boy: The hard shining part of the tooth.
Monitor: What part of our tooth is it?
Boy: The covering of that part that is out of the jawbone.
Monitor: What do you mean by disposed?
Boy: Placed.
Monitor: The root?
Boy: 'Pono', I place.
Monitor: What is crescent-shaped?
Boy: Shaped like the moon before it is a half-moon.
Monitor: Draw a crescent. *Boy draws it on the blackboard.*

Monitor: What is the root of the word?
Boy: 'Cresco', I grow.
Etc., etc.

This is a specimen of an intelligent and untheological question-
naire: its value to exhausted factory children can be imagined. How
far this 'discovery' was in fact universally applied we can only conjecture: there is some reason to hope that its practitioners were less
senseless than its propounders.

COLE and POSTGATE, The Common People, 1938

'Bitzer,' said Thomas Gradgrind. 'Your definition of a horse.'

'Quadruped. Graminivorous. Forty teeth, namely twenty-four
grinders, four eye-teeth, and twelve incisive. Sheds coat in the spring;
in marshy countries, sheds hoofs, too. Hoofs hard, but requiring to
be shod with iron. Age known by marks in mouth.' Thus (and much
more) Bitzer.

'Now girl number twenty,' said Mr Gradgrind. 'You know what
a horse is.'

She curtseyed again, and would have blushed deeper, if she could
have blushed deeper than she had blushed all this time. Bitzer, after
rapidly blinking at Thomas Gradgrind with both eyes at once, and
so catching the light upon his quivering ends of lashes that they
looked like the antennae of busy insects, put his knuckles to his
freckled forehead, and sat down again.

DICKENS, Hard Times, 1854

'When we were little,' the Mock Turtle went on at last, more
calmly, though still sobbing a little now and then, 'we went to school
in the sea. The master was an old Turtle—we used to call him
Tortoise——'

'Why did you call him Tortoise, if he wasn't one?' Alice asked.

'We called him Tortoise because he taught us,' said the Mock Turtle angrily: 'really you are very dull!'

'You ought to be ashamed of yourself for asking such a simple question,' added the Gryphon; and then they both sat silent and looked at poor Alice, who felt ready to sink into the earth. At last the Gryphon said to the Mock Turtle, 'Drive on, old fellow! Don't be all day about it!' and he went on in these words:—

'Yes, we went to school in the sea, though you mayn't believe it——'

'I never said I didn't!' interrupted Alice.

'You did,' said the Mock Turtle.

'Hold your tongue!' added the Gryphon, before Alice could speak again. The Mock Turtle went on:

'We had the best of educations—in fact, we went to school every day——'

'*I've* been to a day-school, too,' said Alice; 'you needn't be so proud as all that.'

'With extras?' asked the Mock Turtle, a little anxiously.

'Yes,' said Alice, 'We learned French and music.'

'And washing?' said the Mock Turtle.

'Certainly not!' said Alice indignantly.

'Ah! then yours wasn't a really good school,' said the Mock Turtle in a tone of great relief. 'Now at *ours* they had at the end of the bill, "French, music, *and washing*—extra." '

'You couldn't have wanted it much,' said Alice; 'living at the bottom of the sea.'

'I couldn't afford to learn it,' said the Mock Turtle, with a sigh. 'I only took the regular course.'

'What was that?' inquired Alice.

'Reeling and Writhing, of course, to begin with,' the Mock Turtle replied; 'and then the different branches of Arithmetic—Ambition, Distraction, Uglification, and Derision.'

'I never heard of "Uglification," ' Alice ventured to say. 'What is it?'

The Gryphon lifted up both its paws in surprise. 'Never heard of uglifying!' it exclaimed. 'You know what to beautify is, I suppose?'

'Yes,' said Alice doubtfully; 'it means—to—make—anything—prettier.'

'Well, then,' the Gryphon went on, 'if you don't know what to uglify is, you are a simpleton.'

Alice did not feel encouraged to ask any more questions about it, so she turned to the Mock Turtle and said, 'What else had you to learn?'

'Well, there was Mystery,' the Mock Turtle replied, counting off the subjects on his flappers—'Mystery, ancient and modern, with Seaography; then Drawling—the Drawling-master was an old conger-eel, that used to come once a week; *he* taught us Drawling, Stretching, and Fainting in Coils.'

'What was *that* like?' said Alice.

'Well, I can't show it to you myself,' the Mock Turtle said; 'I'm too stiff. And the Gryphon never learnt it.'

'Hadn't time,' said the Gryphon; 'I went to the Classical master, though. He was an old crab, *he* was.'

'I never went to him,' the Mock Turtle said, with a sigh; 'he taught Laughing and Grief, they used to say.'

'So he did, so he did,' said the Gryphon, sighing in his turn; and both creatures hid their faces in their paws.

'And how many hours a day did you do lessons?' said Alice, in a hurry to change the subject.

'Ten hours the first day,' said the Mock Turtle; 'nine the next, and so on.'

'What a curious plan!' exclaimed Alice.

'That's the reason they're called lessons,' the Gryphon remarked; 'because they lessen from day to day.'

This was quite a new idea to Alice, and she thought it over a little before she made her next remark. 'Then the eleventh day must have been a holiday?'

'Of course it was,' said the Mock Turtle.

'And how did you manage on the twelfth?' Alice went on eagerly.

Concerning Education

'That's enough about lessons,' the Gryphon interrupted in a very decided tone; 'tell her something about the games now.'

LEWIS CARROLL, *Alice's Adventures in Wonderland*, 1865

Something like a journal of the proceedings of the Evergreens may be interesting to those foreign readers of *Punch*, who want to know the customs of an English gentleman's family and household. There's plenty of time to keep the Journal. Piano strumming begins at six o'clock in the morning; it lasts till breakfast, with but a minute's intermission, when the instrument changes hands, and MISS EMILY practises in place of her sister, MISS MARIA.

In fact, the confounded instrument never stops: when the young ladies are at their lessons, MISS WIRT hammers away at those stunning variations, and keeps her magnificent finger in exercise.

———

I asked this great creature in what other branches of education she instructed her pupils? 'The modern languages,' says she modestly, 'French, German, Spanish, and Italian, Latin and the rudiments of Greek if desired. English of course; the practice of Elocution, Geography and Astronomy, and the Use of the Globes, Algebra, (but only as far as quadratic equations); for a poor ignorant female, you know, MR SNOB, cannot be expected to know everything. Ancient and Modern History no young woman can be without; and of these I make my beloved pupils *perfect mistresses*. Botany, Geology, and Mineralogy, I consider as amusements. And with these I assure you we manage to pass the days at the Evergreens not unpleasantly.'

Only these, thought I—what an education! But I looked in one of MISS PONTO's manuscript song-books and found five faults of French in four words: and in a waggish mood asking MISS WIRT whether DANTE ALGIERY was so called because he was born at Algiers? received a smiling answer in the affirmative, which made me rather doubt about the accuracy of MISS WIRT's knowledge.

THACKERAY, *Book of Snobs*, 1849

I have already animadverted on the bad habits which females acquire when they are shut up together; and, I think, that the observation may fairly be extended to the other sex, till the natural inference is drawn which I have had in view throughout—that to improve both sexes they ought, not only in private families, but in public schools, to be educated together. If marriage be the cement of society, mankind should all be educated after the same model, or the intercourse of the sexes will never deserve the name of fellowship, nor will women ever fulfil the peculiar duties of their sex, till they become enlightened citizens, till they become free by being enabled to earn their own subsistence, independent of men; in the same manner, I mean, to prevent misconstruction, as one man is independent of another. Nay, marriage will never be held sacred till women, by being brought up with men, are prepared to be their companions rather than their mistresses; for the mean doublings of cunning will ever render them contemptible, whilst oppression renders them timid. So convinced am I of this truth, that I will venture to predict that virtue will never prevail in society till the virtues of both sexes are founded on reason; and, till the affections common to both are allowed to gain their due strength by the discharge of mutual duties.

Were boys and girls permitted to pursue the same studies together, those graceful decencies might early be inculcated which produce modesty without those sexual distinctions that taint the mind. Lessons of politeness, and that formulary of decorum, which treads on the heels of falsehood, would be rendered useless by habitual propriety of behaviour.

MARY WOLLSTONECRAFT, *A Vindication of the Rights of Woman*, 1792

It is for those who object to the equalisation of the instruction of boys and girls to show in what respects the two ought to differ, and in what respects the characters of the two sexes are so widely distinct as to involve the necessity of a separate education for each. . . . Now let us ask ourselves for a moment what are the subjects, if any, on which boys should, and girls should not, be taught. I have not been able to hear from anyone the suggestion of even a single subject. . . . I would draw no line of demarcation, so as to limit the extent of knowledge which either boy or girl may acquire. I would throw open the portals of knowledge freely to both. Let each sex acquire what it can. Circumstances will draw a line of demarcation: so will ability and opportunity. There is no necessity for our drawing any other line, and there is extreme injustice in our doing so. I would apply to those differences between the male and female sex, the very same principle I would apply to the different classes of society, the rich and the poor. I say it is unwise and unjust to fix any arbitrary limit to the education the poor are to get. Their poverty already more than sufficiently limits it; and it is for us rather to try and extend the amount of instruction than to endeavour arbitrarily and intentionally to limit it. So with the female sex, I say, let us throw open the gates through which the temple of knowledge is to be entered.

FRANCES BUSS, 'Evidence to the Schools Inquiry Commission', 1865

We enter'd on the boards: and 'Now,' she cried,
'Ye are green wood, see ye warp not. Look, our hall!
Our statues!—not of those that men desire,
Sleek Odalisques, or oracles of mode,
Nor stunted squaws of West or East; but she
That taught the Sabine how to rule, and she
The foundress of the Babylonian wall,
The Carian Artemisia strong in war,
The Rhodope, that built the pyramid,
Clelia, Cornelia, with the Palmyrene
That fought Aurelian, and the Roman brows
Of Agrippina. Dwell with these, and lose
Convention, since to look on noble forms
Makes noble thro' the sensuous organism
That which is higher. O lift your natures up:
Embrace our aims: work out your freedom. Girls,
Knowledge is now no more a fountain seal'd:

Drink deep, until the habits of the slave,
The sins of emptiness, gossip and spite
And slander, die. Better not be at all
Than not be noble. Leave us: you may go:
To-day the Lady Psyche will harangue
The fresh arrivals of the week before;
For they press in from all the provinces,
And fill the hive.'

TENNYSON, 'The Princess', 1847

She began to wonder whether hers had been in some way a specially good school. Things *had* mattered there. Somehow the girls had been made to feel they mattered. She remembered even old Stroodie—the least attached member of the staff—asking her suddenly, once, in the middle of a music-lesson, what she was going to do with her life and a day when the artistic vice-principal—who was a connection by marriage of Holman Hunt's and had met Ruskin, Miriam knew, several times—had gone from girl to girl round the collected fifth and sixth forms asking them each what they would best like to do in life. Miriam had answered at once with a conviction born that moment that she wanted to 'write a book'. It irritated her when she remembered during these reflections that she had not been able to give to Fräulein Pfaff's public questioning any intelligible account of the school. She might at least have told her of the connection with Ruskin and Browning and Holman Hunt, whereas her muddled replies had led Fräulein to decide that her school had been 'a kind of high school'. She knew it had not been this. She felt there was something questionable about a high school. She was beginning to think that her school had been very good. Pater had seen to that—that was one of the things he had steered and seen to. There had been a school they might have gone to higher up the hill where one learned needlework even in the 'first class' as they called it instead of the sixth form as at her school, and 'Calisthenics' instead of drilling—and something called elocution—where the

32

girls were 'finished'. It was an expensive school. Had the teachers there taught the girls . . . as if they had no minds? Perhaps that school was more like the one she found herself in now? She wondered and wondered. What was she going to do with her life after all these years at the good school? She began bit by bit to understand her agony on the day of leaving. It was there she belonged. She ought to go back and go on.

. . . Woven through her retrospective appreciations came a doubt. She wondered whether, after all, her school had been right. Whether it ought to have treated them all so seriously. If she had gone to the other school she was sure she would never have heard of the Aesthetic Movement or felt troubled about the state of Ireland and India. Perhaps she would have grown up a Churchwoman . . . and 'lady-like'. Never.

She could only think that somehow she must be 'different'; that a sprinkling of the girls collected in that school was different, too. The school she decided was new—modern—Ruskin. Most of the girls perhaps had not been affected by it. But some had. She had. The thought stirred her. She had. It was mysterious. Was it the school or herself? Herself to begin with. If she had been brought up differently, it could not, she felt sure, have made her very different—for long—nor taught her to be affable—to smile that smile she hated so. The school had done something to her. It had not gone against the things she found in herself.

DOROTHY RICHARDSON, *Pointed Roofs*, 1915

I may perhaps presume upon my somewhat wide educational experience to say something upon the relative advantages of the home, school, and college system. For some years I was educated by governesses at home, I have been at school in London and Paris. For one year I was head teacher in a boarding school of 100 pupils; for seven years I was teacher at Queen's College, London; for seven years I have been principal of the Ladies' College, Cheltenham. Both in

London and on the Continent, especially in Germany (where it is most usual for the pupils to live at home and attend school) I have taken every opportunity of inquiring into different systems, and my verdict is decidedly in favour of the college system, that is to say, when, and only when, the internal arrangements of the college, and the moral training of the pupils are in the hands of a lady. Of course I must expect to be regarded as a prejudiced person, but it does seem to me that a system which combines home life with school discipline, which brings a girl into contact with many, without necessarily making her the intimate companion of any, which gives her opportunities of observing character before she is called upon to judge in the battle of life, whilst parents are able to correct what is wrong, and to confirm what is right in those judgments, must be one more generally suitable than either of the others.

DOROTHEA BEALE, 'Address to the National Association for the
Promotion of Social Science', 1865

Nor was our ignorance confined to public affairs; we were not prepared for any sort of life. One common criticism of the older 'public school' system is that it produced boys and not men, creatures kept adolescent for so long that when they reached Oxford or Cambridge they could not be trusted to behave themselves without a quantity of regulations and disciplinary officials which made Continental students giggle: this was even truer of the girls. We learned nothing of home-keeping or how to conduct ourselves with the opposite sex, and came out of school—this, I believe, was as true of the products of the 'serious' high schools as of those from Roedean, Wycombe Abbey, or St Leonard's—the most innocent greenhorns in the world.

MARGARET COLE, *Growing up into Revolution*, 1949

'The fault,' Miss Bedford said, 'is possibly with us. We have not changed the language of our morals. Who would blame the children for rejecting outworn phrases like "We must all pull together"? I'm afraid I am beginning to believe in the uselessness of exhortation.' She sat up for a moment, shielded her eyes and gazed down on the top lawn and the grassy terraces, the chestnut trees, the few girls moving there. 'When I retire, Miss Curry, which I do assure you will not be for years, unless, that is, the Upper Fifth continue to make inroads on my sanity, I hope to study this in depth: our lack of power in exhortation. It may just be that our language is outmoded; or it may be that our morals are. It may be that our way of life has had its day and cannot be resurrected. And, perhaps I'll publish . . . incidentally.'

'That will be very interesting,' said Miss Curry, feeling the excited fluttering within her mind and body that she always got when she was embarking on an intellectually deep discussion. 'We could use a fresh approach with benefit.'

'Meanwhile,' the headmistress said, tapping ash into the ashtray which Miss Curry held for her, 'meanwhile, what do we have down there?' She watched the Ambers stroll across the lower lawn towards the cloisters, disappear with bags, with baskets and with rugs. 'We have some girls with badly permed hair, children I mean, who are fat and spotty, having been brought up on wartime rations and post-war austerity. And very badly dressed.'

'I also,' said Miss Curry, 'feel quite sorry for them sometimes.' She had not considered that the head concerned herself with clothes, and was suddenly conscious of her own flowery dress.

'Do you?' said the head, as if acknowledging Miss Curry's own appearance lacked attention.

'Well, rather,' said Miss Curry.

Such other members of the staff as were present after Sunday lunch were reading papers or talking quietly among themselves. But Miss Curry became aware that a hush was falling on the room, and her conversation with the head was being monitored. She lowered her voice, but cleared her throat. 'In some ways, Head,' she said, 'it's rather logical, their attitude.'

'Something cannot be *rather* logical, Miss Curry. Nothing can be *rather* logical!'

'Well, shall we say *entirely* logical? Their attitude, I mean. If we preach as we do the supremacy and integrity of the individual . . .'

The head interrupted, stubbing the cigarette out in the ashtray, and said, 'We do not overtly preach it; we simply let the thought infuse our every action, do we not? This has been increasingly the case ever since Romanticism with a capital *r* took hold upon idealism.'

'What I mean'—Miss Curry tried not to get flustered—'what I mean is that the Amb . . . the Upper Fifth, say, take this ideal at face value, act upon the precept as it were . . . the precept of individuality . . .'

'They act upon the precept, do they?' mused the successor to the Founder. She was a large woman with broad shoulders who had come out near the top of her year at Oxford. She was also a striking woman who nearly always wore a white shirt with a large collar lapping over grey or navy blue. She brushed some ash off the jacket of her linen suit and said, 'I can't believe the Upper Fifth have ever acted on a precept in their lives. And yet I don't know why we are discussing them. They haven't done anything too terrible. I mean they may have made us ponder on the quality of our preparation, as it's called, for life, but by and large they haven't burnt the school down yet, or been raped, or stolen anybody's worldly goods.' She had a long and mournful face, accentuated by the way she wore her hair—in a roll around her head. She now threw back her head and laughed and shook her lantern jaw, and showed her long white teeth. She loved her own jokes more than anything. 'And that would really be taking the precept much too far, do you agree with me, Miss Curry?'

The headmistress strode out through the french windows and across the terrace to the lawn, her hands in the deep pockets of her jacket. Miss Curry watched her go. It must be quite a blow, she thought, for someone of that standing, whose whole work depended on the power of organised speech, to have accepted the uselessness of exhortation and persuasion. A soul in torment, possibly, Miss Curry thought.

Miss Bedford sniffed the air which smelled of hay and thought the flag of St George, which always flew on the chapel staff on Sundays, looked gay, but somehow inappropriate.

ELIZABETH NORTH, *Dames*, 1981

On the morning of September 20, 1907, George Nox, then thirteen, stood in the study of the man who was about to become his Housemaster. . . .

'Well, Nox, you are to begin a new life. You will spend here days that you will cherish all your life. You will look back on them with affection and, I trust, pride. I myself have not forgotten my schooldays. They were spent at this school too, so even at this early stage we have that much in common. Have you questions?'

Nox shook his head, but Mr Dowse insisted on hearing his voice.

'No, sir,' Nox said.

'You know why you are here, Nox?'

Nox paused in his reply. He had learned already that it was not a good thing to know too much, though an equally poor impression was created by total ignorance.

'I am here to learn, sir.'

'Not only that, Nox. You might learn anywhere. You might explore the mind of Horace and Virgil in the seclusion of your home. You might be taught the laws of trigonometry by a man who daily visited you. No, Nox, you are here for more than learning. You will absorb knowledge, certainly. At least I hope you will: we cannot send you into the world an ignoramus.' At this Mr Dowse cackled with laughter that was not reflected in his face. He sniffed, and switched his moustache this way and that. He was silent; Nox thought the peroration was over. He wondered about slipping away and leaving Mr Dowse to his many tasks. He shifted his feet and the Housemaster looked up sharply.

'What is the matter, boy?' Nox thought he looked like some animal he had seen in an encyclopedia, and tried for a moment to establish its name in his mind.

'Nothing is the matter, sir.'

'Then do not display impatience. You are treating me to a discourtesy. Do you understand the meaning of that word?'

'Yes, sir.'

'Good, good. When you leave this school that word shall never be allied with your name. Are you pleased by what I say?'

'Yes, sir.'

'You are about to receive, Nox, the finest form of education in the world. You will learn to live in harmony with your fellows, to give and to take in equal proportions. You will recognize superiority in others and bow to it. You will discover your place, your size, and extent of your self. You follow me? You will find that our school is the world in miniature; and your days here are a rehearsal for your time in that world. You are a privileged person to be allowed such a rehearsal. It means that when you leave here you leave with the advantage of knowing what lies beyond. You must make the most of your advantage. You must apply to the world the laws that apply to this school. You must abide by those rules, and you must see to it that others do the same. In life you will be one of the ones who lead the way; it is expected of you and you must fail neither yourself nor the School. So you see there is more to it all than mere mathematics and Latin. You will learn to take punishment and maybe in time distribute it. You will learn to win and to lose, to smile on misfortune with the same equanimity as you smile on triumph. The goodness that is in you will be carried to the surface and fanned to a flame, the evil will be faced fairly and squarely: you will recognize it and make your peace with it. We shall display the chinks in your armour and you will learn how best to defend yourself. When you are my age, Nox, I hope you will look back and know that we have made a good job of you. That is perhaps a facetious way of putting it, but remember that a touch of humour here and there is not out of place.'

'Yes, sir.'

'I would warn you against many things. I would warn you against playing the buffoon. I would warn you against furtive, underhand ways. Steer a straight course, know what you desire, speak up and look people in the face. Never abuse your body, it leads to madness. You know of what I speak?'

'I think so, sir.'

'Be direct, Nox. If you know, say so. If you do not, seek information.'

'I know what you mean, sir.'

WILLIAM TREVOR, *The Old Boys*, 1964

I was now fifteen, dirty, inky, miserable, untidy, a bad fag, a coward at games, lazy at work, unpopular with my masters and superiors, anxious to curry favour and yet to bully whom I dared. The rule of the election system was that we spoke only to the boys of our own year; we could be beaten for speaking first to a boy in an election above and were expected to enforce the same discipline on those below. All our election were most formal with the year that had arrived beneath us. I got a bad report and was described as 'cynical and irreverent'; *'tu ne cede malis'*, wrote Mr Stone, *'sed contra audentior ito'*.

CYRIL CONNOLLY, *Enemies of Promise*, 1938

Why should a man spend nearly a quarter of a century in being 'educated'? The result is often an arrested development, and stultification, and the 'Third Form stupidity and Sixth Form arrogance that landed us in the Boer War . . . and the political insanity of the Black-and-Tan imbroglio in Ireland', beside the 'schoolboy silliness and bluff that caused the General Strike, and the "Play the Game" attitude,' which . . . helped to make the Great War inevitable.

There are probably still plenty of people who say that their schooldays were the best time of their lives. But I cannot see that hors d'oeuvres are the best part of a meal, or that we should eat so much of them that we are left with no time or room for the soup and the fish. I think that education, like hors d'oeuvres, should whet the appetite for what is to follow. I think it should help people to work hard at things they want to do and are fitted to do, and that they should not be pestered or brutalized with irrelevant drudgery and petty tyranny. I cannot see why boys should not be made as happy as possible, for in my experience people are better when they are happy, and to be happy is not necessarily to be, as schoolmasters seem to think, a spineless hedonist. If the Old School could do something more than it does at present to further these aims, to weaken the prejudices of the mass and cherish and develop the individual, who gives life to civilization—well, I believe I wouldn't mind being seen occasionally in an Old School tie, though as a matter of fact I don't much care for stripes.

WILLIAM PLOMER, in Graham Greene (ed.), *The Old School*, 1934

Sex is the great stimulus and it was not only that but a great mystery as well in those days, without which a boy could have gone through school and not have read a single book outside of his lessons. There should come a time for boys to wait up over windows and it should be forbidden them, to give that encouragement which makes it worth their while.

It is not only sex, which he is not allowed, drives him to look about him, but the everyday conventions of a school are of value to anyone strong or unhappy enough to stand up to the disapproval dislike of them brings. What he comes to learn of how the opinion in his house will react to conduct which does not run along with its own will help him to get by long after he has left, indeed until sooner or later he no longer cares what people think. When they say that going to a public school trains one to come naturally into a room full of strangers they also mean it teaches some boys with two eyes how to deal with an assembly of one-eyed people with a squint. He learns when they face him that they may not see him at all but when they are sideways and their faces aslant then probably they are not thinking of themselves and may be dangerous.

HENRY GREEN, *Pack my Bag*, 1940

Concerning Education

I worked hard at school without thinking of it as work. I was not conscious of being ambitious, or of wanting to do well, or even of imitating my father's zeal in the knowledge that he would be pleased. Whatever the motive was, it had already settled itself in my daily life; a habit, it didn't need to be interrogated or kept up to a mark. I was content to let my life have its definition as work, so that intervals between bouts of study came to appear as lived in the service of work. Jean Dutourd says in *The Man of Sensibility*: 'Work brings its own reward, which is a further dose of work.' There were several subjects at school for which I had little capacity: the mathematical subjects, mostly. But I worked at these, too, and recognised only that my habit had to take a grim turn or enter upon an especially dogged mood before I could take out the textbook in, say, algebra or trigonometry. It didn't occur to me to ask why I should be studying these subjects for which I had no natural talent. One day a boy asked what was the use of studying geometry if you didn't intend being an engineer. The teacher answered: to develop that part of your brain. I found the reason sufficient.

DENIS DONOGHUE, *Warrenpoint*, 1991

THE WORLD OF SCHOOL

School must seem strange at all times, it cannot be natural to
go to school. It is no odder than the world outside, only more
concentrated.

HENRY GREEN, *Pack my Bag*, 1940

———

And so return to work—the MA gown,
    Alphas and Betas, central heating, floor-polish,
Demosthenes on the Crown
    And Oedipus at Colonus.
And I think of the beginnings of other terms
    Coming across the sea to unknown England
And memory reaffirms
    That alarm and exhilaration of arrival:
White wooden boxes, clatter of boots, a smell
    Of changing-rooms—Lifebuoy soap and muddy flannels—
And over all a bell
    Dragooning us to dormitory or classroom,
Ringing with a tongue of frost across the bare
    Benches and desks escutcheoned with initials;
We sat on the hot pipes by the wall, aware
    Of the cold in our bones and the noise and the bell impending.
A fishtail gas-flare in the dark latrine;
    Chalk and ink and rows of pegs and lockers;
The War was on—maize and margarine
    And lessons on the map of Flanders.
But we had our toys—our electric torches, our glass

Dogs and cats, and plasticine and conkers,
And we had our games, we learned to dribble and pass
   In jerseys striped like tigers.
And we had our makebelieve, we had our mock
   Freedom in walks by twos and threes on Sunday,
We dug out fossils from the yellow rock
   Or drank the Dorset distance.
And we had our little tiptoe minds, alert
   To jump for facts and fancies and statistics
And our little jokes of Billy Bunter dirt
   And a heap of home-made dogma.
The Abbey chimes varnished the yellow street,
   The water from the taps in the bath was yellow,
The trees were full of owls, the sweets were sweet
   And life an expanding ladder.
     .   .   .   .

And we found it was time to be leaving
To be changing school, sandstone changed for chalk
   And ammonites for the flinty husks of sponges,
Another lingo to talk
   And jerseys in other colours.
And still the acquiring of unrelated facts,
   A string of military dates for history,
And the Gospels and the Acts
   And logarithms and Greek and the Essays of Elia;
And still the exhilarating rhythm of free
   Movement swimming or serving at tennis,
The fives-courts' tattling repartee
   Or rain on the sweating body.
But life began to narrow to what was done—
   The dominant gerundive—
And number Two must mimic Number One
   In bearing, swearing, attitude and accent.
And so we jettisoned all
   Our childish fantasies and anarchism;
The weak must go to the wall

But strength implies the system;
You must lose your soul to be strong, you cannot stand
    Alone on your own legs or your own ideas;
The order of the day is complete conformity and
    An automatic complacence.
Such was the order of the day; only at times
    The Fool among the yes-men flashed his motley
To prick their pseudo-reason with his rhymes
    And drop his grain of salt on court behaviour.
And sometimes a whisper in books
    Would challenge the code, or a censored memory sometimes,
Sometimes the explosion of rooks,
    Sometimes the mere batter of light on the senses.
And the critic jailed in the mind would peep through the grate
    And husky from long silence, murmur gently
That there is something rotten in the state
    Of Denmark but the state is not the whole of Denmark,
And a spade is still a spade
    And the difference is not final between a tailored
Suit and a ready-made
    And knowledge is not—necessarily—wisdom;
And a cultured accent alone will not provide
    A season ticket to the Vita Nuova;
And there are many better men outside
    Than ever answered roll-call.
But the critic did not win, has not won yet
    Though always reminding us of points forgotten;
We hasten to forget
    As much as he remembers.
And school was what they always said it was,
    An apprenticeship to life, an initiation,
And all the better because
    The initiates were blindfold;
The reflex action of a dog or sheep
    Being enough for normal avocations
And life rotating in an office sleep

As long as things are normal.
Which it was assumed that they would always be;
  On that assumption terms began and ended;
And now, in Nineteen-Thirty-Eight A. D.,
  Term is again beginning.

Louis MacNeice, Autumn Journal, 1939

Saturday, May the 5th.

Hon'd. Father,

My Brother has writ so largely to you that I will not trouble you with
a long one this week. We are about ten in our Latin class (which is
the 4th) among which is one Pepploe, the parson of Preston's son, a
very sober lad; but I can scarce give another in the seat the same
character, except those we brought along with us. We are but four in
our Greek class (which is third) of which the man's son where you
us'd to light when you came to Sedbergh is head. I read the same
books I did when I was Mr Lodge's schollar.

  I like my gallaway very well and I hope when you see it it will
prove to your satisfaction.

Your Dutifull son,
Robert Cotesworth.

P. S. I want a new everyday coat.

Schoolboy letter, 1716, in E. Hughes, North Country Life in the
Eighteenth Century, 1952

Here I sit at the desk again, on a drowsy summer afternoon. A buzz
and hum go up around me, as if the boys were so many blue-bottles.
A cloggy sensation of the lukewarm fat of meat is upon me (we dined
an hour or two ago), and my head is as heavy as so much lead. I
would give the world to go to sleep. I sit with my eye on Mr Creakle
blinking at him like a young owl; when sleep overpowers me for a
minute, he still looms through my slumber, ruling those ciphering

books, until he softly comes behind me and wakes me to plainer perception of him, with a red ridge across my back.

Here I am in the playground, with my eye still fascinated by him, though I can't see him. The window at a little distance from which I know he is having his dinner, stands for him, and I eye that instead. If he shows his face near it, mine assumes an imploring and submissive expression. If he looks out through the glass, the boldest boy (Steerforth excepted) stops in the middle of a shout or yell, and becomes contemplative. One day, Traddles (the most unfortunate boy in the world) breaks that window accidentally with a ball. I shudder at this moment with the tremendous sensation of seeing it done, and feeling that the ball has bounded on to Mr Creakle's sacred head.

Poor Traddles! In a tight sky-blue suit that made his arms and legs like German sausages, or roly-poly puddings, he was the merriest and most miserable of all the boys. He was always being caned—I think he was caned every day that half-year, except one holiday Monday when he was only ruler'd on both hands—and was always going to write to his uncle about it, and never did. After laying his head on the desk for a little while, he would cheer up somehow, begin to laugh again, and draw skeletons all over his slate, before his eyes were dry. I used at first to wonder what comfort Traddles found in drawing skeletons; and for some time looked upon him as a sort of hermit, who reminded himself by those symbols of mortality that caning couldn't last for ever. But I believe he only did it because they were easy, and didn't want any features.

DICKENS, *David Copperfield*, 1849–50

I saw Christ's Hospital . . . founded by a great lady, and already in progress during her lifetime, which hospital finds food and drink and clothes for seven hundred young boys and girls, while reading and writing are taught in special schools in the same, and they are kept there until they are fit for some craft or service, when they are taken away and put out wherever they like, or opportunity offers, boys and girls alike; they are all fine children, taken from poor parents and put in here. They keep their hospital exceedingly clean—in the boys' long apartment are one hundred and forty beds in a row on either side, where they sleep two and two together, and by their beds they have low chests in which to keep their clothes. There are fewer girls in a smaller room.

THOMAS PLATTER, *Travels in England,* 1599

Our dress was of the coarsest and quaintest kind, but was respected out of doors, and is so. It consisted of a blue drugget gown, or body, with ample skirts to it; a yellow vest underneath in winter-time; small clothes of Russia duck; worsted yellow stockings; a leathern girdle; and a little black worsted cap, usually carried in the hand. I believe it was the ordinary dress of children in humble life during the reign of the Tudors. We used to flatter ourselves that it was taken from the monks; and there went a monstrous tradition, that at one period it consisted of blue velvet with silver buttons. It was said, also, that during the blissful era of the blue velvet, we had roast mutton for supper; but that the small-clothes not being then in existence, and the mutton suppers too luxurious, the eatables were given up for the ineffables.

LEIGH HUNT, *Autobiography,* 1850; describing Christ's Hospital in 1792

Ye distant spires, ye antique towers,
That crown the watry glade,
Where grateful Science still adores
Her Henry's holy shade;
And ye, that from the stately brow
Of Windsor's heights th'expanse below
Of grove, of lawn, of mead survey,
Whose turf, whose shade, whose flowers among

Wanders the hoary Thames along
His silver-winding way.

   Ah happy hills, ah pleasing shade,
Ah fields belov'd in vain,
Where once my careless childhood stray'd,
A stranger yet to pain!
I feel the gales, that from ye blow,
A momentary bliss bestow,
As waving fresh their gladsome wing,
My weary soul they seem to soothe,
And redolent of joy and youth,
To breathe a second spring.

   Say, father THAMES, for thou hast seen
Full many a sprightly race
Disporting on thy margent green
The paths of pleasure trace,
Who foremost now delight to cleave
With pliant arm thy glassy wave?
The captive linnet which enthrall?
What idle progeny succeed
To chase the rolling circle's speed,
Or urge the flying ball?

   While some on earnest business bent
Their murm'ring labours ply
'Gainst graver hours, that bring constraint
To sweeten liberty:
Some bold adventurers disdain
The limits of their little reign,
And unknown regions dare descry:
Still as they run they look behind,
They hear a voice in every wind,
And snatch a fearful joy.

Gay hope is theirs by fancy fed,
Less pleasing when possest;
The tear forgot as soon as shed,
The sunshine of the breast:
Theirs buxom health of rosy hue,
Wild wit, invention ever-new,
And lively chear of vigour born;
The thoughtless day, the easy night,
The spirits pure, the slumbers light,
That fly th' approach of morn.

Alas, regardless of their doom,
The little victims play!
No sense have they of ills to come,
Nor care beyond to-day:
Yet see how all around 'em wait
The Ministers of human fate,
And black Misfortune's baleful train!
Ah, shew them where in ambush stand
To seize their prey the murth'rous band!
Ah, tell them, they are men!

THOMAS GRAY, 'Ode on a Distant Prospect of Eton
College', 1747

Our village school was poor and crowded, but in the end I relished it. It had a lively reek of steaming life: boys' boots, girls' hair, stoves and sweat, blue ink, white chalk, and shavings. We learnt nothing abstract or tenuous there—just simple patterns of facts and letters, portable tricks of calculation, no more than was needed to measure a shed, write out a bill, read a swine-disease warning. Through the dead hours of the morning, through the long afternoons, we chanted away at our tables. Passers-by could hear our rising voices in our bottled-up room on the bank; 'Twelve-inches-one-foot. Three-feet-make-a-yard. Fourteen-pounds-make-a-stone. Eight-stone-a-hundred-weight.' We absorbed these figures as primal truths declared by some ultimate power. Unhearing, unquestioning, we rocked to our chanting, hammering the gold nails home. 'Twice-two-are-four. One-God-is-Love. One-Lord-is-King. One-King-is-George. One-George-is-Fifth. . . .' So it was always; had been, would be for ever; we asked no questions; we didn't hear what we said; yet neither did we ever forget it.

So do I now, through the reiterations of those days, recall that schoolroom which I scarcely noticed—Miss Wardley in glory on her high desk throne, her long throat tinkling with glass. The bubbling stove with its chink of red fire; the old world map as dark as tea; dead field-flowers in jars on the windowsills; the cupboard yawning with dog-eared books. Then the boys and the girls, the dwarfs and the cripples; the slow fat ones and the quick boney ones; giants and louts, angels and squinters—Walt Kerry, Bill Timbrell, Spadge Hopkins, Clergy Green, the Ballingers and Browns, Betty Gleed, Clarry Hogg, Sam and Sixpence, Poppy and Jo—we were ugly and beautiful, scrofulous, warted, ring-wormed, and scabbed at the knees, we were noisy, crude, intolerant, cruel, stupid, and superstitious.

Laurie Lee, *Cider with Rosie*, 1959

Hark! how the sire of chits, whose future share
Of classic food begins to be his care,
With his own likeness plac'd on either knee,
Indulges all a father's heart-felt glee;
And tells them, as he strokes their silver locks,
That they must soon learn Latin, and to box;
Then turning he regales his list'ning wife
With all th' adventures of his early life;
His skill in coachmanship, or driving chaise,
In bilking tavern bills, and spouting plays;
What shifts he us'd, detected in a scrape,
How he was flogg'd, or had the luck t' escape;

What sums he lost at play, and how he sold
Watch, seals, and all—till all his pranks are told.
Retracing thus his *frolics*, ('tis a name
That palliates deeds of folly and of shame)
He gives the local bias all it's sway;
Resolves that where he play'd his sons shall play,
And destines their bright genius to be shown
Just in the scene, where he display'd his own.
The meek and bashful boy will soon be taught,
To be as bold and forward as he ought;
The rude will scuffle through with ease enough,
Great schools suit best the sturdy and the rough.
Ah happy designation, prudent choice,
Th' event is sure; expect it; and rejoice!
Soon see your wish fulfill'd in either child,
The pert made perter, and the tame made wild.

WILLIAM COWPER (1731–1800), 'Tirocinium; or, A Review
of Schools'

The Eton of my day still retained its character as a school for the
sons of the aristocracy, the ruling classes, country gentlemen and the
higher military. It was appropriate that an educational system intended for the leisured classes should have something leisurely about
it. It is to be remembered also that in the latter part of the nineteenth
century a change had taken place in the educational purposes of
Eton. More importance had come to be attached to organized games
than to scholarship, and more attention given to the fostering of
character than to the development of the intellect. . . .

All the while I had been at Eton my affection for it had been
growing insensibly. Its beauty, which in the first days had made so
forcible an impression on me, I had come to take as a matter of
course. It was only at the moment of leaving Eton that I realized to
the full my deep attachment to the place, to its buildings, its fields

and trees, the river, the surrounding town with the great Castle dominating the horizon, a conglomeration steeped in the romance of bygone centuries. I knew now how much I loved Eton, at all times, at all seasons; the summer sunshine on the playing fields and the river, the bathing at Cuckoo Weir and Athens, the winter fogs and rain that had so often rescued me from football, the walls and cloisters mysterious in lamplight, the darkness of the lanes and passages as one returned in the dusk from outlying class-rooms, and, to descend to more material things, the strawberries-and-cream in the sock-shops and the hot buns at Little Brown's in the mornings before early school.

Eton was for me an Alma Mater beloved for her beauty more than for any other quality, and the memory of it was the most valuable of her gifts.

In so far as my education was concerned, I had learned nothing, less than nothing, a minus quantity. I had lost what little knowledge I had of foreign languages. In history, geography and science I had been confused rather than instructed. I left Eton with a distaste for the Classics and, what was more serious, a distaste for work itself.

No doubt if I had not been prematurely removed from Eton I should be able to speak more favourably of its contribution to my intellectual development. If I had stayed the full course, I might have been induced to take a more earnest view of my studies; I might have made the acquaintance of some of the Eton figures who appear to have had an ennobling influence on one or two of my contemporaries. It was my misfortune that, with the exception of Arthur Benson, I did not enjoy the tuition of anyone I found particularly inspiring.

It would perhaps be difficult to say what sort of education would have been more suitable for a boy of my disposition. My mind and character were of the kind that develop slowly, and it is possible that, had I been more intensively educated at that period of my life, I might have grown up to be, as Herbert Spencer said of early risers, 'conceited in the morning and stupid in the afternoon'.

LORD BERNERS, *A Distant Prospect,* 1945

Coldly, sadly descends
The autumn evening. The field
Strewn with its dank yellow drifts
Of withered leaves, and the elms,
Fade into dimness apace,
Silent—hardly a shout
From a few boys late at their play!
The lights come out in the street,
In the schoolroom windows;—but cold,
Solemn, unlighted, austere,
Through the gathering darkness, arise
The chapel-walls, in whose bound
Thou, my father! art laid.

MATTHEW ARNOLD, 'Rugby Chapel',
November 1857

A Christian and an Englishman! After all, it was not in the class-room, nor in the boarding-house, that the essential elements of instruction could be imparted which should qualify the youthful neophyte to deserve those names. The final, the fundamental lesson could only be taught in the school chapel; in the school chapel the centre of Dr Arnold's system of education was inevitably fixed. There, too, the Doctor himself appeared in the plenitude of his dignity and his enthusiasm. There, with the morning sun shining on the freshly scrubbed faces of his three hundred pupils, or, in the dusk of evening, through a glimmer of candles, his stately form, rapt in devotion or vibrant with exhortation, would dominate the scene. Every phase of the Church service seemed to receive its supreme expression in his voice, his attitude, his look. During the Te Deum, his whole countenance would light up; and he read the Psalms with such conviction that boys would often declare, after hearing him, that they understood them now for the first time. It was his opinion that the creeds in public worship ought to be used as triumphant hymns of thanksgiving, and, in accordance with this view, although unfortunately he possessed no natural gift for music, he regularly joined in the chanting of the Nicene Creed with a visible animation and a peculiar fervour, which it was impossible to forget.

Lytton Strachey, Eminent Victorians, 1918

School is rather a dim memory to me; all hurry and scurry; beginning in the morning with the sound of the housemaids' feet racing along the passages, as they carried great cans of water for the saucer-baths, which they pulled out from under our beds; and then, all day long, running myself like a hare, from place to place, at the sound of the bell, in the hopeless endeavour not to be late. And then, the continual strain, the effort, of trying to understand, to imitate, to conciliate the indigenous population of that foreign land, where I never could get higher than the tolerance of 'It's only old Génie' from the kinder inhabitants. And when at last the anxious, crowded day was over, there came the distasteful duty of *kissing* five or six mistresses good night. They stood in a row after Prayers, to endure this unhygienic operation from the whole school. (How could they bear it?)

In all that time there is only one vision that I keep: a flash, seen through the garden hedge, of some sheep in the next field, with the frosty, winter light running along their backs. It seemed like something from another world: the real world, to which I should escape again some day. It kept me alive.

I must not be ungrateful: I did learn a great deal at school, and grow and widen, too. I am glad I went there. But it is no use denying it: I don't like boarding schools; although they are better than governesses. Day schools might be better still, but I never went to a day school.

Gwen Raverat (b. 1885), Period Piece, 1952

Now my mother, having come in one day upon the steeplechasing lessons, decided that really something must be done—anyhow for little Mary's better education. Unfortunately for me, she took a fly next day for Marsh, where a community of Sisters of Mercy ran a young ladies' college, a high school, an orphanage, and a penitentiary. It was the bell of the young ladies' college she rang.

The Sisters of Mercy in their grace, with their long black robes and fresh white caps under their flowing veils, and their silver crosses, seemed to her irresistible. The long, white dormitories, the bees-waxed floors, the incense-laden chapel, gave her a sense of that disciplined order and calm she herself longed for, and would love to have imparted to a daughter. But oh, mamma! you did not inquire about the fellow pupils, about the food, the hours of work, the walks two and two in a 'crocodile'. There and then she sealed my fate. I was to be incarcerated in this High Church stronghold as speedily as possible.

For some twenty-four hours after my arrival I was sustained by curiosity; then no prisoner in the Château d'If could have felt more hopeless and forlorn than I did on the second morning of awakening in the frosty dormitory. At six o'clock, a servant lit the gas jet with a loud pop. She then rang a dinner bell round about and all over us, as though she were sprinkling us with the sound. (She was, by the way, a reformed penitent, and she had a wooden arm with a hook to it, like Captain Cuttle.)

Each morning I gulped and tasted my salt tears as her outrageous bell died away down the farther dormitories. Then fear pulled me together and braced my cold fingers for struggling with my buttons, tapes, and tangles; feeling sleepy and forlorn, I rushed down with the belated, and from that moment, all day, I was uttering the White Rabbit's cry, 'I shall be late, I shall be late'. Life became nothing but an unquestioning effort not to be left behind, and not to be too conspicuously incompetent.

I felt hopelessly out of it with the hundred girls, into whose bewildering giggling, chattering, and scrambling I had suddenly been plunged. I did not think I should ever be anything but silent and depressed, so I concluded I should always be out of it. Everyone said, 'Why on earth did you come for the Lent Term? It's the worst of all; even beastlier food than in other terms, and everything's horrible.' As for the food, I will only mention here one dish which we called 'skilly'. This concoction was said to be a recipe from the workhouse. It was simply paste, which, served up in a great white pool for a hundred people, was a very nauseating dish.

When the refectory meal was over on that first day, I was told we were all to assemble for the walk, in the school courtyard; it was bounded on three sides by the ecclesiastical school architecture, and on the fourth by the church. Thither I went, and loitered forlornly in the cold.

A chaplain in a biretta and a long black cassock flapped across it, and all the white pigeons strutting there rose up above his head as he passed on into the church. Other girls were now gathering in twos and threes for the walk; and very soon I was sandwiched between the flowing hair of the girl in front of me and the toes and nose of the girl behind, as the long 'crocodile' swung out of the courtyard and on into the suburbs, slums, and dust-heaps into which the town of Marsh degenerates. And at that very moment I knew Evelina at home would be skating on the frozen floods on the meads! She had written that she could even do the outside edge, and now she would be flying about over the ice in her little sealskin jacket, as free as air, in the fields by the river under the Castle. Here at Marsh I was walking with a perfect muff! For the new girls had no choice of a companion; they were engaged for the walks by girls who could not succeed in getting partners among their contemporaries. Mine had an old face and silly ringlets; her name was Mabel Parsley.

I gathered from her that the 'crocodile' rarely went into fields or open country. We stuck to the roads on the outskirts of Marsh, where the most bedraggled of that town always seemed the only passers-by: low-looking tramps trudging with sacks to the dust-heaps, or women wheeling perambulators full of washing or firewood.

'That's the House of Pity we are passing now,' my partner said, as we turned up a lane and passed a building shut off from the road by a high wall and a solid wooden gate with a great knocker.

'What's that?' I asked.

'Oh, where the penitents are,' she said mysteriously.

'What are they?'

'Oh, bad women,' said Mabel Parsley. 'They do laundry work and are trained there.'

'Oh,' I said.

I had never heard of a harlot, so I supposed they had stolen things, or perhaps slaughtered people in tempers. Some penitents, in white caps, were at the moment carrying their washing baskets across the road, accompanied by a Sister of Mercy. I thought that they seemed to be thoroughly making up now for everything they had done.

Meeting them was the best event on the walk. We 'broke rank' for a little; then the 'crocodile' pieced together its vertebrae again, and we filed home to sit at our desks for more lessons.

My misery increased and increased as I sat there at my desk, facing the crucifix on the schoolroom wall.

I admired the racked figure of Jesus with the dramatically pierced forehead, feet, and hands, and with a kind of exquisite pang of dramatic sympathy I felt the nails drive into my own palms and the thorns into my own forehead. My home-sickness had now become a chronic pain akin to physical sickness. I saw that I should be entirely shut off from my home life, with all its interests so near my heart, and shut in with the beringed and bangled, sweet-eating, 'genteel' herd, amongst whom I had suddenly been dropped.

MARY McCARTHY, *A Nineteenth-Century Childhood*, 1924; describing her schooldays in the 1890s

From the first day, every Eton boy has a room to himself, which is no small thing. For sheer cosiness, there is nothing to beat cooking sausages over a coal-fire in a tiny room, with the shabby dark-red curtains drawn, and the brown tea-pot steaming on the table. And after the rigours of the mornings, we were certainly entitled to a little cosiness at tea-time. For at my tutor's no fires might be lit in boys' rooms till four o'clock, however hard the frost outside, and since the wearing of great-coats was something not 'done' except by boys who had their house-colours or Upper Boats, we shook and shivered from early school till dinner at two o'clock. It is often said that colds are not caught through cold, but I shall never believe it, for we snuffled and snivelled through the Winter Halves, much to the annoyance of 'the Hag', the generic name for all matrons. Miss Hale, Lowry's 'Hag', was the daughter of a former House-master, and although kind, had Spartan standards. She was ready with ammoniated quinine, but deaf to our suggestions that we had colds because we were cold. If there is anything more bleak than to return to your room between schools on a winter's morning, with snow on the ground, to find door and window open, the chairs on the table and Bird, the boys' maid, scrubbing the linoleum floor, I have not met with it. Bigger boys could crowd round the fire in the House Library, but the Lower boys had none at which to dry a handker-chief. I think we did suffer real hardship, without being hardened by it; but it was the only suffering of any sort that we endured, and memory, which works on the principle of the sun-dial, calls up a dozen times the cosiness of tea-time for once that it summons back the shivery catarrh-ridden mornings.

L. E. JONES, *A Victorian Boyhood*, 1955

David was extremely quick at picking up an atmosphere, and he made the perfectly correct conclusion that, though smoking was bad form, swearing was not. But the mention of Maddox roused the thrill and glamour of hero-worship—a hero-worship more complete and entire than is ever accorded by the world of grown-up men and women to their most august idols.

'Oh, go on, tell me about Maddox,' he said.

'I dare say you'll see him. Sure to, in fact. He's not very tall, but he's damned good-looking. He's far the finest bat in the eleven, and the funny thing is he says cricket's rather a waste of time, and hardly ever goes up to a net. He's editor of the school-paper, and played racquets for us at Queen's last year. But what he likes best of all is reading.'

'That's queer,' said David.

' 'Tis rather. He makes all our juniors work too, I can tell you. But he'll help anybody, and he'll always give you a construe of a bit you don't understand, if you've looked out all the words first. And he's only just seventeen—think of that—so that he'll have two more years here. He never plays footer, though he can run like hell, and says Rugby is a barbarous sport; and in the winter, when he's not playing racquets, he just reads and reads. His mother was French, too; rum thing that, and the point is that H. T. (that's Hairy Toe, an awful ass) who teaches French, is English, and Maddox knows about twice as much as he. He makes awful howlers, Maddox says, and pronounces just as if he was a cad. But that's all right, because he is.'

David skipped with uncontrollable emotion.

'Oh, I say, how ripping!' he said. 'But I wish Maddox liked cricket and footer.'

E. F. BENSON, David Blaize, 1916

I first went to this school in September 1914. We unpacked our trunks in a cement passage outside the gymnasium and carried our things upstairs. The school must have re-assembled with an elating sense of emergency, but as I was new I was not conscious of this. Everything seemed so odd that the war was dwarfed, and though one had been made to feel that one was now living in history, one's own biography was naturally more interesting. I found my school-fellows rather terse and peremptory, their snubbing of me had a kind of nobility: whether this arose from the war's or my own newness I did not ask: as I had been told that this was a very good school it was what I had been led to expect. A squad of troops marching past in the dark on the tarmac road, whistling, pointed the headmistress's address to us in the gymnasium that first night of term. Wind kept flapping the window cords on their pulleys, the gas jets whistled and the girls drawn up by forms in resolute attitudes looked rather grim. The headmistress stated that it did not matter if we were happy so long as we were good. At my former school the headmistress had always said she knew we should be good as long as we were happy.

That sounded sunnier. But in my three years at this school I learnt to define happiness as a kind of inner irrational exaltation having little to do with morals one way or the other. That night in the gymnasium I felt some apprehension that my character was to be lopped, or even forcibly moulded, in this place, but this came to be dispelled as the term wore on. The war having well outlasted my schooldays, I cannot imagine a girls' school without a war. The moral stress was appalling. We grew up under the intolerable obligation of being fought for, and could not fall short in character without recollecting that men were dying for us. During my second year, the *Daily Mail* came out with its headline about food-hogs, and it became impossible to eat as much as one wished, which was to over-eat, without self-consciousness. If the acutest food shortage had already set in, which it had not, meals would really have been easier. As it was, we *could* over-eat, but it became unfeeling to do so. The war dwarfed us and made us morally uncomfortable, and we could see no reason why it should ever stop. It was clear, however, that someone must have desired it, or it would not have begun. In my first term, we acted a pageant representing the Allies for the head-mistress's birthday, and later sang songs of the epoch, such as 'We don't want to lose you, but . . .' at a concert in the village, in our white muslin Saturday evening frocks. Most eligible fighters had, however, by this time gone to the war and we can only have made their relatives more hysterical. An excellent bun supper was provided by the village committee, and some of us over-ate.

ELIZABETH BOWEN, 'The Mulberry Tree' (Downe House),
in Graham Greene (ed.), *The Old School*, 1934

The state of affairs was summed up by Archie Fletcher in the last week of the Christmas term.

'This place is simply ghastly now,' he said; 'all the best fellows have gone. Next term we shall have that awful ass Rudd head of the House. Then all the young masters have gone, and we are left with these fossils, fretting because they are too old to fight, and making our lives unbearable because we are too young. As soon as I am old enough I mean to go and fight; but I can't stick the way these masters croak away about the trenches all day long. If you play badly at rugger you are asked what use you will be in a regiment. If your French prose is full of howlers, you are told that slackers aren't wanted in the trenches. Damn it all, we know that all these O. F.'s who are now fighting in France slacked at work and cribbed; and they weren't all in the Fifteen. And splendid men they are, too. These masters forget and panic about. Fernhurst isn't what it was. Last term we had a top-hole set of chaps, and I loved Fernhurst; but I am not going to stick here now. I am going back home till I am eighteen. Then I'll go and fight. This is no place for me.'

ALEC WAUGH, *The Loom of Youth*, 1917

The new girl stopped with her mouth puckered into a button. A look of consternation spread over her face, then passed into a smile.

'I was told I'd have to be jolly careful and mind my p's and q's here!' she remarked cheerily. 'I've been just five minutes in the school, and my first impressions are that Miss Thompson aims at unadulterated dignity, and that Miss Hopkins is concentrated essence of fuss. Am I near?'

'Not so far off!' laughed Laura. 'They can exchange characters sometimes, though. I've seen Miss Hopkins ride her high horse and be dignity personified, and on the other hand I've seen Miss Thompson more ruffled than a head mistress has any business to be. You'll soon get to know them.'

'I suppose I shall. Whether I shall altogether like them is another question.'

'You'll like Silverside!' gushed Irma. 'It's a perfectly delightful school—at least it used to be. We're afraid it is going to be utterly and entirely spoilt now.'

'Why?'

'Because it's being invaded. It used to be quite small and select, more boarders than day girls, you know. And now we've just had a horrible shock—the whole of another day school is being plumped upon us—a school we've always despised. We're too indignant for words.'

Avelyn, who was fumbling with the lock of her box, lifted her head.

'Don't you like them coming?'

'Like them! Sophonisba! How can you ask such a question? We've always looked down on them so fearfully. Why, if we met any of them in the street, we used just to stare straight through them, as if they didn't exist. They wore dark-blue coats and horrid stiff kind of hats with coloured bands, for all the world like an institution. I tell you we simply wouldn't have touched them.'

ANGELA BRAZIL, *For the School Colours*, 1918

Dimsie, though temporarily distracted by the incident of Molly Lamont's hair, and the information given by Erica in her letter, had by no means forgotten the ghost's goloshes, and on the following afternoon she sent a Junior to find Hilary and summon her to an inquiry.

'You don't mind, Jean, do you?' she said to her study-mate. 'There's a little matter that wants going into, and I may just have time before prep. begins. I should really have seen to it yesterday, but I was too busy.'

'Oh, I don't mind!' returned Jean peacefully from the window-seat where she was scribbling in a note-book, 'so long as you get it over before I start work. You're usually going into some little matter or other, and I like to observe your methods. It keeps up my interest in life.'

'Anyhow, it's better for you than eternally writing poetry,' said Dimsie, with a disgusted glance at the note-book. 'Oh, yes! I know I back you up when the others come down on you for being soppy—

and I do think there's no harm in it, up to a point—but there are times when you go beyond that—and get lost to the world—and look goofy—and I'm rather afraid you've got a fit of that coming on now.'

'I haven't, really,' said Jean earnestly. 'It's only that I can't get the right metre for the thing I'm doing. Directly I've found the one that suits it, I shall be all right again. And besides, this is school-work, Dimsie. It's my extra composition for this week—Miss Yorke set it.'

'Well, for goodness' sake get it done, then!' advised Dimsie. 'We'll all feel better when it's safely out of your system. Was that meant to be a knock at the door? Oh, it's you, Hazel Hunt! Did you give Hilary my message?'

Hazel was a very small Junior, and she was looking rather scared.

'No, please, Dimsie—I've looked everywhere I can think of, and I can't find her. She isn't in any of the places you'd expect her to be in.'

'Humph!' said the head girl, and, rising, she stretched her arms above her head with a resigned yawn. 'All right, then, thanks. That reduces us to the places you wouldn't expect, and I'd better look in those myself. Cut along back to your game, infant! I'm quite sure you did your best.'

And she bestowed a reassuring smile on Hazel, who ran off happily.

'Better look in the lower music-room,' counselled Jean lazily. 'In our young days, if we weren't where we ought to be, that's where we generally were—in the winter.'

Dimsie nodded, grinning.

'And in the summer we took to the tool-shed in the wood. Thanks for the hint. Strikes me Puck is up to something—as usual!'

But Jean's outlook was rather more tolerant.

'Oh, I don't know! She might want to get away somewhere by herself and be quiet. It isn't so easy at school.'

Dimsie raised her eyebrows at the idea of Hilary Garth wanting to be quiet anywhere, and went off at once to investigate the possibilities of the lower music-room. On her way over from the school-room wing she glanced at the practising board hanging in the passage, and saw that the next name down for that particular piano was Dolly Ansell's, but this conveyed nothing to her; she had no reason, so far, to connect Dolly's movements with Hilary's. Usually there was very little intercourse between the Upper and Lower 2nd Division.

The basement, when she reached it, had a silent and deserted appearance—much more so than when she had gone ghost-hunting down there, two evenings before, to the strains of the percussion-band; on that occasion it had seemed to be teeming with life. She paused outside the door of the music-room; there was somebody within, because she could hear a faint murmur of quiet voices. An air of ancient peace brooded over all the premises; it hardly seemed as though Hilary could be anywhere about, but Dimsie turned the handle of the door and entered.

What she saw was so completely unexpected that, for a moment, she could only stand speechless, gazing at the tableau before her. Dolly Ansell's music-case lay on the piano, her green serge slip and various other garments lay on the nearest chairs, and Dolly herself (clad in the few under-clothes left to her) stood in the middle of the floor passively submitting while Hilary, red-faced and panting, laced her into a pair of very new-looking flesh-pink stays.

Dolly was the first to catch sight of the intruder. Hilary, kneeling on the rug with her back to the door, was putting all her attention and muscular energy into the task on which she was engaged; but a curious half-strangled yelp of horror from her patient caused her to glance round in alarm, loosening her hold on the laces, whereupon the corsets gaped widely apart.

'What, in the name of all that's astounding——' began Dimsie; but Dolly, with one hop, had got behind the piano, clutching the shortening laces as she fled.

Oh, Hilary! I told you!' she moaned. 'You would try them on down here, and I knew it wasn't safe—I said we should have gone up to the dormitory!'

'Certainly not!' said Hilary firmly. 'We're forbidden to go up to the dormitories in the afternoon without leave, but there's no rule, that I've ever heard, against trying on new corsets in the lower music-room.'

DORITA FAIRLIE BRUCE, *Dimsie Intervenes*, 1937

'Jackson,' said Mike.

'Are you the Bully, the Pride of the School, or the Boy who is Led Astray and takes to Drink in Chapter Sixteen?'

'The last, for choice,' said Mike, 'but I've only just arrived, so I don't know.'

'The boy—what will he become? Are you new here, too, then?'

'Yes! Why, are you new?'

'Do I look as if I belonged here? I'm the latest import. Sit down on yonder settee, and I will tell you the painful story of my life. By the way, before I start, there's just one thing. If you ever have occasion to write to me, would you mind sticking a P at the beginning of my name? P-s-m-i-t-h See? There are too many Smiths, and I don't care for Smythe. My father's content to worry along in the old-fashioned way, but I've decided to strike out a fresh line. I shall found a new dynasty. The resolve came to me unexpectedly this morning. I jotted it down on the back of an envelope. In conversation you may address me as Rupert (though I hope you won't), or simply Smith, the P not being sounded. Cp. the name Zbysco, in which the Z is given a similar miss-in-baulk. See?'

Mike said he saw. Psmith thanked him with a certain stately old-world courtesy.

'Let us start at the beginning,' he resumed. 'My infancy. When I was but a babe, my eldest sister was bribed with a shilling an hour by my nurse to keep an eye on me, and see that I did not raise Cain. At the end of the first day she struck for one-and-six, and got it. We now pass to my boyhood. At an early age, I was sent to Eton, everybody predicting a bright career for me. But,' said Psmith solemnly, fixing an owl-like gaze on Mike through the eyeglass, 'it was not to be.'

'No?' said Mike.

'No. I was superannuated last term.'

'Bad luck.'

'For Eton, yes. But what Eton loses, Sedleigh gains.'

'But why Sedleigh, of all places?'

'This is the most painful part of my narrative. It seems that a certain scug in the next village to ours happened last year to collar a Balliol——'

'Not Barlitt!' exclaimed Mike.

'That was the man. The son of the vicar. The vicar told the curate, who told our curate, who told our vicar, who told my father, who sent me off here to get a Balliol too. Do *you* know Barlitt?'

'His father's vicar of our village. It was because his son got a Balliol that I was sent here.'

'Do you come from Crofton?'

'Yes.'

'I've lived at Lower Benford all my life. We are practically long-lost brothers. Cheer a little, will you?'

Mike felt as Robinson Crusoe felt when he met Friday. Here was a fellow human being in this desert place. He could almost have embraced Psmith. The very sound of the name Lower Benford was heartening. His dislike for his new school was not diminished, but now he felt that life there might at least be tolerable.

'Where were you before you came here?' asked Psmith. 'You have heard my painful story. Now tell me yours.'

'Wrykyn. My father took me away because I got such a lot of bad reports.'

'My reports from Eton were simply scurrilous. There's a libel action in every sentence. How do you like this place from what you've seen of it?'

'Rotten.'

'I am with you, Comrade Jackson. You won't mind my calling you Comrade, will you? I've just become a Socialist. It's a great scheme. You ought to be one. You work for the equal distribution of property, and start by collaring all you can and sitting on it. We must stick together. We are companions in misfortune. Lost lambs. Sheep that have gone astray. Divided, we fall, together we may worry

through. Have you seen Professor Radium yet? I should say Mr
Outwood. What do you think of him?'

'He doesn't seem a bad sort of chap. Bit off his nut. Jawed about
apses and things.'

P. G. WODEHOUSE, *Mike and Psmith*, 1909

At this distance of time I cannot remember precisely what sort of an
overcoat Widmerpool was said to have worn in the first instance.
Stories about it had grown into legend: so much so that even five or
six years later you might still occasionally hear an obtrusive or
inappropriate garment referred to as 'a Widmerpool'; and Templer,
for example, would sometimes say: 'I am afraid I'm wearing
rather Widmerpool socks today', or, 'I've bought a wonderfully
Widmerpool tie to go home in'. My impression is that the overcoat's
initial deviation from normal was slight, depending on the existence
or absence of a belt at the back, the fact that the cut was single- or
double-breasted, or, again, irregularity may have had something to
do with the collar; perhaps the cloth, even, was of the wrong colour
or texture.

ANTHONY POWELL, *A Question of Upbringing*, 1951

The social code of Charterhouse rested on a strict caste system; the
caste marks, or *post-té*'s, being slight distinctions in dress. A new boy
had no privileges at all; a boy in his second term might wear a knitted
tie instead of a plain one; a boy in his second year might wear
coloured socks; the third year gave most of the main privileges—
turned down collars, coloured handkerchiefs, a coat with a long
roll, and so on; fourth year, a few more, such as the right to get up
raffles; but peculiar distinctions were reserved for the bloods. These
included light-grey flannel trousers, butterfly collars, jackets slit up
the back, and the right of walking arm-in-arm.

ROBERT GRAVES, *Goodbye to all that*, 1929

There were about two hundred boys in the school; in the same building, but strictly segregated, and only visible at meal-times, were about a hundred girls. The regimen was Spartan: no hot water for washing at any time of the year; meat and vegetables once a day and otherwise only milk and bread, mostly dry bread. The discipline was strict, though not tyrannical, and strongly religious in tone. There were no amenities—no private rooms, not even a reading-room. A boy who wished to read a book outside class-hours had to read it in the shrill pandemonium of the common playroom—an exercise to which I attribute my unusual ease of concentration. There were no luxuries; pocket money was forbidden, and though there was a certain amount of secret trading, it had usually exhausted itself by the end of the second or third week of the term. All the menial duties were done by the boys themselves; we made our own beds and cleaned our own boots. We wore a uniform which consisted of grey trousers and waistcoat, an Eton jacket of blue facecloth, and a pork-pie cap with a straight flat peak of shiny black leather. In winter we carried grey Inverness capes.

This monastic establishment has changed out of all recognition since my time: it has been brought into the general line of secondary schools, thrown open to day-boys, and generally modernized. But when I was there, it still maintained all the features of a much earlier conception of education, such as we can find described in the novels of Dickens; it was not essentially different from the Christ's Hospital described by Leigh Hunt in his *Autobiography*. For the first year I had the company of my younger brother; and our third brother joined us in the second year. But I have never lived under such a cloud of unhappiness as fell upon me once we had taken a brave farewell of our mother and the guardian uncle who had accompanied us on this first journey. I was by disposition of a quiet nature, but no wild animal from the pampas imprisoned in a cage could have felt so hopelessly thwarted. From fields and hedges and the wide open spaces of the moors; from the natural companionship of animals and all the mutations of farm life, I had passed into a confined world of stone walls, smoky skies, and two hundred unknown and apparently unsympathetic strangers. It is true that among the crowd we soon

learned to distinguish a group of a dozen or twenty in the same
predicament—the 'new boys' or 'newkers' who had arrived on the
same day. And each of us was allotted a 'guardian'—an older boy
whose duty was to initiate us into the ways of the school. But
nothing could relieve the overwhelming desolation of our life, and
this state of anguish continued for at least twelve months.

HERBERT READ, *The Falcon and the Dove*, 1940

Luxuriating backwards in the bath,
I swish the warmer water round my legs
Towards my shoulders, and the waves of heat
Bring those five years of Marlborough through to me,
In comfortable retrospect: 'Thank God
I'll never have to go through them again.'
As with my toes I reach towards the tap
And turn it to a trickle, stealing warm
About my tender person, comes a voice,
An inner voice that calls, 'Be fair! be fair!
It was not quite as awful as you think.'
In steam like this the changing-room was bathed;
Pink bodies splashed hot water on themselves
After the wonderful release from games,
When Atherton would lead the songs we sang.
I see the tall Memorial Reading Room,
Which smelt of boots and socks and water-pipes,
Its deaf invigilator on his throne—
'*Do you tickle your arse with a feather, Mr. Purdick?*'
'*What?*'
'*Particularly nasty weather, Mr. Purdick!*'
'*Oh.*'

And, as the water cools, the Marlborough terms
Form into seasons. Winter starts us off,
Lasting two years, for we were new boys twice—

The World of School

Once in a junior, then a senior house.
Spring has its love and summer has its art:
It is the winter that remains with me,
Black as our college suits, as cold and thin.

    Doom! Shivering doom! Clutching a leather grip
Containing things for the first night of term—
House-slippers, sponge-bag, pyjams, Common Prayer,
My health certificate, photographs of home
(Where were my bike, my playbox and my trunk?)—
I walked with strangers down the hill to school.
The town's first gaslights twinkled in the cold.
Deserted by the coaches, poorly served
By railway, Marlborough was a lonely place;
The old Bath Road, in chalky whiteness, raised
Occasional clouds of dust as motors passed.

JOHN BETJEMAN, *Summoned by Bells*, 1960

You could be a Coll pre. or merely a House pre. You could be a Coll
Blood or merely a House Blood, a Coll Punt (i.e. a pariah, an
unpopular person) or merely a House Punt; and of course a Coll
Tart or merely a House Tart. A Tart is a pretty and effeminate-
looking small boy who acts as a catamite to one or more of his
seniors, usually Bloods. Usually, not always. Though our oligarchy
kept most of the amenities of life to themselves, they were, on this
point, liberal; they did not impose chastity on the middle-class boy
in addition to all his other disabilities. Pederasty among the lower
classes was not 'side', or at least not serious side; not like putting
one's hands in one's pockets or wearing one's coat unbuttoned. The
gods had a sense of proportion.

  The Tarts had an important function to play in making school
(what it was advertised to be) a preparation for public life. They were
not like slaves, for their favours were (nearly always) solicited, not

70

compelled. Nor were they exactly like prostitutes, for the *liaison* often had some permanence and, far from being merely sensual, was highly sentimentalised. Nor were they paid (in hard cash, I mean) for their services; though of course they had all the flattery, unofficial influence, favour, and privileges which the mistresses of the great have always enjoyed in adult society. That was where the Preparation for Public Life came in. It would appear from Mr Arnold Lunn's *Harrovians* that the Tarts at his school acted as informers. None of ours did. I ought to know, for one of my friends shared a study with a minor Tart; and except that he was sometimes turned out of the study when one of the Tart's lovers came in (and that, after all, was only natural) he had nothing to complain of. I was not shocked by these things. For me, at that age, the chief drawback to the whole system was that it bored me considerably. For you will have missed the atmosphere of our House unless you picture the whole place from week's end to week's end buzzing, tittering, hinting, whispering about this subject. After games, gallantry was the principal topic of polite conversation; who had 'a case with' whom, whose star was in the ascendant, who had whose photo, who and when and how often and what night and where. . . . I suppose it might be called the Greek Tradition. But the vice in question is one to which I had never been tempted, and which, indeed, I still find opaque to the imagination. Possibly, if I had only stayed longer at the Coll, I might, in this respect as in others, have been turned into a Normal Boy, as the system promises. As things were, I was bored.

C. S. LEWIS, *Surprised by Joy*, 1955

It was usual in those days for anxious elders to accuse the public schools of almost universal sexual corruption, but in reality we were on the whole an innocent lot. More than sixty years later, I sometimes see an elderly gentleman, bald, stout, with a sad moustache, and I remember that once he was a self-conscious Adonis, top-hat to one side, proud of his reputation as a school tart. We believed in a system of live-and-let-live; we made vulgar jokes; we repeated ribald rhymes to show our sophistication; but very few of us translated vulgar ribaldry into action.

ALAN PRYCE-JONES, *The Bonus of Laughter*, 1987

'I say, Frank, what's wrong with you?' said David.

Frank gave Adams's letter to him.

'Read it,' he said.

David took it. It spoke of the letter written by Hughes to a boy in the house, a letter disgusting and conclusive. . . . Then it spoke of the disgrace Hughes had brought on himself, and the misery he had brought on his father and mother. He read it and gave it back to Frank.

'Well, I'm awfully sorry, just as you are,' he said: 'but if fellows will be brutes——Old Adams seems no end cut up about it. But somehow, I'd ceased to be pals with Hughes. Where's the Swinburne?'

But still Frank did not answer, and David knitted puzzled brows.

'What's up?' he said.

Maddox turned over on to his back, and tilted his hat over his eyes till his face was invisible.

'I might have been Hughes,' he said.

Again the memory of what David always turned his face from came into his mind.

'Oh, rot,' he said lamely, hating the subject.

Maddox was silent a moment.

' 'Tisn't quite rot,' he said. 'But then there came a thing, which I dare say you've forgotten, only I haven't. You came in from playing squash one wet afternoon, and you and your innocence made me suddenly see what a beast I was.'

David could not help giving a little shudder, but the moment after he was ashamed of it.

'I don't care what you were like before,' he said. 'But what I'm

333333

3333333

perfectly sure of is that since then—I remember it very well—you've been all right.'

'Yes.'

'There you are, then!' said David.

Frank was still lying with his hat over his face, but now he pushed it back and looked at David.

'It's all serene for you,' he said, 'because you've always been a straight chap. But it's different for me. I feel just rotten.'

David scratched his head in some perplexity. The whole matter was vague and repugnant to him, and he did not want to hear more or know more. There were such heaps of jolly proper things in the world to be interested in and curious about. But he understood without any vagueness at all and with the very opposite of repulsion, that his friend was in trouble, and that he wanted sympathy with that. So the whole of his devoted little heart went out there. It was bad trouble, too, the worst trouble a fellow could have.

'It must be perfectly beastly for you,' he said, 'and I'm as sorry as I can be. But you're sorry yourself, and what more can a chap do? If you weren't sorry it would be different. There's another thing too, to set against what you've done, and that's how you've behaved to me. You've been an absolute brick to me. You've kept that sort of filth away from me: I know you have.'

David paused for a moment. This morning alone on the hot beach his mind had dwelt long and eagerly on this wonderful friendship, and now, just when it was the very thing that was wanted to comfort Frank, this aspect of it struck him. He remembered how often Frank had, by a seemingly chance word, discouraged him from seeing much of certain fellows in the house; he remembered the night when Hughes came and sat on his bed, and with what extraordinary promptitude Frank had ejected him; he remembered how his dormitory had been changed, and he had been put in Frank's, and had since then slept in the bed next him. All this with swift certainty started into his mind, and with it the policy that lay behind it. Frank had consistently kept nasty things away from him; here was his atonement.

So he went on eagerly.

'I know what you've done for me,' he said, 'You've always—since then—had an eye on me, and kept filth away. I'm no end grateful. And since you've done that, chalk it up on the other side. You've made it easier for me to be decent. Oh, damn, I'm jawing.'

E. F. BENSON, *David Blaize*, 1916

The Angel of Reason, descending
   On my seven year old head
Inscribed this sentence by my bed:
   The pleasure of money is unending
But sex satisfied is sex dead.
   I tested to see if sex died
But, all my effort notwithstanding,
   Have never found it satisfied.

Abacus of Reason, you have been
   The instrument of my abuse,
The North Star I have never seen,
   The trick for which I have no use:
The Reason, gadget of schoolmasters,
   Pimp of the spirit, the smart alec,
Proud engineer of disasters,
   I see phallic: you, cephalic.

Happy those early days when I
   Attended an elementary school
Where seven hundred infant lives
   Flittered like gadflies on the stool
(We discovered that contraceptives
   Blown up like balloons, could fly);
We memorised the Golden Rule:
   Lie, lie, lie, lie.

GEORGE BARKER, 'The True Confessions of
George Barker', 1947

There was only one need that the City Grammar could not meet—girls. There were, of course, a lot of them about. Indeed, more than half of the school's population was female; for as well as containing girls of conspicuous talent the sixth form included others with inadequate School Certificates and little hope of success at A-Level, who simply hung around waiting for places in teachers' training colleges. But none of my peers ever attracted me. In the fifth form I had worshipped from afar the head prefect, whose name I now forget. And in my final term I felt a brief (and unreciprocated) infatuation for a sixteen-year-old replica of Anne Baxter. But neither the older woman to whom I never spoke nor the child who rebuffed my every advance sat with me in class between nine and four. It was, I have no doubt, a weakness in my character. But I could never feel any attraction for a girl who confused the two Home Rule Bills, or could not understand why Andrea del Sarto was not satisfied with being called 'the perfect painter'. The girls I met outside the school did not face the constant humiliation of returned essays with 'C' on the bottom. Nor were they obliged to run about in navy blue knickers holding hockey sticks in their hands as if they were as adept at women's sports as I was at men's games. No doubt the girls I saw outside school were less scholarly than my colleagues and contemporaries in the sixth form. And, Olga George apart, they were certainly less athletic. But their deficiencies were not as cruelly exposed as the shortcomings of Pat Taylor, Pat Coulson, Olga Bennett and Shirley Jago. Towards the very end of what our school magazine would have called my 'school career', I did make an unsuccessful foray in Miss Jago's direction. But when she contemptuously ignored me I felt neither pain nor embarrassment. I simply assumed that she was experiencing the aversion that I felt when I listened to her friends attempting to read Shelley or Keats aloud. Romance was struck dead by one touch of cold philosophy—or (to be more precise) history, English, geography and Latin.

ROY HATTERSLEY, *A Yorkshire Boyhood*, 1983

On the road, a boy from an inferior school, where the parents did not have to pay anything, called me 'One eye!' in a harsh, adult voice. I took no notice, but walked along whistling, my good eye on the summer clouds sailing, beyond insult, above Terrace Road.

The mathematics master said: 'I see that Mr Thomas at the back of the class has been straining his eyesight. But it isn't over his homework, is it, gentlemen?'

Gilbert Rees, next to me, laughed loudest.

'I'll break your leg after school!' I said.

He'd hobble, howling, up to the head master's study. A deep hush in the school. A message on a plate brought by the porter. 'The head master's compliments, sir, and will you come at once?' 'How did you happen to break this boy's leg?' 'Oh! damn and bottom, the agony!' cried Gilbert Rees. 'Just a little twist,' I would say. 'I don't know my own strength. I apologize. But there's nothing to worry about. Let me set the leg, sir.' A rapid manipulation, the click of a bone. 'Doctor Thomas, sir, at your service.' Mrs Rees was on her knees. 'How can I thank you?' 'It's nothing at all, dear lady. Wash his ears every morning. Throw away his rulers. Pour his red and green inks down the sink.'

In Mr Trotter's drawing class we drew naked girls inaccurately on sheets of paper under our drawings of a vase and passed them along under the desks. Some of the drawings were detailed strangely, others were tailed off like mermaids. Gilbert Rees drew the vase only.

'Sleep with your wife, sir?'

'What did you say?'

'Lend me a knife, sir?'

'What would you do if you had a million pounds?'

'I'd buy a Bugatti and a Rolls and a Bentley and I'd go two hundred miles an hour on Pendine sands.'

'I'd buy a harem and keep the girls in the gym.'

'I'd buy a house like Mrs Cotmore-Richard's, twice as big as hers, and a cricket field and a football field and a proper garage with mechanics and a lift.'

'And a lavatory as big as, as big as the Melba pavilion, with plush seats and golden chains and . . .'

'And I'd smoke cigarettes with real gold tips, better than Morris's Blue Book.'

'I'd buy all the railway trains, and only 4A could travel in them.'

'And not Gilbert Rees either.'

'What's the longest you've been?'

'I went to Edinburgh.'

'My father went to Salonika in the War.'

'Where's that, Cyril?'

'Cyril, tell us about Mrs Pussie Edwards in Hanover Street.'

'Well, my brother says he can do anything.'

I drew a wild guess below the waist, and wrote Pussie Edwards in small letters at the foot of the page.

'Cave!'

'Hide your drawings.'

'I bet you a greyhound can go faster than a horse.'

Everybody liked the drawing class, except Mr Trotter.

DYLAN THOMAS, *Portrait of the Artist as a Young Dog*, 1940

The big dormitory was the grimmest part of the House. It was so lofty and cold that it seemed to make people heartless.

Two lips had been painted on one of the beams and all new boys had to pull themselves up by their arms, to kiss them. I remember straining up, and at last reaching the yellow pitch pine and the two crimson lips. They looked indecent, for some reason; as if they were the drawing of another part of the body.

When I kissed them, the taste of varnish and dust came as a shock. I imagined that they would somehow be scented.

I thought of this now as I watched other people trying to kiss them. If they were not quick or could not reach them, they were flicked with wet towels as an encouragement.

I had been told that you could lift the skin off someone's back in this way. I always waited, half in horror, to see a ribbon of flesh come off.

All the handles had been broken off the chambers so that we could play bowls. Being hollow, they looked like white skulls as they spun towards you across the dark linoleum.

The head of the dormitory this term was Woods. He was tall and heavy, and he sometimes wore a pair of black pyjamas which had, at first, created a sensation. He would lie in bed, looking frowsty, the black pyjamas open so that you saw the little black hairs sprouting on his chest.

He used to tell loud stories about his aunt who wanted to be a débutante at forty-three, and insisted on being presented at Court.

Anyone who was going to be beaten had to stay downstairs after prayers. When they came up to the dormitory Woods would say, 'Show us your marks.' Then we would all crowd round and look at the purple marks on the white behind.

DENTON WELCH, *Maiden Voyage*, 1943

The boys, as they talked to the girls from Marcia Blaine School, stood on the far side of their bicycles holding the handlebars, which established a protective fence of bicycle between the sexes, and the impression that at any moment the boys were likely to be away.

The girls could not take off their panama hats because this was not far from the school gates and hatlessness was an offence. Certain departures from the proper set of the hat on the head were over-looked in the case of fourth-form girls and upwards so long as nobody wore their hat at an angle. But there were other subtle variants from the ordinary rule of wearing the brim turned up at the back and down at the front. The five girls, standing very close to each other because of the boys, wore their hats each with a definite difference.

These girls formed the Brodie set. That was what they had been called even before the headmistress had given them the name, in scorn, when they had moved from the Junior to the Senior school at the age of twelve. At that time they had been immediately recognisable as Miss Brodie's pupils, being vastly informed on a lot of subjects irrelevant to the authorised curriculum, as the head-mistress said, and useless to the school as a school. These girls were discovered to have heard of the Buchmanites and Mussolini, the Italian Renaissance painters, the advantages to the skin of cleansing cream and witch-hazel over honest soap and water, and the word 'menarche'; the interior decoration of the London house of the author of *Winnie the Pooh* had been described to them, as had the love lives of Charlotte Brontë and of Miss Brodie herself. They were aware of the existence of Einstein and the arguments of those who considered the Bible to be untrue. They knew the rudiments of astrology but not the date of the Battle of Flodden or the capital of Finland. All of the Brodie set, save one, counted on its fingers, as had Miss Brodie, with accurate results more or less.

By the time they were sixteen, and had reached the fourth form, and loitered beyond the gates after school, and had adapted themselves to the orthodox regime, they remained unmistakably Brodie, and were all famous in the school, which is to say they were held in suspicion and not much liking. They had no team spirit and very little in common with each other outside their continuing friendship with Jean Brodie. She still taught in the Junior department. She was held in great suspicion.

Marcia Blaine School for Girls was a day school which had been partially endowed in the middle of the nineteenth century by the wealthy widow of an Edinburgh book-binder. She had been an admirer of Garibaldi before she died. Her manly portrait hung in the great hall, and was honoured every Founder's Day by a bunch of hard-wearing flowers such as chrysanthemums or dahlias. These were placed in a vase beneath the portrait, upon a lectern which also held an open Bible with the text underlined in red ink, 'O where shall I find a virtuous woman, for her price is above rubies.'

MURIEL SPARK, *The Prime of Miss Jean Brodie*, 1961

There seems to be a large gap
Somewhere about here.
If repression is at work
Then repression works efficiently,
In this sphere.

I don't remember learning about sex
In the school lavatories;
Though I remember the lavatories.

With a great effort I call up
Certain goings-on in the rear rows
Of the Physics class. I can't believe it.
That Welsh master was so sharp
You couldn't blow your nose
Without him glaring.

At one time or another
Some slightly special one or other—
But to kiss a girl
Would have seemed like criminal assault.
There was one called Pearl
Who would quote bits from Rosalind
In *As You Like It*, leaving me confused.
Once at a party I stepped heavily
On her hand, and was appalled.
In a strange way she seemed to like it.
I was glad to go home and study *The Prelude*.

It was homework and rugger; then
It was essays and walks to Grantchester.
Perhaps we were great Platonic lovers then.
Perhaps there is nothing to remember.

D. J. ENRIGHT, 'Ugly Neck', in *The Terrible Shears*, 1973

The World of School

It is very difficult to convey the atmosphere of an English public school for girls to anyone who has the good fortune not to have been sent to one. They are—or at least this one was in my time—run on a male system imperfectly adapted to female needs. We were terribly, terribly keen on games. A carefully fostered and almost entirely spurious interest in house matches was our main subject of conversation. Girls at boarding school ages are suggestible almost beyond belief: trying to recall now the inter-girl talks that took place when authority was not in hearing, I remember snatches of discussion, in which we vied with one another in the single-minded animation expected of us, as to whether Wingfield's second eleven was likely to do better than last year against Aldhelmsted Juniors, these being two of the houses. Now I do not believe that sporting conjecture of this kind comes natural to one girl in twenty; but this was the tradition of the place (officially described as The High Moral Tone of the School) and so this was how we talked, even when alone.

E. ARNOT ROBERTSON (Sherborne), in Graham Greene (ed.),
The Old School, 1934

Anxious to publicise and pay our dues
Contracted here, we, Bernard Noel Hughes
And Philip Arthur Larkin, do desire

To requite and to reward those whom we choose;
To thank our friends, before our time expire,
And those whom, if not friends, we yet admire.

First, our corporeal remains we give
Unto the Science Sixth—demonstrative
Of physical fitness—for minute dissection;

Trusting that they will generously forgive
Any trifling lapses from perfection,
And give our viscera their close attention.

—With one exception: we bequeath our ears
To the Musical Society, and hope
It finds out why they loathed the panatrope—

(And, however pointed it appears,
We leave the wash-bowls twenty cakes of soap)
Item, herewith to future pioneers

In realms of knowledge, we bequeath our books,
And woe pursue who to a master quotes
The funnier of our witty marginal notes.

Likewise, we leave the Modern Sixth the jokes
This year has fostered, and to him who croaks
Of Higher School Certificates, ten sore throats.

To Paul Montgomery, a sturdy comb
To discipline his rough and ruddy strands;
And Mr H. B. Gould we leave . . . alone.

We leave our Latin cribs to William Rider,
And may his shadow never disappear;
To the Zoologists, a common spider;

And, for their services throughout the year,
To the Air Defence Cadets a model glider;
And to the First XV a cask of beer.

Item, to Percy Slater we now send
A candle he can burn at either end,
And hours of toil without the ill-effects;

Item, our school reports we leave the Staff,
To give them, as we hope, a hearty laugh;
And Kipling's 'If' to hang upon their wall.

The World of School

Sympathy for the impossible task
Of teaching us to swim the six-beat crawl
We leave our swimming master. Item, all

Our *Magnets* and our *Wizards* we consign
To the Librarian in the cause of Culture
And may his Library flourish well in future;

Next (now the troops have taken their departure)
With ever-grateful hearts we do assign
To our French master, all the Maginot Line.

Essays, and our notes on style and diction,
We leave our English master, confident
He won't consider them as an infliction.

Our German master, for the sore affliction
Of teaching us, we humbly present
With an Iron Cross (First Class, but slightly bent);

To the Art Master, as the only one
Appreciative (and, Philistines to thwart)
We leave a blue cap and four ties that stun:

And all the Scholarships we never won
We give to those who want things of that sort:
And to the Savings Groups . . . our full support.

Our Games Master we leave some high-jump stands
—The reason why we know he understands—
And to the Carpenter the grass he's mown.

Our badges we resign to future Prefects,
The lines-book, too; to F. G. Smith, our friend,
We leave a compact and a bottle of Cutex;

And all the paper that we never needed
For this *Coventrian*, to Ian Fraser,
And may he triumph where we've not succeeded:

To his subordinates, an ink eraser . . .
And this Magazine itself? Well, there's always a
Lot of people queer enough to read it.

Herewith we close, with Time's apology
For the ephemeral injury,
On this 26th of July, 1940.

The Coventrian, September 1940

PHILIP LARKIN, 'Last Will and Testament',
in *Collected Poems*, 1988

The ideal school of fiction . . . must at all costs be near the sea, preferably standing at the top of precipitous cliffs. The cliffs can either be fallen down, climbed up, or stuck on halfway. Stuck on halfway is best, for the agonizing wait enables Thirza to find the old smugglers' cave and the underground passage and to come bursting back through a secret door right into Miss Pritchard's bathroom at a moment when Miss Pritchard is least expecting her.

Came the whine of rusty hinges, the creak of ancient woodwork, and an odour of musty, forgotten things. Smoothly a portion of the linen-fold panelling slid gently sideways to reveal a dusty, towsled head.
Then: 'It's me,' said a small voice.
Miss Pritchard gasped. 'Good gracious, Thirza, how you startled me,' and her dripping loofah fell back with a splash into the foaming suds.

The school grounds must contain a disused well, down which one of the new girls falls, a tidal river down which one of the new girls is swept away, and a potting shed, inside which the school smart set gives sherbet parties. Within the school there must be a boot-hole, for it is here that a really wicked girl can smoke an occasional cigarette, or put a dab of forbidden powder on her nose or a smear of *Nuit de Penzance* behind her ears.

It is essential, too, that the fire arrangements should be of the flimsiest and most makeshift kind. It is no sort of fun at all if, when the stairs are found to be blazing, Mademoiselle can make an easy way down. No: after screeching from her window in a glorious mixture of imperfect English and troubled French, she must then clamber on to the windowsill and take a spirited header into a laurel bush, emerging with nothing worse than assorted bruises and one or two simple fractures. It is the least we expect of her. Incidentally, how badly in fiction is the *entente cordiale* preserved. Poor Mademoiselle! Her French-speaking table in the dining-room is a riot of second-rate behaviour and dexterously aimed bread-pellets. The stairs outside her bedroom are relentlessly buttered and she comes purler after purler. White mice rush squeaking from any desk that she happens to open, and she cannot go within fifty yards of the cricket-field without receiving a wristy full-toss on a spot where she would least have wished to receive it. Her life is spent uttering a string of '*Mon Dieu! Qu'est-ce que c'est que ça? Ah non!* Zeees is *intolérable!*', surrounded by a positive Sherwood Forest of exclamation marks.

ARTHUR MARSHALL, 'Girls will be Girls', a broadcast in 1954

I opened a volume. The pages were frayed at the edges. A smudged image of a cricketer in a soft cap caught my eye: a hero. The fields inside me opened out into full summer. An inside left's leg lifted into the sky: another hero. The cheers inside me unfroze. A fat bottom was being ejected at speed from a third-class carriage, a fat face yelled silently out of the past. Bunter! Just to glimpse these narrow columns of type placed me at once in the spring of 1940, when my father descended on me from London one glorious weekend and brought me his tattered collection of *Magnet*s to show me for the first time. He had often spoken of Bunter before the war, lightly, as if fearing scorn. Only now did he judge me old enough, at eleven or so, to be entrusted with the physical proof that Greyfriars, and so many traditions inexplicable to infants or foreigners or women, really existed. 'This'll make you laugh, boy,' he said.

Squatting in a hot field behind the bungalow where I was billeted as an evacuee, father showed me my way about that world as he turned the faded page, told me to guard the papers with my life, sat on his haunches to smile at the silly way I laughed, and hurried back by an evening train to his hush-hush war-work in threatened London. 'Don't cry, boy,' he said, shaking his head as the whistle blew and the carriages moved off.

That night in bed I started reading out of duty and soon perked up and my elbow ached and the bulb in the torch started flickering. And thereafter for weeks on end I read back and forth over the territory as it grew familiar, and I learnt with what passion a page of print seized hold of my mind, and how completely a world of which I had no experience not only established dominion over me, but intensified my longings for an equal excitement in the world outside it. Fiction was a rush of truth; facts just got muddled in.

DAVID HUGHES, *But for Bunter*, 1985

The mental world of the *Gem* and *Magnet* . . . is something like this:

The year is 1910—or 1940, but it is all the same. You are at Greyfriars, a rosy-cheeked boy of fourteen in posh tailor-made clothes, sitting down to tea in your study on the Remove passage after an exciting game of football which was won by an odd goal in the last half-minute. There is a cosy fire in the study, and outside the wind is whistling. The ivy clusters thickly round the old grey stones. The King is on his throne and the pound is worth a pound. Over in Europe the comic foreigners are jabbering and gesticulating, but the grim grey battleships of the British fleet are steaming up the Channel and at the outposts of Empire the monocled Englishmen are holding the niggers at bay. Lord Mauleverer has just got another fiver and we are all settling down to a tremendous tea of sausages, sardines, crumpets, potted meat, jam and doughnuts. After tea we shall sit round the study fire having a good laugh at Billy Bunter and discussing the team for next week's match against Rookwood. Everything is safe, solid and unquestionable. Everything will be the same for ever and ever. That approximately is the atmosphere.

GEORGE ORWELL, 'Boys' Weeklies', in *Inside the Whale*, 1940

CUSTOMS, ANECDOTES, INCIDENTS

Deborah Delora, she liked a bit of fun—
She went to the baker's and she bought a penny bun;
Dipped the bun in treacle and threw it at her teacher—
Deborah Delora: what a wicked creature!

ANON.

─────

As it was an hour and a half before school would commence, I hastened home, and having spent all my money, begged aunt Milly to give me some; she gave me a shilling, and with that I bought as much gunpowder as I could procure, more than a quarter of a pound.

I then returned to the school, looked into the school-room, and found it empty; I quickly raised up the claret case, under which the fireworks had been placed, put the powder under it, leaving only sufficient for a very small train, which would not be perceived in the green baize covering; having so done, I left the school-room immediately, and rejoined my companions. I had a piece of touchwood, as all the boys had, to let off their fireworks with, and this I lighted and left in a corner until the bell should summon us into school.

Oh! how my heart beat when I heard the sound, so full was I of anxiety lest my project should fail.

Once more we were all assembled. Mr O'Gallagher, surveying, with the smile of a demon, the unhappy and disappointed faces of the boys, was again perched upon his throne, the rod on one side, the ferrule on the other, and the ruler, that dreaded truncheon of command, clenched in his broad fist.

I had the touchwood lighted and concealed in my hand; gradually I moved downwards, until at last, unperceived by Mr O'Gallagher, I was behind him, and close to my train of gunpowder. I gave one look to ascertain if he had observed me; his eye was roving over the school for some delinquent to throw his ruler at; fearful that he might turn round to me, I no longer hesitated, and the touchwood was applied to the train.

Ignorant as I was of the force of gunpowder, it was with astonishment mingled with horror that I beheld, in a second, the claret case rise up as if it had wings, and Mr O'Gallagher thrown up to the ceiling enveloped in a cloud of smoke, the crackers and squibs fizzing and banging, while the boys in the school uttered a yell of consternation and fear as they rushed back from the explosion, and afterwards, tumbling over one another, made their escape from the school-room.

The windows had all been blown out with a terrible crash, and the whole school-room was now covered by the smoke. There I stood in silent dismay at the mischief which I had done. The squibs and crackers had not, however, all finished popping before I heard the howling of Mr O'Gallagher, who had fallen down upon the centre school-room table.

I was still in the school-room half suffocated, yet not moving away from where I stood, when the neighbours, who had been alarmed by the explosion and the cries of the boys, rushed in, and perceiving only me and Mr O'Gallagher, who still howled, they caught hold of us both, and bore us out in their arms. It was high time, for the school-room was now on fire, and in a few minutes more the flames burst out of the windows, while volumes of smoke forced through the door and soon afterwards the roof.

The engines were sent for, but before they could arrive or water be procured, the whole tenement was so enveloped in flames that it could not be saved. In an hour, the *locale* of our misery was reduced to ashes. They had put me on my legs as soon as we got clear of the school-room, to ascertain whether I was hurt, and finding that I was not, they left me.

I never shall forget what my sensations were, when I beheld the flames and volumes of smoke bursting out; the hurry, and bustle, and confusion outside; the working of the engines, the troops marched up from the barracks, the crowd of people assembled, and the ceaseless mingling of tongues from every quarter; and all this is my doing, thought I—mine—all mine.

I felt delighted that I had no partner or confederate; I could, at all events, keep my own secret. I did, however, feel some anxiety as to Mr O'Gallagher, for, much as I detested him, I certainly had no intention to kill him; so, after a time, I made inquiries, and found that he was alive, and in no danger, although very much bruised, and somewhat burnt.

CAPTAIN MARRYAT, *Percival Keene*, 1842

At one point the school was burnt down. It happened during a cricket match between the staff and the school's chartered accountants. Francis Huxley discovered the fire in, I think, a linen cupboard. He ran out to the cricket field to give the alarm. We all ran back to the main building, now burning well. A waiter known as Jilly George was throwing top hats out of the headmaster's study, and later had to be rescued when he was overcome by smoke.

After the fire we went home for several weeks while they put up temporary huts to replace the part of the school that had been burnt down. We all wondered who had started the fire. Rumour said it was a small boy, who, when we wore ties on Sundays instead of open-necked shirts, always tied the knot of his tie very small.

'It's not nice for small boys to have small knots in their ties,' the matron used to say to him, pulling him about as she re-tied his tie. 'Not nice.'

JOHN GALE, *Clean Young Englishman*, 1965

Walking one day in the street, he chanced to displease a stout lad, who doubled his fist to beat him; but another boy interfered to claim benefit of clergy for the studious George. 'You must not meddle with *him*,' he said; 'let *him* alone, for he ha' got l'arning.'

His father observed this bookish turn, and though he had then no higher view of him in life than that he should follow his own example, and be employed in some inferior department of the revenue service, he resolved to give George the advantage of passing some time in a school at Bungay, on the borders of Norfolk, where it was hoped the activity of his mind would be disciplined into orderly diligence. I cannot say how soon this removal from the paternal roof took place; but it must have been very early, as the following anecdote will show:—The first night he spent at Bungay he retired to bed, he said, 'with a heavy heart, thinking of his fond, indulgent mother.' But the morning brought a new misery. The slender and delicate child had hitherto been dressed by his mother. Seeing the other boys begin to dress themselves, poor George, in great confusion, whispered to his bedfellow, 'Master G——, can you put on your shirt?—for—for I'm afraid I cannot.'

Soon after his arrival he had a very narrow escape. He and several of his schoolfellows were punished for playing at soldiers, by being put into a large dog-kennel, known by the terrible name of 'the black hole'. George was the first that entered: and, the place being crammed full with offenders, the atmosphere soon became pestilentially close. The poor boy in vain shrieked that he was about to be suffocated. At last, in despair, he bit the lad next to him violently in the hand. 'Crabbe is dying—Crabbe is dying,' roared the sufferer; and the sentinel at length opened the door, and allowed the boys to rush out into the air. My father said, 'A minute more, and I must have died.'

I am unable to give any more particulars of his residence at Bungay. When he was in his eleventh or twelfth year, it having now been determined that he should follow the profession of a surgeon, he was removed to a school of somewhat superior character, kept by Mr Richard Haddon, a skilful mathematician, at Stowmarket, in the same county; and here, inheriting his father's talent and predilection for mathematical science, he made considerable progress in such pursuits. The Salt-master used often to send difficult questions to

Mr Haddon, and, to his great delight, the solution came not unfrequently from his son; and, although Haddon was neither a Porson nor a Parr, his young pupil laid, under his care, the foundations of a fair classical education also. Some girls used to come to the school in the evenings, to learn writing; and the tradition is, that Mr Crabbe's first essay in verse was a stanza of doggerel, cautioning one of these little damsels against being too much elevated about a new set of blue ribbons to her straw bonnet.

Life of Crabbe, by his son, 1834

The punishment of a schoolboy for telling tales or for any act of treachery, coming immediately under the summary jurisdiction of his peers, is *bumping*: and this is performed by prostrating the coatless culprit on his back, in the immediate vicinity of a large block of wood, or of a wall. A strong boy seizes the right ankle and wrist, another the left, and lift him off the ground; and after a preparatory vibration or two to give a due momentum, he comes in violent contact with the block, *a posteriori*. This is repeated six or eight more times, according to the enormity of ᴛhe offence, or the just resentment of the executioners.

EDWARD MOOR, at school in the 1770s, in *Suffolk Words*, 1823

The schoolchild, in his primitive community, conducts his business with his fellows by ritual declaration. His affidavits, promissory notes, claims, deeds of conveyance, receipts, and notices of resignation, are verbal, and are sealed by the utterance of ancient words which are recognized and considered binding by the whole community.

This juvenile language of significant terms and formulas appears to be a legacy of the days when the nation itself was younger and more primitive (a medieval knight offered his opponent 'barlay', and children today in the north-west seek respite with the same cry);

and much of this language, like the country dialects, varies from one region of Britain to another. Of barbarian simplicity, the schoolchild code enjoins that prior assertion of ownership in the prescribed form shall take the place of litigation; and that not even the deliberately swindled has redress if the bargain has been concluded by a bond word. Further, it will be noticed that the gestures with which the significance of the language is stressed, for example, spitting, crossing fingers, and touching cold iron, are gestures which have been an accepted part of ritual since times long before our own.

IONA and PETER OPIE, *Lore and Language of Schoolchildren*, 1959

The boys have played two tricks upon me which were these—they first proposed to play at 'King of the Cobblers' and asked if I would be king, to which I agreed. Then they made me sit down and sat (on the ground) in a circle round me, and told me to say 'Go to work' which I said, and they immediately began kicking me and knocking me on all sides. The next game they proposed was 'Peter, the red lion,' and they made a mark on a tombstone (for we were playing in the church-yard) and one of the boys walked with his eyes shut, holding out his finger, trying to touch the mark; then a little boy came forward to lead the rest and led a good many very near the mark; at last it was my turn; they told me to shut my eyes well, and the next minute I had my finger in the mouth of one of the boys, who had stood (I believe) before the tombstone with his mouth open. For 2 nights I slept alone, and for the rest of the time with Ned Swire. The boys play me no tricks now. The only fault (tell Mama) that there has been was coming in one day to dinner just after grace. On Sunday we went to church in the morning, and sat in a large pew with Mr Fielding, the church we went to is close by Mr Tate's house, we did not go in the afternoon but Mr Tate read a discourse to the boys on the 5th commandment. We went to church again in the evening. Papa wished me to tell him all the texts I had heard preached upon, please to tell him that I could not hear it in the morning nor hardly one sentence of the sermon, but the one in the evening was 1 Cor. i. 23. I believe it was a farewell sermon, but I am not sure. Mrs Tate has looked through my clothes and left in the trunk a great many that will not be wanted. I have had 3 misfortunes in my clothes etc. 1st I cannot find my tooth-brush, so that I have not brushed my teeth for 3 or 4 days, 2nd I cannot find my blotting paper, and 3rd I have no shoe-horn. The chief games are, football, wrestling, leap frog, and fighting. Excuse bad writing.

Yr affec[t] brother CHARLES.

LEWIS CARROLL, letter to his brother, 1844

He was at length placed in a classical school, just then established by a certain Frank Glass. It was situated near the village of Tobermore, four miles from Grillagh as the crow flies, five by the road. Of the school-house itself, and the difficulties experienced in getting possession of it, Dr Cooke has left a graphic account:—'We were compelled to remove five times in search of accommodation. We had flitted like fieldfares in the commencement of bad weather. The house we got at last had two window-frames, but no glass. One was well secured against light by earthen sods; the other was open for some light we must have, and it served to admit, in company with the light, a refreshing portion of rain and snow. We were furnished with one table, whereat our Master sat for audience and judgment. Stones were the seats. I had myself the only stool in the house; but, the master being too tender to sit on a cold stone, I was robbed of the stool, "to save him", as he said, "from the colic". By a penny subscription and the aid of a glazier, we shut out the snow; and, in process of time, we substituted for the stone seats slabs of oak from the neighbouring bog. We thus became wonderfully content, for we had the best Master and the most comfortable school-house in all the country.'

The direct path to school lay through fields, over a swampy bog, and across a ford of the river Moyola, which often swept down, a swollen torrent, from the Dungiven mountains. Most parents would have thought a daily walk to and from Tobermore impracticable for a boy of Henry's age, and most boys would have shrunk in fear from such a difficult, if not dangerous path. But Mrs Cooke was not an ordinary woman; and fear was never a word in the vocabulary of her son. He was of slender make, but wiry and agile. Among other boyish feats he had learned to walk, and run, and gambol on stilts; and he had often astonished the sober matrons of Maghera by stalking past their upper windows. What he had learned and practised for amusement was now, by the thoughtfulness of his mother, turned to good account.

Henry was enrolled a pupil in the new classical school. His first morning's journey he never forgot. It left an indelible impress on his memory. Probably, too, it may have had some influence in fixing his principles, and moulding his whole subsequent career; for he often referred to the incident. It was in the year '98, one of the darkest in Ireland's history. The country was convulsed with rebellion. The neighbourhood of Maghera swarmed with daring bandits, who found an asylum among the mountains, and lived by rapine, caring little what party they spoiled. Henry, thoughtless of danger, strapped his satchel on his back, poised his long stilts on his shoulder, and set out for school. His mother accompanied him, anxiety filling her heart. On reaching the ford of the Moyola, they found the river swollen: to pass it on foot was impossible. Henry mounted his stilts, crossed the torrent by a few vigorous strides, and stepped safely on the opposite bank. Carefully concealing his stilts in the heath, he tripped gaily onward. When at some distance, he chanced to look back, and saw the tall figure of his mother standing on a mound with outstretched arm, pointing towards Cairntogher. Turning his eyes to the place indicated, a scene presented itself which might well have struck terror into the stoutest heart. A farm-steading was in flames—the house of a loyal man fired by the rebels. The sight was not new to Henry. Young as he was, he had witnessed many such; yet seventy years afterwards, when narrating the incident at his own table, he said the whole scene was as vividly pictured before his mind as the day on which it occurred.

J. L. PORTER, *The Life and Times of Henry Cooke*, 1871;
Cooke was born *c.*1788

Speaking to the children at the school about the Collect for the 2nd Sunday after the Epiphany and God's peace I asked them what beautiful image and picture of peace we have in the xxiii Psalm. 'The Good Shepherd', said I, 'leading His sheep to——?' 'To the slaughter,' said Frederick Herriman promptly. One day I asked the children to what animal our Saviour is compared in the Bible. Frank Matthews confidently held out his hand. 'To an ass,' he said.

REVD FRANCIS KILVERT, *Diary (1875)*, 1938–40

'Fetch that stool,' said Mr Brocklehurst, pointing to a very high one from which a monitor had just risen. It was brought.

'Place the child upon it.'

And I was placed there, by whom I don't know. I was in no condition to note particulars; I was only aware that they had hoisted me up to the height of Mr Brocklehurst's nose, that he was within a yard of me, and that a spread of shot orange and purple silk pelisses and a cloud of silvery plumage extended and waved below me.

Mr Brocklehurst hemmed.

'Ladies,' said he, turning to his family; 'Miss Temple, teachers, and children, you all see this girl?'

Of course they did, for I felt their eyes directed like burning-glasses against my scorched skin.

'You see she is yet young; you observe she possesses the ordinary form of childhood; God has graciously given her the shape that he has given to all of us; no signal deformity points her out as a marked character. Who would think that the Evil One had already found a servant and agent in her? Yet such, I grieve to say, is the case.'

A pause, in which I began to steady the palsy of my nerves, and to feel that the Rubicon was passed, and that the trial, no longer to be shirked, must be firmly sustained.

'My dear children,' pursued the black marble clergyman, with pathos, 'this is a sad, a melancholy occasion, for it becomes my duty to warn you that this girl, who might be one of God's own lambs, is a little castaway; not a member of the true flock, but evidently an interloper and an alien. You must be on your guard against her; you must shun her example; if necessary, avoid her company, exclude her from your sports, and shut her out from your converse. Teachers, you must watch her, keep your eyes on her movements, weigh well her words, scrutinize her actions, punish her body to save her soul,— if, indeed, such salvation be possible,—for (my tongue falters while I tell it) this girl, this child, the native of a Christian land,—worse than many a little heathen who says its prayers to Brahma and kneels before Juggernaut,—this girl is—a liar!'

CHARLOTTE BRONTË, *Jane Eyre,* 1847

According to tradition, Keate was positively fond of using the birch. On one occasion, it is said, the names of a batch of candidates for Confirmation were by mistake sent to him on a 'bill' like that used for reporting boys for punishment. The boys tried to explain the matter, but Keate only flogged them the harder for what he considered a sacrilegious trick to escape punishment. All this happened in the time when the boys lived under 'dames' in the boarding-houses. As the school life has become better regulated and the care of the boys has come more and more into the hands of the masters, the discipline of the prepostors and captains has become better. The head-master has only half a dozen boys or so to *swish* each term.

JOHN CORBIN, *Schoolboy Life in England,* 1898;
Eton, mid-nineteenth century

Eton.
March 1st, 1825.

My dearest Mother,

A most awful and horrible warning not to fight in the playing-fields happened last night. Owing to Wood (a boy at Hawtrey's) having bullied Ashley minimus, one of Lord Shaftesbury's sons, who was above him in the school, but considerably inferior both in size and strength, the latter offered to fight him in the playing-fields, a challenge which he immediately accepted, and they actually fought for two hours and a quarter. As Ashley, who fought most bravely, naturally became weak, he drank half a pint of brandy, which was too much for him, and after renewing the fight for some time afterwards, he fainted and died in consequence of the brandy and the blows on his temples at ten o'clock in the evening. Wood also was very much hurt: he is now dangerously ill and was taken home this morning at half past nine. Poor Ashley is the only boy who has been killed in fighting, except one about 40 years ago, since the school has been founded. I do trust this will serve as a warning for the future against this dangerous system, and I daresay Dr Keate will do his utmost to prevent a thing so disgraceful to the school and so fateful in its consequences. A Coroner's inquest is to be held over the body of the poor fellow this morning, and I am quite horrorstruck when I think that a boy so much liked as Ashley minimus and in the full vigour of health should in one evening be cut off from us by the abominable folly of fighting. I saw Sir John Chapman to-day. He told me he would send my gargle to-night; and I believe he thinks Wood's case is extremely dangerous—it is so awful that I shall not easily be able to forget it. . . .

James Milnes Gaskell, *An Eton Boy 1820–30*,
ed. Charles Milnes Gaskell, 1939

'Bolder,' said Squeers, tucking up his wristbands and moistening the palm of his right hand to get a good grip of the cane, 'you are an incorrigible young scoundrel, and as the last thrashing did you no good, we must see what another will do towards beating it out of you.'

With this, and wholly disregarding a piteous cry for mercy, Mr Squeers fell upon the boy and caned him soundly: not leaving off indeed, until his arm was tired out.

'There,' said Squeers, when he had quite done; 'rub away as hard as you like, you won't rub that off in a hurry. Oh! you won't hold that noise, won't you? Put him out, Smike.'

The drudge knew better from long experience, than to hesitate about obeying, so he bundled the victim out by a side door, and Mr Squeers perched himself again on his own stool, supported by Mrs Squeers, who occupied another at his side.

'Now let us see,' said Squeers. 'A letter for Cobbey. Stand up, Cobbey.'

Another boy stood up, and eyed the letter very hard while Squeers made a mental abstract of the same.

'Oh!' said Squeers: 'Cobbey's grandmother is dead, and his Uncle John has took to drinking, which is all the news his sister sends, except eighteenpence, which will just pay for that broken square of glass. Mrs Squeers, my dear, will you take the money?'

The worthy lady pocketed the eighteenpence with a most business-like air, and Squeers passed on to the next boy as coolly as possible.

'Graymarsh,' said Squeers, 'he's the next. Stand up, Graymarsh.'

Another boy stood up, and the schoolmaster looked over the letter as before.

'Graymarsh's maternal aunt,' said Squeers when he had possessed himself of the contents, 'is very glad to hear he's so well and happy, and sends her respectful compliments to Mrs Squeers, and thinks she must be an angel. She likewise thinks Mr Squeers is too good for this world; but hopes he may long be spared to carry on the business. Would have sent the two pair of stockings as desired, but is short of money, so forwards a tract instead, and hopes Graymarsh will put his trust in Providence. Hopes above all, that he will study in everything to please Mr and Mrs Squeers, and look upon them as his only friends; and that he will love Master Squeers, and not object to sleeping five in a bed, which no Christian should. Ah!' said Squeers, folding it up, 'a delightful letter. Very affecting indeed.'

It was affecting in one sense, for Graymarsh's maternal aunt was strongly supposed, by her more intimate friends, to be no other than his maternal parent; Squeers, however, without alluding to this part of the story (which would have sounded immoral before boys), proceeded with the business by calling out 'Mobbs,' whereupon another boy rose, and Graymarsh resumed his seat.

'Mobbs's mother-in-law,' said Squeers, 'took to her bed on hearing that he would not eat fat, and has been very ill ever since. She wishes to know by an early post where he expects to go to, if he quarrels with his vittles, and with what feelings he could turn up his nose at the cow's liver broth, after his good master had asked a blessing on it. This was told her in the London newspapers—not by Mr Squeers, for he is too kind and too good to set anybody against anybody—and it has vexed her so much, Mobbs can't think. She is sorry to find he is discontented, which is sinful and horrid, and hopes Mr Squeers will flog him into a happier state of mind; with which view she has also stopped his halfpenny a week pocket-money, and given a double-bladed knife with a corkscrew in it to the Missionaries, which she had bought on purpose for him.'

DICKENS, Nicholas Nickleby, 1838–9

Harrow, Jan. 29, 1847.—When I left you, I went to school and came back to pupil room, and in the afternoon had a solitary walk to the skating pond covered with boys. . . . In the evening two big boys rushed up, and seizing Buller (another new boy) and me, dragged us into a room where a number of boys were assembled. I was led into the midst. Bob Smith whispered to me to do as I was bid and I should not be hurt. On the other side of the room were cold chickens, cake, fruit, &c., and in a corner were a number of boys holding open little Dirom's mouth, and pouring something horrible stirred up with a tallow-candle down his throat. A great boy came up to me and told me to sing or to drink some of this dreadful mixture. I did sing—at least I made a noise—and the boys were pleased because I made no fuss, and loaded me with oranges and cakes.

Jan. 21.—What do you think happened last night? Before prayers I was desired to go into the fifth form room, as they were having some game there. A boy met me at the door, ushered me in, and told me to make my salaam to the Emperor of Morocco, who was seated cross-legged in the middle of a large counterpane, surrounded by twenty or more boys as his serving-men. I was directed to sit down by the Emperor, and in the same way. He made me sing, and then jumped off the counterpane, as he said, to get me some cake. Instantly all the boys seized the counterpane and tossed away. Up to the ceiling I went and down again, but they had no mercy, and it was up and down, head over heels, topsy-turvy, till some one called out 'Satis'—and I was let out, very sick and giddy at first, but soon all right again.

Jan. 23.—Yesterday I was in my room, delighted to be alone for once, and very much interested in the book I was reading, when D. came in and found the fire out, so I got a good licking. He makes me his fag to go errands, and do all he bids me, and if I don't do it, he beats me, but I don't mind much.

Feb. 10.—To-day at 5 minutes to 11, we were all told to go into the Speech-room (do you remember it?), a large room with raised benches all round and a platform in the middle and places for the monitors. I sat nearly at the top of one of these long ranges. Then Dr Vaughan made a speech about snow-balling at the Railway Station (a forbidden place), where the engine-drivers and conductors had been snow-balled, and he said that the next time, if he could not find out the names of the guilty individuals, the whole school should be punished. To-day the snow-balling, or rather ice-balling (for the balls are so hard you can hardly cut them with a knife), has been terrific: some fellows almost have their arms broken with them.

Feb. 21.—I have been out jumping and hare-and-hounds, but we have hard work now to escape from the slave-drivers for racket-fagging. Sometimes we do, by one fellow sacrificing himself and shutting up the others head downwards in the turn-up bedsteads, where they are quite hidden; and sometimes I get the old woman at the church to hide me in the little room over the porch till the slave-drivers have passed. . . .

Harrow, Sept. 10.—Alas! our form is under Mr Oxenham. He has the power of flogging, and does flog very often for the least fault, for he really enjoys it. He is such an old man, very old, very sharp, very indolent, very preachy. Sometimes he falls asleep when we are in form, and the boys stick curl-papers through his hair, and he never finds it out. He always calls his boys 'stupid little fools', without meaning anything particular by it.

Augustus Hare, *The Story of My Life*, 6 vols., 1896–1900;
29 Jan. is a misprint for 20 Jan.

I witnessed one morning on Ludgate Hill, as I passed to school in the omnibus, a not unusual spectacle in those days. At the turning to the Old Bailey a man who had been hanged that morning was still suspended in the air, preparatory to being cut down. It was not then quite nine o'clock, and an hour was always allowed to intervene. This was about 1845.

W. Carew Hazlitt, *Memoirs*, 1897

The boys at first wore a uniform approved and partly designed by the Prince Consort, and it remarkably resembled that of the porters and ticket-collectors of the South Eastern railway on which Wellington College was situated. This gave rise to little confusions. Lord Derby, for instance, when paying a visit to the College on the annual Speech-day, presented the outward half of his return ticket to a boy who had come down to the station to meet his mother, and the boy was not as respectful as he should have been to a member of the Governing body, and permitted himself to say something unbecoming to a well-behaved ticket-collector. It was therefore better to modify the uniform than risk the recurrence of such incidents. The Prince Consort was still inclined to think that German academical methods were in many points more desirable than the freer and more self-governing notions of the English public school in which senior boys have a hand in discipline; he did not approve of the fagging system, he did not like compulsory games, and he objected to masters (other than the head master) having the power to cane their pupils, for one master (so he pointed out) would almost certainly be stronger than another, and a more savage disciplinarian, and thus certain boys would suffer more than others for similar faults, which was obviously unfair. Then there was the question of the school chapel: he thought (with a great deal of reason) that contemporary English architecture was in a very poor way and proposed that the new chapel should be an exact model of the chapel at Eton, one-third of the size and built of brick. But with that sound wisdom which always characterized him, he very soon saw that the English were not as the Germans, and that German methods were incompatible with English ideas, and up to the time of his most lamentable death in 1861 he backed up the head master, who indeed was a very forcible man, with the utmost zeal and goodwill, and Wellington developed on native lines.

E. F. BENSON, *As We Were*, 1930

The first Master [of Wellington College] was Edward White Benson, destined afterwards to become successively Chancellor of Lincoln, Bishop of Truro, and Archbishop of Canterbury. He was more equable in those later periods, but at Wellington his was a most volcanic personality. It is said that at the beginning of January 1859 he faced the sixty shivering boys who had arrived on that day, and delivered an address so terrifying in its threats that on the first night of the first term of Wellington the entire school ran away. Probably this is mere legend. But Benson's occasional ferocity is beyond dispute. Fred Benson has recorded that none of the family dared to approach him when he was in one of his black moods. From time to time he had a violent altercation with some member of his staff, followed by a hardly less violent reconciliation. Then the Master and assistant master would shed copious tears together, after the true pattern of Victorian emotionalism. On the other side of the account must be set his tireless energy, his immense driving power, his high ideals and the resolute courage with which he pursued them. If often he terrified the boys, he inspired them also. If his wishes ran contrary to those of the Governors and the Prince Consort, always he got his way. By the sheer force of his personality, in an amazingly short time he had transformed what had been designed as a charitable institution into one of the leading Public Schools.

ANTHONY C. DEANE, *Time Remembered*, 1945

Then a dozen big boys seized hold of a blanket dragged from one of the beds. 'In with Scud, quick, there's no time to lose.' East was chucked into the blanket. 'Once, twice, thrice, and away!' up he went like a shuttlecock, but not quite up to the ceiling.

'Now, boys, with a will,' cried Walker, 'once, twice, thrice, and away!' This time he went clean up, and kept himself from touching the ceiling with his hand, and so again a third time, when he was turned out, and up went another boy. And then came Tom's turn. He lay quite still, by East's advice, and didn't dislike the 'once, twice, thrice'; but the 'away' wasn't so pleasant. They were in good wind now, and sent him slap up to the ceiling first time, against which his knees came rather sharply. But the moment's pause before descending was the rub, the feeling of utter helplessness, and of leaving his whole inside behind him sticking to the ceiling. Tom was very near shouting to be set down, when he found himself back in the blanket, but thought of East, and didn't: and so took his three tosses without a kick or a cry, and was called a young trump for his pains.

He and East, having earned it, stood now looking on. No catastrophe happened, as all the captives were cool hands, and didn't struggle. This didn't suit Flashman. What your real bully likes in tossing, is when the boys kick and struggle, or hold on to one side of the blanket, and so get pitched bodily on to the floor; it's no fun to him when no one is hurt or frightened.

'Let's toss two of them together, Walker,' suggested he. 'What a cursed bully you are, Flashey!' rejoined the other. 'Up with another one.'

And so no two boys were tossed together, the peculiar hardship of which is, that it's too much for human nature to lie still then and share troubles; and so the wretched pair of small boys struggle in the air which shall fall a-top in the descent, to the no small risk of both falling out of the blanket, and the huge delight of brutes like Flashman.

But now there's a cry that the præpostor of the room is coming; so the tossing stops, and all scatter to their different rooms; and Tom is left to turn in, with the first day's experience of a public school to meditate upon.

THOMAS HUGHES, *Tom Brown's Schooldays*, 1857

At last the bell of the school chapel began to ring, and they went in to the afternoon service. Eric usually sat with Duncan and Llewellyn, immediately behind the benches allotted to chance visitors. The bench in front of them happened on this afternoon to be occupied by some rather odd people, viz. an old man with long white hair, and two ladies remarkably stout, who were dressed with much juvenility, although past middle age. Their appearance immediately attracted notice, and no sooner had they taken their seats than Duncan and Llewellyn began to titter. The ladies' bonnets, which were of white, trimmed with long green leaves and flowers, just peered over the top of the boys' pew, and excited much amusement; particularly when Duncan, in his irresistible sense of the ludicrous, began to adorn them with little bits of paper. But Eric had not yet learnt to disregard the solemnity of the place, and the sacred act in which they were engaged. He tried to look away and attend to the service, and for a time he partially succeeded, although, seated as he was between the two triflers, who were perpetually telegraphing to each other their jokes, he found it a difficult task, and secretly he began to be much tickled.

At last the sermon commenced, and Llewellyn, who had imprisoned a grasshopper in a paper cage, suddenly let it hop out. The first hop took it to the top of the pew; the second perched it on the shoulder of the stoutest lady. Duncan and Llewellyn tittered louder, and even Eric could not resist a smile. But when the lady, feeling some irritation on her shoulder, raised her hand, and the grasshopper took a frightened leap into the centre of the green foliage which enwreathed her bonnet, none of the three could stand it, and they burst into fits of laughter, which they tried in vain to conceal by bending down their heads and cramming their fists into their mouths. Eric, having once given way, enjoyed the joke uncontrollably, and the lady made matters worse by her uneasy attempts to dislodge the unknown intruder, and discover the cause of the tittering, which she could not help hearing. At last all three began to laugh so violently that several heads were turned in their direction, and Dr Rowlands's stern eye caught sight of their levity. He stopped short in his sermon, and for one instant transfixed them with his indignant glance. . . .

Next morning Dr Rowlands, in full academicals, sailed into the fourth-form room. His entrance was the signal for every boy to rise, and after a word or two to Mr Gordon, he motioned them to be seated. Eric's heart sank within him.

'Williams, Duncan, and Llewellyn, stand out!' said the Doctor. The boys, downcast eyes and burning cheeks, stood before him. 'I was sorry to notice,' said he, 'your shameful conduct in chapel yesterday afternoon. As far as I could observe, you were making yourselves merry in that sacred place with the personal defects of others. The lessons you receive here must be futile indeed if they do not teach you the duty of reverence to God, and courtesy to man. It gives me special pain, Williams, to have observed that you, too, a boy high in your remove, were guilty of this most culpable levity. You will all come to me at twelve o'clock in the library.'

Frederic W. Farrar, *Eric; or, Little by Little*, 1858

From where they were the boys in the boat could not see what the nature of the excitement was, and therefore paddled on with a view to satisfy their curiosity.

As they came up to the lock Paul suddenly exclaimed, 'That's young Greenfield!'

'What!' said Oliver—'Stephen?'

'Yes, and—what *on earth* are they doing to him?'

The boat being low down under the bank, it was impossible to see what was going on on the tow-path. Oliver, however, having once heard Stephen's name, ordered Paul to put them into the opposite bank quick, where they could land.

While this was being done a shriek from the bank sent the blood suddenly to the faces of the two friends. It was Stephen! They dashed ashore, and in a moment were across the lock and on the spot. The spectacle which met their eyes as they came up was a strange one. The central figure was the luckless Stephen, in the clutches of three or four disreputable fellows, one of whom was Cripps the younger, who, with loud laughter at the boy's struggles and brutal unconcern at his terror, were half dragging, half carrying him towards the water's edge.

Beside them stood Loman, flushed, excited, and laughing loudly. Poor Stephen, very unlike himself, appeared to be utterly cowed and terrified, and uttered shriek upon shriek as his persecutors dragged him along.

'Oh, don't! Please, Cripps! Don't let them, Loman—don't let them drown me!' he shouted.

A laugh was the only answer.

It was at this moment, and just when, to all appearances, the boy was about to be thrown into the water, that Oliver and Wraysford appeared on the scene.

Their appearance was so sudden and unexpected that the fellows, even though they did not know who the two boys were, were momentarily taken aback and dropped their prey.

With a bound Oliver sprang furiously on Cripps, who happened to be nearest him, and before that respectable gentleman knew where he was, had dealt him a blow which sent him staggering back in the utmost alarm and astonishment. Wraysford, no less prompt, tackled one of the other blackguards, while Stephen, now released, and cured of his momentary terror by the appearance of the rescuers, did his share manfully with one of the others.

The contest was short and sharp. A pair of well-trained athletic schoolboys, with a plucky youngster to help them, are a match any day for twice the number of half-tipsy cads. In a minute or two the field was clear of all but Cripps, who appeared, after his short experience, by no means disposed to continue the contest single-handed. As for Loman, he had disappeared.

TALBOT BAINES REED, *The Fifth Form at St Dominic's*, 1887

The eight or nine seniors, their faces very set and sober, were ranged in chairs round Carson's severely Philistine study. Tulke was not popular among them, and a few who had had experience of Stalky & Company doubted that he might, perhaps, have made an ass of himself. But the dignity of the Sixth was to be upheld. So Carson began hurriedly:

'Look here, you chaps, I've—we've sent for you to tell you you're a good deal too cheeky to the Sixth—have been for some time—and—and we've stood about as much as we're goin' to, and it seems you've been cursin' and swearin' at Tulke on the Bideford road this afternoon, and we're goin' to show you you can't do it. That's all.'

'Well, that's awfully good of you,' said Stalky, 'but we happen to have a few rights of our own, too. You can't, just because you happen to be made prefects, haul up seniors and jaw 'em on spec, like a house-master. *We* aren't fags, Carson. This kind of thing may do for Davies tertius, but it won't do for us.'

'It's only old Prout's lunacy that we weren't prefects long ago. You know that,' said M'Turk. 'You haven't any tact.'

'Hold on,' said Beetle. 'A prefects' meetin' has to be reported to the Head. I want to know if the Head backs Tulke in this business?'

'Well—well, it isn't exactly a prefects' meeting,' said Carson. 'We only called you in to warn you.'

'But all the prefects are here,' Beetle insisted. 'Where's the difference?'

'My Gum!' said Stalky. 'Do you mean to say you've just called us in for a jaw—after comin' to us before the whole school at tea an' givin' 'em the impression it was a prefects' meeting? 'Pon my Sam, Carson, you'll get into trouble, you will.'

'Hole-an'-corner business—hole-an'-corner business,' said M'Turk, wagging his head. 'Beastly suspicious.'

RUDYARD KIPLING, *Stalky and Co.*, 1899

I was not content, however, to be the cipher that I found myself, and when I had been at school for about a year, I 'broke out', greatly, I think, to my own surprise in a popular act. We had a young usher whom we disliked. I suppose, poor half-starved phthisic lad, that he was the most miserable of us all. He was, I think, unfitted for the task which had been forced upon him; he was fretful, unsympathetic, agitated. The school-house, an old rambling place, possessed a long cellar-like room that opened from our general corridor and was lighted by deep windows, carefully barred, which looked into an inner garden. This vault was devoted to us and to our play-boxes: by a tacit law, no master entered it. One evening, just at dusk, a great number of us were here when the bell for night-school rang, and many of us dawdled at the summons. Mr B., tactless in his anger, bustled in among us, scolding in a shrill voice, and proceeded to drive us forth. I was the latest to emerge, and as he turned away to see if any other truant might not be hiding, I determined upon action. With a quick movement, I drew the door behind me and bolted it, just in time to hear the imprisoned usher scream with vexation. We boys all trooped upstairs, and it is characteristic of my isolation that I had not one 'chum' to whom I could confide my feat.

That Mr B. had been shut in became, however, almost instantly known, and the night-class, usually so unruly, was awed by the event into exemplary decorum. There, with no master near us, in a silence rarely broken by a giggle or a cat-call, we sat diligently working, or pretending to work. Through my brain, as I hung over my book, a thousand new thoughts began to surge. I was the liberator, the tyrannicide; I had freed all my fellows from the odious oppressor. Surely, when they learned that it was I, they would cluster round me; surely, now, I should be somebody in the school-life, no longer a mere trotting shadow or invisible presence. The interval seemed long; at length Mr B. was released by a servant, and he came up into the school-room to find us in that ominous condition of suspense.

EDMUND GOSSE (b. 1850), *Father and Son*, 1907

'Oh, chuck them away,' said his friend, 'or give them to a porter. It would be a rotten affair if any of the fellows in the house knew. You'd come here with a bad name.'

David's face fell for a moment, for those were gold-tipped cigarettes, which he had thought would probably be so exceedingly the right thing. Hughes noticed this, and gave consolation, for really Blaize was extremely presentable.

'I say, Blazes,' he said, 'I'm awfully glad to see you, and we'll have a ripping time. But it's best to tell you what's the right thing and what isn't, don't you think?'

David responded cordially to this.

'Rather,' he said, 'and it's jolly good of you. Thanks, awfully. Do tell me if there's anything else.'

Hughes gave him another critical glance, as solemn as a tailor's when looking at the fit of a coat that he wants to be a credit to him.

'Oh well, that buttonhole,' he said. 'I think I should take that out. Only tremendous swells wear them, and even then it's rather "side".'

David instantly plucked out the offending vegetable. He probably would have torn out a handful of his hair, if crisp yellow locks showed 'side'. Hughes nodded at him approvingly.

'Now you're first-rate,' he said. 'Oh, just send your stick up with your luggage. Now come on. You look just as if you were at Marchester already. You see I got leave for you to come and brew— have tea, you know—in my study this afternoon, and it would have been beastly for both of us, if you weren't up to Adams's form, and it turned out that you smoked, or kept white mice, or something hopeless.'

E. F. BENSON, *David Blaize*, 1916

One day some of the schoolchildren came rushing into the School house to tell Mr Evans that Sarah Chard Cooper, the gardener's little granddaughter, was running about the school as if she were mad and they could not stop her. The children added that they believed Sarah was drunk. Mr Evans went out immediately to see what was the matter and he found the little girl running wildly round and round the school with her hair streaming, and her eyes glaring and starting out of her head. They could not stop her, she slipped through their hands and rushed past them, running round in circles plainly quite beside herself. It was true the child was drunk. Her grandmother Mrs Cooper confessed afterwards laughing that she had been drinking brandy herself and had given the child some.

REVD FRANCIS KILVERT, *Diary (1872)*, 1938–40

The first master I was 'up to' was Mr 'Hoppy' Daman, a grotesque little man, whose antics, resembling those of a monkey-on-a-stick, combined with a most peculiar voice, made it impossible for anyone to take him seriously. A stranger visiting his division-room might well have imagined that knock-about humour was one of the subjects taught at Eton.

Then there was 'Pecker' Rouse (so called, I imagine, on account of his odd hen-like gestures), who moved about with shuffling footsteps and a suspicious air, peeping, as Percy Lubbock describes him, furtively at the day, as though he had too often caught it in the act of insulting him. He taught mathematics, as far as I can remember. In spite of his diffidence, he was rather bad-tempered. I was told that he was totally incapable of keeping order among the boys in his house, and the sounds of tumult that could be heard therein as one passed by seemed to prove it. Mr Rouse was continually being subjected to booby traps and practical jokes. Strings were stretched across the passages in his house precipitating him into baths, and his umbrella was frequently filled with confetti so that he was enveloped in a miniature snowstorm when he opened it in the street. It was hardly to be wondered at that he was suspicious and bad-tempered.

LORD BERNERS, *A Distant Prospect*, 1945

6 March 1946

To the Headmaster

Sir—It is with considerable regret that I inform you that things cannot go on as they are at present unless some change is made. Had it been some small matter such as the school radiators, which have been stone cold for the last three days, I should have come to see you in the ordinary way, or the shortage of nibs and blotting-paper about which I have spoken fifty times to Rawlinson already, but it is *not*. A schoolmaster has plenty to do without that sort of thing in any case. But either there is discipline in a school or there is not. That is my point. And if there is no discipline I for one will have no part in it. I have not given up what might have been the best years of my life to Burgrove, in order to have my boot-laces tied to the legs of my desk at the end of it and so be prevented from rising to my feet when parents are shown into my classroom, as I always do. This is not the first time an attempt has been made to make me look ridiculous in front of other people, nor is it the last, as I am well aware, after seeing Matron sneaking into your study this very afternoon with some garbled version no doubt of an incident outside the School Museum which could never have happened if people would stop misrepresenting my slightest action and making mare's nests at my expense out of nothing at all.

I have always done my best and put the interests of the school first, but if it is to be put about that I made an unprovoked attack with a cutlass on a boy of eleven years during the after-lunch rest-period, I can only say that the sooner I tender my resignation the better for all concerned. That the boy, Malcolm, was not even a member of my Mathematical Set would have been enough, one might have supposed, to scotch such a ridiculous story at the outset. But apparently it is not. The sword was not, as it happens, a cutlass, but a scimitar. There is no cutlass in the School Museum. But those who are responsible for spreading unfounded gossip of this kind about me are not likely to allow a trifle of that nature to stand in their way. I should be thankful, perhaps, that I am not accused of throwing assegais, of which a large number were presented to the school last term by Mr Tallboys and hang on the west wall at present, pending some other arrangement. He has also promised an elk's head and some West African wood-carvings.

I am determined to put a stop to this kind of thing. I have as much right to handle the weapons in the Museum as anyone. More. The Museum is in my charge, as was settled at the Masters' Meeting in January, and Malcolm had no business to be there in the rest-period. Does Matron deny my right to take down the scimitar and dust it? If so, let her deny it to my face and I will very soon make clear to her where her jurisdiction ends and mine begins. She would be better employed in seeing that the boys are resting on their beds after lunch than in trying to interfere with the way I run the Museum.

I have little more to say. I consider that Malcolm's behaviour in dashing out of the Museum crying, 'Spare me! Spare me!' the moment he caught sight of me with the sword in my hand was little short of downright impertinence. The boy should be thrashed. That I should run after him to tell him to be quiet was not only a perfectly natural thing to do, it was my duty. And I shall continue to do my duty, with or without Matron's permission, for so long as I remain on the Staff here at Burgrove.

That that time is likely to be short we are both well aware. My resignation is in your hands. Should you wish to accept it, there is no more to be said, except to thank you for many happy years and much kindness and to ask you as a special favour that some arrangement be made to expedite the return of my laundry before I depart. I should of course in the ordinary way approach Matron on this matter, but you will understand, in the circumstances, that that is quite impossible. I have a few books which may be of use to the boys' library.

Should you desire me to withdraw my resignation I will do so, provided:

That a full apology is made by Matron in the presence of the whole Staff.

That Malcolm is thrashed, or otherwise punished at your discretion.

That other arrangements are made for the management of the School Museum, which it is now painful for me to enter.

I will take steps to deal with the comparatively trivial matter of the boot-laces myself.

(Signed) ARTHUR J. WENTWORTH.

[*A copy of the note sent by the Headmaster to Wentworth, in answer to the foregoing Memorandum, has come into my hands. It seems to clear the matter up.*]

From the Headmaster

Dear A. J.—I don't know what all the fuss is about. Matron came to see me this afternoon about gym-shoes, not cutlasses.

I have seen Malcolm and told him not to be a silly little fool.

The man I had with me when I entered your classroom this morning was not a parent, or not, at any rate, in the sense in which we use the term; he had come to see about the breakdown in the central heating system. I cannot allow you to resign on the grounds that you were unable to stand up when a plumber came into your room.

So please put your personal feelings on one side—and remember, Wentworth, that the School must come first.

(Signed) G. S.

H. F. ELLIS, *The World of A. J. Wentworth, B. A.*, 1949

Irma, half undressed, paused in the act of pulling off her stockings, and made the important suggestion:

'I say, let's play a trick on the prefects!'
'What a blossomy idea!'
'They richly deserve it!'
'It would be just top-hole!'
'What could we do?'
'Ah, that's just the question, my good child!' said Laura, putting a thoughtful finger to her forehead. 'There's an art in ragging. It ought to be done delicately. We don't want clumsy tricks, such as apple-pie beds. As for booby traps, they're vulgar and dangerous; I wouldn't soil my fingers with making one. It must be something that will annoy them, but not harm them or anybody else. I haven't got a brain wave yet, but perhaps ideas may come.'
'Suppose we go and reconnoitre,' proposed Avelyn.
'A very jinky notion. We might get an idea on the spot.'

ANGELA BRAZIL, *For the School Colours,* 1918

I used to speculate on which of my contemporaries would distinguish themselves after they left school. The war upset these calculations. Many dull boys had brief brilliant military careers, particularly as air-fighters, becoming squadron and flight commanders. 'Fuzzy' McNair, the Head of the school, won the VC as a Rifleman. Young Sturgess, who had been my study fag, distinguished himself more unfortunately by flying the first heavy bombing machine of a new pattern across the Channel on his first trip to France: he made a perfect landing (having mistaken his course) at an aerodrome behind the German lines. A boy whom I had admired during my first year at Charterhouse was the Honourable Desmond O'Brien: the only Carthusian of that time who cheerfully disregarded all school rules. Having cut skeleton-keys for the library, chapel, and science laboratories, he used to break out of his house at night and carefully disarrange things there. O'Brien had the key to the headmaster's study too and, entering one night with an electric torch, carried off a memorandum which he showed me: 'Must expel O'Brien.' He had a wireless receiving-station in one

of the out-of-bounds copses on the school grounds; and discovered
a ventilator shaft down which he could hoot like an owl into the
library without detection. Once we were threatened with the loss of
a half-holiday because some member of the school had catapulted a
cow, which died of shock, and nobody would own up. O'Brien was
away at the time, on special leave for a sister's wedding. A friend
wrote to tell him about the half-holiday. He sent Rendall a telegram:
'Killed cow sorry coming O'Brien.' At last Rendall did expel him for
having absented himself from every lesson and chapel for three
whole days. O'Brien was killed, early in the war, while bombing
Bruges.

ROBERT GRAVES, *Goodbye to all that,* 1929

The innumerable forms of minor torture, bullying, and mischief
which boys can serve to boys, as a portent of the ways of the adult
world, have been written about too much because of the deep
impression they make on the infant mind. There were com-
pensations: the tiny joys, equally pristine and impressive, which
the grown man and woman have to relinquish as their sensibility
hardens. It was a pleasure to chew pieces of orange-peel in school, or
those withered tubers called 'tiger-nuts', or a dried bean called
'locusts', bought in the one-room sweet-shop in a slum dwelling
opposite the school gate, kept by a crone who subsisted upon the
farthings thus gathered from the scholars.

I recall, too, the seasonal games, such as the mid-summer sport of
'cherry-oggs', when ingenious boys made castle façades of cardboard,
with doors through which their mates were invited to pitch dried
cherry stones, so many being paid out if the stone passed through. I
have no doubt that some of the more persistent of those promoters
are now successfully running football pools.

After the 'cherry-ogg' season, which ended with the expert
manipulators carrying large cotton bags full of this stony currency,
there followed the autumnal jousting with horse chestnuts, or

'conkers'. A certain amount of research went into this game, in the matter of toughening the nuts by soaking them in oil and drying them. One social factor worth recording is that a boy's word as to the promotion of his 'conker' was always accepted. It might be a 'fiver' or a 'tenner'; or it might have smashed a hundred adversaries. No doubt was ever thrown on the claim by its wielder. . . .

With the coming of cold weather, iron hoops were heard trundling to school, driven by boys with an iron hook in a wooden handle. Both hook and hoop wore smooth and polished under this mutual friction, while the skill of the trundler in guiding the hoop, turning, stopping and bouncing it, served as an apprenticeship to later dexterity with a bicycle; a skill transmitted perhaps hereditarily to sons and grandsons, to emerge in the driving of sports cars and the piloting of jet planes.

These are only three of the group games which enriched street and school-yard life, kindling mass enthusiasm overnight, and as suddenly being dropped to give place to another. Towards the coming of spring, which brought radio-activity even to the dust of those Battersea streets, a racial craving for colour seized the children and they would be seen walking abstractedly along the pavements, or crossing roads recklessly in front of the hooves of wagon- and omnibus-horses, while giving all their attention to a cotton-reel into one end of which they had hammered four tin-tacks. Round these tacks they wound a thread of coloured wool from a ball carried in the pocket. With a pin, or a sharpened match-stick, they raised a second turn of the wool over the tacks. This operation of alternate treatment of each round produced a tubular rope that made its way slowly through the central hole of the cotton-reel. Inch by inch, foot by foot, it grew, coloured according to the choice of the young weaver in his selection of skeins. When this rainbow rope was long enough it was made into reins, sometimes with the addition of knitted harness. For weeks, during the lengthening evenings of March and April, these gay caparisons would be worn by one boy, as the horse, and held by another, as the driver.

RICHARD CHURCH, *Over the Bridge*, 1955

'You got me to promise to come,' he said. 'It's up to you to do the rest.'

'Cold feet?' asked Merrys, in accents calculated to embarrass and wound the hearer.

'Yes, if you want to know, I *have* got cold feet,' said Skene, firmly. 'But I *said* I'd come with you, so I'm coming. But that's *all* I'm going to do.'

'All right, then,' said Merrys. 'I only wish it was Conway's bike, though,' he added, in a different tone. 'The silly, sickening, unfair beast! I'd jolly well smash it up for him as well as borrow it, if I had it.'

'No, you wouldn't, chump. There'd be a row, and everything would come out.'

Merrys did not contest this, but went off to spy out the lie of the land with a view to sneaking the bicycle. Mr Loveday's potting-sheds, garage and kitchen premises were out of bounds to his boys, but there were ways and means of circumventing this law.

'I say, Stallard,' said Merrys, presenting himself before his House captain as that august man was dismembering a bloater which he had just cooked for himself over his study fire, 'I'm awfully sorry, but I've dropped a gym. shoe out of the dorm. window, and I think it's got caught in a bush. May I go round and pick it up?'

'How the devil *could* it drop out of the dorm. window?' demanded Stallard, irritated, for a bloater must be eaten hot, in his opinion, or not at all. Fagging was not part of the official system at Spey, and he did not want the trouble of cooking another bloater if this one grew cold and, in his view, inedible.

'Please, Stallard, I had cleaned it, and shoved—put it on the window-ledge to dry, and, as I went to move away, I suppose I must have caught it with the edge of my hand, sort of, and——

'Oh, go to hell and get it!' said Stallard, hitching his chair nearer the table and picking up a fork and a bit of bread. 'And no messing about, do you hear!'

'Oh, yes, Stallard. Thanks a lot.'

Merrys then ran round to the forbidden territory, found the coast clear, collared the bicycle, hid it in the bushes and rejoined his comrade. Both were studious during Prep., both ate large suppers of bread and margarine, both responded to Call-Over in the hearty, trumpet-voice of virtue, and both (having sworn the two boys in their dormitory to secrecy) descended on to the roof of Mr Loveday's outhouse, crept past a chimney-stack, slithered down a drainpipe, and so gained the kitchen garden unheard, unseen and unthought-of, at exactly ten minutes past nine.

GLADYS MITCHELL, Tom Brown's Body, 1949

And at that happy school in Byron House
Only one harbinger of future woe
Came to me in those far, sun-gilded days—
Gold with the hair of Peggy Purey-Cust—
Two other boys (my rivals, I suppose)
Came suddenly round a corner, caught my arms
And one, a treacherous, stocky little Scot,
Winded me with a punch and 'Want some more?'
He grunted when I couldn't speak for pain.
Why did he do it? Why that other boy,
Who hitherto had been a friend of mine,
Was his accomplice I could not divine,
Nor ever have done. But those fatal two
Continued with me to another school—
Avernus by the side of Highgate Hill.

Let those who have such memories recollect
Their sinking dread of going back to school.
I well remember mine. I see again
The great headmaster's study lined with books
Where somewhere, in a corner, there were canes.
He wrapped his gown, the great headmaster did,
About himself, chucked off his mortar-board
And, leaning back, said: 'Let's see what you know,

How many half-crowns are there in a pound?'
I didn't know. I couldn't even guess.
My poor fond father, hearing nothing, smiled;
The gold clock ticked; the waiting furniture
Shone like a colour plate by H. M. Brock . . .
No answer—and the great headmaster frown'd;
But let me in to Highgate Junior School.

JOHN BETJEMAN, *Summoned by Bells*, 1960

When I went to Haileybury the conditions of life for boys were hard, though perhaps wholesomely bracing. The school stands high up and I think it must always be cold there in winter. At the beginning of my first term, England was in the grip of a severe frost. I can distinctly recollect taking my sponge to bed with me, the only means of preventing it being frozen into a hard stone when I wanted to use it next morning. The form room which I was supposed to occupy out of school hours was lighted only by a skylight and was approached by descending three steps from the level of the quadrangle outside. It was a room which would not be tolerated in the meanest parochial school to-day. But I could not even use it as a sheltering habitation or seek warmth from its fire. The older boys in the form, one of them in particular, made the lives of smaller boys a perfect hell to them. I came too late into public school life to experience the full rigour of the bullying which used to go on, the sort of thing described in *Tom Brown*, which certainly persisted long after his time. But even in my day the lives of small and weak boys were made desperately unpleasant for them. There were humiliating tortures to which we were submitted if we ventured to put our noses inside the form-room, where we had a perfect right to go. The result was that during that first bitterly cold term I spent most of my hours out of school in walking forlornly round and round the quadrangle in the company of others as unfortunate as myself. All that term I think I must have been unhappy, for, years afterwards, I came across some verses I wrote at the time. They were very doleful, so I suppose I must have been suffering a good deal when I wrote them.

GEORGE A. BIRMINGHAM [J. O. Hanney], *Pleasant Places*, 1934

Nothing was stranger at preparatory schools in the 1920s than the way in which a sudden spree was visited on the inmates. Without a word of warning, everybody up-anchored and shot off to somewhere else. At Stirling Court one summer's day a special treat was announced. We were all to go by charabanc, as a bus was then called, to watch a professional cricket match at Portsmouth. The outing meant, at least, no school work and even the more anti-cricket boys were in merry mood as we clambered on board. Williamson and I, deep in chat as was our custom, settled ourselves in. We were only mildly surprised to observe that the expedition was not being led by the games master but by a strangely-scented rotundity who taught Latin, was said to debauch the maids and pawn confiscated penknives, and survived but one shaky term. Off we went and on reaching the ground it was apparent that the game had been in progress for some time. Philip Mead, of whom even I had heard, was batting.

When we had found our seats, our first concern, after the hour's drive, was to make for the lavatory, an open-air and rather whiffy square construction of brick, conveniently close. As we hastened in, a solitary figure drew all eyes. In a corner, and facing outwards, an aged and decrepit clergyman was standing, smiling encouragement and wildly waggling. At our fairly tender years this was a startling spectacle and one hardly knew where to look. Where not to look was plain to all. Subsequent visits found him, hope on hope ever, still there and still at it. Not a cricket-lover, evidently.

ARTHUR MARSHALL, 'The Crooked Bat', in *Girls will be Girls*, 1974

Bootham School was Georgian rather than Victorian—George IV, not George V. I do not think it can have changed much since Joseph

Simpson started a school in Walmgate at the other end of York in 1823—a school where John Bright, our most distinguished old boy, had been even unhappier than I was. Bootham's official name, still I hope used, was York Quarterly Meeting Friends' Boys School. We were given full Quaker training. We attended York Meeting on Sunday mornings, walking through the city in bowler hats. The girls from our sister school, The Mount, sat across the aisle. They were known as Mount Hags, and social contacts with them were few. The more harmless inmates of The Retreat, the Quaker lunatic asylum, were also allowed to attend. On one legendary occasion, before my time, one of them rose up and cried, 'Oh for the bubbling up of strawberry jam'. Not a boy sniggered.

A. J. P. Taylor, *A Personal History*, 1983

My father now hit upon a plan which filled me with delight. About a mile from the New House rose the large red-brick walls and towers of Campbell College, which had been founded for the express purpose of giving Ulster boys all the advantages of a public school education without the trouble of crossing the Irish Sea. My clever cousin, Uncle Joe's boy, was already there and doing well. It was decided that I should go as a boarder, but I could get an *exeat* to come home every Sunday. I was enchanted. I did not believe that anything Irish, even a school, could be bad; certainly not so bad as all I yet knew of England. To 'Campbell' I accordingly went.

I was at this school for so short a time that I shall attempt no criticism of it. It was very unlike any English public school that I have ever heard of. It had indeed prefects, but the prefects were of no importance. It was nominally divided into 'houses' on the English pattern, but they were mere legal fictions; except for purposes of games (which were not compulsory) no one took any notice of them. The population was socially much more 'mixed' than at most English schools; I rubbed shoulders there with farmers' sons. The boy I most nearly made a friend of was the son of a tradesman who had recently been going the rounds with his father's van because the driver was illiterate and could not keep 'the books'. I much envied him this pleasant occupation, and he, poor fellow, looked back on it as a golden age. 'This time last month, Lewis,' he used to say, 'I wouldn't have been going in to Preparation. I'd have been coming home from my rounds and a wee teacloth laid for me at one end of the table and sausages to my tea.'

I am always glad, as a historian, to have known Campbell, for I think it was very much what the great English schools had been before Arnold. There were real fights at Campbell, with seconds, and (I think) betting, and a hundred or more roaring spectators. There was bullying, too, though no serious share of it came my way, and there was no trace of the rigid hierarchy which governs a modern English school; every boy held just the place which his fists and mother-wit could win for him. From my point of view the great drawback was that one had, so to speak, no home. Only a few very senior boys had studies. The rest of us, except when seated at table for meals or in a huge 'preparation room' for evening 'Prep', belonged nowhere. In out-of-school hours one spent one's time either evading or conforming to all those inexplicable movements which a crowd exhibits as it thins here and thickens there, now slackens its pace and now sets like a tide in one particular direction, now seems about to disperse and then clots again. The bare brick passages echoed to a continual tramp of feet, punctuated with cat-calls, scrimmages, gusty laughter. One was always 'moving on' or 'hanging about'—in lavatories, in store rooms, in the great hall. It was very like living permanently in a large railway station.

C. S. LEWIS, *Surprised by Joy*, 1955

Every morning we showed up with no homework done, none at all. This was due, so we declared to a man, to the fact that we'd had sick headaches, all of us. And all our mothers were too busy to write the customary notes, 'excuses', explaining this. Young Mr Heslop (Hessy for short) gulped and goggled over the mass-afflicted but he had to let it go. In any case, he would never have bothered my desk much.

I was back on the boys' side of the room now, sharing a seat with a cross-eyed, cow-licked lad called Warmy, to whom the fairies had given but one talent: he could regurgitate at will. He did and all. Whenever the situation got difficult, he'd gasp out, 'Please, sir, A'm gannin' te——' and begin to retch. He wasn't kidding either. An obstinate and disbelieving teacher got the lot over his boots and trousers as the upheaving Warmy butted blindly into him. Now if I'd any awkward inquiries about homework to deal with, I'd only to give Warmy a nudge, and the little horror obliged at once.

Of course, we were killing our goose. More and more frequently there swept into our uproar the scholarship teacher from next door. A bull-like man, pock-marked and with a habit of irritably scratching at his arse, he was used to quelling his class and keeping them quelled. He had no aversion to giving corporal punishment, and this was very well known indeed. Now we found one sad morning that he was to supervise our homework, while the wretched Hessy sat withdrawn at his desk pretending to be busy with papers. He'd brought his own strap with him, we noticed, and we were prepared to believe that it was specially treated to cause the maximum pain or at any rate stiff with the blood of generations of victims. The sick headache excuse was no excuse to him. Most of us prepared to plead guilty and take a belting. That seemed to suit him too, probably because it was quicker and he wanted to get back to his own class, the little scholarship marvels who were quiet as mice even in his absence. Up and down the aisles, boy after boy stepped out of his desk, the strap flailed, and boy after boy sat down again hugging his aching palms. It came to us anon. Poor old Warmy for the first time in a life of public service couldn't be sick. He felt sick, I dare say, he looked sick but he couldn't be. He was belted first and ordered off to the lavatory afterwards, ignominiously. I took mine next, rather badly because I under-estimated the teacher's swing and got the first one too high up the wrist where it would leave a weal. Altogether, you might say, a poorish morning and worse to come: later that day, it was plain, we should have to do homework.

JACK COMMON (b. 1903), *Kiddar's Luck*, 1951

The grown-ups decided to send Mary to Malvern girls college, there was an awful fuss getting her clothes ready, Daddy didn't like the idea of her going much but Mammie wanted her to be like our Hillersdon cousins who were all at large boarding schools. When all the preparations were finished, off Mary went looking pretty green and Mammie departed for a few days rest at Hillersdon but she was soon summonsed back by a telegram saying Mary had run away from school and they couldn't trace her. The next day she was discovered eating buns on a station and Daddy brought her home again, Mammie was simply fourious but Daddy was in the position of saying 'I told you so' and made a great fuss of Mary when she came home. The school refused to have her back which upset Mammie still more. In the end she was sent to a much smaller school with Beatrix as her companion, neither of them liked it very much but they didn't attempt to run away.

BARBARA COMYNS, *Sisters by a River*, 1947

Gambling with death was instigated by Eileen Carver, whose un-willing lieutenant I became. We entered upon a carnival of bravado, or alternatively incipient commando training, wall-top running, roof-top running, roof mountaineering (the roofs of the Hall were steep) and blindfold bicycling being the early stages. She was a small, taut, pale, wiry London girl, alarmingly taciturn, demon at basketball only. She had ruthlessly slighted the rest of our crazes, so far. A withheld personality, apt to become a searing one. Afternoon 'nature rambles' over Harpenden Common or through hitherto friendly Hertfordshire thickets and lanes became, that autumn, darkened by apprehension: what might not she challenge us to do next? When it came to balancing, at a run, *eyes shut*, along the sky-high parapet of a railway bridge, several defaulted. She did not so much as look at them. Worst was to be the day of the deadly nightshade—for as that a spray of berries glistening under a hedge was identified by two embryonic botanists. 'If *you* eat those, if you even touch those, you die!' 'Rot,' returned our Leader, in her most languid tone. 'How do you know it's rot?' She flickered those sum-ming-up eyes from face to face, then said: 'Well, all right—at least *I* am.' She plucked a palmful of berries and gulped them down.

ELIZABETH BOWEN, *Pictures and Conversations*, 1974

The most fearful disgrace which Marlborough can thrust you into is the basket. Your friends desert you. It only happens a few times a year, but it is as bad as expulsion. In after-life Marlburians chatting about old times in the bars of local golf clubs will say: 'Oh—Betjeman!—not much of a chap. He was put in the basket, wasn't he?' It is in the power of that tough autocrasy, 'Big Fire', to put you in the basket.

This is the process. There are two large wastepaper baskets in the Upper School. During the half hour after 6.30 tea, before 'prep.' begins, 'Big Fire' (with the captains watching at the door) comes in and seizes the victim. His clothes are taken off save his shirt, and he is thrust into one of the baskets, filled with apple cores and wastepaper, by the fags. Sometimes ink, sometimes paper and some-times only obloquy is poured on his head. He is allowed to remain on exhibition until just before prep. begins, when he is allowed to go and 'stamped out' of the building. When he returns to prep., the master in charge asks why he is late. 'Put in the basket, sir.' The master nods. It does a fellow good. He has probably been suspected of thieving or worn coloured socks before he had been in Upper School three times or . . . never mind. Boys know each other best. There is nothing like the moral indignation of someone who is fifteen or sixteen. Besides the fellow was unpopular.

JOHN BETJEMAN, in *Little Innocents*, 1932

I noticed that we were passing through a rusty pair of open gates. Ahead stretched an uphill drive lined with clumps of faded ponticums. At the end of it as though barring the way to eternity straddled the vast red brick mausoleum of my dying hopes, covered with virginia creeper and fire escapes. Out of the front door of this lugubrious edifice were streaming dozens of grey flannelled, be-capped midgets, dressed exactly alike, carrying cricket bats and pads, interspersed with a few white-flannelled giants in striped jackets and straw boaters. As I learned afterwards, the 4th of June happened to be a half-holiday, and the exodus of boys and masters on to the playing field coincided with our ill-fated arrival. The spectacle before us was now too much for my tender-hearted mother. 'How hideous!' she exclaimed. 'How perfectly hideous! How could the de Frevilles . . . ?' She gave an ill-concealed gulp and a few silent tears blazed a trail down her faintly rouged cheeks. The remark had an electrical effect upon the cabby. He actually gave a snort and lashed the hollow flanks of the old horse, which suddenly plunged into a lolloping canter just as we were approaching the carriage sweep.

My mother and I, both now sobbing uncontrollably, were pitch-forked by the unexpected jolt against the tuck-box. Instantly there was a harsh sound of rending woodwork. The tuck-box gave a wobble, then a lurch and disappeared through the floor boards, which clattered to the ground, our feet with them. The noise was alarming, the spectacle exceedingly humiliating. The two of us, shocked beyond measure, had no alternative to running inside the carriage as fast as our legs could carry us. Any other course would have invited instant and perhaps fatal injury, for we would have been knocked down by the seat we had precipitately left and then been crushed by the axle or the wheels. But the faster we ran and the louder we shouted to that brute of a cabby, who never once so much as turned his head in our direction, the more the old horse took the bit between its teeth. Round and round the sweep we went, and over and over the remains of the tuck-box, of which the contents— for the lid and bottom had broken off with the fall—made a ghastly contusion on the drive. Strawberries, petits-beurres biscuits, asparagus, cream and pheasants' feathers were churned into the gravel by a succession of wheels, and human and equine feet. My mother had the presence of mind to seize me by the arm and pull me along with her, or I should inevitably have been lost. Just before we completed the fourth round of the sweep one of the white-flannelled giants managed to catch hold of the bridle and, by dint of being dragged several yards along the gravel to the absolute detriment of his immaculate ducks, brought the sweating horse to a standstill.

The scene witnessed by the entire school was indescribable. My mother was hauled from the wreckage in a fit of hysterical giggles. Her dress was torn to shreds and her long hair was down to her waist. My plight was even more pitiable. In the mêlée I had completely lost my trousers. In fact it was a mercy that they had come off truly and properly: a miracle that the trailing extremities had not got caught in the wheel spokes, and possibly squeezed or throttled me to death. The two of us were then stretched on the grass and restored by the matron with sal volatile. All this while the abominable cabby was bending over us, making demands in dumb show for his fare and reparation money for the damage to his victoria.

The final ignominy was having to explain who we were. It transpired that my mother had failed to notify the headmaster that we were coming that afternoon. And although in later years she strenuously denied it, I have often wondered whether she had ever entered me for the school in the first place, or merely assumed that the headmaster would welcome any stray child whose parents dropped in on the off chance. Welcome me, or rather accept me he did. The kindest thing he could have done would have been to send us both packing there and then. As it was, the boys who witnessed our arrival never allowed me to forget it.

James Lees-Milne, *Another Self,* 1970

The science room smelt unevenly of the Canongate on that day of the winter's walk with Miss Brodie, the bunsen burners, and the sweet autumnal smoke that drifted in from the first burning leaves. Here in the science room—strictly not to be referred to as a laboratory—lessons were called experiments, which gave everyone the feeling that not even Miss Lockhart knew what the result might be, and anything might occur between their going in and coming out and the school might blow up.

Here, during that first week, an experiment was conducted which involved magnesium in a test-tube which was made to tickle a bunsen flame. Eventually, from different parts of the room, great white magnesium flares shot out of the test-tubes and were caught in larger glass vessels which waited for the purpose. Mary Macgregor took fright and ran along a single lane between two benches, met with a white flame, and ran back to meet another brilliant tongue of fire. Hither and thither she ran in panic between the benches until she was caught and induced to calm down, and she was told not to be so stupid by Miss Lockhart, who already had learnt the exasperation of looking at Mary's face, its two eyes, nose and mouth, with nothing more to say about it.

MURIEL SPARK, *The Prime of Miss Jean Brodie*, 1961

It was the first Sunday evening of the Spring term. The Anglicans had marched in crocodile to morning service: the few Dissenters had gone off to their chapel in anarchy. All had eaten mutton and cabbage and walked afterwards by the sea under Mr Chaplin's gold-rimmed eye. The period immediately after tea was set aside for letter writing.

Mr Chaplin was reading the last of the letters. 'Snape minor!' he called. A small boy stood up. 'What on earth does this mean, Snape? "I swolled a marpell." ' A balloon of laughter went up, as though Mr Chaplin had made an exquisite joke.

'I did, sir,' said Snape minor.

ROY FULLER, *The Ruined Boys*, 1959

I went to a small preparatory school, only about 25 of us, and as in most such schools we were called by our surnames. I was Curtis. No one had any idea what my Christian name was. We were 25 little surnames.

It was in my second year that, for the first time, a brother enrolled and complications began to arise. There were now two Smiths, and a decision had to be made about what to call them. The headmaster chose a very simple route, which was to call them, as he naturally found himself doing, Young Smith and Old Smith. It was a happy summer.

The real trouble started two terms later when another, this time unrelated, Smith arrived. There was discussion in the staff room about changing to a numerical system—Smith 1, Smith 2, Smith 3—or to a classical nomenclature—Major, Minor, Minimus—but the headmaster felt he should stick to his guns. So the new term began with Old Smith still Old Smith, the new Smith taking his position as Young Smith, and the former Young Smith, a soft-faced 10-year-old, picked out as Middle-Aged Smith.

Unfortunately, the mother of Old Smith and his younger (middle-aged) brother had not finished her child-bearing, and only two terms later their young brother arrived to take his position in the school. The option was open to rename everyone again, but it was decided this would cause too much disruption, so the youngest Smith entered the school as Very Young Smith.

He was joined, a term later, by Young Smith's younger brother. By now, the headmaster had become adept at the Smith business. The new Smith became Very Young Smith, Very Young Smith became Young Smith, and very cunningly, Young Smith moved into a gap that had until now been neglected—and became, at the age of nine, Teenage Smith.

At this point the headmaster was strongly advised against admitting any more Smiths. But a fee is a fee in a fee-paying school, and when Mr Smith, the managing director of a large travel firm, came to enrol his son, the boy was accepted. Now there really was a problem. The choice seemed to be between the new boy—a very jolly, fat boy—becoming Foetus Smith, or everyone moving upwards. With relief, we plumped for the Foetus. Old Smith remained Old Smith and all was well with the world. The rugby fifteen was a strong side, and we beat Haileybury at judo for the first time.

Tragically, this paradise didn't last for long. Mr Smith the managing director turned up the next term with another son—who set off the long-dreaded domino effect. Foetus Smith became Very Young Smith; Very Young Smith was now just Young; Young Smith became a Teenager overnight; Teenage Smith, still nine, became Middle-Aged; Middle-Aged found himself drifting into Old Age; and Old Smith, at the age of 12, became Senile Smith.

Everyone gritted their teeth and got down to normal living, never expecting that the managing director and his wife had another Smithlet up their sleeves. His arrival the next term was greeted with horror. Very little time at all was now spent on studies—whole classes, weeks of school time, were dedicated to memorising the Smiths and their names. Geography had been dropped off the curriculum altogether to make space . . . And now, just as the oldest Smith was getting used to being Senile, and the once Foetal Smith was growing into his new-found youth, it was all change once more.

But what to change to? For a while the headmaster toyed with the suggestion of the biology master that the new boy should become Spermatozoa Smith. This would have had the double advantage of leaving everyone else unaltered, and of teaching the school a valuable lesson in sex-education.

But the English master pointed out that the new Smith's entry test had not revealed the sharpest of minds, and he warned against the psychological scarring that might result from the poor boy being stuck with a name he couldn't spell. So the long trek was on again. The Sperm became a Foetus, the Foetus became Very Young, and poor Senile Smith found himself, at the age of 12½, Dead.

RICHARD CURTIS, *Independent*, 31 December 1991

That senior English master tended to come in five or ten minutes late for the first session after the midday break. One day—I expect I wanted to show I could be a bit of a devil—I threw a stink bomb across the classroom eight or nine minutes before he was normally due, not realising that the smell would still be there when he did arrive; in fact, he came in earlier than usual and the rotten eggs were at their most potent. He sniffed and asked, more magisterially than angrily: 'Which boy is responsible for this?' There was a pause and then I stood up and said: 'Sir, it was I.' 'At least your admission is grammatical, Hoggart. You will be in detention for the whole of this week, for one hour.' It being Monday, I arrived home an hour late each night and deserved at least that. Whether I lied to cover my lateness I do not remember; certainly, no one at Newport Street guessed what had happened; they would have been unduly distressed if they had.

A silly little story but I suppose I tell it because the peculiar dignity and decisiveness of the master impressed me. He neither raged nor purported to be amused. He did what he had to do and forgot it and I do not imagine he told anyone except the master on detention duty; certainly he never held it against me. My impulse to throw the stink bomb would have come as much as anything from reading Frank Richards in the *Magnet* and *Gem*; those magazines had a more powerful hold on our grammar-school imaginations than the *Wizard* or *Hotspur*. Pseudo-public-school culture had overhauled street culture.

RICHARD HOGGART, *A Local Habitation*, 1988

One Monday morning a remarkable apparition turned up, with a complaint. She had a man's cloth cap on backwards, a very fancy sprigged smock over an ancient grey skirt and boy's football boots. I met her at the door and asked her what she wanted. She said that she wanted to take me by the hair of my head and drag me down to the canal and put me in it. I said she had better come in and talk it over.

There is no need to conclude from that that I am one of those debonair young people who belong spiritually to the cloak-and-sword era. It was simply that I had heard that kind of thing so often that I was able to translate it immediately into what it signified in polite English, which was, 'I am afraid I have a complaint to make.'

She stamped in, looking at the posters on the walls, 'Beauty Spots of England', with the lively interest of a savage in a strange environment, and I left her standing in the hall while I went to find the Head. On my way I nearly fell over the caretaker, who was on his hands and knees scrubbing the patch where Teddie Hunt had been sick a few minutes before. I noticed that he was laying on the soap very thickly and the water scarcely at all. The soap was paid for by the Government and he had to fetch the water from an outside tap. I remember this so clearly because those two incidents were really responsible for changing several lives. If they had not happened, I suppose we might all still have been in our nice comfortable little rut, as we were then.

I met Miss Harford in the cloakroom, where she was making sure that all the windows were open. She was very keen on fresh air. I said, 'A parent to see you, Miss Harford,' and went back to my own classroom. Little Miss Thornby, who had been watching the class for me, told me that the woman was the parent of the seven little Hunts, and that she used to do some scrubbing for her sister and had stolen the artistic overall from her.

A few minutes later Miss Harford called me out to ask me whether Georgie Hunt was in school. I said he had gone down to the clinic. This inspired Mrs Hunt to a tremendous flow of eloquence. She said that education was one thing, though she herself couldn't see the sense of keeping great lads and girls in school, when they might be out at work and would rather be in the factory and bringing home a bit to help their poor parents who slaved for them night and day, but that dragging them down to the clinic and pulling them about and frightening the lives out of them was quite another, and a bloody scandal besides. Miss Harford said that if she was going to use bad language, she was afraid she would have to ask the corner policeman to see her off the premises. Mrs Hunt replied that it was all very well for some as thought they had the law on their side to be so mealy-mouthed, but that a lot of old maids couldn't be expected to feel the same about children as them who had borne and brought up, not only Georgie, but six others besides, and who should know better what was good for a child but its own mother? And if there wasn't a stop put to this dragging children who had nothing the matter with them down to the clinic and pulling them about something disgraceful, she herself would have the law on someone, policemen or no policemen.

Miss Harford said that if Mrs Hunt doubted the legality of Georgie's appointment down at the medical clinic, she had better come across to my room and have a look at the printed clinic card, all properly stamped and signed. I thought this was a good idea. Printed papers have a wonderfully convincing effect on parents of Mrs Hunt's stamp.

RUTH ADAM, I'm Not Complaining, 1938

Will and Tegwyn stood very still. William Evans, ignoring them, went back to his desk, and took up his book. He continued to read aloud.

' "They have not," continued Gruffydd, "the sinew for our sinew, the hearts for our hearts, the blood for our blood. On the mountains they are lost. In the valleys they are fearful. We, by the shadow of this rock, by the light of this sun . . ." '

Will was not listening. He was thinking of Brychan, following his movements. It was normal, in the school, to send a boy out to cut a stick for caning. Sometimes, even, you cut your own, the one you would be hit with. The precise instructions William Evans had found necessary from experience; without them, the merest switch would be brought. 'Couldn't reach up to no others, sir, my knife's too blunt.' But the ruling majority of the boys had a method which had been passed from brother to brother. A thick enough stick would be cut, if ordered, but then they would take a bud, about a foot from the thin end, and cut a T, carefully, in the soft skin around it. Lifting the edges of the skin, they would bore in with the point of the knife, cutting across the fibres, and then the skin would be smoothed back, and a lick of mud smeared over the T. As the stick hit the hand, it should break. The victim, forewarned (a tampered stick was always handed thick end first) would then yell as if he had been hit too hard. Always, when a stick broke, William Evans failed to send for another. He knew his own temper, and was quickly cautious. An obvious trick, such as ducking the hand so that the stick hit the desk, was certain to be punished, but 'boring' em', so far as the boys knew, had never been discovered. Will waited, thinking of Brychan, knowing he could rely on him. He seemed almost to see the fine incision in the freckled skin. The door opened, and Brychan was back.

William Evans stopped reading, and put out his hand for the stick. Brychan gave it to him, thick end first. Will felt Tegwyn close against his body. There was a smell of fresh cow-muck, from his boots.

'Discipline,' William Evans said, standing above the boys. 'Discipline, now, in every walk of life is essential. Hold out your hands.'

The boys obeyed. Will noticed that Tegwyn's hand was much thicker than his own. On the ends of the fingers there was a smear of bright yellow pollen.

'You, boy, for lateness,' William Evans said, and swung the stick.

Tegwyn took the cut on his fingers, without cry or movement. The stick did not break. Will saw Brychan anxiously watching.

'And you, boy, for inattention and disturbance.'

The stick swung again, and Will, looking at Brychan, yelled before it even reached his hand. At the same time he pushed his hand forward, so that the cut came on the bottom of the palm. The stick broke, and Will turned and jumped about, lifting his hand to his mouth and licking. The palm in fact hardly hurt at all.

RAYMOND WILLIAMS, *Border Country*, 1960

'The Under Thirteen Netball team lost 5 to 3 to the Sacred Heart Under Thirteens, the Under Fifteens won 4 to 2 and the Over Fifteens lost 9 to 3. Well done, Under Fifteens!'

Puny applause.

'And now from something pleasant to something less pleasant. I want these three girls to come up on the platform: Janice Webb, Dolores Kellog, Mavis Sloat.'

To the faint minstrelsy of blowing noses and filing nails three white-faced prisoners walked down the gangway and mounted the dock. Heads screwed round and teachers, too, craned forward as at a public execution. The piano teacher sat on her hands.

'These girls, all fourth year leavers, beat up—yes, you may well gasp—beat up a second year girl on the way home from school last night. In addition to this display of utter bestiality, there are no other words to describe it . . .'

The voice rose to a shriek and, her fat figure shaking with rage in her gown, she pointed the finger of accusation at the prisoners.

'. . . In addition to this bestiality, not one of these girls was wearing her beret. These girls, I call them girls for want of a better word, these girls shall learn that violence reaps a reward of recrimination. They will not be rejoining their classes. They have disgraced their parents and the School. Look at them, and be warned. They are guttersnipes and shall be dealt with as such.'

She flung out of the shocked and silent hall.

The Head Girl read out the Lost Property Notices.

SHENA MACKAY, *Dust Falls on Eugene Schlumburger*, 1964

A rather solitary boy—
we were hardly aware of him until
one day, when we were in 5C,
in Assembly, as the Assistant Head
was intoning the Lord's Prayer, he sang

If you go down to the woods today
    You'd better not go alone,
It's lovely down in the woods today
    But safer to stay at home

loud and was removed during the second verse.

About a week later, in Chemistry,
Mr Watts discovered him writing up
his account of the preparation of
sodium thiosulphate crystals
in an unusual manner i.e.
he would do a few lines and then invert
his exercise book before scrawling
the next bit—alternate paragraphs
upside-down. When asked why, he replied
'In Japan the natives eat fish raw.'

Some days later, he seized Mr Hotchkiss
(a small History teacher) by the throat
crying 'At the roadside rooks snatch voles!'.

About three-quarters of the way through
the Autumn Term, he left (I believe
to conclude his education elsewhere).

PETER READING, 'Alma Mater', in *Tom O'Bedlam's Beauties*, 1981

AT ODDS WITH THE SYSTEM

If I describe a day's work in that dusty, dingy, ill-ventilated schoolroom, there will not be a qualified teacher in the world beneath the age of fifty who will not consider it frightful. A lifetime ago it would have seemed perfectly normal schooling.

H. G. WELLS, *Experiment in Autobiography*, 1934

When Miss Sharp had performed the heroical act mentioned in the last chapter, and had seen the Dictionary, flying over the pavement of the little garden, fall at length at the feet of the astonished Miss Jemima, the young lady's countenance, which had before worn an almost livid look of hatred, assumed a smile that perhaps was scarcely more agreeable, and she sank back in the carriage in an easy frame of mind, saying—'So much for the Dictionary; and, thank God, I'm out of Chiswick.'

Miss Sedley was almost as flurried at the act of defiance as Miss Jemima had been; for, consider, it was but one minute that she had left school, and the impressions of six years are not got over in that space of time. Nay, with some persons those awes and terrors of youth last for ever and ever. I know, for instance, an old gentleman of sixty-eight, who said to me one morning at breakfast, with a very agitated countenance, 'I dreamed last night that I was flogged by Dr Raine.' Fancy had carried him back five and fifty years in the course of that evening. Dr Raine and his rod were just as awful to him in his heart, then, at sixty-eight, as they had been at thirteen. If the Doctor, with a large birch, had appeared bodily to him, even at the age of threescore and eight, and had said in awful voice, 'Boy, take down your pant . . . !' Well, well, Miss Sedley was exceedingly alarmed at this act of insubordination.

'How could you do so, Rebecca?' at last she said, after a pause.

'Why, do you think Miss Pinkerton will come out and order me back to the black-hole?' said Rebecca, laughing.

'No: but——'

'I hate the whole house,' continued Miss Sharp, in a fury. 'I hope I may never set eyes on it again. I wish it were in the bottom of the Thames, I do; and if Miss Pinkerton were there, I wouldn't pick her out, that I wouldn't. Oh! how I should like to see her floating in the water, yonder, turban and all, with her train streaming after her, and her nose like the beak of a wherry.'

'Hush!' cried Miss Sedley.

'Why, will the black footman tell tales?' cried Miss Rebecca, laughing. 'He may go back and tell Miss Pinkerton that I hate her with all my soul; and I wish he would; and I wish I had a means of proving it too. For two years I have only had insults and outrage from her. I have been treated worse than any servant in the kitchen. I have never had a friend or a kind word, except from you. I have been made to tend the little girls in the lower school-room, and to talk French to the Misses, until I grew sick of my mother-tongue. But that talking French to Miss Pinkerton was capital fun, wasn't it? She doesn't know a word of French, and was too proud to confess it. I believe it was that which made her part with me; and so thank Heaven for French. *Vive la France! Vive l'Empereur! Vive Bonaparte!*'

W. M. Thackeray, *Vanity Fair*, 1847–8

The right Education of the Female Sex, as it is in a manner everywhere neglected, so it ought to be generally lamented. . . . Certainly Mans Soul cannot boast of a more sublime Original than ours; they had equally their efflux from the same eternal Immensity, and therefore capable of the same improvement by good Education. Vain man is apt to think we were meerly intended for the Worlds propagation, and to keep its humane inhabitants sweet and clean; but, by their leaves, had we the same Literature, he would find our brains as

fruitful as our bodies. Hence I am induced to believe, we are de-
barred from the knowledg of humane learning, lest our pregnant
Wits should rival th'towring conceits of our insulting Lords and
Masters.

———————

I cannot but complain of, and must condemn the great negligence of
Parents, in letting the fertile ground of their Daughters lie fallow, yet
send the barren Noddles of their Sons to the University, where they
stay for no other purpose than to fill their empty Sconces with idle
notions to make a noise in the Country.

———————

There is no instruction more moving, than the example of your
living. By that line of yours they are to conform their own. Take
heed then lest the damp of your own life extinguish the light of your
Childrens. As you are a kind Mother to them be a careful Monitor
about them; and if your business will permit, teach them your self,
with their letters, good manners. For there is an in-bred, filial fear in
Children to their Parents, which will beget in them more attention
in hearing, and retention in holding what they hear.

HANNAH WOOLLEY, *The Gentlewoman's Companion,* 1675

I love to rise in a summer morn,
 When the birds sing on every tree;
The distant huntsman winds his horn,
 And the skylark sings with me:
 Oh what sweet company!

But to go to school in a summer morn,—
 Oh it drives all joy away!
Under a cruel eye outworn,
 The little ones spend the day
 In sighing and dismay.

Ah then at times I drooping sit,
 And spend many an anxious hour;

Nor in my book can I take delight,
  Nor sit in learning's bower,
  Worn through with the dreary shower.

How can the bird that is born for joy
  Sit in a cage and sing?
How can a child, when fears annoy,
  But droop his tender wing,
  And forget his youthful spring?

Oh father and mother, if buds are nipped,
  And blossoms blown away;
And if the tender plants are stripped
  Of their joy in the springing day,
  By sorrow and care's dismay,—

How shall the summer arise in joy,
  Or the summer fruits appear?
Or how shall we gather what griefs destroy,
  Or bless the mellowing year,
  When the blasts of winter appear?

WILLIAM BLAKE, 'The Schoolboy', in *Poems,*
Songs of Experience, 1794

My education was averted in a dank atmosphere of Portuguese
laurels, dim Victorian rooms, and surrealist ineptitude. The school,
which was in a part of the Home Counties rapidly being transformed
from rural into dormitory-suburb, was what was known as private—
and my strongest feeling about it now is so it should have been.

In fact, I look back with bewilderment at its very existence, one
which ended during the war, not by the clean strike of a bomb but
by creeping insolvency brought to crisis point and extinction by
evacuation. Surely such cartoon schools can't survive today? How
did it then?

At this time, in the middle Thirties, it had been in existence for twenty years or so. Upon its foundation optimistic efforts had been made to furnish it with the trappings of 'tradition'. It had a stylish name. We wore bright caps with enormous peaks. We had a motto and a school song. We, boarders and day boys, were regularly enjoined to uphold the school's honour by such measures as remaining aloof from the grammar school pupils at the bottom of the hill, or by not skulking in the laurel jungle smoking Park Drive cigarettes (the same price as Weights and Woods, but which seemed to be regarded by us trainee-smokers as a superior brand more appropriate to betray the school's honour with). But by the time I arrived there the thin Greyfriars varnish had cracked and flaked, exposing the forlorn shanty-town structure beneath.

The school consisted of two big sham-grand mansions—built, I suppose, by prosperous tradesmen in the 1890s—with the intervening wall knocked down and with their own stucco now falling down. (A new boy trying to cringe into invisibility on his first day there received a horrid head wound when a plaster gargoyle detached itself from the guttering and felled him to the path; he recovered consciousness but never his self-confidence.) A dogged dignity was maintained around the main entrance, where the brass and floorboards were kept polished. But when the corridor reached the classrooms reality bared its mouldy teeth: rickety desks, wormy woodwork, and walls, on which the muddy distemper had worn bare, which appeared to have been viciously pelted with shrapnel. When, for a few minutes a day, the sun managed to penetrate to the classroom windows, it fell back baffled by the curds of undisturbed dust which gave the panes the look of that thick, frosted glass put in lavatories. (The lavatories themselves were unmentionable.)

The reason for the infrequency of direct sunlight was the rank luxuriance of the neglected grounds. Monkey-puzzle trees, Chinese conifers, rhododendrons, and those thickets of speckled laurel, all for many a year untrimmed and unchecked, swarmed in sinister profusion. Flower beds remained only as smudgy outlines, like ancient earthworks seen from an aircraft, under the long, tough grass of the insurgent lawns. Gravel paths were mattresses of thistles and dandelions. Across what had once been a tennis court a grey, tattered net looped like a lowered flag. In one corner was a heap of splintered planking lapped by nettles. This, I learned, had been the bicycle shed until it abruptly collapsed one day, and the rumour never ceased to circulate that still there under the debris was the skeleton of an insignificant boarder, buried with his Raleigh; he had never been missed. . . .

It was an odd atmosphere in which to acquire knowledge, or even any respect for knowledge, but at least we probably acquired a wider experience of the vagaries and oddballs of the adult world than most school-incarcerated boys, for ours was a kind of transit-hide-out for the educational underworld. I don't know how wage rates and union conditions applied in those days. I can only suppose that the school was run on scab labour. I can remember few of the teachers, because they were there so briefly, for a term or less. Most had the furtive air of being on the run. They were often failed undergraduates, sent down or fleeing from what one suspected as being an unsavoury mess of one kind or another, or decrepit, ageing unqualified nomads in the grip of alcohol or nervous derangement.

KENNETH ALLSOP, in Brian Inglis (ed.), *John Bull's Schooldays*, 1961

After Sunday meeting we returned to our class room and wrote home. Mr Jones wrote the principal news of the week—football matches against other schools and such like—on the blackboard and we copied it. At the foot of the sheet we were allowed to add a personal message of our own. Then Mr Jones inspected our letter—upsidedown in order to respect the privacy of our little postscript. At the end of my first letter I wrote: 'I hate this place. I hate this school. I cannot make my bed like a parcel.'

These remained my sentiments. Presumably my parents were upset, but they never considered removing me to somewhere more tolerable. Once a term they came to the local hotel for the weekend, and I had some escape from school life. Otherwise the dreary round was unbroken. Lessons made little impact on me though I always managed to be top of my class. What I particularly disliked was the period, devised by Mrs Jones, called 'Stiff Reading'. For an hour we had to read some solid book, not a work of fiction. I did not mind these solid books, most of which I should have read in any case. But I resented being denied any relief at other times—no Sexton Blake, no comics, nothing but improving works.

Nature study, always a feature of Quaker schools, was my special bugbear. I tried one variety after another, always in vain. I tried Aquarium. My tadpoles died. I could not catch newts. My tank smelled. I tried Astronomy and could never identify the stars. I even tried Lichen, the dreariest study known to man. Worst of all was the Flower List. This was a great printed sheet, issued to each boy, with the names of some 200 flowers and space for even rarer ones. We had to collect these flowers on our Sunday walk and then name them to Mr Jones the next morning. Some boys scored well over a hundred in no time. I never got more than half a dozen—daisy, dandelion, buttercup and after that, what? My flowers had all withered by Monday and the water in my jam jar stank. The whole affair was a nightmare to me.

A. J. P. TAYLOR, *A Personal History*, 1983

My dear, dear Mother,

If you don't let me come home, I die—I am all over ink, and my fine clothes have been spoilt—I have been tost in a blanket, and seen a ghost.

I remain, my dear, dear mother,
Your dutiful and most unhappy son,
FREDDY

P.S. Remember me to my father.

The Life and Times of Frederick Reynolds Written by Himself, 1826;
on his second day at Westminster, mid-eighteenth century

Since this custom of educating by the lash is suffered by the gentry of Great Britain, I would prevail only that honest heavy lads may be dismissed from slavery sooner than they are at present, and not whipped on to their fourteenth or fifteenth year, whether they expect any progress from them or not. Let the child's capacity be forthwith examined, and he sent to some mechanic way of life, without respect to his birth, if nature designed him for nothing higher: let him go before he has innocently suffered, and is debased into a dereliction of mind for being what it is no guilt to be, a plain man. I would not here be supposed to have said, that our learned men of either robe who have been whipped at school, are not still men of noble and liberal minds; but I am sure they would have been much more so than they are, had they never suffered that infamy.

RICHARD STEELE (1672–1725), 'On Flogging Schoolboys'

The Form Master's observations about punishment were by no means without their warrant at St James's School. Flogging with the birch in accordance with the Eton fashion was a great feature in its curriculum. But I am sure no Eton boy, and certainly no Harrow boy of my day, ever received such a cruel flogging as this Headmaster was accustomed to inflict upon the little boys who were in his care and power. They exceeded in severity anything that would be tolerated in any of the Reformatories under the Home Office. My reading in later life has supplied me with some possible explanations of his temperament. Two or three times a month the whole school was marshalled in the Library, and one or more delinquents were haled off to an adjoining apartment by the two head boys, and there flogged until they bled freely, while the rest sat quaking, listening to their screams. This form of correction was strongly reinforced by frequent religious services of a somewhat High Church character in the chapel. Mrs Everest was very much against the Pope. If the truth were known, she said, he was behind the Fenians. She was herself Low Church, and her dislike of ornaments and ritual, and generally her extremely unfavourable opinion of the Supreme Pontiff, had prejudiced me strongly against that personage and all religious practices supposed to be associated with him. I therefore did not derive much comfort from the spiritual side of my education at this juncture. On the other hand, I experienced the fullest applications of the secular arm.

How I hated this school, and what a life of anxiety I lived there for more than two years. I made very little progress at my lessons, and none at all at games. I counted the days and the hours to the end of every term, when I should return home from this hateful servitude and range my soldiers in line of battle on the nursery floor. The greatest pleasure I had in those days was reading. When I was nine and a half my father gave me *Treasure Island*, and I remember the delight with which I devoured it. My teachers saw me at once backward and precocious, reading books beyond my years and yet at the bottom of the Form. They were offended. They had large resources of compulsion at their disposal, but I was stubborn. Where my reason, imagination or interest were not engaged, I would not or I could not learn. In all the twelve years I was at school no one ever succeeded in making me write a Latin verse or learn any Greek except the alphabet. I do not at all excuse myself for this foolish neglect of opportunities procured at so much expense by my parents and brought so forcibly to my attention by my Preceptors. Perhaps if I had been introduced to the ancients through their history and customs, instead of through their grammar and syntax, I might have had a better record.

Winston Churchill, *My Early Life*, 1930

It so chanced . . . that in what proved the closing scene in my term of school attendance, I was rather unfortunate than guilty. The class to which I now belonged read an English lesson every afternoon, and had its rounds of spelling; and in these last I acquitted myself but ill; partly from the circumstance that I spelt only indifferently, but still more from the further circumstance, that, retaining strongly fixed in my memory the broad Scotch pronunciation acquired at the dames' school, I had to carry on in my mind the double process of at once spelling the acquired word, and of translating the old sounds of the letters of which it was composed into the modern ones. Nor had I been taught to break the words into syllables; and so, when required one evening to spell the word '*awful*', with much deliberation—for I had to translate, as I went on, the letters *a-w* and *u*—I spelt it word for word, without break or pause, as a-w-f-u-l. 'No,' said the master, 'a-w, *aw*, f-u-l, *awful*; spell again.' This seemed preposterous spelling. It was sticking in an *a*, as I thought, into the middle of the word, where, I was sure, no *a* had a right to be; and so I spelt it as at first. The master recompensed my supposed contumacy with a sharp cut athwart the ears with his tawse; and again demanding the spelling of the word, I yet again spelt it as at first. But on receiving a second cut, I refused to spell it any more; and, determined on overcoming my obstinacy, he laid hold of me and attempted throwing me down. As wrestling, however, had been one of our favourite Marcus' Cave exercises, and as few lads of my inches wrestled better than I, the master, though a tall and tolerably robust fellow, found the feat considerably more difficult than he could have supposed. We swayed from side to side of the school-room, now backwards, now forwards, and for a full minute it seemed to be a rather a moot point on which side the victory was to incline. At length, however, I was tripped over a form; and as the master had to deal with me, not as master usually deals with pupil, but as one combatant deals with another, whom he has to beat into submission, I was mauled in a way that filled me with aches and bruises for a full month thereafter. I greatly fear that, had I met the fellow on a lonely road five years subsequent to our encounter, when I had become strong enough to raise breast-high the 'great lifting stone of the Dropping Cave,' he would have caught as sound a thrashing as he ever gave to little boy or girl in his life; but all I could do at this time was to take down my cap from off the pin, when the affair had ended, and march straight out of school. And thus terminated my school education.

HUGH MILLER (b. 1802), *My Schools and Schoolmasters*, 1854

There is yet a further Reason, why Masters and Teachers should raise no Difficulties to their Scholars; but on the contrary should smooth their Way, and readily help them forwards, where they find them stop. Children's Minds are narrow and weak, and usually susceptible but of one Thought at once. Whatever is in a Child's Head, fills it for the time, especially if set on with any Passion. It should therefore be the Skill and Art of the Teacher to clear their Heads of all other Thoughts whilst they are learning of any Thing, the better to make room for what he would instill into them, that it may be received with Attention and Application, without which it leaves no Impression. The natural Temper of Children disposes their Minds to wander. Novelty alone takes them; whatever that presents, they are presently eager to have a Taste of, and are as soon satiated with it. They quickly grow weary of the same thing, and so have almost their whole Delight in Change and Variety. It is a Contradiction to the natural State of Childhood for them to fix their fleeting Thoughts. Whether this be owing to the Temper of their Brains, or the Quickness or Instability of their animal Spirits, over which the Mind has not yet got a full Command; this is visible, that it is a Pain to Children to keep their Thoughts steady to any thing. A lasting continued Attention is one of the hardest Tasks can be imposed on them; and therefore, he that requires their Application, should endeavour to make what he proposes as grateful and agreeable as possible; at least he ought to take care not to join any displeasing or frightful Idea with it. If they come not to their Books with some Kind of Liking and Relish, 'tis no wonder their Thoughts should be perpetually shifting from what disgusts them; and seek better Entertainment in more pleasing Objects, after which they will unavoidably be gadding.

'Tis, I know, the usual Method of Tutors, to endeavour to procure Attention in their Scholars, and to fix their Minds to the Business in Hand, by Rebukes and Corrections, if they find them ever so little wandering. But such Treatment is sure to produce the quite contrary Effect. Passionate Words or Blows from the Tutor fill the Child's Mind with Terror and Affrightment, which immediately takes it wholly up, and leaves no Room for other Impressions. I

believe there is no body that reads this, but may recollect what
Disorder hasty or imperious Words from his Parents or Teachers
have caused in his Thoughts; how for the Time it has turned his
Brains, so that he scarce knew what was said by or to him. He
presently lost the Sight of what he was upon, his Mind was filled
with Disorder and Confusion, and in that State was no longer
capable of Attention to any thing else.

JOHN LOCKE, 'Some Thoughts Concerning Education', 1693

That I got on tolerably well at Harrow, even with my 'armour' on,
is a proof that I never was ill-treated there. I have often, however,
with Lord Eustace Cecil (who was at Harrow with me), recalled since
how terrible the bullying was in our time—of the constant cruelty at
Harris's, where the little boys were always made to come down and
box in the evening for the delectation of the fifth form:—of how
little boys were constantly sent in the evening to Famish's—half-way
to the cricket-ground, to bring back porter under their greatcoats,
certain to be flogged by the head-master if they were caught, and to
be 'wapped' by the sixth form boys if they did not go, and infinitely
preferring the former:—of how, if the boys did not 'keep up' at
football, they were made to cut large thorn sticks out of the hedges,
and flogged with them till the blood poured down outside their
jerseys. Indeed, what with fagging and bullying, servility was as
much inculcated at Harrow in those days as if it was likely to be a
desirable acquirement in after life.

I may truly say that I never learnt anything useful at Harrow, and
had little chance of learning anything. Hours and hours were wasted
daily on useless Latin verses with sickening monotony. A boy's
school education at this time, except in the highest forms, was
hopelessly inane.

I have often heard since much of the immoralities of a public-
school life, but I can truly say that when I was there, I saw nothing
of them. A very few boys, however, can change the whole character

of a school, especially in a wrong direction. I do not think that my morals were a bit the worse for Harrow, but from what I have heard since of all that went on there even in my time, I can only conclude it was because—at that time certainly '*je n'avais pas le goût du péche*,' as I once read in a French novel.

Augustus Hare, *The Story of my Life*, 6 vols., 1896–1900;
Harrow, 1843–8

The young gentlemen were prematurely full of carking anxieties. They knew no rest from the pursuit of stoney-hearted verbs, savage noun-substantives, inflexible syntactic passages, and ghosts of exercises that appeared to them in their dreams. Under the forcing system, a young gentleman usually took leave of his spirits in three weeks. He had all the cares of the world on his head in three months. He conceived bitter sentiments against his parents or guardians, in four; he was an old misanthrope, in five; envied Curtius that blessed refuge in the earth, in six; and at the end of the first twelve-month had arrived at the conclusion, from which he never afterwards departed, that all the fancies of the poets, and lessons of the sages, were a mere collection of words and grammar, and had no other meaning in the world.

But he went on, blow, blow, blowing, in the Doctor's hothouse, all the time; and the Doctor's glory and reputation were great, when he took his wintry growth home to his relations and friends.

Dickens, *Dombey and Son*, 1848

With what disgust have I heard sensible women, for girls are more restrained and cowed than boys, speak of the wearisome confinement, which they endured at school. Not allowed, perhaps, to step out of one broad walk in a superb garden, and obliged to pace with steady deportment stupidly backwards and forwards, holding up their heads and turning out their toes, with shoulders braced back, instead of bounding, as Nature directs to complete her own design, in the various attitudes so conducive to health. The pure animal spirits, which make both mind and body shoot out, and unfold the tender blossoms of hope, are turned sour, and vented in vain wishes or pert repinings, that contract the faculties and spoil the temper; else they mount to the brain, and sharpening the understanding before it gains proportionable strength, produce that pitiful cunning which disgracefully characterizes the female mind—and I fear will ever characterize it whilst women remain the slaves of power!

MARY WOLLSTONECRAFT, *A Vindication of the Rights of Woman*, 1792

The latch of the door clicked, and they entered the big room. Ursula glanced down the place. Its rigid, long silence was official and chilling. Half way down was a glass partition, the doors of which were open. A clock ticked re-echoing, and Miss Harby's voice sounded double as she said:

'This is the big room—Standard Five-Six-and-Seven.—Here's your place—Five—'

She stood in the near end of the great room. There was a small high teacher's desk facing a squadron of long benches, two high windows in the wall opposite.

It was fascinating and horrible to Ursula. The curious, unliving light in the room changed her character. She thought it was the rainy morning. Then she looked up again, because of the horrid feeling of being shut in a rigid, inflexible air, away from all feeling of the ordinary day; and she noticed that the windows were of ribbed, suffused glass.

The prison was round her now! She looked at the walls, colour washed, pale green and chocolate, at the large windows with frowsy geraniums against the pale glass, at the long rows of desks, arranged in a squadron, and dread filled her. This was a new world, a new life, with which she was threatened. But still excited, she climbed into her chair at her teacher's desk. It was high, and her feet could not reach the ground, but must rest on the step. Lifted up there, off the ground, she was in office. How queer, how queer it all was! How different it was from the mist of rain blowing over Cossethay. As she thought of her own village, a spasm of yearning crossed her, it seemed so far off, so lost to her.

She was here in this hard, stark reality—*reality*. It was queer that she should call this the reality, which she had never known till to-day, and which now so filled her with dread and dislike, that she wished she might go away. This was the reality, and Cossethay, her beloved, beautiful, well-known Cossethay, which was as herself unto her, that was minor reality. This prison of a school was reality. Here, then, she would sit in state, the queen of scholars! Here she would realize her dream of being the beloved teacher bringing light and joy to her children! But the desks before her had an abstract angularity that bruised her sentiment and made her shrink. She winced, feeling she had been a fool in her anticipations. She had brought her feelings and her generosity to where neither generosity nor emotion were wanted. And already she felt rebuffed, troubled by the new atmosphere, out of place.

D. H. LAWRENCE, *The Rainbow*, 1915

For a reason which all English readers will understand ... I am humiliated and embarrassed at having to record that as time went on I came to dislike the fagging system. No true defender of the Public Schools will believe me if I say that I was tired. But I was—dog-tired, cab-horse tired, tired (almost) like a child in a factory. Many things besides fagging contributed to it. I was big and had possibly outgrown my strength. My work in Form was almost beyond me. I was having a good deal of dental trouble at the time, and many nights of clamorous pain. Never, except in the front line trenches (and not always there) do I remember such aching and continuous weariness as at Wyvern. Oh, the implacable day, the horror of waking, the endless desert of hours that separated one from bed-time! And remember that, even without fagging, a school day contains hardly any leisure for a boy who does not like games. For him, to pass from the form-room to the playing field is simply to exchange work in which he can take some interest for work in which he can take none, in which failure is more severely punished, and in which (worst of all) he must feign an interest.

I think that this feigning, this ceaseless pretence of interest in matters to me supremely boring, was what wore me out more than anything else. If the reader will picture himself, unarmed, shut up for thirteen weeks on end, night and day, in a society of fanatical golfers—or, if he is a golfer himself, let him substitute fishermen, theosophists, bimetallists, Baconians, or German undergraduates with a taste for autobiography—who all carry revolvers and will probably shoot him if he ever seems to lose interest in their conversation, he will have an idea of my school life. Even the hardy Chowbok (in *Erewhon*) quailed at such a destiny. For games (and gallantry) were the only subjects, and I cared for neither. But I must seem to care for both, for a boy goes to a Public School precisely to be made a normal, sensible boy—a good mixer—to be taken out of himself; and eccentricity is severely penalised.

C. S. Lewis, *Surprised by Joy*, 1955

I have my doubts upon allowing the system of *fagging:*—it may inculcate subordination, on one side, but it encourages tyranny, on the other;—it may, perhaps, curb the overweening spirit of the heir apparent to an Earldom, when the son of a rich shop-keeper sends him upon a message;—it may, also, fill the child of a wholesale dealer with notions of equality, unfit for his future commerce;—and, as great boys fag the smaller, (both being free-born little men,) it seems that 'might overcomes right,'—which is the principle of the African Slave-Trade.

At all events, it must strike the impartial, that blacking shoes, and running on errands, are rather redundant parts of a liberal education.

George Colman the Younger (b. 1762), *Random Records*, 1830

It is almost impossible to convey to any one who has had no experience in teaching girls any notion of the wholly unsystematic and confused state of their education. A lively, we *wish* we could say an exaggerated, sketch of some of its most striking defects is to be found in Mr Bryce's valuable report presented to the Schools' Inquiry Commission. The great majority of English girls are educated either at home with the help of governesses and masters, or at exceedingly small schools, whether day-schools or boarding-schools. Parents prefer these small schools because they believe they approach the most nearly to that which is their ideal of instruction for girls, and what in theory is very beautiful, home-education; but in nothing whatever is there a greater divergence between the theory and the actual, and in many cases the only possible practice, than in this matter of home-education for girls.

ELIZABETH WOLSTENHOLME-ELMY, 'The Education of Girls', 1869

Roedean may not have been the stupidest school in England, but it certainly ranked high. The action of punishing a girl for finishing her preparation too quickly by depriving her of access to the Library seems to me indicative, and intellectual achievement rated in public opinion just nothing at all (by which I do not mean that it was maltreated); we did not follow the School Story example and persecute our 'swots' or 'sweats'. Nobody minded if you were top of your form, which was very easy to achieve; but it was no advantage to you. And no one—or practically no one—discussed the subject-matter of lessons (as distinct from the awfulness of the sums or the unfairness of the piece of translation set) outside the class-room, or indeed any cognate subject such as politics. We had no debating society, and the only reference to politics (other than a joke or two about suffragettes) which I remember was when a young and untried history mistress suddenly observed in the middle of a lesson, 'Now we are coming to a man about whom I cannot trust myself to speak calmly!' The monster turned out to be Disraeli; we looked up in mild surprise, but did not pursue the matter. We talked about other things—games, theatrical stars such as Lewis Waller (no film stars then), and male athletes, and places for summer holidays. Also about who was 'keen' on whom; it was customary to have an emotional attachment to a senior girl, or to feign one if you had not. But we never imitated the 'scandalous' side of public school life faintly, nor did we resemble the characters of Colette. One or two girls sometimes told slightly vulgar stories, but our language and our behaviour was otherwise clean as a whistle.

MARGARET COLE, *Growing Up Into Revolution*, 1949

My dear old school goes back to-day,
Fumbling for tips and 'Goodbye, old boy,'
   Shall we give it a cheer?
Let us pray for its members, past and present,
Let us remember how unpleasant
   Most of them were.

To-morrow there'll be the same old rags,
The disgusted prefects going with fags,
   The long walks in the woods,
The despondent scribbling in worn-out rears,
The long discussions in comfy chairs
   On eternal goods.

Remember how, in capitals, WOMAN
Was thought of as tart or as superhuman,
   Remember the vague
Nimbus of undefined emotion
Round the words 'Country', 'Duty', 'Devotion',
   Poppies, Earl Haig.

They took me to see the working class,
I stood there feeling unwanted, an ass,
   By the London docks.

If they haven't the reputation of sinners
Toc H gives people occasional dinners,
   As sly as a fox.

But most of us never saw the slums,
The marching we knew was done to drums
   And in uniform . . .
Remember how sex was a festering sore,
How they plastered it over more and more
   As a 'matter of form'.

Interception of notes became a game,
Their only amusement, the penalty Shame.
   They knew their cues.
'Sex is God's and you mustn't touch it,
It's a beautiful shoe whose very latchet
   You may not loose.'

So we were onanists; beds at night
Used to respond with continual slight
   Creaks of their springs.
But this was love's face in a mirror
That showed fatigue, not joy or terror,
   Eyes hollow rings.

Remember the countless Latin proses,
The poems we read, about girls and roses,
   Ethereal feelings,
Lofting shots from the sensual bunker,
Buds untouched by a worldly canker,
   Sublime as ceilings.

Remember, we prayed like anything
For Peace and the Forces of the King,
   Land, sea and air,
While sexual activity became

Hockey or Rugger, any game,
　　To tough and tear.

A host of rules; but it was these,
The attitudes of the authorities,
　　That made us bitter;
And now we realise that we,
Try as we may, can never be
　　A boundary hitter.

Emotionally we're almost dead,
To have stunned us, hit us on the head,
　　Would have been better;
Our white-hot desires were twisted
Inwards by their frightful, boasted
　　'Obedience to the letter.'

What should be love in us is hate,
Habits of feeling continued late
　　Are with us still.
We keep alive on a series of kicks,
Occasional women and Hollywood flicks.
　　We feel rather ill.

The outside world for us was a fable,
A topic that sat at the breakfast table,
　　Renowned for sin.
We were trained up a different wall
And the result is that after all
　　We don't fit in.

My dear old school goes back to-day;
I shouldn't cheer it, shout 'Hooray!'
　　Because you know too well
That those who smile because it's new
Will find out in a year or two
　　What parsons mean by Hell.

This poem, written in the summer of 1934, was published later that year in Esmond Romilly's anti-Public School magazine *Out of Bounds*. As a result, Mr Malim sent me a letter saying that it would not be a good thing for me to visit the school for at least three years.

GAVIN EWART, 'The Fourth of May', in *The Collected Ewart*, 1980

My father wrote his articles, reviews—
the postman brought him books—though now I'd say
that A. S. Neill is not the latest news,
his was the brightest star of many a day.
When those brave volumes of *The Dominie,*
his Log—Dismissed—In Doubt, dropped through the door—
his later books I'd name less certainly—
my father felt more surely than before
that he was right to head his romping class
to frolic in the quarry on Cavehill,
or march them to the baths to learn to swim.
Inspectors could not let such treason pass
when there were proper elements to fill
the squared timetable. They admonished him.

JOHN HEWITT, 'A Dominie's Log', in *Kites in Spring:
A Belfast Boyhood*, 1980

Shops and dwellings of the type of my home were 'run up' any-how. Slum conditions appeared almost at once in courts and muddy by-ways. Yet all around were open fields and common land, Bromley Common, Chislehurst Common, great parks like Sundridge Park and Camden, and to the south the wide heathery spaces about Keston Fish Ponds and Down.

The new order of things that was appearing in the world when I was born, was already arousing a consciousness of the need for universal elementary education. It was being realized by the ruling classes that a nation with a lower stratum of illiterates would compete at a disadvantage against the foreigner. A condition of things in which everyone would read and write and do sums, dawned on the startled imagination of mankind. The British and the National Schools, which had existed for half a century in order to make little Nonconformists and little Churchmen, were organized into a state system under the Elementary Education Act of 1871 and supplemented by Board Schools (designed to make little Unsectarian Christians). Bromley was served by a National School. That was all that the district possessed in the way of public education. It was the mere foundation of an education. It saw to the children up to the age of thirteen or even fourteen, and no further. Beyond that the locality had no public provision for technical education or the development of artistic or scientific ability whatever. Even that much of general education had been achieved against considerable resistance. There was a strong objection in those days to the use of public funds for the education of 'other people's children', and school pennies were exacted weekly from the offspring of everyone not legally indigent.

But side by side with that nineteenth-century National School under the Education Act, the old eighteenth-century order was still carrying on in Bromley, just as it was still carrying on in my mother's mind. In the eighteenth century the lower classes did not pretend to read or write, but the members of the tenant-farmer, shopkeeper, innkeeper, upper servant stratum, which was then, relatively to the labourers, a larger part of the community, either availed themselves of the smaller endowed schools which came down from the mental stir of the Reformation, or, in the absence of any such school in their neighbourhood, supported little private schools of their own. These private schools were struggling along amidst the general dissolution, shuffling and reconstruction of society that was already manifest in the middle nineteenth century, and the Academy of Mr Thomas Morley was a fairly well preserved specimen, only slightly modernized, of the departing order of things.

He had opened school for himself in 1849, having previously filled the post of usher at an old-established school that closed down in that year. He was Scotch and not of eminent academic attainments; his first prospectus laid stress on 'writing in both plain and ornamental style, Arithmetic logically, and History with special reference to Ancient Egypt'. Ancient Egypt and indeed most of the History except lists of dates, pedigrees and enactments, had dropped from the school outlook long before I joined it, for even Bromley Academy moved a little with the times, but there was still great stress on copperplate flourishes, long addition sums and book-keeping. Morley was a bald portly spectacled man with a strawberry nose and ginger-grey whiskers, who considered it due to himself and us to wear a top hat, an ample frock-coat, and a white tie, and to carry himself with invariable dignity and make a frequent use of 'Sir.' Except for a certain assistance with the little ones from Mrs Morley, a stout ringleted lady in black silk and a gold chain, he ran the school alone. It was a single room built out over a scullery; there were desks round the walls and two, of six places each, in the centre, with a stove between which warmed the place in winter. His bedroom window opened upon the schoolroom, and beneath it, in the corner of the room, was his desk, the great ink bottle from which the ink-wells were replenished, the pile of slates and the incessant cane, with which he administered justice, either in spasmodic descents upon our backs and hindquarters, or after formal accusations, by smacks across the palm of the hand. He also hit us with his hands anywhere, and with books, rulers and anything else that came handy, and his invective and derision were terrific. Also we were made to stand on the rickety forms and hold out books and slates until our arms ached. And in this way he urged us—I suppose our numbers varied from twenty-five to thirty-five—along the path of learning that led in the more successful instances to the examinations, conducted by an association of private schoolmasters, for their mutual reassurance, known as the College of Preceptors (with special certificates for book-keeping) and then to jobs as clerks.

About half the boys were boarders drawn from London public houses or other homes unsuitable for growing youth. There were a few day-boarders from outlying farms, who took their dinner in the house. The rest were sons of poorish middle-class people in the town. We assembled at nine and went on to twelve and again from two to five, and between these hours, except when the windows were open in warm weather, the atmosphere grew steadily more fœtid and our mental operations more sluggish and confused.

H. G. Wells, *Experiment in Autobiography*, 1934

I began to collect my things together. All the school books had to be left in a big pile on my table. I took my games clothes up to the dormitory to be packed. Geoffrey and I went together to the Armoury to return our uniforms. The long, thin sergeant called 'Pull Through' was there. I smelt the oil rags and metal for the last time. We made jokes about someone's initials which were F. L.

In school that afternoon we each had to write a chapter of a ghost story. This is the only lesson I have ever enjoyed or remembered.

Borrowing from the Bible, I wrote, 'The hair of my flesh stood up.' How everyone laughed when it was read out! I described the red damask walls, the silver sconces, and the great bed crowned with mouldy ostrich feathers. It was very romantic.

When the marks for the term were read out I was fourteenth, a not very distinguished place. Geoffrey was a little above me, and right at the top of the form was someone we both looked on as simple. Either we were quite wrong or very lazy.

On our way back to the House I stopped at the Art School to collect my drawings and say good-bye to Mr Williams. He was in a corner, bending over someone's drawing, giving it a big, grey wash. The boy was hating it. His work was being spoilt for him. Masters never understand this.

When Williams saw me he pushed his round shoulders back and said, 'Well, good-bye, Welch. Go on with your drawing. Don't let them make you do anything else.'

I felt flattered. I decided that I wanted to be a painter. I collected my drawings and went out feeling warm and comfortable.

Geoffrey was annoyed because I had kept him waiting. He knocked off my hat and trod on it. It looked like a big, crushed egg, pale and fragile in the darkness. For a moment I was horrified, then I remembered that tomorrow was the last day.

We ate all we could at tea so that we should have nothing left in our lockers.

DENTON WELCH, *Maiden Voyage*, 1943

There was a highly competitive house system in the Senior school, whose four houses were named Holyrood, Melrose, Argyll, and Biggar. Miss Mackay saw to it that the Brodie girls were as far as possible placed in different houses. Jenny was put in Holyrood, Sandy with Mary Macgregor in Melrose, Monica and Eunice went into Argyll, and Rose Stanley into Biggar. They were therefore obliged to compete with each other in every walk of life within the school and on the wind-swept hockey fields which lay like the graves of the martyrs exposed to the weather in an outer suburb. It was the team spirit, they were told, that counted now, every house must go all out for the Shield and turn up on Saturday mornings to yell encouragement to the house. Inter-house friendships must not suffer, of course, but the team spirit . . .

This phrase was enough for the Brodie set who, after two years at Miss Brodie's, had been well directed as to its meaning.

'Phrases like "the team spirit" are always employed to cut across individualism, love and personal loyalties,' she had said. 'Ideas like "the team spirit" ', she said, 'ought not to be enjoined on the female sex, especially if they are of that dedicated nature whose virtues from time immemorial have been utterly opposed to the concept. Florence Nightingale knew nothing of the team spirit, her mission was to save life regardless of the team to which it belonged. Cleopatra knew nothing of the team spirit if you read your Shakespeare. Take Helen of Troy. And the Queen of England, it is true she attends international sport, but she has to, it is all empty show, she is concerned only with the King's health and antiques. Where would the team spirit have got Sybil Thorndike? *She* is the great actress and the rest of the cast have got the team spirit. Pavlova . . .'

Perhaps Miss Brodie had foreseen this moment of the future when her team of six should be exposed to the appeal of four different competing spirits, Argyll, Melrose, Biggar, and Holyrood. It was impossible to know how much Miss Brodie planned by deliberation, or how much she worked by instinct alone. However, in *this*, the first test of her strength, she had the victory.

MURIEL SPARK, *The Prime of Miss Jean Brodie*, 1961

Dr M.'s favourite technique for inculcating love of the Latin language was to invite a boy to kneel on a platform in front of the class with hands stretched out in front and the feet, behind, raised off the ground. This is a very difficult thing to do. The boy was then made to open his mouth and a chalk duster inserted into it. If he fell forward on to his hands or relaxed backward so that his feet touched the ground he would be beaten around the head. Thus balanced precariously on the fulcrum of his knees and emitting animal grunts he would be invited to agree by a nodding of the head that he was a rogue, a ne'er-do-well, a stupid oaf who ought to be out digging roads and not wasting teachers' time and taxpayers' money here in St Columb's. Outside class Dr M. walked quietly and read his breviary. He was said to be an extremely clever and a very saintly man. Not all techniques were quite so sophisticated. Father F. might simply knock a boy unconscious and tell two of his class-mates to 'cart him outside. I'm not having him here, lying about in my class-room.' These were exceptions, but exceptions which were tolerated, in no way regarded as outrageous. Had lay teachers behaved so, there might have been protest from parents, but one did not question the activities of priests.

EAMONN MCCANN, *War and an Irish Town*, 1974

Brightness of brightness shimmers and is gone;
The music founders to the cries of children,
Screaming of bells, the rattle of milk bottles,
Footfall echoes of jails and hospitals.

At Odds with the System

I think I have been sitting here half my life,
Feet on desk, drumming a confiscated penknife
On a pile of unsatisfactory homework.
Careful, kids; my bite is worse than my bark.
I love them, but not even the greatest lover
Can stay on form five days a week for ever
And not start reading, over the loved head,
Book titles on the shelf behind the bed.
At five to two the lunch hour nears its end
And gulls come down on the deserted playground,
One at a time, to search the litter bins.
This is the moment my fantasy begins
And I drive with a generous lady, long since lost,
Against the traffic to the glittering west,
Startling the hens in drowsy villages,
Cushioned with money, time and privileges.
O chalky teachers, you would gladly do
Without your pensions to be with me too!
The fields are bright with sunlight after rain,
The skies are clear, the music starts again . . .

DEREK MAHON, 'Teaching in Belfast',
in *Poems 1962–1978*, 1979

Edmund went out of my life. He was one of those selected for scholarship cramming, a good selection it proved since he won his scholarship all right, in fact, I believe he won two. I was rejected, a good rejection too, confirmed fairly regularly in after-life by many other authorities given the opportunity of showing me the door. The chosen assembled in a corner class-room, and settled down in an atmosphere of earnest quiet; the rejects were herded into a somewhat scruffy room next door where chaos and rebellion reigned. Occasionally during our hilarities we might peer through the glass partition at the fifty busy pens toiling away next door; and you might catch one wandering gaze from a misplaced crammee longing to be out of it. Perhaps it was this contrast in our fates that made our lot so wild and would-be tough: we had been judged unfit for educational advancement—were we not then, licensed to be of bad behaviour? If that was it, the circumstances then ruling favoured the attitude demanded by our psychological state. War had been declared during the holidays; a couple of teachers had gone to it, and one of the vacant places was filled by a very young man of little experience and hardly any natural authority. We got him, or he got us, poor fellow.

In no time we discovered that he didn't like belting us. He was one of those who can strike only in anger, and then with no sureness because half of him was in recoil from his own emotion just as it was overwhelming him. A thin gangling young man with a long neck and a large Adam's apple, he seemed to be caught in the act of gulping and this impression was strongest at the very times when he was trying to seem the authentically fearsome figure of authority outraged. Half the class were defying him in various ways, behind his back and all around, as he struggled to deal with the boy before him. That boy was mass-supported, obstinately and cunningly cheeky. The teacher's anger mounted; he whirled round to his desk and pulled out the strap. A stride and he stood over the boy, his Adam's apple working and the strap pulled through his trembling fingers. But he couldn't strike, or if he did it was nothing of a blow and he was so obviously distressed by it, we—and the boy, though he didn't forget to yell—thoroughly enjoyed his upset. Seeing that this was no good, he thought he'd try more humane punishments. Double your homework was one. Now we would have thought that a dirty trick if we'd really had to do what he set. But we didn't, and he hadn't the power to insist. Then he had an idea he might bring a rebel to shame by making him go and sit among the girls. I, myself, was one of the first to come under this sentence. I lumbered out of the boys' aisles grinning and receiving considerable encouragement from my pals and made my way to the only vacant seat on the girls' side of the class.

JACK COMMON (b. 1903), *Kiddar's Luck*, 1951

Some there are who get on the wrong track
Early on, victims of nannies or parents at odds
With each other or myopia or fatness,
Butterfingers spending their lives going back,
Plunging the darkness for pieces of suffering.
These remember only misery and scorn, the curt nods
Of masters responsive to more appetizing pupils,
The feeling of being failures and feeling
Failure to be irrevocable, their own and God's,
Who had made them eccentric, ugly or comic.
But, later, from lessening oblivion, humiliation, distil
Subtle essences, no need to be popular;
Tortures of childhood are made into *objets d'art*.
These fatten at High Table, turn novelist or critic.

Others, however, restless in unsexy beds, assistants
At private or public schools, obscure servants
Of trade in a crumbling empire, dream of the distance
Time has put between them and their prospects
So certain once as they moved with confidence,
Taking the Greeks as text and pretext,
Through enviable teams and prizes, romantic friendships
That grew less interesting, like their scholarship.
The features, too, have hardened, grown coarse
Where once scrawled lines of nose and lip
Were tender. Shrinking each year, these must force
Themselves back to the orchard where the golden apple
Falls and their friends wear puzzled faces,
And those they barely noticed, lagging in all the races,
Are the ones they have to grapple.

ALAN ROSS, 'The Golden Apples', in *Blindfold Games*, 1986

I still find it difficult to write with detachment about the Roedean of
my youth; and must, therefore, make it perfectly clear that I am not

in any way referring to present-day Roedean which may, for all I know, be as different from mine as chalk from cheese. Also, I have no doubt that at fourteen I was an awkward child with many unattractive traits, who might have found some difficulty in fitting into any community. I do not for a moment suggest that my experience at school was all the school's fault. But considering that up till September, 1907, I got on reasonably well with my contemporaries, that I left my home perfectly prepared to like school and to like my schoolfellows, and that as soon as I got away from school to college I found it perfectly easy to get on with my contemporaries there, I cannot accept that in September, 1907, I turned abruptly into the kind of creature with whom it was impossible for any normal human being to enjoy associating.

My early terms were almost pure misery—the kind of misery which no one can realise who has not had the experience of being thoroughly unpopular, not by reason of any defiance or independence of your own (which would at least provide a martyr's crown) but simply because you cannot fit the pattern, because, as small boys would say, 'you *stink*'; you do not know why, and your best efforts seem only to result in making you stink worse. It is far sharper in a residential community without private rooms where you can never, for thirteen long weeks at a time, get away from seeing your own personality mirrored in the eyes of others—and watching them move away from the vision in repulsion. To have no one—no one at all—who wants to speak to you, to giggle with you, or to be seen alive or dead with you; to find any group to which you try unobtrusively to attach yourself melting mysteriously away, leaving you in naked and patent quarantine; to hear voices saying, '*Margaret Postgate*? No, thank you . . .'

MARGARET COLE, *Growing Up Into Revolution*, 1949

It was a dull autumn day and Jill Pole was crying behind the gym.

She was crying because they had been bullying her. This is not going to be a school story, so I shall say as little as possible about Jill's school, which is not a pleasant subject. It was 'Co-educational', a school for both boys and girls, what used to be called a 'mixed' school; some said it was not nearly so mixed as the minds of the people who ran it. These people had the idea that boys and girls should be allowed to do what they liked. And unfortunately what ten or fifteen of the biggest boys and girls liked best was bullying the others. All sorts of things, horrid things, went on which at an ordinary school would have been found out and stopped in half a term; but at this school they weren't. Or even if they were, the people who did them were not expelled or punished. The Head said they were interesting psychological cases and sent for them and talked to them for hours. And if you knew the right sort of things to say to the Head, the main result was that you became rather a favourite than otherwise.

C. S. Lewis, *The Silver Chair*, 1953

I first began to realise that not everyone thought the public schools an unmixed blessing when I was about eight and a half and had just begun to attend a preparatory school; and indeed it was Uncle Isaak, a genial and generous godfather (though an unofficial one, I suppose, since he was a Jew) and a very amusing companion who was the first (in my experience) to sound a note of dissent. His charge . . . was that the older and more famous public schools looked down on the others. . . .

'The thing is,' he said, 'that these places were mostly founded to educate poor local boys who had shown ability. Then the rich got into the act. Here, they realised, was a good thing going cheap— nothing a rich man likes better than bargain prices. What was more, it got your trouble-making children out of the way for most of the year . . . very handy this, as the old way of doing it—sending 'em as pages to another rich man's castle—was just going out of fashion. So they used their influence to hog the vacancies or make extra ones at all the most conveniently situated foundations; and from then on, where you should have had poor humble boys who were grinding away at their Latin Grammar (on which they depended for their livelihood), you now had the idle and flashy sons of great merchants and noblemen, who knew that they were being *dumped* and resented it. So what did they do? They took it out on such of the poor scholars who were still around the place, and then, when they had more or less dispossessed them altogether, took it out on the grammar schools (i.e. those schools which for one reason or another had never appealed to rich parents and therefore hadn't grown smart like Eton or Winchester) in which the poor scholars took refuge. Then, in the nineteenth century, a whole lot of new public schools were set up to supply empire-builders, and of course these were despised by the old lot almost more than the grammar schools were . . . because, whereas the grammar schools were absolutely genuine in their own kind, the new public schools were just shoddy imitations of the grand ones. 'But you are not to think,' Isaak used to say as we pottered about the summer landskip, 'that this last fact *excuses* the famous schools for taking such attitudes toward the weaker ones. The assumption of superiority is the most offensive thing in the sight of God.'

Simon Raven, The Old School, 1986

I had to leave for Edinburgh by the morning train a few years ago— I was living at St Andrews at the time—and as I walked to the station I passed the children going to school. It was a dismal morning draped with discoloured rags of clouds like a great washing; a few drops of rain splashed down at meaningless intervals; sodden leaves were plastered to the pavements and low walls. I watched the children, their satchels on their backs, walking through the school gate and trudging towards a door in the high wall; there was little sound anywhere, for it was an unfrequented street; everything had an air of secrecy. I can give no idea of the dreariness of the scene; the earth bleared and wet; the dejected children. I seemed to see an enormous school, higher even than this one, and millions of children all over the world creeping towards it and disappearing into it. The picture rose of itself, and it brought back a still Sunday evening in

Wyre, when my mother and I had gone for a walk. The walk took us past the school, which, being shut, had a clean, forsaken look. My heart beat faster as we drew near, and I looked with dread at the ragged grass of the playground, not pounded now by the boots of the other boys, but lying peaceful and lost. I lingered to glance at the classroom windows, and my head grew hot and tight, as if I had been shut in a clothes cupboard. That was the feeling which my first year at school gave me, a feeling of being shut in some narrow, clean, wooden place: it must be known to every one who has attended a school, and the volume of misery it has caused will not bear thinking of. One day it made me so sick that Miss Angus took me outside and told me to sit down in a grassy field. It was a warm summer day. She came out later and told me to go home.

EDWIN MUIR, *An Autobiography*, 1940

To sum up my schooling:

My knowledge of English literature derived chiefly from my home. Most of my hours in the form room for ten years had been spent on Latin and Greek, History and Mathematics. Today I remember no Greek. I have never read Latin for pleasure and should now be hard put to it to compose a simple epitaph. But I do not regret my superficial classical studies. I believe that the conventional defence of them is valid; that only by them can a boy fully understand that a sentence is a logical construction and that words have basic inalienable meanings, departure from which is either conscious metaphor or inexcusable vulgarity. Those who have not been so taught—most Americans and most women—unless they are guided by some rare genius, betray their deprivation. The old-fashioned test of an English sentence—will it translate?—still stands after we have lost the trick of translation.

Those who passed through the Sixth at Lancing might spell atrociously, for our written work was seldom read and then only to criticise style or meaning; spelling was regarded as too elementary for attention. Those of us who 'specialised' in History had a vague conspectus of the succession of events in the Mediterranean from the time of Pericles, a rather more detailed knowledge of English History from the time of Henry VII, and of European History from the War of the Austrian Succession to the battle of Sedan. We could translate literary French unseen, but spoke it with outrageous accents and without knowledge of idiom. In verse the classical metres had been well drummed into us—'drummed' is the right word. The syllables and rhythms resounding into our ears were to deafen us to modern verse which followed different patterns. We were completely ignorant of Geography and all the natural sciences. In Mathematics we had advanced scarcely at all since we left our preparatory schools. Our general information was of the kind that makes *The Times* cross-word puzzle soluble.

My education, it seems to me, was the preparation for one trade only; that of an English prose writer. It is a matter of surprise that so few of us availed ourselves of it.

EVELYN WAUGH, A Little Learning, 1964

SCHOOLS AND
SCHOOLMASTERS

Here lie Willie Michie's banes;
    O Satan, when ye tak him,
Gie him the schoolin' of your weans,
    For clever deils he'll mak them!

ROBERT BURNS (1759–1796), 'On a Schoolmaster,
in Cleish Parish, Fifeshire'

What a griefe may this justly be unto us, when one shall come, and
crie out of us, to our faces: My sonne hath bene under you six or
seven years, and yet is not able so much as to reade English well;
much lesse to construe or understand a peece of Latin, or to write
true Latin, or to speake in Latin in any tolerable sort, which he might
have bene well able to have performed, if that you had taken that
course and those good paines with him which you might have done;
for in such a schoole others much yonger than mine are able to do it.
Another shall complaine: My sonne comes on never a whit in his
writing. Besides that his hand is such, that it can hardly be read; he
also writes so false English, that he is neither fit for trade, nor any
employment wherein to use his pen. . . .

Moreover, how must this needs trouble us, when manie shall crie
out of our severitie: some shall wish, I would my child had never
known him. If he had not dealt so cruelly with my child, he had bene
a scholar, whereas now he is undone. Or when our scholars coming
to mans estate, shall curse us, for that by our blowes they were made
dunses or deafe (though this often times unjustly) or to hate all
learning. . . . Or when they shall thus complaine: Our Maister had
not anie care of our government and manners. He never taught us

172

the feare of the Lord, nor made the least conscience to plant anie
Religion or grace in us.

JOHN BRINSLEY the Elder, A Consolation for our
Grammar Schooles, 1622

Let then our Reverend Master be ador'd
And all our gratefull Penns his praise Record;
I dare not name my selfe, yet what I am
From his examples and his precepts came.
Our Noblest witts from his instructive care
Have grac'd the Senate and have judg'd the Bar;
But, above all, the Muses sacred Band
Have been transplanted from his Eden Land.

DRYDEN, 1684; on the grammarian Lewis Maidwell at
Westminster School

His method of teaching was this. In a morning he would exactly and
plainly construe and parse the lessons to his scholars; which done, he
slept his hour (custom made him critical to proportion it) in his desk
in the school; but woe to any scholar that slept the while. Awaking,
he heard them accurately; and Atropos might be persuaded to pity,
as soon as he to pardon, where he found just fault. The prayers of
cockering mothers prevailed with him as much as the requests of
indulgent fathers, rather increasing than mitigating his severity on
their offending child. . . . it may be truly said (and safely for one out
of his school) that others have taught as much learning with fewer
lashes. Yet his sharpness was the better endured, because unpartial;
and many excellent scholars were bred under him. . . .

THOMAS FULLER, *The Worthies of England*, 1662

In the village where I was born there was four readers successively in
six years, ignorant men, and two of them immoral in their lives, who

173

were all my schoolmasters. In the village where my father lived, there was a Reader of about eighty years of age that never preached, and had two churches about twenty miles distant. His eyesight failing him, he said Common Prayer without book: but for the reading of the Psalms and chapters, he got a common thresher and day labourer one year, and a taylor another year (for the clerk could not read well) and at last he had a kinsman of his own (the excellentest stage-player in all the country, and a good gamester and a good fellow) that got Orders and supplied one of his places. After him another younger kinsman, that could write and read, got Orders. And at the same time another neighbour's son that had been a while at school turned minister, and . . . when he had been a preacher about twelve or sixteen years he was fain to give it over, it being discovered that his Orders were forged by the first ingenious stage-player. After him another neighbour's son took Orders. When he had been a while an attorney's clerk, and a common drunkard, and tipled himself into so great poverty that he had no other to live. . . . These were the schoolmasters of my youth (except two of them) who read Common Prayer on Sundays and holy days, and taught school and tipled on the week-days, and whipped the boys when they were drunk, so that we changed them very oft.

Autobiography of Richard Baxter, 1645–1691

Indeed, Johnson was very sensible how much he owed to Mr Hunter. Mr Langton one day asked him, how he had acquired so accurate a knowledge of Latin, in which, I believe, he was exceeded by no man of his time; he said, 'My master whipt me very well. Without that, Sir, I should have done nothing.' He told Mr Langton, that while Hunter was flogging his boys unmercifully, he used to say, 'And this I do to save you from the gallows.' Johnson, upon all occasions, expressed his approbation of enforcing instruction by means of the rod: 'I would rather,' said he, 'have the rod to be the general terror to all, to make them learn, than tell a child, if you do thus, or thus, you will be more esteemed than your brothers or sisters. The rod produces an effect which terminates in itself. A child is afraid of being whipped, and gets his task, and there's an end on't; whereas, by exciting emulation and comparisons of superiority, you lay the foundation of lasting mischief; you make brothers and sisters hate each other.'

BOSWELL, *Life of Johnson*, 1791

I still recollect, with pleasure, the country day-school: where a boy trudged in the morning, wet or dry, carrying his books, and his dinner, if it were at a considerable distance; a servant did not then lead master by the hand, for, when he had once put on coat and breeches, he was allowed to shift for himself, and return alone in the evening to recount the feats of the day close at the parental knee. His father's house was his home, and was ever after fondly remembered; nay, I appeal to many superior men, who were educated in this manner, whether the recollection of some shady lane where they conned their lesson; or, of some stile, where they sat making a kite, or mending a bat, has not endeared their country to them?

MARY WOLLSTONECRAFT, *A Vindication of the Rights of Woman*, 1792

Fordlow National School was a small grey one-storied building, standing at the cross-roads at the entrance to the village. The one large classroom which served all purposes was well lighted with several windows, including the large one which filled the end of the building which faced the road. Beside, and joined on to the school, was a tiny two-roomed cottage for the schoolmistress, and beyond that a playground with birch trees and turf, bald in places, the whole being enclosed within pointed, white-painted palings.

The only other building in sight was a row of model cottages occupied by the shepherd, the blacksmith, and other superior farm-workers. The school had probably been built at the same time as the houses and by the same model landlord; for, though it would seem a hovel compared to a modern council school, it must at that time have been fairly up-to-date. It had a lobby with pegs for clothes, boys' and girls' earth-closets, and a backyard with fixed wash-basins, although there was no water laid on. The water supply was contained in a small bucket, filled every morning by the old woman who cleaned the schoolroom, and every morning she grumbled because the children had been so extravagant that she had to 'fill 'un again'.

The average attendance was about forty-five. Ten or twelve of the children lived near the school, a few others came from cottages in the fields, and the rest were the Lark Rise children. Even then, to an outsider, it would have appeared a quaint, old-fashioned little gathering; the girls in their ankle-length frocks and long, straight pinafores, with their hair strained back from their brows and secured on their crowns by a ribbon or black tape or a bootlace; the bigger boys in corduroys and hobnailed boots, and the smaller ones in home-made sailor suits or, until they were six or seven, in petticoats.

FLORA THOMPSON, *Lark Rise to Candleford,* 1939

Perhaps there is not a foundation in the country so truly English, taking that word to mean what Englishmen wish it to mean—something solid, unpretending, of good character, and free to all. More boys are to be found in it, who issue from a greater variety of ranks, than in any school in the kingdom; and as it is the most various, so it is the largest, of all the free schools. Nobility do not go there, except as boarders. Now and then a boy of a noble family may be met with, and he is reckoned an interloper, and against the charter; but the sons of poor gentry and London citizens abound; and with them an equal share is given to the sons of tradesmen of the very humblest description, not omitting servants. I would not take my oath—but I have a strong recollection, that in my time there were two boys, one of whom went up into the drawing-room to his father, the master of the house; and the other, down into the kitchen to *his* father, the coachman. One thing, however, I know to be certain, and it is the noblest of all, namely, that the boys themselves (at least it was so in my time) had no sort of feeling of the difference of one another's ranks out of doors. The cleverest boy was the noblest, let his father be who he might. Christ Hospital is a nursery of tradesmen, of merchants, of naval officers, of scholars; it has produced some of the greatest ornaments of their time; and the feeling among the boys themselves is, that it is a medium between the patrician pretension of such schools as Eton and Westminster, and the plebeian submission of the charity schools.

LEIGH HUNT, *Autobiography,* 1850; at Christ Hospital in 1792

Beside yon straggling fence that skirts the way,
With blossom'd furze unprofitably gay,
There, in his noisy mansion, skill'd to rule,
The village master taught his little school;
A man severe he was, and stern to view;
I knew him well, and every truant knew;
Well had the boding tremblers learn'd to trace
The day's disasters in his morning face;
Full well they laugh'd, with counterfeited glee,
At all his jokes, for many a joke had he;
Full well the busy whisper, circling round,
Convey'd the dismal tidings when he frown'd;
Yet he was kind; or if severe in aught,
The love he bore to learning was in fault;
The village all declar'd how much he knew;
'Twas certain he could write, and cypher too;
Lands he could measure, terms and tides presage,
And e'en the story ran that he could gauge.
In arguing too, the parson own'd his skill,
For e'en though vanquish'd, he could argue still;

While words of learned length and thund'ring sound
Amazed the gazing rustics rang'd around,
And still they gaz'd, and still the wonder grew,
That one small head could carry all he knew.

GOLDSMITH, The Deserted Village, 1770

Henry . . . had the best elementary training available. The first school he attended was at Ballymacilcurr, a mile from his father's house. It was a fair sample of the infant school of the country and the period. The house was a thatched cabin. The seats were black oak sticks from the neighbouring bog. A fire of peat blazed, or rather smoked, in the middle of the floor, and a hole in the roof overhead served for a chimney. The teacher was a Mr Joseph Pollock, or Poak, as he was familiarly called—a tall lanky Scotchman, distinguished by an enormous nose, a tow wig, a long coat of rusty black, leather tights, grey stockings, brogues, and a formidable hazel rod. On occasions of state, such as the hearing of one of the advanced scholars or a judicial investigation of some mad prank, the Master was accustomed to raise the hazel rod to his shoulder, and with a grand air place astride his nose a huge pair of black horn spectacles. Thus equipped, he felt himself a king, and the urchins trembled at his nod.

J. L. PORTER, The Life and Times of Henry Cooke, 1871;
Cooke was born c.1788

School began in earnest next day. A profound impression was made upon me, I remember, by the roar of voices in the schoolroom suddenly becoming hushed as death when Mr Creakle entered after breakfast, and stood in the doorway looking round upon us like a giant in a story-book surveying his captives.

Tungay stood at Mr Creakle's elbow. He had no occasion, I thought, to cry out 'Silence!' so ferociously, for the boys were all struck speechless and motionless.

Mr Creakle was seen to speak, and Tungay was heard, to this effect.

'Now, boys, this is a new half. Take care what you're about, in this new half. Come fresh up to the lessons, I advise you, for I come fresh up to the punishment. I won't flinch. It will be of no use your rubbing yourselves; you won't rub the marks out that I shall give you. Now get to work, every boy!'

When this dreadful exordium was over, and Tungay had stumped out again, Mr Creakle came to where I sat, and told me that if I were famous for biting, he was famous for biting, too. He then showed me the cane, and asked me what I thought of *that*, for a tooth? Was it a sharp tooth, hey? Was it a double tooth, hey? Had it a deep prong, hey? Did it bite, hey? Did it bite? At every question he gave me a fleshy cut with it that made me writhe; so I was very soon made free of Salem House (as Steerforth said), and was very soon in tears also.

DICKENS, *David Copperfield*, 1849–50

Within a silent street, and far apart
From noise of business, from a quay or mart,
Stands an old spacious building, and the din
You hear without, explains the work within;
Unlike the whispering of the nymphs, this noise
Loudly proclaims a 'Boarding-School for Boys';
The master heeds it not, for thirty years
Have render'd all familiar to his ears;
He sits in comfort, 'mid the various sound
Of mingled tones for ever flowing round;
Day after day he to his task attends,—
Unvaried toil, and care that never ends:
Boys in their works proceed; while his employ
Admits no change, or changes but the boy;
Yet time has made it easy;—he beside
Has power supreme, and power is sweet to pride
But grant him pleasure;—what can teachers feel,

Dependent helpers always at the wheel?
Their power despised, their compensation small,
Their labour dull, their life laborious all;
Set after set the lower lads to make
Fit for the class which their superiors take;
The road of learning for a time to track
In roughest state, and then again go back:
Just the same way on other troops to wait,—
Attendants fix'd at learning's lower gate.

GEORGE CRABBE (b. 1754), 'The Borough', 1810

When it came to my turn to receive education, it was not in London but in Brighton that the ladies' schools most in estimation were to be found. There were even then (about 1836) not less than a hundred such establishments in the town, but that at No. 32, Brunswick Terrace, of which Miss Runciman and Miss Roberts were mistresses, and which had been founded some time before by a celebrated Miss Poggi, was supposed to be *nec pluribus impar*. It was, at all events, the most outrageously expensive, the nominal tariff of £120 or £130 per annum representing scarcely a fourth of the charges for 'extras' which actually appeared in the bills of many of the pupils. My own, I know, amounted to £1,000 for two years' schooling.

I shall write of this school quite frankly, since the two poor ladies, well-meaning but very unwise, to whom it belonged have been dead for nearly thirty years, and it can hurt nobody to record my conviction that a better system than theirs could scarcely have been devised had it been designed to attain the maximum of cost and labour and the minimum of solid results. It was the typical Higher Education of the period, carried out to the extreme of expenditure and high pressure.

Profane persons were apt to describe our school as a Convent, and to refer to the back door of our garden, whence we issued on our dismal diurnal walks, as the 'postern'. If we in any degree resembled nuns, however, it was assuredly not those of either a Contemplative or Silent Order. The din of our large double schoolrooms was something frightful. Sitting in either of them, four pianos might be heard going at once in rooms above and around us, while at numerous tables scattered about the rooms there were girls reading aloud to the governesses and reciting lessons in English, French, German, and Italian. This hideous clatter continued the entire day till we went to bed at night, there being no time whatever allowed for recreation, unless the dreary hour of walking with our teachers (when we recited our verbs), could so be described by a fantastic imagination. In the midst of the uproar we were obliged to write our exercises, to compose our themes, and to commit to memory whole pages of prose. On Saturday afternoons, instead of play, there was a terrible ordeal generally known as the 'Judgment Day'. The two schoolmistresses sat side by side, solemn and stern, at the head of the long table. Behind them sat all the governesses as Assessors. On the table were the books wherein our evil deeds of the week were recorded; and round the room against the wall, seated on stools of penitential discomfort, we sat, five-and-twenty 'damosels', anything but 'Blessed', expecting our sentences according to our ill-deserts. It must be explained that the fiendish ingenuity of some teacher had invented for our torment a system of imaginary 'cards', which we were supposed to 'lose' (though we never gained any) whenever we had not finished all our various lessons and practisings every night before bed-time, or whenever we had been given the mark for 'stooping', or had been impertinent, or had been 'turned' in our lessons, or had been marked 'P' by the music master, or had been convicted of 'disorder' (e.g., having our long shoe-strings untied), or, lastly, had told lies! Any one crime in this heterogeneous list entailed the same penalty, namely, the sentence, 'You have lost your card, Miss So-and-so, for such and such a thing', and when Saturday came round, if three cards had been lost in the week, the law wreaked its justice on the unhappy sinner's head! Her confession having been wrung from her at the awful judgment-seat above described, and the books having been consulted, she was solemnly scolded and told to sit in the corner for the rest of the evening! . . .

That a pupil in that school should ever become an artist, or authoress, would have been looked upon by both Miss Runciman and Miss Roberts as a deplorable dereliction. Not that which was good in itself or useful to the community, or even that which would be delightful to ourselves, but that which would make us admired in society, was the *raison d'être* of each acquirement. Everything was taught us in the inverse ratio of its true importance. At the bottom of the scale were Morals and Religion, and at the top were Music and Dancing; miserably poor music, too, of the Italian school then in vogue, and generally performed in a showy and tasteless manner on harp or piano.

Life of Frances Power Cobbe as told by Herself, 1894

Rugby, October 27th 1837

My dear Sir,—You said when I had the Pleasure of seeing you at Rugby, that your Son wished to be considered as a Boy as long as he could, and was not impatient to be regarded as a young Man. I think it must have been from some such boyish rather than manly Feeling that on Friday last, which was a whole Holyday, after having been told that it could not be granted, he took Leave for himself, and went out for a long Walk and was absent during the whole of Dinner, at which, as the only Preposter in the House, it was his especial Duty to have attended. It was only last half Year that I spoke very strongly to him on a similar great irregularity,—when he went down to the Inn and remained there without Leave till ten o' Clock at Night, to visit a former School Acquaintance who was passing through Rugby. I did not think that any Thing of the Sort would occur again, and I did not therefore mention it to you. Now however I think that I ought to acquaint you with both Cases,—for these extreme Carelessnesses of his Duty make it really impossible to feel the same Confidence in his Sense of Propriety as to Conduct; and would alter the Terms in which I should have been glad to have recommended him, had an Opportunity offered, to the Provost of Oriel. I was greatly surprised at the second Instance of a similar Fault:—not of Course that what he did was wrong in itself,—I have no Doubt that he merely took a long Walk,—but a Neglect of official Duty in one in his Part of the School really argues some Want of Manliness of Character,—and I need not say that it is very mischievous in Point of Example. I am very sorry to be obliged to make this Communication;—but I am happy to say that in all other Respects my favourable Opinion of him continues quite unchanged.

With my best Compliments to Mrs Hutchins, I remain,
My dear Sir,
Very faithfully your's,
T. ARNOLD

Letter from Thomas Arnold, 1837

By introducing morals and religion into his scheme of education, he altered the whole atmosphere of Public School life. Henceforward the old rough-and-tumble, which was typified by the régime of Keate at Eton, became impossible. After Dr Arnold, no public school could venture to ignore the virtues of respectability. Again, by his introduction of the prefectorial system, Dr Arnold produced far-reaching effects—effects which he himself, perhaps, would have found perplexing. In his day, when the school hours were over, the boys were free to enjoy themselves as they liked; to bathe, to fish, to ramble for long afternoons in the country, collecting eggs or gathering flowers. 'The taste of the boys at this period,' writes an old Rugbæan who had been under Arnold, 'leaned strongly towards flowers'; the words have an odd look to-day. The modern reader of *Tom Brown's Schooldays* searches in vain for any reference to compulsory games, house colours, or cricket averages. In those days, when boys played games they played them for pleasure; but in those days the prefectorial system—the system which hands over the life of a school to an oligarchy of a dozen youths of seventeen—was still in its infancy, and had not yet borne its fruit. Teachers and prophets have strange after-histories; and that of Dr Arnold has been no exception. The earnest enthusiast who strove to make his pupils Christian gentlemen and who governed his school according to the principles of the Old Testament has proved to be the founder of the worship of athletics and the worship of good form. Upon those two poles our public schools have turned for so long that we have almost come to believe that such is their essential nature, and that an English public schoolboy who wears the wrong clothes and takes no interest in football is a contradiction in terms. Yet it was not so before Dr Arnold; will it always be so after him? We shall see.

LYTTON STRACHEY, *Eminent Victorians*, 1918

'Have you made up your mind, my dear,' said Mrs Garth, laying the letters down.

'I shall go to the school at York,' said Mary. 'I am less unfit to teach in a school than in a family. I like to teach classes best. And, you see, I must teach: there is nothing else to be done.'

'Teaching seems to me the most delightful work in the world,' said Mrs Garth, with a touch of rebuke in her tone. 'I could understand your objection to it if you had not knowledge enough, Mary, or if you disliked children.'

'I suppose we never quite understand why another dislikes what we like, mother,' said Mary, rather curtly. 'I am not fond of a schoolroom: I like the outside world better. It is a very inconvenient fault of mine.'

'It must be very stupid to be always in a girls' school,' said Alfred, 'Such a set of nincompoops, like Mrs Ballard's pupils walking two and two.'

'And they have no games worth playing at,' said Jim. 'They can neither throw nor leap. I don't wonder at Mary's not liking it.'

'What is it that Mary doesn't like, eh?' said the father, looking over his spectacles and pausing before he opened his next letter.

'Being among a lot of nincompoop girls,' said Alfred.

'Is it the situation you had heard of, Mary?' said Caleb, gently, looking at his daughter.

'Yes, father: the school at York. I have determined to take it. It is quite the best. Thirty-five pounds a-year, and extra pay for teaching the smallest strummers at the piano.'

GEORGE ELIOT, *Middlemarch*, 1871–2

'Now, if Mr M'Choakumchild,' said the gentleman, 'will proceed to give his first lesson here, Mr Gradgrind, I shall be happy, at your request, to observe his mode of procedure.'

Mr Gradgrind was much obliged. 'Mr M'Choakumchild, we only wait for you.'

So, Mr M'Choakumchild began in his best manner. He and some one hundred and forty other schoolmasters, had been lately turned at the same time, in the same factory, on the same principles, like so many pianoforte legs. He had been put through an immense variety of paces, and had answered volumes of head-breaking questions. Orthography, etymology, syntax, and prosody, biography, astronomy, geography, and general cosmography, the sciences of compound proportion, algebra, land-surveying and levelling, vocal music, and drawing from models, were all at the ends of his ten chilled fingers. He had worked his stony way into Her Majesty's most Honourable Privy Council's Schedule B, and had taken the bloom off the higher branches of mathematics and physical science, French, German, Latin, and Greek. He knew all about all the Water Sheds of all the world (whatever they are), and all the histories of all the peoples, and all the names of all the rivers and mountains, and all the productions, manners, and customs of all the countries, and all their boundaries and bearings on the two and thirty points of the compass. Ah, rather overdone, M'Choakumchild. If he had only learnt a little less, how infinitely better he might have taught much more!

DICKENS, *Hard Times*, 1854

The Government Inspector, Mr Shadrach Pryce, came to inspect our school today. He brought his wife with him and they came to my rooms for a glass of wine and a biscuit after the inspection, refusing anything more substantial. He seemed to me a pleasant kindly fair examiner and the children passed a good examination. We presented 35 for examination out of an average attendance of 51, while Hay school, which was examined yesterday, presented only 42 out of an average attendance of 105. Passed two hours at the school house in the afternoon, talking over the examination with the Evanses who were very much pleased and satisfied with the result.

REVD FRANCIS KILVERT, *Diary (1871)*, 1938–40

It was made a matter of general congratulation about me that I was English. The flavour of J. R. Green's recently published (1874) History of the English People had drifted to me either directly or at second-hand, and my mind had leapt all too readily to the idea that I was a blond and blue-eyed Nordic, quite the best make of human being known. England was consciously Teutonic in those days, the monarchy and Thomas Carlyle were strong influences in that direction; we talked of our 'Keltic fringe' and ignored our Keltic infiltration; and the defeat of France in 1870–71 seemed to be the final defeat of the decadent Latin peoples. This blended very well with the anti-Roman Catholic influence of the eighteenth-century Protestant training, a distrust and hostility that remained quite vivid when much else of that teaching had faded. We English, by sheer native superiority, practically without trying, had possessed ourselves of an Empire on which the sun never set, and through the errors and infirmities of other races were being forced slowly but steadily—and quite modestly—towards world dominion.

All that was quite settled in my head, as I carried my green-baize satchel to and fro between Morley's school and my dismal bankrupt home, and if you had suddenly confronted me with a Russian prince or a rajah in all his glory and suggested he was my equal, I should either have laughed you to scorn or been very exasperated with you about it.

I was taught no history but English History, which after some centuries of royal criminality, civil wars and wars in France, achieved the Reformation and blossomed out into the Empire; and I learnt hardly any geography but British geography. It was only from casual reading that I gathered that quite a number of things had happened and quite a number of interesting things existed outside the world of English affairs. But I looked at pictures of the Taj Mahal, the Colosseum and the Pyramids in very much the same spirit as I listened to stories about the Wonders of Animal Intelligence (beavers, bees, birds' nests, breeding habits of the salmon, etc.). They did not shake my profound satisfaction with the self, the township, the county, the nation, the Empire and the outlook that was mine.

H. G. WELLS, Experiment in Autobiography, 1934

The modern prep. school boy commonly regards his headmaster with a good deal of respect—though with a diabolically keen eye for his mannerisms—and with some degree of affection; he seems a sagacious old thing, whose advice may well be worth following. The master feels that the boys, though they may lapse occasionally into mischievous young imps, deserve as a rule to be treated as sensible human beings. Occasionally at some prep. schools to-day I fancy that the boys are permitted to be just a shade too casual in their attitude towards the staff, and that a trifle more discipline would be an improvement. But no-one would desire a return to the Victorian tradition of antagonism, of terms made up of skirmishes and pitched battles, with intervals at best of neutrality.

Dr Grimstone in *Vice Versa*—with whom I trust the reader is well acquainted—was a portrait painfully true to life. In fact, Guthrie, who wrote as 'F. Anstey', told me that the Doctor and life at Crichton House were drawn with accuracy from the prep. school at Highgate which he himself had attended. And Newlands, the academy to which I was sent, resembled in many ways that at which

Mr Bultitude failed to have the happiest time of his life. It was expensive, the house and playing-fields were spacious, the teaching, so far as elementary classics and English were concerned, enabled all the boys to do well in the Public Schools entrance exams. But the Principal, who was also the owner of the place, had no right to be a schoolmaster. By the boys, for some reason never known to me, he was always called 'the Jowler'—which had no resemblance to his real surname, but may as well be used here. The Jowler was what is euphemistically known as 'temperamental'. On perhaps two days in a week he would be amiability itself; every bit of good work, or well-played innings in a match, was enthusiastically praised and lavishly rewarded. Even a string of blunders in a construe or an exercise occasioned nothing worse than some rather elephantine chaff. But on the other five days he varied only from a cold and bitter moroseness to frequent fits of almost frenzied rage. No-one could do anything right, the most dutiful reply to a question might be 'gross impertinence', and gross impertinence meant a painful ceremony in the study. Other punishments, often for quite imaginary offences, descended upon everyone, and I fancy that on these days his wife and his staff suffered almost as much as the boys. The one set of people from whom he contrived to conceal this behaviour were the parents; to them he always seemed a model of geniality and kindness; sometimes he was even capable of so mean a trick as to open boys' Sunday letters before they went to post; if anyone had dared to describe the Jowler's proceedings truthfully, horrible retribution followed.

ANTHONY C. DEANE, *Time Remembered*, 1945

'Ever since I have devoted myself to the cause of tuition,' continued the Doctor, 'I have made it my object to provide boys under my roof with fare so abundant and so palatable that they should have no excuse for obtaining extraneous luxuries. I have presided myself at their meals, I have superintended their very sports with a fatherly eye—'

Here he paused, and fixed one or two of those nearest him with the fatherly eye in such a manner that they writhed with confusion.

'He's wandering from the point,' thought Paul, a little puzzled.

'I have done all this on one understanding—that the robustness of your constitutions, acquired by the plain, simple, but abundant regimen of my table, shall not be tampered with by the indulgence in any of the pampering products of confectionery. They are absolutely and unconditionally prohibited—as every boy who hears me now knows perfectly well!'

'And yet' (here he began gradually to relax his self-restraint and lash himself into a frenzy of indignation), 'what do I find? There are some natures so essentially base, so incapable of being affected by kindness, so dead to honour and generosity, that they will not scruple to conspire or set themselves individually to escape and baffle the wise precautions undertaken for their benefit. I will not name the dastards at present—they themselves can look into their hearts and see their guilt reflected there—'

At this every boy, beginning to see the tendency of his denunciations, tried hard to assume an air of conscious innocence and grieved interest, the majority achieving conspicuous failure.

'I do not like to think,' said Dr Grimstone, 'that the evil has a wider existence than I yet know of. It may be so; nothing will surprise me now. There may be some before me trembling with the consciousness of secret guilt. If so, let those boys make the only reparation in their power, and give themselves up in an honourable and straightforward manner!'

To this invitation, which indeed resembled that of the duck-destroying Mrs Bond, no one made any response. They had grown too wary, and now preferred to play a waiting game.

'Then let the being—for I will not call him boy—who is known to me, step forth and confess his fault publicly, and sue for pardon!' thundered the Doctor, now warmed to his theme.

But the being declined from a feeling of modesty, and a faint hope that somebody else might, after all, be the person aimed at.

'Then I name him!' stormed Dr Grimstone; 'Cornelius Coggs—stand up!'

Coggs half rose in a limp manner, whimpering feebly, 'Me, sir? Oh, please sir—no, not me, sir!'

'Yes, you, sir, and let your companions regard you with the contempt and abhorrence you so richly merit!' Here, needless to say, the whole school glared at poor Coggs with as much virtuous indignation as they could summon up at such short notice; for contempt is very infectious when communicated from high quarters.

'So, Coggs,' said the Doctor, with a slow and withering scorn, 'so you thought to defy me; to smuggle compressed illness and concentrated unhealthiness into this school with impunity? You flattered yourself that after I had once confiscated your contraband poisons, you would hear no more of it! You deceived yourself, sir! I tell you, once for all, that I will not allow you to contaminate your innocent schoolmates with your gifts of surreptitious sweetmeats; they shall not be perverted with your pernicious peppermints, sir; you shall not deprave them by jujubes, or enervate them with Turkish Delight! I will not expose myself or them to the inroads of disease invited here by a hypocritical inmate of my walls. The traitor shall have his reward!'

All of which simply meant that the Doctor, having once had a small boy taken seriously ill from the effects of overeating himself, was naturally anxious to avoid such an inconvenience for the future.

F. ANSTEY, *Vice Versa*, 1882

Suddenly his grip on David's shoulder tightened, and his eye fixed itself on the back of a small boy who was sitting on the wire railing at the edge of the field, unconscious of their approach.

'Ferrers Minor, I think,' he called out in an awful voice.

The Head thought right, and Ferrers Minor presented his startled and dejected countenance.

'Did you, or did you not, know the rule about sitting on the railings?' demanded the Head.

'Yes, sir,' said Ferrers Minor.

'Then this is wilful disobedience,' thundered the Head. 'I will not be bullied by you, Ferrers Minor, nor have you disregard the rules with which you are perfectly well acquainted. I suppose you wish to make a fool of me, to hold me up to ridicule for having the impertinence to frame rules which Mr Ferrers Minor keeps or not, as he finds convenient. Was that your plan?'

'N-no, sir,' said Ferrers Minor.

'Then I will make a plan for you instead, and it is that you write out in your best copy-hand "I will not sit on the railings like an ass" a hundred times. You may go, Ferrers Minor.'

But Rhadamanthus, the inexorable terror, had only mounted his judgment throne for a moment, and came down off it again. His grip relaxed, and he patted David's shoulder.

'And now for our literature lesson,' he said. 'It's too hot to hold it in the museum, isn't it, Blaize, when we can sit under the trees instead. Let's have it out here: go in, will you, and tell the class to come out. And, personally, I shall take my coat off, and anybody else who likes to do the same of course may.'

E. F. BENSON, *David Blaize*, 1916

The Roman Catholic Convent on the other side of the street was a lively source of interest. Seeing the children straggling along to school there, they looked the same as any others. But we knew they weren't. Like natives in the clutches of a witch-doctor, we knew they were being taught to believe all the wrong things. Smug in one's 'proper' religion, one saw them as heretic lambs being led to the slaughter. Masses, rosaries, and confessions, rules which, if broken, would send them slap to hell, wafted vaguely over them. Even the little creatures being dragged along by an elder sister were going to have everything messed up for them. Sometimes a nun came out and shepherded them in. In their blue habits and enormous white head-dresses so closely resembling the arrangement of Sunday's clean table napkins, they did not look like religious jailers. But they were and they wouldn't get us! Sometimes we caught sight of the priest near the church which was farther down the street. In black, right up to his neck, he looked like a crow. How crammed he must be, we thought, with other people's sins. But under the seal of the confessional he had to carry them, tightly shut up inside him, like the contents of a registered parcel.

By this time the pavement was thickening with the pupils of the Bishop's School. We eyed the girls in their boaters with blue bands as they eyed us in our boaters with scarlet bands with the permanent hostility and curiosity of different schools.

GERALDINE SYMONS, *Children in the Close*, 1959

As Miss Holmes went from class to class, she carried the cane and laid it upon the desk before her; not necessarily for use, but as a reminder, for some of the bigger boys were very unruly. She punished by a smart stroke on each hand. 'Put out your hand,' she would say, and some boys would openly spit on each hand before proffering it. Others murmured and muttered before and after a caning and threatened to 'tell me feyther'; but she remained calm and cool, and after the punishment had been inflicted there was a marked improvement—for a time.

It must be remembered that in those days a boy of eleven was nearing the end of his school life. Soon he would be at work; already he felt himself nearly a man and too old for petticoat government. Moreover, those were country boys, wild and rough, and many of them as tall as she was. Those who had failed to pass Standard IV and so could not leave school until they were eleven, looked upon that last year as a punishment inflicted upon them by the school authorities and behaved accordingly. In this they were encouraged by their parents, for a certain section of these resented their boys being kept at school when they might be earning. 'What do our young Alf want wi' a lot o' book-larnin'?' they would say. 'He can read and write and add up as much money as he's ever likely to get. What more do he want?' Then a neighbour of more advanced views would tell them: 'A good education's everything in these days. You can't get on in the world if you ain't had one,' for they read their newspapers and new ideas were percolating, though slowly. It was only the second generation to be forcibly fed with the fruit of the tree of knowledge: what wonder if it did not always agree with it.

Meanwhile, Miss Holmes carried her cane about with her. A poor method of enforcing discipline, according to modern educational ideas: but it served. It may be that she and her like all over the country at that time were breaking up the ground that other, later comers to the field, with a knowledge of child psychology and with tradition and experiment behind them, might sow the good seed.

She seldom used the cane on the girls and still more seldom on the infants. Standing in a corner with their hands on their heads was their punishment.

Flora Thompson, Lark Rise to Candleford, 1939

My teachers then, old registers attest
were certain maiden ladies. I recall
Miss Mary Murdoch, ancient, tubby, small,
that bad left leg in need of frequent rest,
and Maggie Thompson, lean, with greying hair,
by Uncle Willie courted for a time;
he married someone else, a heinous crime
the guilt for which I felt she made me share.

And Annie Earls, with large and flashing teeth,
long-legged and tall, spray-spitting when distraught,
her glasses glinting, scolding, often kind.
Yet should I rake forever down beneath
the wilted debris of those days I'd find
I could not isolate one word they taught.

John Hewitt, 'My Teachers', in Kites in Spring, 1980

I was given cards of sums to work out, or the names of rivers and capes to learn by heart, and these dull tasks prevented me from crossing the Atlantic in a wind-jammer, or rounding up buffalo with the Sioux Indians, or serving with Midshipman Easy against the French.

Mr Meek's suspicions of my integrity communicated themselves to the Headmaster and the pupil-teachers who from time to time assisted in the class-rooms. One of these young men, trying to waken me to a sense of duty, took me by the ear and pulled so hard that the lobe broke away. Blood streamed, consternation followed, and for a whole morning I was a school hero.

Mother interviewed the Headmaster next day; but she did not improve matters, for he was an august figure enthroned above all minor strife. His name was John Burgess, and he was ten feet high. He carried his head flung back, with a grim mouth and chin set against the world. He wore large brown shoes, highly polished and hooded by spats, summer and winter. He flung out these feet at an aggressive angle as he advanced (rather than walked). He was terrifying.

His throne was set at the end of the big hall, surrounded by windows, so that he sat in a blaze of light that hovered round his severely brushed hair. His pince-nez flashed fire. In front of his desk, as a kind of altar, stood a long chest, open during school hours to reveal a set of canes of varying thickness and colour, from light switches to heavy cudgels; some straw-blonde, others dour as mahogany as though impregnated with congealed blood. Lying on the array of canes was the Punishment Book, the register of shame. A record of every chastisement was entered therein, after the event, with a broad pen, and in deliberate calligraphy that possessed an Hebraic quality, as though the angry god of the Old Testament himself had made the entry.

Boys sent by their class-masters for punishment by Mr Burgess had to stand in the hall, toeing a white line in front of The Desk. To wait there, facing the grim figure, or even the empty throne, the open chest of canes within sight, was ample torture, especially if the ordeal were prolonged from a quarter to half an hour.

RICHARD CHURCH, Over the Bridge, 1955

For the rest of the day, major and minor bells announced classes, meals, recreations, and prayers. Each hour of study began with an invocation to the Holy Ghost and ended with a recommendation to Our Lady. Three times a day we recited the Angelus and, at half-past six, the whole school assembled for the rosary or for prayers to the patron saints of hygiene, St Philomena and St Roch. After supper came a brief indoor recreation, then night prayers in the chapel and bed. We undressed with another ritual of bells and our last spoken words, like our first, were 'Wash away my sins'.

At first I used to curl up in bed for warmth as I did at home but I was cured of this evil habit by an old French nun.

'Suppose, my child,' she said gently, 'that you died in the night. Would that be a becoming posture in which to meet Our dear Lord?'

And she taught me to lie on my back 'like a Christian' with my feet thrust well down into the cold sheets and my hands crossed on my chest. She taught me, too, to imitate St Theresa by letting my last thoughts dwell on the Agony in the Garden, and to murmur the name of Jesus just before I fell asleep.

ANTONIA WHITE (at Lippington), in Graham Greene (ed.),
The Old School, 1934

In his farewell talk about sex to school-leavers Mr Bull would warn boys not to waste 'it', leaving one with the anxiety that if one did, 'it' might suddenly run out, a terrible prospect. He was rather vague in his description of sexual feeling, making it seem that it came upon one without warning, so that if there was no girl present the chance was lost. It was not clear how often the urge came or what happened if it did not come to the girl at the same time. What Mr Bull did emphasize, though, was that making love was the most wonderful feeling in the world, so that one was left hoping that occasionally the person, the place and the desire would coincide.

ALAN ROSS, *Blindfold Games*, 1986

There was one more formality before we new boys were absorbed into the School at large. The Headmaster, Dr Warre, addressed us. It was in Upper School. The occasion was, for us, tremendous. There he stood, waiting, this great square man, with a broad silk band round his middle, gazing at a high window, and chewing the inside of his cheek, as was his habit. He looked all justice and authority. 'Come up here, boys, don't be afraid.' An enormous voice rumbled from the depths of him. And then he spoke to us, paternally, dropping his final G's, moving his strong lips as one does to a lip-reader, now in a vibrant bass, now in a sudden tenor. He spoke of our responsibility as Etonians; he was encouraging and kind. Then, out of the blue, came an astonishing admonition. He told us to beware of 'filth', to avoid even talking 'filth'. I was completely baffled. I knew a great deal about filth, after that summer among the footpaths and bushes of Valais. But here, at Eton? Could he be telling us to look where we trod, because of the occasional dog-mess on the pavements?

L. E. JONES, *A Victorian Boyhood*, 1955

For prayers on the opening day an unbelievable apparition, dressed in an old check suit, tripped into Big Hall with Mr Bye and Mr Hake—a fat little gentleman with red hair and red pointed beard and more bug-whiskers about his countenance than Bug-Whiskers himself—and pirouetted on a pair of tiny buttoned boots to Mr Rouvier-Toddy's chair. At first glance he was a joke, a joy, a caricature, a subject for baiting such as none of us had ever seen or imagined. All the time he wore an idiotic smile, his lips pursed together and his eyes heavenward, in an expression half pi and half whimsical, rich in promise of great days. This was Mr Jarvis Rickle. He bore out his promise royally.

He made our third Beaver, or Frenchie-beard as we called it; joining the barbed company of Virgil Vivian with his ghoulish little black Imperial, and Paul with his fine orange-coloured spade.

(Augusta's hairy white face-covering was not a true beard.)

Form IVA had more of this new man than any other form had, and more of him than of any other master. The first class with him, straight after prayers that first morning, was of good omen. His voice and speech were more than worthy of his appearance.

'Good morning, my friends,' he began, in a sweet coy little voice and a sweet clipped little accent, rubbing his palms together and smiling in sheer ecstasy. 'Glad indeed am I to make your acquaintance. Fruitful may our joint labours be. Perchance you will favour me with your names; I would always fain know the names of my friends. Wist ye not?'

' 'E's not reight in 'is 'ead,' muttered Albert Edward.

G. P. DENNIS, *Bloody Mary's*, 1934

The headmaster of a national school
chalks *Ginkel* on the blackboard
as a flag snicks a big *NO*
over the mudflats and barracks;
the city is like a locked yard
that's caked with grey pigeon-cack;
the Chief stalks, stalks, like the Kaiser
and crowds bristle at the docks.
Krekk! kkrek! the stubborn particles
trek through my carbon-dater,
each chipping past like a spiked curse
stamped with these numbers: 1–9–1–2.

I'd be dead chuffed if I could catch
the dialects of those sea-loughs,
but I'm scared of all that's hard
and completely subjective:
those quartzy voices in the playground
of a school called Rosetta Primary

whose basalt and sandstone have gone
like Napoleon into Egypt.

TOM PAULIN, 'Politik', in *Liberty Tree*, 1983

The room was almost full. The prefects, instead of lolling disdain-fully in the back row, were ranged like councillors beneath the central throne. This was an innovation of Mr Pembroke's. Carruthers, the head boy, sat in the middle, with his arm round Lloyd. It was Lloyd who had made the matron too bright: he nearly lost his colours in consequence. These two were very grown up. Beside them sat Tewson, a saintly child in spectacles, who had risen to this height by reason of his immense learning. He, like the others, was a school prefect. The house prefects, an inferior brand, were beyond, and behind came the indistinguishable many. The faces all looked alike as yet—except the face of one boy, who was inclined to cry.

'School,' said Mr Pembroke, slowly closing the lid of the desk—'school is the world in miniature.' Then he paused, as a man well may who has made such a remark. It is not, however, the intention of this work to quote an opening address. Rickie, at all events, refused to be critical: Herbert's experience was far greater than his, and he must take his tone from him. Nor could any one criticize the exhortations to be patriotic, athletic, learned, and religious, that flowed like a four-part fugue from Mr Pembroke's mouth. He was a practised speaker—that is to say, he held his audience's attention. He told them that this term, the second of his reign, was *the* term for Dunwood House; that it behoved every boy to labour during it for his house's honour, and, through the house, for the honour of the school. Taking a wider range, he spoke of England, or rather of Great Britain, and of her continental foes. Portraits of empire builders hung on the wall, and he pointed to them. He quoted imperial poets. He showed how patriotism has broadened since the days of Shakespeare, who, for all his genius, could only write of his country as—

This fortress built by Nature for herself
Against infection and the hand of war;
This happy breed of men, this little world;
This precious stone set in the silver sea.

And it seemed that only a short ladder lay between the preparation-room and the Anglo-Saxon hegemony of the globe. Then he paused, and in the silence came 'sob, sob, sob', from a little boy, who was regretting a villa in Guildford and his mother's half acre of garden.

The proceeding terminated with the broader patriotism of the school anthem, recently composed by the organist. Words and tune were still a matter for taste, and it was Mr Pembroke (and he only because he had the music) who gave the right intonation to

'Perish each laggard! Let it not be said
That Sawston such within her walls hath bred.'

'Come, come,' he said pleasantly, as they ended with harmonies in the style of Richard Strauss. 'This will never do. We must grapple with the anthem this term. You're as tuneful as—as day-boys!' Hearty laughter, and then the whole house filed past them and shook hands.

'But how did it impress you?' Herbert asked, as soon as they were back in their own part. Agnes had provided them with a tray of food: the meals were still anyhow, and she had to fly at once to see after the boys.

'I liked the look of them.'

'I meant rather, how did the house impress you as a house?'

'I don't think I thought,' said Rickie rather nervously. 'It is not easy to catch the spirit of a thing at once. I only saw a room full of boys.'

'My dear Rickie, don't be so diffident. You are perfectly right. You only did see a roomful of boys. As yet there's nothing else to see. The house, like the school, lacks tradition. Look at Winchester. Look at the traditional rivalry between Eton and Harrow. Tradition is of incalculable importance, if a school is to have any status. Why should Sawston be without?'

'Yes. Tradition is of incalculable value. And I envy those schools that have a natural connexion with the past. Of course Sawston has a past, though not of the kind that you quite want. The sons of poor tradesmen went to it at first. So wouldn't its traditions be more likely to linger in the Commercial School?' he concluded nervously.

'You have a great deal to learn—a very great deal. Listen to me. Why has Sawston no traditions?' His round, rather foolish, face assumed the expression of a conspirator. Bending over the mutton, he whispered, 'I can tell you why. Owing to the day-boys. How can traditions flourish in such soil? Picture the day-boy's life—at home for meals, at home for preparation, at home for sleep, running home with every fancied wrong. There are day-boys in your class, and, mark my words, they will give you ten times as much trouble as the boarders—late, slovenly, stopping away at the slightest pretext. And then the letters from the parents! "Why has my boy not been moved this term?" "Why has my boy been moved this term?" "I am a dissenter, and do not wish my boy to subscribe to the school mission." "Can you let my boy off early to water the garden?" Remember that I have been a day-boy house-master, and tried to infuse some *esprit de corps* into them. It is practically impossible. They come as units, and units they remain. Worse. They infect the boarders. Their pestilential, critical, discontented attitude is spreading over the school. If I had my own way—'

He stopped somewhat abruptly.

'Was that why you laughed at their singing?'

'Not at all. Not at all. It is not my habit to set one section of the school against the other.'

E. M. FORSTER, *The Longest Journey*, 1907

The day began with the school assembled by forms round the walls of the gymnasium; 'toeing the line' under the orders of the prefects, who had a pretty free hand in cuffing us; a boy was posted to watch for the approach of the masters. At the call of '*Cave*' silence fell. Mr

Grenfell bounded up the three brass-bound steps and said 'Good morning, gentlemen.' We in chorus cried: 'Good morning, sir.' We then recited the Lord's Prayer (in 1914 the prayer for those in danger on the seas was added to our devotions); any necessary announcements were made and we were dispersed to our classes; except on Saturday mornings, when an alarming ceremony occurred.

Mr Grenfell then appeared with a ledger in which were recorded the results of the masters' meeting on the preceding afternoon. First he read the names of those commended. 'Geoghegan minor, plus three for Latin. Where is Geoghegan minor? Let me see him. Fine boy, Geoghegan minor . . . Mackenzie, plus five for Mathematics *and* French. Keep it up, Mackenzie. I am very pleased with you.'

Then with a dramatic change of tone: 'We will now turn to the other side. What is this I find? *Fletcher.* Fletcher has been idle. Stand out, Fletcher.' Mr Grenfell glared and bristled. Fletcher cringed. 'What does this mean? Idle? We had better understand one another, young man. You do not come here to be idle. And I am going to see that you work. Any idling, Fletcher, and'—with great vehemence and a blow of his fist on the table—'I'll be down on you like a ton of bricks.' Then he would turn to the assistant masters grouped behind him. 'Keep your eyes on Fletcher, gentlemen. Any more trouble, send him to me, and he knows just what he'll get.'

Evelyn Waugh, A Little Learning, 1964

These were the years of the 1914–18 war. Most of the staff had been called up and were away, fighting and dying in Flanders mud. Their replacements were a curious collection of oddities—among others, an Indian with an imperfect command of English who instructed us in chemistry, a lady with a shrill, genteel voice for whom we wrote compositions, an elderly mathematics master with rather obviously dyed hair and a frenzied moustache who desperately flung chalk at us when, as frequently happened, we failed to get his point. I can remember them all, in their tattered gowns—this one genial, that one erudite, and this other seemingly malignant as he sat, dark and glowering, while one stumbled over French irregular verbs.

I rode to and from school on my bicycle. The very air was full of the hysteria of war. There were old boys who appeared resplendent in their uniforms. We ourselves had a school cadet corps which we were compelled to join. The headmaster was in charge of it, with the rank of a major, and shambled along at the head of us when we had occasion to march through the streets, his uniform, as even my ignorant eye could detect, in strange disarray.

When, later, at Cambridge and elsewhere, I got to know the products of public schools, the thing that struck me about them was their passionate entanglement in their schooldays. At first I rather envied them this, and wished that I, too, had memories of famous cricket matches, a private, exclusive slang, and all the other outward and visible manifestations of belonging to an inward and invisible *élite*, self-contained and economically and socially advantageous. On further consideration, however, I changed my attitude. It seemed to me that the great advantage of the sort of education I had was precisely that it made practically no mark upon those subjected to it. Scholastic and other deficiencies were more than compensated for by the fact that one's first vivid impressions of life were provided, not by a closed and essentially homosexual community of schoolboys under the direction of masters who had themselves been through the same process, but by men and women actually living and earning their livings. How much I preferred the ribald, noisy, dangerous world to any walled garden, however elegantly arranged and full of summer fragrance! No one ever seems to forget Eton. I easily forgot my Borough Secondary School.

MALCOLM MUGGERIDGE, in Brian Inglis (ed.),
John Bull's Schooldays, 1961

I was never a ringleader, even in such minor escapades as blocking up the form-room keyhole with paper, or writing out French 'rep' on

the master's own blackboard. I deplore this timidity, but I am glad
I did not try to overcome it, for the role of revolutionary would
not have suited me and I profited more by sitting receptive at the feet
of my pastors and masters than I should have done by buzzing,
mosquito-like, about their ears. If they despised me for this attitude
they were, on the whole, magnanimous enough not to show it. Thus,
though I never won the plaudits of my fellows for (say) powder-
ing my form-master's neck with a substance called Russian Flea, I
escaped the counter-attacks for which some of the staff were justly
famous. My first form-master did not seize me by the short hair
above the ears, or make me sit on a form alone, with the flex of
the reading-lamp twisted lightly round my neck, a painless but
humiliating position, nor did he ever say to me, 'Whatever you look
like, boy, don't look like Mrs. . . .' (naming the wife of one of his
colleagues). In V^1 I kept careful watch over my vocabulary, and
managed to avoid the phrase 'stir up' (almost inevitable in construing many Latin authors) and the thunderous exclamation 'Porridge!'
with which E. G. always greeted it. Nor had he occasion to address
to me the famous harangue beginning, 'Boy, you have said what
you know to be wrong, next you'll do what you know to be wrong,
then . . .' and so on through a series of ever blacker crimes, culminating in the murder of one's grandmother and death by hanging. The
form-master of the Lower Sixth was a man with an extremely fine
mind, an impressive presence, a wonderful command of English,
and a tongue that was justly dreaded. He was formidable even in his
lighter moments. As he passed one's desk he would say: 'If you put
your hat there I shall tread on it, and I weigh fourteen stone.' When
one made a blunder he forbore for a moment from comment;
perhaps he was thinking it out, for it was generally devastating when
it came. But in more genial moods he would remark, 'If you ever say
that again I shall fall on you with my teeth and my umbrella'; or,
with a slightly hissing intake of breath, 'May I appeal to Heaven to
strike me pink.'

L. P. HARTLEY (at Harrow), in Graham Greene (ed.),
The Old School, 1934

I arrived at Eton in the afternoon of January 22, 1922. My father, bowler-hatted, and my mother, carefully dressed down for the occasion, were with me, and we brought between us a hip bath of brown tin, a folding chair upholstered in red rep, and a few suitable pictures—by Cecil Aldin it might be, bright with tally-ho heartiness.

It was not a happy day. My room in Cotton Hall House looked down on the lavatories, which echoed with regular regurgitations, and smelled commandingly of Jeyes Fluid. There was a folding bed in one corner, a deal 'burry' for clothes and books, a wall cupboard for tea-cup and plate, a red-covered ottoman for gym-shoes and flannel shorts, and by the grate a coal-scuttle, only filled three times a week for a fire to be lit in the evening. Four days of that week I could, in winter, write my name in the damp on the meanly-flowered wallpaper.

We had called on m'tutor, Mr Whitworth, a florid schoolmaster with a slightly dotty wife, and on m'dame, Miss Dix. I was the only new boy in the house, and so I was briefly an object of curiosity. I had never before been sent to a boarding-school, partly because my parents simply forgot, and partly because I was thought to be so precociously clever and so highly-strung that I was daily in danger of a brainstorm. That this was utter rubbish did not prevent my undergoing a lamentable apprenticeship to life, held back from any possible proficiency in learning, schoolboy athletics—in those days the main commitment of school existence—or plain awareness of the world, except from the hothouse comfort of an overheated nursery, or, worse, an overheated drawing-room.

So there we sat, in a miasma of Jeyes Fluid, while partly I dreaded the moment of being left alone, and partly I longed for it, so as to celebrate my escape into the society of other boys.

From this distance of over sixty years I look back on the three of us as though on a faded daguerreotype. My father is very much the colonel, with mouse-coloured hair and moustache, gold watch-chain—he considered wrist-watches, like suede shoes and, Heaven knows, pocket-combs, marks of the beast (an effeminate beast); my mother ran to strapped shoes, mink capes, a regimental brooch in diamonds—the Coldstream, of course—and sufficient but not obtrusive pearls; I, to judge by surviving photographs, have a deceptively angelic appearance, inevitably muffish and on this very day no doubt glandular with emotion. We sit by the empty grate with nothing much to say, while from the passage outside my room sounds the scuffle of small boys arriving after the Christmas holidays, the scrape of suitcases on linoleum, and a banging door or two. I remember hoping not to cry.

ALAN PRYCE-JONES, *The Bonus of Laughter*, 1987

Assistant masters came and went. By no means all of them had university degrees. Some liked little boys too little and some too much. According to their tastes they mildly mauled us in the English scholastic way, fondling us in a manner just short of indecency, smacking us and pulling our hair in a manner well short of cruelty. Some could in their turn be tormented. Some were surly and, it seemed, old; some young and facetious; most of them boasted. Then and for many years later prep-school masters were drawn from a heterogeneous and undefinable underworld into which—little did I know it—I was myself destined to descend.

EVELYN WAUGH, *A Little Learning*, 1964

He sighed with relief. He had got the job. He was safe.
Putting on his gown, he prepared for the long years to come
That he saw, stretching like aisles of stone
Before him. He prepared for the unreal life
Of exercises, marks, honour, speech days and games,
And the interesting and pretty animals that inspired it all,
And made him a god. No, he would never fail.

Others, of course, had often spoken of the claims
Of living: they were merely desperate.
His defence of Youth and Service silenced it.

It was acted as he planned: grown old and favourite,
With most Old Boys he was quite intimate—
For though he never realised it, he
Dissolved. (Like sugar in a cup of tea.)

PHILIP LARKIN, 'Schoolmaster', in *Collected Poems*, 1988

Watson's was divided into three sections, the elementary school, the junior school, and the senior school. I entered the junior school at the age of nine, after leaving Class 'H'. Here we still had one teacher for all subjects, and for the first two years they were still women teachers. But in the Autumn of 1923, when I entered the third year of the junior school, I came under the redoubtable 'Dub-Dub', Mr W. W. Anderson, a man with a reputation throughout the school as a stern disciplinarian and a teacher of old-fashioned strictness and thoroughness. He was within a few years of retirement when I came to know him as a teacher, a dour old Scot with a grey and ginger moustache and very little hair. His methods were old-fashioned, but remarkably effective. He battered the boys with a brand of irony all his own, and after bellowing at one of them for some error or piece of forgetfulness he would lean back against the mantel and say sardonically: 'You think I'm hard on you, don't you? You think I'm a Turk? You think I'm a Tartar? You're going to complain to your parents about me?' He would then pause and remove his gold-rimmed pince-nez glasses. 'Go home and tell your mother I'm a Tartar. Tell her I'm a Turk.' And he would give a curious little sibilant titter which sounded like 'sih, sih, sih'.

Dub-Dub never used the tawse, but he had his own way of keeping discipline. He was more feared, I think, than any other master in the school, and it was rumoured among the boys that he was not allowed to use the strap because once, away back in the 1880's or '90's, he had broken a boy's wrist with it. But I doubt if this was true. His moods of sternness made one tremble, and his levity had something of the quality of a jocund rattlesnake. He could get the most extraordinary effects out of the simplest sentences. If he threatened (as he occasionally did) to throw a boy out of the class-room, he would say, in a peculiarly intense intonation, 'I'll change your name to Walker.' That threat, with its monstrous pun (it meant 'I'll make you walk out of the room') always hushed a class to immediate stillness. 'Change it to Walker,' he'd repeat, meditatively. Then, suddenly: 'Give your dear mother my compliments and tell her I'm a Turk.'

DAVID DAICHES (b. 1913), *Two Worlds*, 1957; an Edinburgh
Jewish Childhood

In 1934 I appeared at the City of London School, a large, rather oppressively dignified building on the Victoria Embankment. It had lots of identical passages and a vast agoraphobic playground filled with self-possessed boys in black coats and striped trousers. At this time I was an undersized, law-abiding, timid person. Fear made me vomit on the first few mornings, but I quickly found that this was excessive. Nobody ever used me unkindly, except perhaps King (Science III), who at tuck-shop time every morning would greet me with 'Hallo, Curly' and ruffle my hair, which I currently wore in two brilliantined flaps. His bearing, the tone of his voice and the redness of his own hair made me afraid to punch him. I was soon reconciled, however, and began to be fascinated by the social possibilities of this immense new environment. My fellows, I saw dimly, were drawn from a wide variety of social strata: accents varied from those that discomforted me to those that made me feel superior. But example at once taught me to put such attitudes aside. To be accepted you had only to be amiable; to be liked you needed pre-eminently to be able to raise a laugh occasionally—but here the most vapid clowning served as well as wit.

Efficient mimics of the staff were especially highly regarded. I developed an imitation of the headmaster: 'Get it right, not wrong. Black, not white. Cat, not dog.' This measure had the double advantage of securing esteem and providing a counterpoise to the terrified veneration I felt for my original. As at every school one ever hears about, the masters were imitable eccentrics almost to a man. This can only partly be put down to the stylizing effects teaching has on demeanour. What is also at work in this situation is the nature of the observer. To the pre-pubertial eye all grown-up behaviour is so fantastic as to defeat discrimination; the youth in his last year or two at school is already taking out naturalization papers for the adult world. It is the boy in his early teens who sees that world with the delighted, faintly hostile astonishment of the tourist, who is entertained to the limits of endurance by its quaint tribal customs, its grotesque ritual dances, its capering, scowling, gesticulating witch-doctors. And if he later becomes a novelist he must strive to recapture, not indeed the undifferentiating vision of childhood, but the adolescent's coldly wondering stare.

However that may be, I shall never forget Mr Marsh sucking the earpiece of his glasses, or Mr Penn accusing us all of having eaten his biscuits, or Mr Carruthers's imperturbability when Rumsey and I dropped the suitcase full of broken glass—a long-treasured riot-mechanism—at the back of the room. I remember these things not as facts, but as little mental films with a complete set of sound effects. The most noteworthy figure of all, I realize now, was Mr Copping, who played (one at a time) the flute and the double-bass, who spoke with an Attic Greek accent of the fifth century, who once captivated us all by replying with incomparable, table-turning deftness to a disingenuous question from Rigden about castration: 'I don't know whether any of you have ever been to a horse-fair', the answer led off—I can hear those Periclean tones now. As I do so I marvel at the way the 1938 version of Mr Copping still seems older than the 1958 version of me, a trick of time which will no doubt remain as effective in 1978.

KINGSLEY AMIS, *What Became of Jane Austen?*, 1970

Twenty years ago, Seaford's prep schools began to disappear, like mighty dinosaurs creeping off to die: parents in Esher and Tunbridge Wells tended instead to send their children to local schools as weekly boarders or day boys or girls; headmasters and governing bodies were made gratifyingly aware of the property value of the many acres of land they were sitting on; blackboards and canes and rolls of honour were committed to the flames, and the games fields that had been so distinctive a feature of the town were covered with desirable residences suitable for retired tobacconists. Particularly melancholy was the disappearance of the buildings themselves: Edwardian prep schools, like golf clubs, embody English institutional architecture at its best, and Seaford in its heyday was chock-a-block with white mullioned windows, overhung balconies with curious box-like fire escapes attached, dormer windows with mattresses propped out to dry, belfries, weather-vaned clock towers and well-raked gravel drives. Our particular school was a low-slung, rambling building: like many south coast houses of the 'cocktail shaker' vintage it had a green roof, and was covered with white painted pebbledash. Like all the Seaford schools, it stood amidst cosy suburban streets; it was, however, insulated by tree-lined playing fields; and in the small garden in front stood the school flagpole and a small slatted white box on legs that housed the all-important Meteorological Instruments.

JEREMY LEWIS, *Playing for Time*, 1987

Back again. Day one. Fingers blue with cold. I joined the lengthening
   queue.
Roll-call. Then inside: chalk-dust and iced milk, the smell of watered
   ink.
Roods, perches, acres, ounces, pounds, tons weighed imponderably in
   the darkening
Air. We had chanted the twelve-times table for the twelfth or thir-
   teenth time
When it began to snow. Chalky numerals shimmered down; we
   crowded to the window—

*These are the countless souls of purgatory, whose numbers constantly
   diminish*

And increase; each flake as it brushes to the ground is yet another soul
   released.
And I am the avenging Archangel, stooping over mills and factories
   and barracks.
I will bury the dark city of Belfast forever under snow: inches, feet,
   yards, chains, miles.

   CIARAN CARSON, 'Slate Street School', in *The Irish For No,* 1987

That was the last of Cockburn. When I think of the place I see first
the classrooms of the sixth form, with a teacher glad to have a small
group of clever children and doing his or her best to introduce them
to a wider world. I think second of walking home at about 4.15 or so
in the middle of winter, when the street-lights have already begun to
come on. I would look round as I finished crossing the clinkered
'Moor' and still see over the house-tops half a mile away the pale
yellow glow of its classrooms and corridors and its cupolas standing
up half silvery-grey in the near-darkness. It exercised as powerful a
pull on my imagination as Oxford's dreaming spires on Matthew
Arnold's or Christminster on Jude the Obscure's.

   RICHARD HOGGART, *A Local Habitation,* 1988

A DREADFUL SCHISM IN THE
BRITISH NATION

High wind . . . They turn their backs to it, and push.
Their crazy strides are chopped in little steps.
And all their lives, like that, they'll have to rush
Forwards in reverse, always holding their caps.

DOUGLAS DUNN, 'Glasgow Schoolboys, Running Backwards',
in *Selected Poems*, 1986

Believe me—and I have spent a great part of ten years in watching
some three hundred and twenty elementary schools,—we may prate
of democracy, but actually, a poor child in England has little more
hope than had the son of an Athenian slave to be emancipated into
that intellectual freedom of which great writings are born.

SIR ARTHUR QUILLER-COUCH, *The Art of Writing*, lectures 1913–14;
published 1916

As to my schooling, I think never a year pass'd me till I was 11, or 12,
but 3 months or more at the worst of times was luckily spared for my
improvement, first with an old woman in the village, and latterly
with a master at a distance from it. Here soon as I began to learn to
write, the readiness of the Boys always practising urged and
prompted my ambition to make the best use of my absence from
school, as well as at it, and my master was always surprised to find me
improved every fresh visit, instead of having lost what I had learned
before; for which, to my benefit, he never failed to give me tokens of

encouragement. Never a leisure hour pass'd me without making use of it; every winter night, our once unlettered hut was wonderfully changed in its appearance to a schoolroom. The old table, which, old as it was, doubtless never was honoured with higher employment all its days than the convenience of bearing at meal times the luxury of a barley loaf, or dish of potatoes, was now covered with the rude beggings of scientifical requisitions, pens, ink, and paper,—one hour, hobbling the pen at sheephooks and tarbottles, and another, trying on a slate a knotty question in Numeration, or Pounds, Shillings and Pence; at which times my parents' triumphant anxiety was pleasingly experienced; for my mother woud often stop her wheel, or look off from her work, to urge with a smile of the warmest rapture in my father's face her prophesy of my success, saying 'she'd be bound I shoud one day be able to reward them with my pen for the trouble they had taken in giving me schooling.'

JOHN CLARE (b. 1793), *Autobiography*, first published 1931

I am the second of four sons by the same father and mother; namely, Robert Hogg and Margaret Laidlaw. My progenitors were all shepherds of this country. My father, like myself, was bred to the occupation of a shepherd,—and served in that capacity until his marriage with my mother; about which time, having saved some substance, he took a lease of the farms of Ettrickhouse and Ettrickhall. He then commenced dealing in sheep—bought up great numbers, and drove them both to the English and Scottish markets; but, at length, owing to a great fall in the prices of sheep, and the absconding of his principal debtor, he was ruined, became bankrupt, every thing was sold by auction, and my parents were turned out of doors without a farthing in the world. I was then in the sixth year of my age, and remember well the distressed and destitute condition that we were in. At length the late worthy Mr Brydon of Crosslee took compassion upon us,—and, taking a short lease of the farm of Ettrickhouse, placed my father there as his shepherd, and thus afforded him the means of supporting us in life for a time. This gentleman continued to interest himself in our welfare until the day of his untimely death, when we lost the best friend that we had in the world. It was on this mournful occasion that I wrote the 'Dialogue in a Country Church-Yard.'

At such an age, it cannot be expected that I should have made great progress in literature. The school-house, however, being almost at our door, I had attended it for a short time,—and had the honour of standing at the head of a juvenile class, who read the Shorter Catechism and Proverbs of Solomon. At the next Whitsunday after our expulsion from the farm, I was obliged to go to service; and, being only seven years of age, was hired by a farmer in the neighbourhood to herd a few cows. Next year, my parents took me home during the winter quarter, and put me to school with a lad named Ker, who was teaching the children of a neighbouring farmer. Here I advanced so far as to get into the class who read in the Bible. I had likewise, for some time before my quarter was out, tried writing; and had horribly defiled several sheets of paper with copy-lines, every letter of which was nearly an inch in length.

Thus terminated my education. After this I was never another day at any school whatever. In all I had spent about half a year at it. It is true, my former master denied me; and when I was only twenty years of age, said, if he was called to make oath, he would swear I never was at his school. However, I know I was at it for two or three months; and I do not choose to be deprived of the honour of having attended the school of my native parish; nor yet that old John Beattie should lose the honour of such a scholar. I was again, that very spring, sent away to my old occupation of herding cows. This employment, the worst and lowest known in our country, I was engaged in for several years under sundry masters, till at length I got into the more honourable one of keeping sheep.

JAMES HOGG, *The Mountain Bard*, 1807

There will still be a number of families who, though not properly of the class of poor, yet find it difficult to give education to their children, and such children, under such a case, would be in a worse condition than if their parents were actually poor. A nation under a well regulated government should permit none to remain un-instructed. It is monarchical and aristocratical governments, only, that require ignorance for their support. . . . Public schools do not answer the general purpose of the poor. They are chiefly in corporation-towns, from which the country towns and villages are excluded; or, if admitted, the distance occasions a great loss of time. Education, to be useful to the poor, should be on the spot; and the best method, I believe, to accomplish this, is to enable the parents to pay the expense themselves. There are always persons of both sexes to be found in every village, especially when growing into years, capable of such an undertaking. Twenty children, at ten shillings each (and that not more than six months in each year), would be as much as some livings amount to in the remote parts of England; and there are often distressed clergymen's widows to whom such an income would be acceptable. Whatever is given on this account to children answers two purposes: to them it is education, to those who educate them it is a livelihood.

THOMAS PAINE, *The Rights of Man*, 1791

Despite all the platitudes repeated in most textbooks as to the 'educational initiatives' of the Churches at this time, the Sunday schools were a dreadful exchange even for village dame's schools. 18th-century provision for the education of the poor—inadequate and patchy as it was—was nevertheless provision *for education*, in some sort, even if . . . it was little more than naming the flowers and herbs. In the counter-revolutionary years this was poisoned by the dominant attitude of the Evangelicals, that the function of education began and ended with the 'moral rescue' of the children of the poor. Not only was the teaching of writing discouraged, but very many Sunday school scholars left the schools unable to read, and in view of the parts of the Old Testament thought most edifying this at least was a blessing. Others gained little more than the little girl who told one of the Commissioners on Child Labour in the Mines: 'if I died a good girl I should go to heaven—if I were bad I should have to be burned in brimstone and fire: they told me that at school yesterday, I did not know it before.'

E. P. THOMPSON, *The Making of the English Working Class*, 1967

And the Master shall take particular care of the Manners and Behaviour of the Poor Children.

And by all proper methods shall discourage and correct the beginnings of Vice, and particularly, Lying, Swearing, Cursing, taking God's name in vain, and the Prophanation of the Lord's Day etc. . . .

3. The Master shall teach them the true spelling of Words, and Distinction of Syllables, with the Points and Stops, which is necessary to true and good Reading, and serves to make the Children more mindful of what they Read.

4. As soon as the Boys can read competently well, the Master shall teach them to write a fair legible Hand, with the Grounds of Arithmetick, to fit them for Services or Apprentices.

NOTE. The Girls learn to read etc. and generally to knit their Stockings and Gloves, to Mark, Sew, make and mend their Cloaths, several learn to write, and some to spin their Cloaths.

[5, 6. To provide for Church going on Sundays and Saints' days and twice daily Prayers in School from the Prayer-Book.]

7. [Names-calling at beginning of School] . . . Great Faults as Swearing, Stealing etc. shall be noted down in monthly or weekly bills to be laid before the Subscribers or Trustees every time they meet, in order to their correction or expulsion.

8. [Holidays.]

9. [Provides that the School is to be free, no charge whatever being made.]

10. [The children are to be sent to school clean.]

11. The Children shall wear their Caps, Bands, Cloaths, and other marks of Distinction every Day, whereby their Trustees and Benefactors may know them, and see what their Behaviour is abroad.

> Charity Schools 1699–1718, a form of a subscription for
> a charity school, in Arthur F. Leach, *Educational Charters
> and Documents 598 to 1909*, 1911

The Christ's Hospital boy feels that he is no charity-boy; he feels it in the antiquity and regality of the foundation to which he belongs; in the usage which he meets with at school, and the treatment he is accustomed to out of its bounds; in the respect, and even kindness, which his well-known garb never fails to procure him in the streets of the metropolis; he feels it in his education, in that measure of classical attainments which every individual at that school, though not destined to a learned profession, has it in his power to procure— attainments which it would be worse than folly to put it in the reach of the labouring classes to acquire: he feels it in the numberless comforts, and even magnificences, which surround him; in his old and awful cloisters, with their traditions; in his spacious schoolrooms, and in the well-ordered, airy, and lofty rooms where he sleeps; in his stately dining-hall, hung round with pictures by Verrio, Lely, and others, one of them surpassing in size and grandeur almost any other in the kingdom; above all, in the very extent and magnitude of the body to which he belongs, and the consequent spirit, the intelligence, and public conscience which is the result of so many various yet wonderfully combining members. Compared with this last-named advantage, what is the stock of information (I do not here speak of book-learning, but of that knowledge which boy receives from boy), the mass of collected opinions, the intelligence in common, among the few and narrow members of an ordinary boarding-school?

> CHARLES LAMB, *Last Essays of Elia*, 1833

. . . she was about to relapse into her former studious mood. Again I ventured to disturb her. 'Can you tell me what the writing on that stone over the door means? What is Lowood Institution?'

'This house where you are come to live.'

'And why do they call it "Institution"? Is it in any way different from other schools?'

'It is partly a charity school; you and I, and all the rest of us, are charity-children. I suppose you are an orphan. Are not either your father or your mother dead?'

'Both died before I can remember.'

'Well, all the girls here have lost either one or both parents, and this is called an institution for educating orphans.'

'Do we pay no money? Do they keep us for nothing?'

'We pay, or our friends pay, fifteen pounds a year for each.'

'Then why do they call us charity-children?'

'Because fifteen pounds is not enough for board and teaching, and the deficiency is supplied by subscription.'

'Who subscribes?'

'Different benevolent-minded ladies and gentlemen in this neighborhood and in London.'

'Who was Naomi Brocklehurst?'

'The lady who built the new part of this house, as that tablet records, and whose son overlooks and directs everything here.'

'Why?'

'Because he is the treasurer and manager of the establishment.'

'Then this house does not belong to that tall lady who wears a watch, and who said we were to have some bread and cheese.'

'To Miss Temple? Oh, no! I wish it did; she has to answer to Mr Brocklehurst for all she does. Mr Brocklehurst buys all our food and all our clothes.'

'Does he live here?'

'No; two miles off, at a large hall.'

'Is he a good man?'

'He is a clergyman, and is said to do a great deal of good.'

CHARLOTTE BRONTË, *Jane Eyre*, 1847

A Dreadful Schism in the British Nation

For our Mechanics' Literary Club
I study Tacitus. It takes all night
At this rough country table which I scrub
Before I sit at it, by candlelight,
Spreading my books on it. I think respect
Must work like love in any intellect.
   Difficult Latin sticks in my throat
   And the scarecrow wears my coat.

What put me up to it, this partnership
Of lexicon and text, these five books thieved,
These two books borrowed, handed down, this grip
Of mind on mind, this work? Am I deceived?
Is literature a life proved much too good
To have its place in our coarse neighbourhood?
   Difficult Latin sticks in my throat
   And the scarecrow wears my coat.

In Paisley when they read the Riot Act
We faced the horsemen of the 10th Hussars.
Men's bones were broken, angry heads were cracked—
Provosts, sheriffs, guns and iron bars.
We thrashed the poet William Motherwell,
That depute-sheriff and the law's law-minstrel.
   Difficult Latin sticks in my throat
   And the scarecrow wears my coat.

Between us and our lives were bayonets.
They shone like water. We were crooked with thirst,
That hot dry bubbling when your whole life sweats.
'If you want life', they said, 'you must die first.'
Thus in a drought of fear Republic died
On Linen Street, Lawn Street and Causeyside.
   Difficult Latin sticks in my throat
   And the scarecrow wears my coat.

A Dreadful Schism in the British Nation

Beneath our banners I was marching for
My scholarship of barley, secret work
On which authority must slam its door
As Rome on Goth, Byzantium on Turk.
I'm left to guess their books, which precious line,
Eluding me, is never to be mine.
    Difficult Latin sticks in my throat
    And the scarecrow wears my coat.

Frost, poverty, rare, rare, the rapid rain . . .
What good can come of study, I must have.
I read it once, then read it twice again.
Fox, whittrick, dog, my horse, my new-born calf—
Let me recite my life, my animals and clay,
My candlelight, my fuddled melody.
    Difficult Latin sticks in my throat
    And the scarecrow wears my coat.

Such hard work urges me to turn each line
As firmly as I plough a furrow straight,
By doing so make this work clandestine,
Mix its affections with both love and hate.
So, Tacitus, old friend, though not to me,
Allow me master your authority.
    Difficult Latin sticks in my throat
    And the scarecrow wears my coat.

DOUGLAS DUNN, 'The Student, of Renfrewshire, 1820',
in *Selected Poems*, 1986

A Composition which ought to be spoken by the Son of a
Parishioner, in the presence of the Feoffees and Visitors, at the
Kidderminster Grammar School, at every public examination,
until the Free Boys are in possession of their ancient rights.

'Here I appear a suitor for your care,
Trusting you'll listen to my simple prayer;
The son of parents humble but discreet,
I lay my just petition at your feet.—
A time there was when our free school was FREE,
When all were taught regardless of a fee,
When those devoid of means possessed the right
To bless their children with scholastic light,
And boys who had poor parents fared the same
As those who claimed the rich man's favoured name.
Nor age, nor faith, were ever brought to bear
Upon the claims of all, the school to share.—
But now, alas! rules, laws, and schemes are made,
To bar Dissenters and the sons of trade;
Some are too young and some too old, forsooth,
And some too poor to mix with boarding youth!
And some, the sons of parents long since dead,
Whose guardians scarce can give them daily bread,
Are told, unless the classics are their aim,
To go to other schools of meaner name!—
Did not the founder of this school decree,
That every parish boy should be taught free?
That not the proudest parents' proudest heir,
Should be preferred 'mongst those who sought its care,
Nor lands, nor gold, nor pedigree should be
Esteemed above the sons of low degree?—
Boys have gone hence of humble rank and birth,
Who in the world proved men of sterling worth.

GEORGE GRIFFITH, *Going to Markets and Grammar Schools*,
1870; an autobiography

I have often absented myself the whole Sunday at this time, nor could the chiming bells draw me from my hiding place to go to church; tho' at night I was sure to pay for my absence from it by a strong snubbing. I at length got an higher notion of learning by going to school, and every leisure minute was employ'd in drawing squares and triangles upon the dusty walls of the barn. This was also my practice in learning to write. I also devour'd for these purposes every morsel of brown or blue paper, (it mattered not which) that my mother had her tea and sugar lapt in from the shop. But this was in cases of poverty, when I could not muster three farthings for a sheet of writing paper.

The saying of 'a little learning is a dangerous thing' is not far from fact. After I left school for good, (nearly as wise as I went, save reading and writing) I felt an itching after everything. I now began to provide myself with books of many puzzling systems. Bonnycastle's Mensuration, Fenning's Arithmetic, and Algebra, was now my constant teachers, and as I read the rules of each Problem with great care, I persevered so far as to solve many of the questions in those books; my pride fancy'd itself climbing the ladder of learning very rapidly; on the top of which, harvests of unbounded wonders was conceived to be bursting upon me, and was sufficient fire to prompt my ambition. But in becoming acquainted with a neighbour, one John Turnill, who was a good mathematical scholar, I found I was not sufficient to become master of these things without better assistance, as a superficial knowledge of them was next to nothing, and I had no more.

JOHN CLARE (b. 1793), Autobiography, first publ. 1931

Every winter's day each brought two sods of turf for the fire, which was kept burning in the centre of the school: there was a hole in the roof that discharged the functions of a chimney. Around this fire, especially during cold and severe weather, the boys were entitled to sit in a circle by turns. The enjoyment of this right occasioned a great deal of squabbling. The seats about the fire were round stones. I remember we had one scholar, named Sam Nelson, son of a most respectable man who lived within ten yards of our house. Sam was about eighteen years of age, a fine strapping young fellow, possessed of a great deal of dry humour. In consequence of his age and respectability he usually sat at the fire beside the master, who used to indulge in a variety of anecdotes for Sam's entertainment. Sam, on the other hand, returned anecdote for anecdote, or in other words, lie for lie. Now the master had small and extremely well-made feet, and wore the neatest possible shoes, made by the renowned Paddy Mellon. Whilst sitting beside him at the fire, Sam did no literary business whatever, but generally kept fiddling with a short bit of stick with which he seemed to amuse himself, as it were, by beating now the knuckles of one hand and then those of the other. Let us conceive Pat in the act of relating some egregious lie, for he was as great a liar as Sam, when, after a start, and the pause of a moment, he bounces to his feet, and finds a live coal burning in through his shoe and sticking to his very skin. This was Sam's ingenuity, who had laid the coal against his foot during the conversation by the aid of the stick. The trick was well understood by the whole school, who enjoyed it richly; indeed, so much so that screams of laughter burst out in several directions among the scholars. Pat, on looking round to ascertain the persons of those who amused themselves at his expense, found every face solemnly attentive upon the business in hand, and, consequently, though conscious that the matter was enjoyed by the whole school, found it impossible to fix upon any individual for punishment. He sat in a malignant state of meditation for some time, after which he arranged the boys upon their stone seats around the walls of the school, and desired them to remain at their peril without change in that particular position. He then went out, and after some time returned with a large furze-bush in his hand, and, commencing at the right hand side of the door, swept it round against their naked shins until he had completed the circuit, afterwards returning in the contrary direction, ending where he had begun. Thus did he make himself certain that none of those who enjoyed Sam Nelson's practical joke had escaped him.

I need not assure my readers that he contrived to get more butter from his pupils than five families like his could consume. Indeed, it was well known that his wife Nancy sold a great deal of butter in Clogher market, although it was equally well known that they had

no cow. I am now painting the state of education and society in the
north when I was a boy.

Life of William Carleton, 1896

The building in which we met was a low, long, straw-thatched
cottage, open from gable to gable, with a mud floor below, and an
unlathed roof above; and stretching along the naked rafters, which,
when the master chanced to be absent for a few minutes, gave noble
exercise in climbing, there used frequently to lie a helm, or oar, or
boathook, or even a foresail,—the spoil of some hapless peat-boat
from the opposite side of the Firth. The Highland boatmen of Ross
had carried on a trade in peats for ages with the Saxons of the town;
and as every boat owed a long-derived perquisite of twenty peats to
the grammar school, and as payment was at times foolishly refused,
the party of boys commissioned by the master to exact it almost
always succeeded, either by force or stratagem, in securing and
bringing along with them, in behalf of the institution, some spar, or
sail, or piece of rigging, which, until redeemed by special treaty, and
the payment of the peats, was stowed up over the rafters. These peat-
expeditions, which were intensely popular in the school, gave noble
exercise to the faculties. It was always a great matter to see, just as
the school met, some observant boy appear, cap in hand, before the
master, and intimate the fact of an arrival at the shore, by the simple
words, 'Peat-boat, Sir.' The master would then proceed to name a
party, more or less numerous, according to the exigency; but it
seemed to be matter of pretty correct calculation that, in the cases in
which the peat claim was disputed, it required about twenty boys to
bring home the twenty peats, or, lacking these, the compensatory sail
or spar.

HUGH MILLER (b. 1802), *My Schools and Schoolmasters*, 1854

As I could not get a school with a name, and rations 'to match', I set
up on my own account. I took a room in an old projecting-storied

building, called St Leonard's Hospital; yes, and also put a paper in my window, expressive of my business, with 'N.B. No connection' appended thereto. In the 'old hospital' I opened a school for boys and girls to learn plain work. There can be no surprise excited at my 'keeping a school', anybody could make a schoolmaster. People must live; and as well to keep a school as do anything else; every sixpence will buy a loaf; and to be a schoolmaster is one of the few comfortable trades which require no previous training. It has pleased the guardian spirit of England's mind and morals to furnish her with ready-made 'maisters and dames' fitted for school; and I was one of them. O privileged nation!

I was not quite so easy in my new stool as there are many of the rulers of the birch; I had scarcely time to 'Ahem!' and measure the distance from wall to wall, and tuck my hands under my coat tails, before I began to count over my qualifications for a teacher. *Imprimis*: I could read a little, write a decent hand, and figure simples and a few compounds; but the practice 'made me mad'. True I had a few boys to teach, and the sixpennies of those who did pay were useful; but others of them forgot to bring their pence on Mondays. Some of their mothers promised to pay another time; perhaps they may, but as it is now beyond the 'limitations' they need not fear an arrest from me. Again, I had to counter direct opposition in my new line, from the Orthodox. It was charged against me, that I refused to *beat* the boys because they could not 'say their spellings', and that, with such mildness, the boys would be saucy, and overbearing; and those who did read under me, read their books more like reading a play, than the Bible; that by teaching them to read 'poetry and stuff', the boys would, at some future time, all run away from their masters, or parents, and turn players. With such reports current, my school was soon at a discount; I struggled on for a time, but the school returns were insufficient for my family. By necessity I kept the school, until prejudice prevented it from keeping me. In vain I looked around for some means of support; I could discover none, except by a return to my former vocation in the Theatre.

CHRISTOPHER THOMSON (b. 1799), *The Autobiography of an Artisan*, 1847

A Dreadful Schism in the British Nation

Poor *Reuben Dixon* has the noisiest school
Of ragged lads, who ever bow'd to rule;
Low in his price—the men who heave our coals,
And clean our causeways, send him boys in shoals:
To see poor Reuben, with his fry beside,—
Their half-check'd rudeness and his half-scorn'd pride,—
Their room, the sty in which th' assembly meet,
In the close lane behind the Northgate-street;
T' observe his vain attempts to keep the peace,
Till tolls the bell, and strife and troubles cease,—
Calls for our praise; his labour praise deserves,
But not our pity; Reuben has no nerves:
'Mid noise and dirt, and stench, and play, and prate,
He calmly cuts the pen or views the slate.

GEORGE CRABBE (b. 1754), 'The Borough', 1810

Mrs Garth at certain hours was always in the kitchen, and this morning she was carrying on several occupations at once there—making her pies at the well-scoured deal table on one side of that airy room, observing Sally's movements at the oven and dough-tub through an open door, and giving lessons to her youngest boy and girl, who were standing opposite to her at the table with their books and slates before them. A tub and a clothes-horse at the other end of the kitchen indicated an intermittent wash of small things also going on.

Mrs Garth, with her sleeves turned above her elbows, deftly handling her pastry—applying her rolling-pin and giving ornamental pinches, while she expounded with grammatical fervour what were the right views about the concord of verbs and pronouns with 'nouns of multitude or signifying many', was a sight agreeably amusing. She was of the same curly-haired, square-faced type as Mary, but handsomer, with more delicacy of feature, a pale skin, a solid matronly figure, and a remarkable firmness of glance. In her snowy-frilled cap she reminded one of that delightful Frenchwoman whom we have all seen marketing, basket on arm. Looking at the mother, you might hope that the daughter would become like her, which is a prospective advantage equal to a dowry—the mother too often standing behind the daughter like a malignant prophecy— 'Such as I am, she will shortly be.'

'Now let us go through that once more,' said Mrs Garth, pinching an apple-puff which seemed to distract Ben, an energetic young male with a heavy brow, from due attention to the lesson. ' "Not without regard to the import of the word as conveying unity or plurality of idea"—tell me again what that means, Ben.'

(Mrs Garth, like more celebrated educators, had her favourite ancient paths, and in a general wreck of society would have tried to hold her 'Lindley Murray' above the waves.)

'Oh—it means—you must think what you mean,' said Ben, rather peevishly. 'I hate grammar. What's the use of it?'

'To teach you to speak and write correctly, so that you can be understood,' said Mrs Garth, with severe precision. 'Should you like to speak as old Job does?'

'Yes,' said Ben, stoutly; 'it's funnier. He says, "Yo goo"—that's just as good as "You go".'

'But he says, "A ship's in the garden", instead of "a sheep",' said Letty, with an air of superiority. 'You might think he meant a ship off the sea.'

'No, you mightn't, if you weren't silly,' said Ben. 'How could a ship off the sea come there?'

'These things belong only to pronunciation, which is the least part of grammar,' said Mrs Garth. 'That apple peel is to be eaten by the pigs, Ben; if you eat it, I must give them your piece of pastry. Job has only to speak about very plain things. How do you think you would write or speak about anything more difficult, if you knew no more of grammar than he does? You would use wrong words, and put words in the wrong places, and instead of making people understand you, they would turn away from you as a tiresome person. What would you do then?'

'I shouldn't care, I should leave off,' said Ben, with a sense that this was an agreeable issue where grammar was concerned.

'I see you are getting tired and stupid, Ben,' said Mrs Garth, accustomed to these obstructive arguments from her male offspring. Having finished her pies, she moved towards the clothes-horse, and said, 'Come here and tell me the story I told you on Wednesday, about Cincinnatus.'

'I know! he was a farmer,' said Ben.

GEORGE ELIOT, Middlemarch, 1871–2

During January, February, and part of March, the deep snows, and after their melting the almost impassable roads, prevented our stirring beyond the garden walls, except to go to church; but within these limits we had to pass an hour every day in the open air. Our clothing was insufficient to protect us from the severe cold. We had no boots; the snow got into our shoes and melted there; our ungloved hands became numbed and covered with chilblains, as were our feet. I remember well the distracting irritation I endured from this cause every evening, when my feet inflamed, and the torture of thrusting the swelled, raw, and stiff toes into my shoes in the morning. Then the scanty supply of food was distressing. With the keen appetites of growing children, we had scarcely sufficient to keep alive a delicate invalid. From this deficiency of nourishment resulted an abuse, which pressed hardly on the younger pupils; whenever the famished great girls had an opportunity, they would coax or menace the little ones out of their portion. Many a time I have shared between two claimants the precious morsel of brown bread distributed at tea-time; and after relinquishing to a third half the contents of my mug of coffee, I have swallowed the remainder with an accompaniment of secret tears, forced from me by the exigency of hunger.

Sundays were dreary days in that wintry season. We had to walk two miles to Brocklebridge Church, where our patron officiated. We set out cold, we arrived at church colder. During the morning service we became almost paralyzed. It was too far to return to dinner, and an allowance of cold meat and bread, in the same penurious propor-

tion observed in our ordinary meals, was served round between the
services.

At the close of the afternoon service we returned by an exposed
and hilly road, where the bitter winter wind, blowing over a range of
snowy summits to the north, almost flayed the skin from our faces.

CHARLOTTE BRONTË, *Jane Eyre*, 1847

Mr Wopsle's great-aunt kept an evening-school in the village; that
is to say, she was a ridiculous old woman of limited means and
unlimited infirmity, who used to go to sleep from six to seven every
evening, in the society of youth who paid twopence per week each,
for the improving opportunity of seeing her do it. . . .

The Educational Scheme or Course established by Mr Wopsle's
great-aunt may be resolved into the following synopsis. The pupils
ate apples and put straws down one another's backs, until Mr
Wopsle's great-aunt collected her energies, and made an indiscrimi-
nate totter at them with a birch-rod. After receiving the charge with
every mark of derision, the pupils formed in line and buzzingly
passed a ragged book from hand to hand. The book had an alphabet
in it, some figures and tables, and a little spelling—that is to say, it
had had once. As soon as this volume began to circulate, Mr
Wopsle's great-aunt fell into a state of coma; arising either from sleep
or a rheumatic paroxysm. The pupils then entered among themselves
upon a competitive examination on the subject of Boots, with the
view of ascertaining who could tread the hardest upon whose toes.
This mental exercise lasted until Biddy made a rush at them and
distributed three defaced Bibles (shaped as if they had been un-
skilfully cut off the chump-end of something), more illegibly printed
at the best than any curiosities of literature I have since met with,
speckled all over with ironmould, and having various specimens of
the insect world smashed between their leaves. This part of the
Course was usually lightened by several single combats between
Biddy and refractory students. When the fights were over, Biddy
gave out the number of a page, and then we all read aloud what we

could—or what we couldn't—in a frightful chorus; Biddy leading with a high shrill monotonous voice, and none of us having the least notion of, or reverence for, what we were reading about. When this horrible din had lasted a certain time, it mechanically awoke Mr Wopsle's great-aunt, who staggered at a boy fortuitously, and pulled his ears. This was understood to terminate the Course for the evening, and we emerged into the air with shrieks of intellectual victory. It is fair to remark that there was no prohibition against any pupil's entertaining himself with a slate or even with the ink (when there was any), but that it was not easy to pursue that branch of study in the winter season, on account of the little general shop in which the classes were holden—and which was also Mr Wopsle's great-aunt's sitting-room and bed-chamber—being but faintly illuminated through the agency of one low-spirited dip-candle and no snuffers.

DICKENS, *Great Expectations*, 1860–1

The following is the simple narrative of one of the teachers at the B—street school. 'Mr—tells me you wish to know something of the origin of our school. I was invited on the first of October, 1843, (i.e. to assist in establishing a school of the kind) by the city missionary. It appears that the missionary had given out that this school was to be opened on the Sunday for boys who had no shoes or clothes to go to other schools. About six or seven of us met in the little room in B—street, on the Sunday afternoon, little expecting what we should have to contend with. We opened our school this first Sunday afternoon, with about twenty lads from twelve to twenty years of age: their object, as I afterwards found, was to have a lark. We attempted to teach them, but they immediately wished to leave the school; this we opposed: the boys got resolute, so did some of the teachers. This very soon broke out into open rebellion, and had the teachers been *all* as resolute as some were, we should all have had our heads broken. Some of the teachers used great violence, and when the boys saw the blood flowing from one of the boys, in consequence of one of the teachers holding him so tight by the neck, I could see and hear that they were urging one another to the attack. I stood a calm spectator, but I at once saw the necessity of breaking up the conspiracy, by diverting their minds to a new object, and holding out a prospect of some reward to those who were not so forward in the rebellion; and thus we managed to divide them. We soon got several of the bigger boys on our side, and such a scene followed as I shall never forget: some swearing, some dancing, some whistling, and the teachers looking some of them as pale as death, and some quite exhausted: and thus we got over our first afternoon. Some of the teachers I have never seen since: most of the boys were reformed.

ANON., *Ragged Schools*, 1851

My education in consciousness of class was swift and progressive. When I was eleven I won a scholarship from the board school to the King Edward's Grammar School at Barnfield, and in a way I was luckier than I knew. The school at Barnfield had not yet been built, and the teaching was carried on at the High School in the centre of the town. These grammar schools, which in a way were branches of the old High School, were new institutions. The High School had been founded for the poor boys of the town, but after three hundred years it had become the school for the middle-class. I suppose the grammar schools were established in order to make good, at least in some degree, the wishes of the founder. I would have been proud to go to the Barnfield building, had it existed, but I am sure my feelings of awe would have been nothing compared to those I had on going to the High School. It was in what is now called Victorian Gothic— Pugin was the architect—but for me Gothic and Victorian Gothic were one and the same, and Pugin's school, with its pinnacles, its fretted windows, great oak beams and leaded lights, was venerability itself. It was as awesome as a cathedral (and almost as dark), and I responded to it ardently. My spirit soared each morning as I entered: I saw it, as it were, as the nursery of greatness, and I too would be great. And none of this was dimmed at all by the fact that we were not of the High School and Pugin's building (they've built a cinema and a Marks & Spencers where it used to stand) and that we were ignored by the High School boys proper. They left us coldly alone as often as they saw us, for in fact we were taught separately by different masters and attended at different hours. This crude manifestation of class I was young enough to take for granted without rancour. I knew that the boys of the High School were the sons of the town's industrialists and professional men; I had nothing in common with them. The one thing I envied them was that they learned both Greek and Latin, whereas Latin was deemed enough for us. Nor was I bothered at all by the class differences between myself and the other boys of the Barnfield School. At the board school, I had been in the highest rank of the social hierarchy; here, I was certainly in the lowest, indeed so lowly as to comprise a rank all of my own. Yet I did not care and was not seriously aware of it. In a way, I was lucky, as I see now. I knew very well how great the odds were against my being there at all. True, I had my scholarship, but there were still books to be bought, and there had had to be new clothes. Indeed, the only reason I was able to go was that Lizzie and Edwin and Horace were now at work, so that, for the time being at any rate, we were not so straitened in means as we had been. At the same time, there were no compulsory games and no special clothes for games. Had there been, that alone might well have prevented my going; nor indeed was there any uniform at all, save for the mortar-board that I wore with such pride. I was the first boy from Fussell Street ever to go to any school higher than a board school and I was proud of it.

WALTER ALLEN, *All in A Lifetime*, 1959; a novel based on the life of Walter Allen's father—called Billy Ashted in the book —who was born in working-class Birmingham in 1875

Lord Cumnor had certainly a little time for gossip, which he con- trived to combine with the failing of personal intervention between the old land-steward and the tenantry. But, then, the countess made up by her unapproachable dignity for this weakness of the earl's. Once a year she was condescending. She and the ladies, her daughters, had set up a school; not a school after the manner of schools now-a-days, where far better intellectual teaching is given to the boys and girls of labourers and workpeople than often falls to the lot of their betters in worldly estate; but a school of the kind we should call 'industrial', where girls are taught to sew beautifully, to be capital housemaids, and pretty fair cooks, and, above all, to dress neatly in a kind of charity uniform devised by the ladies of Cumnor Towers:—white caps, white tippets, check aprons, blue gowns, and ready curtseys, and 'please, ma'ams', being *de rigueur.*

Now, as the countess was absent from the Towers for a considerable part of the year, she was glad to enlist the sympathy of the Hollingford ladies in this school, with a view to obtaining their aid as visitors during the many months that she and her daughters were away. And the various unoccupied gentlewomen of the town responded to the call of their liege lady, and gave her their service as required; and along with it, a great deal of whispered and fussy admiration. 'How good of the countess! So like the dear countess—always thinking of others!' and so on; while it was always supposed that no strangers had seen Hollingford properly, unless they had been taken to the countess's school, and been duly impressed by the neat little pupils, and the still neater needlework there to be inspected. In return, there was a day of honour set apart every summer, when with much gracious and stately hospitality, Lady Cumnor and her daughters received all the school visitors at the Towers, the great family mansion standing in aristocratic seclusion in the centre of the large park, of which one of the lodges was close to the little town.

ELIZABETH GASKELL, *Wives and Daughters,* 1864–6

A girl is not expected to serve God in Church or State and is therefore not invited to the University or the grammar-school; but she may, if poor, be wanted to contribute to the comfort of her betters, as an apprentice or servant, and the charity schools are therefore open to her. . . . The children are dressed in a hideous costume; they are subject to many restraints of a humiliating kind which are presumed to be appropriate in a charity school, but which would not be tolerated in a free and open boarding school by parents who paid for their children's maintenance. The fact that all the scholars come from one class, and that a low one, causes the tone of thinking and of social life to become narrow and enervating, and the absence of stimulus, aid, or supervision from without renders the teachers satisfied with educational results of the most meagre kind.

JOSHUA FITCH, 1873

At Ripley Hall work was important and classes were based firmly on ability. Yet for us girls, in spite of the board in the dining-room, there were no prizes quite like a scholarship to Eton or Winchester, opening up prospects of later glories, Firsts in Greats, shining careers in the Diplomatic Service, the Judiciary or Parliament, as there supposedly were for our brothers. Indeed, in my year only one girl took a scholarship exam, and that not to a major girls' school. Some of us did not even sit Common Entrance.

Miss Leefield was, I suspect, a feminist of sorts, but without a proper constituency. The wishes of our parents were not that we should become hockey blues and blue-stockings like herself, but, rather, that a decent education would help us later to earn a living until in the ideal outcome we found good husbands and had children of our own. At the time and indeed for a number of years afterwards, I did not know, did not really know, that women went to university and had careers. Schoolteachers might have—some of them—but they were different and hardly human.

SARAH WINTLE, 'Prep School Girl', in *London Review of Books*, 4 April 1985 (1950s)

It has to be remembered what ordinary boarding school life was like 150 years ago. Most girls slept two to a bed (it was warmer as well as economical of space). Washing conditions and sanitation were primitive, epidemics frequent. At the time of the 1864–7 Schools Inquiry Commission few schools of any sort were equipped, as Red Maids' was, with gas lighting, warm water, warm-air heating and a basement bathroom—though it has to be said that these were installed in premises that the inspectors considered to be in an unhealthy part of Bristol, with far too little space for play. (In 1837 it had been decided not to move the children to a new building erected for them, on the grounds that 'the very beauty and magnificence of the edifice' would unfit them for 'the closer and humbler dwellings it must necessarily be their lot in after life to inhabit'.) However, there was very little recreation generally for any girls until the late Victorian period; boarding school diet was often not much better than the charity hospitals' (though probably more appetizingly presented), and the pupils were watched with the same vigilance and kept constantly occupied. And as for the unreformed boys' public schools, you had to be very fit to survive: the squalor, dissipation and violence at Eton in the Georgian period were notorious; even worse were the atrocities that went on in Long Chamber at night. Here the 'Collegers' were locked up between 8.30 at night and seven next morning, and 'there were many things done, which one cannot but remember with horror and regret'. At all boys' schools flogging was the rule, for errors in construing quite as much as for more serious lapses. In short, it is only comparatively recently that school could be said to be at all pleasurable, or even healthy.

GILLIAN AVERY, *The Best Type of Girl*, 1991

St Jude's was a small school run in connection with the church of the parish, a very poor parish. We lived on the fringe of it: if you walked from our house, which was situated in a decent if rather dingy lower-middle-class street, in the opposite direction from the church—down our street and then to the left along Munster Road—you came to the abodes of the rich, or so I conceived them, though prosperous middle class was probably the correct designation of the people who dwelt in those square black houses with their ugly laurel-walled

gardens on which the sun so rarely shone. But in the direction of St
Jude's Church and school, now to become my four-times-daily walk,
at every few steps darkness and poverty grew amain: narrower, dirtier
streets; smells, gloom, squalor, puddles, offal—till the school was in
sheer slums.

G. P. DENNIS, *Bloody Mary's*, 1934

But what about school then, says you. Ah now, with school begins
his contact with the upstairs world which so far he has only known
of as buffered off by his parents. And school, which is the council
school, of course, is in origin quite alien to working-class life. It does
not grow from that life; it is not 'our' school, in the sense in which
other schools can be so spoken of by the folk of other classes. The
government forced them on us, and the real shaping of the working-
class boy goes on after they are shut. That is a very important point
to remember: that school in working-class life expresses nothing of
that life; it is an institution clapped on from above. Thus all his life
a man from this environment will regard many knowledges and skills
with a suspicion which is incomprehensible to those who found that
learning to be their natural birthright. He will fumble with a foreign
language as though he had a secret shame in being found learning it
at all; and in this, for there are always these harkings-back, he is of
closer kin to the nineteenth century middle-class than to the nimble-
tongued young bourgeois of to-day.

In the council schools you are taught a respect for white collars,
punctuality (the best prizes usually go for this), a certain amount of
docility, patriotism, religion, and the rest of the half-hearted precepts
which schoolteachers are unwillingly pushed into spreading. Also, of
course, the indispensable mechanical proficiencies necessary to every
citizen nowadays: reading, writing, and elementary arithmetic.
Other subjects, history, geography, science, are by way of meaningless decoration. Only an occasional starved enthusiast teaches them
seriously at all. So school is a half-hearted affair, and the children
know that it is half-hearted. There cannot be a disciplined way of life

taught there as in the public schools, though nowadays you get many
foolish attempts at imitations of it, for you are not preparing these
boys for any lordly functions, and you have not the honesty plainly
to shape them for the job they are going to get.

JACK COMMON (b. 1903), *The Freedom of the Streets*, 1938

[Moses] was only awakened from his day-dream by the brazen
clanging of a bell. It was the bell of the great Ghetto school, sum-
moning its pupils from the reeking courts and alleys, from the garrets
and the cellars, calling them to come and be Anglicised. And they
came—in a great straggling procession recruited from every lane and
by-way: big children and little children; boys in blackening corduroy
and girls in washed-out cotton; tidy children and ragged children;
children in great shapeless boots gaping at the toes; sickly children
and sturdy children and diseased children; bright-eyed children and
hollow-eyed children; quaint, sallow, foreign-looking children and
fresh-coloured, English-looking children; with great pumpkin heads,
with oval heads, with pear-shaped heads; with old men's faces, with
cherubs' faces, with monkeys' faces; cold and famished children
and warm and well-fed children; children conning their lessons
and children romping carelessly; the demure and the anæmic; the
boisterous and the blackguardly, the insolent, the idiotic, the vicious,
the intelligent, the exemplary, the dull—spawn of all countries—all
hastening at the inexorable clang of the big school-bell to be ground
in the same great blind, inexorable Governmental machine. Here,
too, was a miniature fair, the path being lined by itinerant tempta-
tions. There was brisk traffic in toffy and grey peas and monkey-
nuts, and the crowd was swollen by anxious parents seeing tiny or
truant offspring safe within the school-gates. The women were bare-
headed or beshawled, with infants at their breasts and little ones
toddling at their sides; the men were greasy and musty and squalid.
Here a bright, earnest little girl held her vagrant big brother by
the hand, not to let go till she had seen him in the bosom of his
class-mates. There a sullen wild-eyed mite in petticoats was being

dragged along, screaming, towards distasteful durance. It was a drab picture—the bleak, leaden sky above, the sloppy, miry stones below, the frowsy mothers and fathers, the motley children.

ISRAEL ZANGWILL, *Children of the Ghetto*, 1892

The church 'of the establishment' to which our school belonged had been built about 1830. It stood on the north flank of the parish, whilst on the south rose an infantry barracks—both buildings being erected, some thought, to keep the lower orders on their knees. Our seat of learning, attached to the church, had opened its doors in 1839, several years before Friedrich Engels, whose factory stood close by, wrote about the district. In all justice we pupils could have sung, with Ernest Jones, 'We're low—we're low—we're very, very low.' And they provided us with education to match. Year after year inspectors came and condemned our great sooty edifice by the marshalling yards. They damned the unqualified staff, the stinking rooms, the appalling cultural results. In all, they reported, a place of educational ill repute, even by the low standards of the times. But I found it delightful. So did all my siblings, and we blubbered and complained if anything occurred to stop attendance. Then, whatever inspectors might say, we scholars had reason at least for spiritual pride. 'The religious tone of this school,' reported the Bishop's examiners, 'is excellent'!

ROBERT ROBERTS, *A Ragged Schooling*, 1976

The real trouble with the Council school is that there is no machinery by which continuation classes can be made compulsory. No boy should be given a clearance certificate until, say, he has made himself proficient in one of the modern languages. As matters are at present, a boy leaves school more or less illiterate, with no other qualification than that required for a van or errand boy. But mostly, I think, the real deficiency in the system is that he is not taught to speak. Well acquainted as I am with the peculiar intonation of the street boy, I am frequently at a loss to understand what he is talking about. This stricture not only applies to London, but to the provinces. The horrible articulation of the average Council-trained youth is a terrible handicap to him in after life. Indeed, the only difference that exists between the Council boy and the public school boy is his voice. The nasal whine of the Cockney schoolboy is an offence. And there is really no reason in the world why he should be allowed to go into the world under such a disadvantage.

EDGAR WALLACE, A Short Autobiography, 1932

And here it is worth noticing a rather curious fact, and that is that the school-story is a thing peculiar to England. So far as I know there are extremely few school-stories in foreign languages. The reason, obviously, is that in England education is mainly a matter of status. The most definite dividing line between the petite-bourgeoisie and the working class is that the former pay for their education, and within the bourgeoisie there is another unbridgeable gulf between the 'public' school and the 'private' school. It is quite clear that there are tens and scores of thousands of people to whom every detail of life at a 'posh' public school is wildly thrilling and romantic. They happen to be outside that mystic world of quadrangles and house-colours, but they yearn after it, day-dream about it, live mentally in it for hours at a stretch. The question is, Who are these people? Who reads the *Gem* and *Magnet*?

Obviously one can never be quite certain about this kind of thing. All I can say from my own observation is this. Boys who are likely to go to public schools themselves generally read the *Gem* and *Magnet*, but they nearly always stop reading them when they are about twelve; they may continue for another year from force of habit, but by that time they have ceased to take them seriously. On the other hand, the boys at very cheap private schools, the schools that are designed for people who can't afford a public school but consider the

Council schools 'common', continue reading the *Gem* and *Magnet* for several years longer. A few years ago I was a teacher at two of these schools myself. I found that not only did virtually all the boys read the *Gem* and *Magnet*, but that they were still taking them fairly seriously when they were fifteen or even sixteen. These boys were the sons of shopkeepers, office employees, and small business and professional men, and obviously it is this class that the *Gem* and *Magnet* are aimed at. But they are certainly read by working-class boys as well. They are generally on sale in the poorest quarters of big towns, and I have known them to be read by boys whom one might expect to be completely immune from public-school 'glamour'. I have seen a young coal-miner, for instance, a lad who had already worked a year or two underground, eagerly reading the *Gem*. Recently I offered a batch of English papers to some British legionaries of the French Foreign Legion in North Africa; they picked out the *Gem* and *Magnet* first. Both papers are much read by girls, and the Pen Pals department of the *Gem* shows that it is read in every corner of the British Empire, by Australians, Canadians, Palestine Jews, Malays, Arabs, Straits Chinese, etc., etc. The editors evidently expect their readers to be aged round about fourteen, and the advertisements (milk chocolate, postage stamps, water pistols, blushing cured, home conjuring tricks, itching powder, the Phine Phun Ring which runs a needle into your friend's hand, etc., etc.) indicate roughly the same age; there are also the Admiralty advertisements, however, which call for youths between seventeen and twenty-two. And there is no question that these papers are also read by adults. It is quite common for people to write to the editor and say that they have read every number of the *Gem* or *Magnet* for the past thirty years.

GEORGE ORWELL, 'Boys' Weeklies', in *Inside the Whale*, 1940

Under Miss Holmes, the children had been weaned from the old free life; they had become accustomed to regular attendance, to sitting at a desk and concentrating, however imperfectly. Although they had not learned much, they had been learning to learn. But Miss Holmes's ideas belonged to an age that was rapidly passing. She believed in the established order of society, with clear divisions, and had done her best to train the children to accept their lowly lot with gratitude to and humility before their betters. She belonged to the past; the children's lives lay in the future, and they needed a guide with at least some inkling of the changing spirit of the times. The new mistresses, who came from the outside world, brought something of this spirit with them. Even the transient and unappreciated Miss Higgs, having given as a subject for composition one day 'Write a letter to Miss Ellison, telling her what you did at Christmas', when she read over one girl's shoulder the hitherto conventional beginning 'Dear and Honoured Miss', exclaimed 'Oh, no! That's a *very* old-fashioned beginning. Why not say, "Dear Miss Ellison?" ' An amendment which was almost revolutionary.

Miss Shepherd went further. She taught the children that it was not what a man or woman had, but what they were which mattered. That poor people's souls are as valuable and that their hearts may be as good and their minds as capable of cultivation as those of the rich. She even hinted that on the material plane people need not necessarily remain always upon one level. Some boys, born of poor parents, had struck out for themselves and become great men, and everybody had respected them for rising upon their own merits. She would read them the lives of some of these so-called self-made men (there were no women, Laura noticed!) and though their circumstances were too far removed from those of her hearers for them to inspire the ambition she hoped to awaken, they must have done something to widen their outlook on life.

Meanwhile the ordinary lessons went on. Reading, writing, arithmetic, all a little less rather than more well taught and mastered than formerly. In needlework there was a definite falling off. Miss Shepherd was not a great needle-woman herself and was inclined to cut down the sewing time to make way for other work. Infinitesimal stitches no longer provoked delighted exclamations, but more often a 'Child! You will ruin your eyes!' As the bigger girls left who in their time had won county prizes, the standard of the output declined, until, from being known as one of the first needlework schools in the district, Fordlow became one of the last.

FLORA THOMPSON, *Lark Rise to Candleford,* 1939

Still hardly accepted as members of a profession, teachers in Church and State schools fought respectfully for social recognition. Sons and daughters very often from top working-class families, they felt the need to conform as closely as possible to what they knew of middle-class standards. Disseminators among the poor of bourgeois morals, culture and learning, they remained economically tied to the lower orders, living in genteel poverty with an income little higher than that of the skilled manual worker. In 1905, after increases in that year, our headmaster received £120 per annum and his assistants £110. As the century grew older both the economic and the social gap between teachers and the skilled manual workers widened: teaching became a 'profession' and its members establishment figures in the lower middle class.

Under appalling conditions in our school the staff worked earnestly but with no great hope. The building itself stood face on to one of the largest marshalling yards in the North. All day long the roar of a work-a-day world invaded the school hall, where each instructor, shouting in competition, taught up to sixty children massed together. From the log book it is clear that rarely did a week pass with all teachers present. 'Miss F.' or 'Mr D. absent today—ulcerated throat' appears throughout with monotonous regularity.

Fortunately for the size of the classes, anything up to a quarter of the pupils would stay away too, perhaps in sympathy. One of our dominies, a frail young Scot, had, we thought, the disgusting habit of coughing into his handkerchief, then staring into it. We could not as yet spot the active consumptive looking anxiously for signs of haemorrhage.

His Majesty's inspectors seemed permanently dissatisfied with us. These gentlemen we learned to recognise: they came in pairs like comedians, addressing us with some unction. Teachers feared them as they feared the Lord; scholars knew and enjoyed their terror. Many the looks of gratitude we, the bright boys, got for responding smartly to these god-like questioners.

One inspector early in the century had complained that 'Classrooms are insufficient [four for 450 pupils] and one is without desks. Yet writing is taught in it, thus inducing awkward attitudes and careless work.' Error, though, was easily emendable; scholars wrote on slates and made erasures with saliva and cuff. In a school nearby, however, this method was frowned on. There the pupil wishing to 'rub out' had to raise a hand and a monitor swung to him a damp sponge fastened to the end of a rod. Another inspector deplored the fact that all our 'offices' were without doors, 'even those under the classroom'. Doorless privies, our school managers believed, eliminated 'certain practices' among the pupils. They were mistaken. One HMI urged an innovation—'a cloakroom with taps and bowls'. Months later the 'washing appliances' were installed—cold water taps and bowls—'two for the girls' end; two for the boys' '. The uproar from the street another inspector found 'intolerable'. 'Wooden blocks laid down', he thought, instead of the 'cobbles' (setts), 'would be a great boon.' The blessing remained unconferred fifty years even later, when the school fell down. Time and again others condemned the wretched lighting (open gas jets) and the stench of classrooms. They seem, however, to have overlooked the 'pit'. Under a shed where we gathered when it rained, our small play yard contained a hole six feet square and six feet deep, with a loose lid, into which all the school's refuse was shot, to be removed at intervals. Meanwhile we salvaged what we could. One pupil spent so much time there, looking for 'treasure', that he was known among his contemporaries even thirty years after as 'Dusty Dan'.

ROBERT ROBERTS, *The Classic Slum*, 1971

I imagine that what we felt to be breadth in those distant days could today be thought narrow enough. I can recollect no consciousness, in the early nineteen hundreds, among masters or boys, of the coming social revolution. The first crack in our solid unawareness came with a boy, Charles Lister, who joined the Labour Party while still at Eton. But to the rest of us Keir Hardie in his cloth cap was a joke. We rode on the backs of the workers with the insouciance of the man who sat on the back of a whale, believing it to be an island. We were taught to be sorry for the very poor, and went in batches to visit the Eton Mission at Hackney Wick, but it could never have entered our heads that some of the boys we met there might well, in our lifetime, be among Her Majesty's Ministers. But for all this obtuseness, this assurance of a social stability which in fact was so soon to break up, I believe we did acquire, unconsciously, a set of values which has enabled many of us to accept the loss of privilege with equal minds. If we seriously over-valued prowess at games, we set no value at all on money or social position, and among my thousand contemporaries I can only remember two snobs. One was a Master, whose snobbery cost him the loss of all influence or respect; the other a boy, whom we laughed at. (He stuck to his guns and, becoming a Courtier, went to Heaven in this world.) The Revolution came; and in a changed society, the Etonians who sold their country homes and took to washing-up after supper are not, I believe, among the least cheerful or the most regretful.

L. E. JONES, *A Victorian Boyhood*, 1955

How docile we were, how orderly! Empire Day,
Armistice Day, and all that religious instruction!
They were training us to die for something—
It meant nothing, only holidays and queer emotions.

Forty years later, walking in Canton, I encounter
A mass of orderly children—they are listening
Intently, with every sign of agreement,
To a horror story about red-haired imperialists.

I slope past fearfully. But to them I'm no more
Than a comical flower in this well-kept park.
Keeping one's eyes on teacher is far more important.
As yet they haven't learnt to connect.

D. J. ENRIGHT, 'Training', in *The Terrible Shears*, 1973

Far far from gusty waves, these children's faces
Like rootless weeds the torn hair round their paleness;
The tall girl with her weighed-down head; the paper-
seeming boy with rat's eyes; the stunted unlucky heir
Of twisted bones, reciting a father's gnarled disease,
His lesson from his desk. At back of the dim class
One unnoted, mild and young: his eyes live in a dream
Of squirrel's game, in tree room, other than this.

On sour cream walls, donations; Shakespeare's head
Cloudless at dawn, civilized dome riding all cities;
Belled, flowery, Tyrolese valley; open-handed map
Awarding the explicit world, of every name but here.
To few, too few, these are real windows: world and words and
    waving
Leaves, to heal. For these young lives, guilty and dangerous
Is fantasy of travel. Surely, Shakespeare is wicked

To lives that wryly turn, under the structural Lie,
Toward smiles or hate? Amongst their heap, these children
Wear skins peeped through by bones, and spectacles of steel
With mended glass, like bottle bits in slag.
Tyrol is wicked; map's promising a fable:
All of their time and space are foggy slum,
So blot their maps with slums as big as doom.

Unless, dowager, governor, these pictures, in a room
Columned above childishness, like our day's future drift

Of smoke concealing war, are voices shouting
O that beauty has words and works which break
Through coloured walls and towers. The children stand
As in a climbing mountain train. This lesson illustrates
The world green in their many valleys beneath:
The total summer heavy with their flowers.

STEPHEN SPENDER, 'An Elementary School Classroom',
in *Collected Poems, 1928–53*

The War made an enormous difference to our manners and modes . . . the fact was that before the War the boys were a distinctly rough crowd. How I got through these elementary school years as well as I did is rather a mystery to me now. I seem to remember a good deal of going out of the way to avoid trouble; sometimes I recommended myself to the protection of some older and stronger ruffian, much as a weaker Saxon might recommend himself to a feudal lord. I must have been a good deal more diplomatic than I subsequently became when I was capable of standing up for myself. And it was a great advantage that natural tastes and sympathies led me to consort with the girls, who were chiefly my friends in these earlier years. My brother, who had no such gifts but his own strong right arm, and being five years older was among the senior boys, was for ever in trouble fighting with them. I hope he enjoyed it: I wouldn't have had such a life for anything. I remember one occasion when several of the big boys gave him a 'hammering', hitting him over the head and shoulders with their big red handkerchiefs which they had filled with stones and tied up for the purpose. No such things happened to me, though I was completely incapable of defending myself. I remember thinking him—with the superior wisdom of nine to fourteen—a fool for getting involved with them.

Anyway, whether it is illusion or no, I have the impression that after the War elementary schools like ours became much less rough and raw, and altogether quieter. For one thing there were so many fewer children; for another, their parents had been a bit educated

by the War and liked fighting and quarrelling among themselves rather less; then, more recently, the elder children have been
skimmed off to the senior schools. But I think it is no illusion—the
War brought about profound changes in English society; working
people became better off and their standards changed. The changes
have gone through all classes: in the older Universities the pre-war
rowdiness has largely come to an end; the public schools have
become immensely less harsh and rigorous than they were.

A. L. Rowse, *A Cornish Childhood,* 1942

I liked going to school very much but I didn't learn enough. I always
wanted to learn more. But we were too poor to be sent anywhere
else. I was always quick at a lot of things, I never missed a class. But
I always remember those—their parents were teachers and they had
a good job. Now those were the children that always won the
scholarship. If they got a scholarship they went to Mount St
Joseph's. They had to pay so much because my niece won and her
father had to pay for her. Well I longed to go but my mother and
father was too poor, they couldn't have us going there. I have known
a lot of people get to the top if they've been educated. Always
through education. And I think that's the greatest thing you can
have if you want to get on in the world, but get on in the proper
manner, not be a snob. I think it's the best thing out.

When I left school we had to go to work and some of these girls
that had won scholarships and got on and had a good education
they'd broke away from us. They went on their own, they didn't
seem to come to us like they used to do before they went to these
high schools. They broke away. I noticed there was some kind of
distinction between the girls who went to a high school and those
that had to go out working for a living. I've always wanted to go to
a nice school and wear uniform. It's strange that, isn't it?

Florence Atherton (b. 1898 in Lancashire), in Thea
Thompson (ed.), *Edwardian Childhoods,* 1981

A Dreadful Schism in the British Nation

Bog-brown glens, mica schist rocks, waterfalls
Gulching down screes, a rain-logged mountain slope
With scrawny pine-trees twisted by mad gales,
They see from my ball-yard, and abandon hope.

Wild boys my workshops chasten and subdue
Learn here the force of craft. Few can escape
My rack of metal, wood, thread, hide: my screw
Of brotherhood: the penny stitched in a strap.

Podded in varnished pews, stunted in beds
Of cruciform iron, they bruise with sad, hurt shame:
Orphans with felons, bastards at loggerheads
With waifs, branded for life by a bad name.

One, almost hanged in my boot-room, has run free
Dressed as a girl, saved by a thieving gypsy.

RICHARD MURPHY, 'Letterfrack Industrial School',
in *New Selected Poems*, 1989

Discipline in schools inevitably reflected the class pattern of society beyond the walls. Teachers were only too well aware from the physique, clothing, and cleanliness of their charges just how far each one stood from the social datum line. In spite of their compassion for the neglected and deprived (not always in evidence), some teachers publicly scolded the condition of their dirty and ill-dressed pupils, too often forgetting the poverty from which they came. It was difficult for a child to keep himself clean in a house where soap came low on the list of necessaries. Children of the quality they might reprimand but seldom punished; the rest were caned (it seldom amounted to much) with fair indiscrimination.

ROBERT ROBERTS, *The Classic Slum*, 1971

We had to take an examination to see if we were clever enough to go for a scholarship for Huntingdon Street school where they had to pay you see. It wasn't like the scholarships there are today. Huntingdon Street school had the boys and girls of better class people, business people mostly, and if they'd got one or two vacancies they'd let them in from the board schools. The fees weren't heavy fees. One or two of the girls used to tell me, 'My father pays so much a year for us.' You got in free you see because you'd been top of your class. I'd been in the top class at Bath Street so long they were getting tired of me. I shouldn't be quite ten when I went there. And I stayed there until I was thirteen and could leave.

Before I went to Huntingdon Street school I can remember our children in my class we were made to make a dress or whatever we got on last so very long, we weren't allowed to come to the table without a white pinafore on. And you had to wear one. And Mother wouldn't let me go to Huntingdon Street without a pinafore. And I can hear the gasp when I walked in with this. It was quite a nice pinafore. It was white. And the teacher said to me, 'You could have hung your pinafore up in the cloakroom, Annie.'

I said, 'But Mother wouldn't let me—I'd soil my dress perhaps.' You see.

She said, 'Well it's the rules here we don't have you in here with a pinafore.' A lot of snobbishness there was. And so of course I was made to—in fact I rolled it up in a bundle and put it in me schoolbook bag when I got towards school so that I wouldn't have to be immolated again. But Mother was very cross about it. I told Grace and somehow or other it came out. She didn't mean it to do. So she says, 'You'd better not take them any more. If that's the regulations.' She said, 'I wonder what the dresses look like underneath.'

We all had our own pegs in the cloakroom. And I'd hung me hat up on this my own peg. And they were very long cloakrooms. And as I got to the bottom that hat hit me on the back—it had been thrown at me—my hat. And I heard this girl say, 'I'm not going to put mine with the dirty Bath Street lot' and you couldn't live it down. And the headmistress was a snob. I always remember her name, Mrs Thorn. And I heard her once say, some little thing we'd

done—'What would you expect from that place.' Quite a few of the
girls who were fairly comfortable, had good positions and got lovely
clothes and that kind of thing and—they'd sort of pull aside, they
wouldn't pass you on the stairs if they could help it. And they used
to look at us as if we were tramps in the street. And of course it used
to get my back up a bit and I said to one girl, I said, 'Well, I shan't
contaminate you and I'm not a tramp either.'

ANNIE WILSON (b. 1898 in Nottingham), in Thea Thompson (ed.),
Edwardian Childhoods, 1981

I remember the skin diseases of kids
I sat among at Rood End Infants School.
'We try to keep the clean books for the clean children,'
The weary, kind Headmaster told my mother.

JOHN ADLARD, *The Lichfield Elegies*, 1991

I'm 11. And I don't really know
my Two Times Table. Teacher says it's disgraceful
But even if I had the time, I feel too tired.
Ron's 5, Samantha's 3, Carole's 18 months,
and then there's Baby. I do what's required.

Mum's working. Dad's away. And so
I dress them, give them breakfast. Mrs Russell
moves in, and I take Ron to school.
Miss Eames calls me an old-fashioned word: Dunce.
Doreen Maloney says I'm a fool.

After tea, to the Rec. Pram-pushing's slow
but on fine days it's a good place, full

of larky boys. When 6 shows on the clock
I put the kids to bed. I'm free for once.
At about 7—Mum's key in the lock.

GAVIN EWART, 'Arithmetic', in *The Collected Ewart*, 1980

When I was fourteen or fifteen I was an odious little snob, but no
worse than other boys of my own age and class. I suppose there is no
place in the world where snobbery is quite so ever-present or where
it is cultivated in such refined and subtle forms as in an English
public school. Here at least one cannot say that English 'education'
fails to do its job. You forget your Latin and Greek within a few
months of leaving school—I studied Greek for eight or ten years,
and now, at thirty-three, I cannot even repeat the Greek alphabet—
but your snobbishness, unless you persistently root it out like the
bindweed it is, sticks by you till your grave.

At school I was in a difficult position, for I was among boys who,
for the most part, were much richer than myself, and I only went to
an expensive public school because I happened to win a scholarship.
This is the common experience of boys of the lower-upper-middle
class, the sons of clergymen, Anglo-Indian officials, etc., and the
effects it had on me were probably the usual ones. On the one hand
it made me cling tighter than ever to my gentility; on the other hand
it filled me with resentment against the boys whose parents were
richer than mine and who took care to let me know it. I despised
anyone who was not describable as a 'gentleman', but also I hated the
hoggishly rich, especially those who had grown rich too recently.
The correct and elegant thing, I felt, was to be of gentle birth but to
have no money. This is part of the *credo* of the lower-upper-middle
class. It has a romantic, Jacobite-in-exile feeling about it which is
very comforting.

But those years, during and just after the war, were a queer time
to be at school, for England was nearer revolution than she has been
since or had been for a century earlier. Throughout almost the whole

nation there was running a wave of revolutionary feeling which has since been reversed and forgotten, but which has left various deposits of sediment behind. Essentially, though of course one could not then see it in perspective, it was a revolt of youth against age, resulting directly from the war. In the war the young had been sacrificed and the old had behaved in a way which, even at this distance of time, is horrible to contemplate; they had been sternly patriotic in safe places while their sons went down like swathes of hay before the German machine guns. Moreover, the war had been conducted mainly by old men and had been conducted with supreme incompetence. By 1918 everyone under forty was in a bad temper with his elders, and the mood of anti-militarism which followed naturally upon the fighting was extended into a general revolt against orthodoxy and authority. At that time there was, among the young, a curious cult of hatred of 'old men'. The dominance of 'old men' was held to be responsible for every evil known to humanity, and every accepted institution from Scott's novels to the House of Lords was derided merely because 'old men' were in favour of it. . . . For several years it was all the fashion to be a 'Bolshie', as people then called it. England was full of half-baked antinomian opinions. Pacifism, internationalism, humanitarianism of all kinds, feminism, free love, divorce-reform, atheism, birth-control—things like these were getting a better hearing than they would get in normal times. And of course the revolutionary mood extended to those who had been too young to fight, even to public schoolboys. At that time we all thought of ourselves as enlightened creatures of a new age, casting off the orthodoxy that had been forced upon us by those detested 'old men'. We retained, basically, the snobbish outlook of our class, we took it for granted that we should continue to draw our dividends or tumble into soft jobs, but also it seemed natural to us to be 'agin the government'. We derided the OTC, the Christian religion, and perhaps even compulsory games and the Royal Family, and we did not realise that we were merely taking part in a world-wide gesture of distaste for war. Two incidents stick in my mind as examples of the queer revolutionary feeling of that time. One day the master who taught us English set us a kind of general knowledge paper of which one of the questions was, 'Whom do you consider the ten greatest men now living?' Of sixteen boys in the class (our average age was about seventeen) fifteen included Lenin in their list. This was at a snobbish expensive public school, and the date was 1920, when the horrors of the Russian Revolution were still fresh in everyone's mind. Also there were the so-called peace celebrations in 1919. Our elders had decided for us that we should celebrate peace in the traditional manner by whooping over the fallen foe. We were to march into the school-yard, carrying torches, and sing jingo songs of the type of 'Rule Britannia'. The boys—to their honour, I think—guyed the whole proceeding and sang blasphemous and seditious words to the tunes provided. I doubt whether things would happen in quite that manner now. Certainly the public schoolboys I meet nowadays, even the intelligent ones, are much more right-wing in their opinions than I and my contemporaries were fifteen years ago.

GEORGE ORWELL, The Road to Wigan Pier, 1937

I can't say that we were given any real sense of the problems of the world, or of how to attack them, other than in vague ideals of service, but then I have never heard of any school that did, and my own convictions are perhaps too extreme for me to expect to see them acted upon. Indeed it is impossible to see how any school, which is not directly attached in some way to an industrial or agricultural unit, and where boys and staff are both drawn from the monied classes, can hope to see the world picture of that class objectively. The mass production of gentlemen is their *raison-d'être*, and one can hardly suggest that they should adopt principles which would destroy them. The fact remains that the public schoolboy's attitude to the working-class and to the not-quite-quite has altered very little since the war. He is taught to be fairly kind and polite, provided of course they return the compliment, but their lives and needs remain as remote to him as those of another species. And I doubt very much if the same isn't true of the staff as well. I do remember hearing however that a master was sacked for taking part in left-wing politics outside the school, which if true, and I cannot vouch for the accuracy of the story, seems to me a shameful thing.

The only concrete suggestion I have to make here is that the staff might give up wearing those ridiculous black clothes (if they still do) which made them look like unsuccessful insurance agents, and certainly did not increase our respect for them; if we were allowed—and rightly—to wear blazers and flannel trousers, the staff as well might surely be allowed a sensible costume.

I suppose no one ever remembers actually being taught anything, though one remembers clearly enough when one failed to learn. My efforts at engineering which must have been as distressing to the very nice military man who taught that subject as they were boring to me—the sum total of my achievement was two battered ash-trays and any number of ruined tools—are still vivid.

Where one was more successful, one remembers only the idiosyncrasies of the masters, that X shouted in class—a horrible habit—that Y would come up behind one on a bicycle ride and pinch one's seat, that Z wore his cap like a racing-tout, and so on. For, as people, those who at one time or another have taught me stand out in my memory very clearly, far more clearly in fact than my friends, and this seems a common experience.

It is perhaps as well that teachers can never realize how intensely aware of their personalities their charges are, because if they could they would be too terrified to move or to open their mouths. A single act or remark is quite sufficient to queer the pitch. For example a certain master once caught me writing poetry in prep, writing a poem which I knew to be a bad one. He said, 'You shouldn't waste your sweetness on the desert air like this, Auden'; to-day I cannot think of him without wishing him evil.

W. H. AUDEN, 'Honour' (Gresham's School), in Graham Greene (ed.), *The Old School*, 1934

Because of our reduced circumstances my parents could not afford to send Peter and me to one of the posher preparatory schools.

(They were both old-fashioned Tories.) We attended the local Public Elementary School where, out of a large class of nearly forty pupils, we were almost the only middle-class children. Most of the others lived on 'the wrong side' of the Lisburn Road. Their clothes were different from ours—woollen balaclavas, laced boots with studs in the soles. Alongside them Peter and I must have appeared chubby and well-scrubbed. I noticed at once the skinny knees and snotty noses, but most of all the accent, abrasive and raucous as a football rattle. This I soon acquired in order to make myself less unacceptable. 'Len' us a mey-ek'—'Lend me a make' (a ha'penny). At home I would try to remember to ask for 'a slice of cake' and not 'a slice a' cey-ek', to refer to the 'door' and the 'floor' rather than 'doo-er' and 'floo-er'. By the age of six or seven I was beginning to lead a double life, learning how to recreate myself twice daily.

I made friends with the other pupils and started to explore the Lisburn Road. Belfast's more prosperous citizens have usually been careful to separate themselves safely from the ghettoes of the bellicose working classes. An odd exception is the Lisburn Road which runs south from the city centre. Intermittently for about three miles workers' tiny two-up-and-two-down houses squint across the road at the drawing rooms of dentists, doctors, solicitors: on the right, as you drive towards Lisburn, gardenless shadowy streets, on the left rhododendrons and rose bushes. Belfast laid bare, an exposed artery.

I spent much of my childhood drifting from one side to the other, visiting the homes of my new friends: the lavatory outside in the yard, stairs ascending steeply as you entered, low ceilings and no elbow-room at all. My first tea at Herbie Smith's was fried bread sprinkled with salt. Herbie came to our house and gasped when he saw the size of our back garden. For the first time I felt ashamed of our relative affluence. Our separate drawing and dining rooms, the hall with its wooden panelling, the lavatory upstairs were all novelties to Herbie. He seemed curious rather than envious. Every corner of the home I had taken for granted was illuminated by his gaze as by wintry sunlight.

Another pupil John McCluskey was often caned for being late. He delivered papers for Younger the newsagent. If the *Belfast Newsletter* was delayed, John without complaint or explanation would be standing at 9.30 in front of the class, his hand presented to the whistling cane and then hugged under his armpit as he stumbled over schoolbags to his desk. Should I have told the teacher that he delivered papers to *our* house? Sometimes, as though to drown his sorrows, John would swig the blue-grey sludge from one of the small white inkwells. Every December my father gave me a half-crown as a Christmas box for the paper boy, as he called him. I never told my father that the paper boy was in my class. On the doorstep John McCluskey and I behaved like strangers and avoided each other's eyes as the half-crown changed hands. Later in class the transaction would not be mentioned.

MICHAEL LONGLEY, 'Tu'penny Stung', in *Poetry Review*, 74: 4 (1985)

Public School boys are not merely conservatives; they are by nature totalitarian reactionaries. Nowhere else but in the Public Schools does the spirit of the Drones Club and Blandings Castle live on with such loyal enthusiasm; nowhere else may such embryo fogeyism or blimpishness pass quite unquestioned. Nowhere else is Socialism, that 'attempted corner in ideas', treated with such lofty disdain; and yet nowhere is an oligarchy of such uncompromising severity accepted without demur. Totalitarian reaction! And, if they cannot have it both ways, they would generally plunk for totalitarianism. They live in a régime that is by constitution and by popular rumour a free one, certainly freer at Eton than at many other schools, yet they subjugate themselves to a society in which in practice they have neither freedom of will, freedom of choice, nor freedom of action. They would never question this. To give one relevant example; it is remarkable that the existing rights of appeal against summary corporal punishment (to the housemaster, to the Headmaster and, by fanciful but untested tradition, to the President of Pop) remain virtually uninvoked. In fact they live a life of utter subservience to—

well, to an ideology, and what is more remarkable very few of them
think or talk of politics at all.

DAVID BENEDICTUS, *The Fourth of June*, 1962

> *The grace of Tullies eloquence doth excell*
> *any Englishmans tongue . . . my barbarous stile . . .*

The tongue our leaders use to cast their spell
was once denounced as 'rude', 'gross', 'base' and 'vile'

How fortunate we are who've come so far!

We boys can take old Hansards and translate
the British Empire into SPQR
but nothing demotic or too up-to-date,
and *not* the English that I speak at home,
not Hansard standards, and if Antoninus
spoke like delinquent Latin back in Rome
he'd probably get gamma double minus.

And so the lad who gets the alphas works
the hardest in his class at his translation
and finds good Ciceronian for Burke's:

a dreadful schism in the British nation.

TONY HARRISON, 'Classics Society, Leeds Grammar School
1552–1952', in *The School of Eloquence*, 1978

FRIENDS AND ENEMIES

At school each other's prompters, day by day.
Companions in the frolic or the fray . . .

CRABBE, 'The Schoolfellow', in *Posthumous Tales*, 1834

———

I found by experience, what before I could not believe, that every young gentleman, at his first coming to a boarding school, is generally looked upon with a great deal of contempt by the upper Scholars, who sometimes think too much of themselves. I asked one a question, he turned from me without condescending to give me an answer; a second laughed at me; and a third even gave me a knock on the pate.

'Master Michel Angelo', *Juvenile Sports and Pastimes*, 1776

This little child, while he was studying
His little primer, which he undertook,
Sitting at school, heard other children sing
O Alma Redemptoris from their book.
Close as he dared he drew himself to look,
And listened carefully to work and part
Until he knew the opening verse by heart.

He had no notion what this Latin meant
Being so young, so tender too, so green;
But in the end, one morning there, he went

And asked a comrade what the song might mean
And why it was in use. He was so keen
To know it that he went upon his knees
Begging the boy explain it if he please.

His comrade was a boy of senior station
And answered thus: 'This song in times gone by
Was made, they say, in prayer and salutation,
To greet our blessed Lady, now on high,
That she may reach to help us when we die,
And be our succour. That is all I know.
I can learn singing, but my grammar's slow.'

CHAUCER, 'The Prioress's Tale', in The Canterbury Tales,
probably begun c.1387

Unhappily, Dr Morgan was at that time dissatisfied with some points in the progress of his head class; and, as it soon appeared, was continually throwing in their teeth the brilliancy of my verses at eleven or twelve, by comparison with theirs at seventeen, eighteen, and even nineteen. I had observed him sometimes pointing to my-self, and was perplexed at seeing this gesture followed by gloomy looks, and what French reporters call 'sensation', in these young men, whom naturally I viewed with awe as my leaders,—boys that were called young men, men that were reading Sophocles (a name that carried with it the sound of something seraphic to my ears), and who never had vouchsafed to waste a word on such a child as myself. The day was come, however, when all that would be changed. One of these leaders strode up to me in the public play-ground; and, delivering a blow on my shoulder, which was not intended to hurt me, but as a mere formula of introduction, asked me, 'What the devil I meant by bolting out of the course, and annoying other people in that manner? Were "other people" to have no rest for me and my verses, which, after all, were horribly bad?' There might have been some difficulty in returning an answer to this address, but none was required. I was briefly admonished to see that I wrote worse for the future, or else—. At this *aposiopesis* I looked inquiringly at the speaker, and he filled up the chasm by saying, that he would 'annihilate' me.

THOMAS DE QUINCEY, *Confessions of an English Opium-Eater*, 1821; Bath Grammar School

Hark to that happy shout!—the school-house door
  Is open thrown, and out the younkers teem;
Some run to leap-frog on the rushy moor,
  And others dabble in the shallow stream,
Catching young fish, and turning pebbles o'er
  For mussel-clams. Look in that mellow gleam,
Where the retiring sun, that rests the while,
  Streams through the broken hedge! How happy seem
Those friendly schoolboys leaning o'er the stile,
  Both reading in one book!—Anon a dream,
Rich with new joys, doth their young hearts beguile,
  And the book's pocketed right hastily.
Ah, happy boys! well may ye turn and smile,
  When joys are yours that never cost a sigh.

JOHN CLARE, 'Evening Schoolboys', in *Poems*, 1935

I never heard to what influence or agency the improvement of the school was due, but as it existed down to 1850 it was little better than a charity school of a high grade. There was once a year a strange piece of archaism in the shape of an Examination or Probation Day, when we had to put in an appearance at eight o'clock in the morning, and to have our breakfast on the premises. All the arrangements were of the meanest and most barbarous character. Except that the *menu* was differentiated by the modern introduction of sausage rolls, three-cornered-tarts, and Bath buns, the scene was perchance, in its general

costume, not dissimilar from what it had been in the founder's lifetime. Of course the Merchant Taylors' Company could not afford to
find us our modest repast. For 200 boys it might have involved them
in an outlay of £10.

It long used to be considered a good joke to lay hold of every
newcomer to the establishment, and throw him into a large clothes-
chest upstairs as an introductory ceremony; it was at any rate a dry
christening; and if it did no good, it did little harm. It is curious how
a mere accident gave me a peculiar ascendency over nearly the whole
school. While I was in the fifth form, a schoolfellow (Fat Nelham)
attacked me one day, and I went for him. I was very strong, and I
thrashed him well. My reputation and prestige were placed on the
most solid foundation from that hour till the day on which I left. I
was honoured by the *sobriquet* of the 'Black Sheep', not by reason of
any misdemeanour of which I had to plead guilty, but on account of
the awe which my exploit inspired.

W. CAREW HAZLITT, *Memoirs*, 1897

Ye scenes of my childhood, whose loved recollection
Embitters the present, compared with the past;
Where science first dawn'd on the powers of reflection,
And friendships were formed, too romantic to last;

Where fancy yet joys to retrace the resemblance
Of comrades, in friendship and mischief allied;
How welcome to me your ne'er fading remembrance,
Which rests in the bosom, though hope is denied!

Again I revisit the hills where we sported,
The streams where we swam, and the fields where we fought;
The school where, loud warn'd by the bell, we resorted,
To pore o'er the precepts by pedagogues taught.

LORD BYRON, 'On a Distant View of the Village and
School of Harrow on the Hill', 1806

Eton,
May 22nd.

My dearest Mama,
I am sorry to say that my tormentors have not ceased to torment me
in the open manner which you speak of. This morning, I confess, I
am very sorry that I took my prayer book into Church, for on my return they took it from me by main force and kicked it backwards and
forwards through the mud, which has sadly injured it. They were
not, however, content with this, but about 6, after having carried
their main object of enclosing me in a corner, threw large bricks and
stones at me for a considerable time. Two or three hit me, but thank
God none on the face; many, however, whizzed close to my head—
the smallest were about the size of a half crown and the largest
of a common brick, most of them large pieces of the latter. It is
wonderful that I have escaped almost unhurt. Both my arms are of
the most beautiful mulatto colour with kicks and blows, and I
cannot use my left one much. I think how very fortunate I have been
not to lose an eye. I hope I shall not be disfigured when you come to
Eton.

JAMES MILNES GASKELL, *An Eton Boy 1820–30*,
ed. Charles Milnes Gaskell, 1939

Where are my friends? I am alone;
    No playmate shares my beaker:
Some lie beneath the churchyard stone,
    And some—before the Speaker;
And some compose a tragedy,
    And some compose a rondo;
And some draw sword for Liberty,
    And some draw pleas for John Doe.

Tom Mill was used to blacken eyes
    Without the fear of sessions;
Charles Medlar loathed false quantities

As much as false professions;
Now Mill keeps order in the land,
   A magistrate pedantic;
And Medlar's feet repose unscanned
   Beneath the wide Atlantic.

Wild Nick, whose oaths made such a din,
   Does Dr Martext's duty;
And Mullion, with that monstrous chin,
   Is married to a Beauty;
And Darrell studies, week by week,
   His Mant, and not his Manton;
And Ball, who was but poor at Greek,
   Is very rich at Canton.

And I am eight-and-twenty now;—
   The world's cold chains have bound me;
And darker shades are on my brow,
   And sadder scenes around me:
In Parliament I fill my seat,
   With many other noodles;
And lay my head in Jermyn Street,
   And sip my hock at Boodle's.

But often, when the cares of life
   Have set my temples aching,
When visions haunt me of a wife,
   When duns await my waking,
When Lady Jane is in a pet,
   Or Hoby in a hurry,
When Captain Hazard wins a bet,
   Or Beaulieu spoils a curry,—

For hours and hours I think and talk
   Of each remembered hobby;
I long to lounge in Poets' Walk,

To shiver in the lobby;
I wish that I could run away
From House, and Court, and Levée,
Where bearded men appear today
Just Eton boys grown heavy.

WINTHROP MACKWORTH PRAED (1802–39),
'Schoolfellows'

Tom's heart beat quick as he passed the great school field or close, with its noble elms, in which several games at football were going on, and tried to take in at once the long line of grey buildings, beginning with the chapel, and ending with the school-house, the residence of the head-master, where the great flag was lazily waving from the highest round tower. And he began already to be proud of being a Rugby boy, as he passed the school gates, with the oriel window above, and saw the boys standing there, looking as if the town belonged to them, and nodding in a familiar manner to the coach-man, as if any one of them would be quite equal to getting on the box, and working the team down street as well as he.

One of the young heroes, however, ran out from the rest, and scrambled up behind; where, having righted himself, and nodded to the guard, with 'How do, Jem?' he turned short round to Tom, and, after looking him over for a minute, began—

'I say, you fellow, is your name Brown?'

'Yes,' said Tom, in considerable astonishment; glad, however, to have lighted on some one already who seemed to know him.

'Ah, I thought so; you know my old aunt, Miss East, she lives somewhere down your way in Berkshire. She wrote to me that you were coming to-day, and asked me to give you a lift.'

Tom was somewhat inclined to resent the patronizing air of his new friend, a boy of just about his own height and age, but gifted with the most transcendent coolness and assurance, which Tom felt to be aggravating and hard to bear, but couldn't for the life of him help admiring and envying—especially when young my lord begins

263

hectoring two or three long loafing fellows, half porter, half stable-man, with a strong touch of the blackguard; and in the end, arranges with one of them, nicknamed Cooey, to carry Tom's luggage up to the school-house for sixpence.

'And heark 'ee, Cooey, it must be up in ten minutes, or no more jobs from me. Come along, Brown.' And away swaggers the young potentate, with his hands in his pockets, and Tom at his side.

'All right, sir,' says Cooey, touching his hat, with a leer and a wink at his comrades.

'Hullo tho',' says East, pulling up, and taking another look at Tom, 'this'll never do—haven't you got a hat?—we never wear caps here. Only the louts wear caps. Bless you, if you were to go into the quadrangle with that thing on, I—don't know what'd happen.' The very idea was quite beyond young Master East, and he looked unutterable things.

THOMAS HUGHES, *Tom Brown's Schooldays,* 1857

'I say,' he said presently, 'do you love your father?'

'Yes,' said Philip, colouring deeply; 'don't you love yours?'

'Oh yes . . . I only wanted to know,' said Tom, rather ashamed of himself now he saw Philip colouring and looking uncomfortable. He found much difficulty in adjusting his attitude of mind towards the son of Lawyer Wakem, and it had occurred to him that if Philip disliked his father, that fact might go some way towards clearing up his perplexity.

'Shall you learn drawing now?' he said by way of changing the subject.

'No,' said Philip. 'My father wishes me to give all my time to other things now.'

'What! Latin, and Euclid, and those things?' said Tom.

'Yes,' said Philip, who had left off using his pencil and was resting his head on one hand while Tom was leaning forward on both elbows and looking with increasing admiration at the dog and the donkey.

'And you don't mind that?' said Tom with strong curiosity.

'No, I like to know what everybody else knows. I can study what I like by and by.'

'I can't think why anybody should learn Latin,' said Tom. 'It's no good.'

'It's part of the education of a gentleman,' said Philip. 'All gentlemen learn the same things.'

'What! Do you think Sir John Crake, the master of the harriers, knows Latin?' said Tom, who had often thought he should like to resemble Sir John Crake.

'He learnt it when he was a boy, of course,' said Philip. 'But I dare say he's forgotten it.'

'Oh, well, I can do that, then,' said Tom, not with any epigrammatic intention, but with serious satisfaction at the idea that, as far as Latin was concerned, there was no hindrance to his resembling Sir John Crake. 'Only you're obliged to remember it while you're at school, else you've got to learn ever so many lines of "Speaker". Mr Stelling's very particular—did you know? He'll have you up ten times if you say "nam" for "jam" . . . he won't let you go a letter wrong, *I* can tell you.'

'Oh, I don't mind,' said Philip, unable to choke a laugh; 'I can remember things easily. And there are some lessons I'm very fond of. I'm very fond of Greek history and everything about the Greeks. I should like to have been a Greek and fought the Persians, and then have come home and have written tragedies, or else have been listened to by everybody for my wisdom, like Socrates, and have died a grand death.'

GEORGE ELIOT, The Mill on the Floss, 1860

At his school Tony made two friends, Austin Freeman and George Wilkinson.

George Wilkinson was a sturdy, thick-set boy with a bluff pink face, profusely freckled, and red hair. He was Tony's age. Austin Freeman was two years older; he was a large boy and bony; he had a dough-coloured face, thick grey eyes, full lips, a heavy nose, and a mat of black hair hung over his forehead.

Tony was tall for his age and slender, with quick blue eyes and an eager, forward-thrusting face under a shock of light hair.

George Wilkinson was great on history, and Austin Freeman, in a heavy, plodding sort of way, was good at mathematics. But Freeman had his limitations. He hated Homer.

One day he and Tony were swinging on a birch bough on the Heath, when Tony said suddenly:

'Do you like Homer?'

'I do not,' said Freeman firmly. 'I consider him a frightfully overrated poet. There's a lot of rot talked about Homer. About his making words like the sound of things. Poluphoisboio. Poluphoisboio doesn't sound a bit like murmuring.'

MAY SINCLAIR, *History of Anthony Waring*, 1927; the novel is about
a character born in 1850

My friends were of every kind—good, bad, and indifferent—including even a loutish youth, in some respects not unlike the traditional school bully, who on nearly my first day had pursued me into a remote corner of the playground with obviously bloodthirsty intentions, which had suddenly turned to extreme friendliness after he had gripped me by the shoulders and given me a shake or two. This surprising change of heart had been witnessed by another small boy, who presumed on it to approach nearer, was hailed with a sort of ogreish chuckle, and suffered such instant and outrageous punishment that in a way it was half comic.

FORREST REID, *Apostate*, 1926

The wide playgrounds were swarming with boys. All were shouting and the prefects urged them on with strong cries. The evening air was pale and chilly and after every charge and thud of the footballers the greasy leather orb flew like a heavy bird through the grey light. He kept on the fringe of his line, out of sight of his prefect, out of the reach of the rude feet, feigning to run now and then. He felt his body small and weak amid the throng of players and his eyes were weak and watery. Rody Kickham was not like that: he would be captain of the third line all the fellows said.

Rody Kickham was a decent fellow but Nasty Roche was a stink. Rody Kickham had greaves in his number and a hamper in the refectory. Nasty Roche had big hands. He called the Friday pudding dog-in-the-blanket. And one day he had asked:

—What is your name?

Stephen had answered: Stephen Dedalus.

Then Nasty Roche had said:

—What kind of a name is that?

And when Stephen had not been able to answer Nasty Roche had asked:

—What is your father?

Stephen had answered:

—A gentleman.

Then Nasty Roche had asked:

—Is he a magistrate?

He crept about from point to point on the fringe of his line, making little runs now and then. But his hands were bluish with cold. He kept his hands in the side pockets of his belted grey suit. That was a belt round his pocket. And belt was also to give a fellow a belt. One day a fellow said to Cantwell:

—I'd give you such a belt in a second.

Cantwell had answered:

—Go and fight your match. Give Cecil Thunder a belt. I'd like to see you. He'd give you a toe in the rump for yourself.

That was not a nice expression. His mother had told him not to speak with the rough boys in the college.

JAMES JOYCE, *A Portrait of the Artist as a Young Man*, 1916

I liked the smell of school, I liked hanging up my coat with the rest. Most of my time I was either the only girl at a boys' school or the only but one, and the other either much older or much younger. But I didn't know or understand other girls—I felt I was a boy who unfairly was not allowed to play rugger (and had no wish to play cricket). The only wretched thing was that when I started school I had also to start wearing black stockings which went right up under my button-below-the-knee knickers. How did they stay up? I think I must have had what was called a liberty bodice with long suspenders attached; I doubt if suspender design has changed very much in half a century. Apart from that I wore a blue serge skirt and a blue jersey, but I did at least have a school blazer with badge. I remember in my first term a boy approaching me with a tin and asking if I would like some bread and cheese. Not being allowed to eat cheese ('It wouldn't agree with you, dear') and supposing myself not to like it, I hesitated. But when he opened the tin it was hawthorn buds which I ate happily and still eat, though they seem rather tasteless now. I felt I was being admitted into the society. It was a nice feeling.

Naomi Mitchison, *Small Talk*, 1973

'I play nearly as rotten a game as you do, Fluff,' John said; 'but Scaife expects us to be Torpids, so we jolly well have to buck up. That bruise over your eye has taken off your painted-doll look. Now, if you're going to blub, you'd better get behind that hedge.'

Fluff exploded.

'This is a beastly hole,' he cried. 'And I loathe it. I'm going to write to my father and beg him to take me away.'

'You ought to be at a girls' school.'

'I hate everything and everybody. I thought you were my friend, the only friend I had.'

John was somewhat mollified.

'I am your friend, but not when you talk rot.'

'Verney, look here, if you'll be decent to me, I *will* try to stick it out. I wish I was like you; I do indeed. I wish I was like Scaife. Why, I'd sooner be the Duffer, freckles and all, than myself.'

John looked down upon the delicately-tinted face, the small, regular, girlish features, the red, quivering mouth. Suddenly he grasped that this was an appeal from weakness to strength, and that he, no older and but a little bigger than Fluff, had strength to spare, strength to shoulder burdens other than his own.

'All right,' he said stiffly; 'don't make such a fuss!'

'You'll have me for a friend, Verney?'

'Yes; but I ain't going to kiss your forehead to make it well, you know.'

'May I call you John, when we're alone? And I wish you'd call me Esmé, instead of that horrid "Fluff".'

John pondered deeply.

'Look here,' he said. 'You can call me John, and I'll call you Esmé, when we're Torpids. And now, you'd better cut back to the house. I must think this all out, and I can't think straight when I look at you.'

'May I call you John once?'

'You are the silliest idiot I ever met, bar none. Call me "John", or "Tom Fool", or anything; but hook it afterwards!'

'Yes, John, I will. You're the only boy I ever met whom I really wanted for a friend.' He displayed a radiant face, turned suddenly, and ran off. John watched him, frowning, because Fluff was a good little chap, and yet, at times, such a bore!

HORACE ANNESLEY VACHELL, *The Hill,* 1905

The school years, with their echoes of *Stalky and Co,* no less than *Eric, or Little by Little,* make merry reading. In the late twenties and the thirties it became fashionable for youngish writers to turn and rend the schools that had nurtured them. In tortured sentences they explained how tedious was the OTC, how trying the footer, how dreary the staff. Occasionally there were moments of excitement and light—a sonnet in the school magazine, perhaps, or one's gouache of the sanatorium specially commended by Mr Tunstall: but by and large the authors had all seen something nasty in the boot-hole and were not going to forget it.

No trace of sourness creeps into Rupert Ray's account, though one could have easily forgiven him a mild outburst on the subject of corporal punishment. This is excessive and takes quaint forms. He is beaten on the knuckles by Mr Radley for passing notes, and caned, in the same morning, for tampering with the classroom clock. His house-master gives him ten strokes in class for alleged impudence, the headmaster smacks him in the face and then beats him for breaking bounds, and here comes Mr Radley again, lashing out with a cane at Rupert's left palm (the other one has to be protected so that he can write out a thousand lines of Cicero) to discourage rebelliousness. Tears and a pep-talk follow this last chastisement, Mr Radley absent-mindedly holding the damaged hand the while. Shortly after, Doe is beaten up by the prefects and reduced to a semi-conscious state. But one feels less sympathy for the exhibitionist Doe. Manhandling doesn't come amiss to him. 'Do you know, I really think I like Radley better than anyone else in the world. I simply loved being whacked by him.'

Doe and Ray (yes, there's a joke about it) are born worshippers and Mr Radley is the first of their many heroes. He is none other than S. T. Radley, the finest bat in the Middlesex team, assistant house-master at Bramhall House, over six feet tall, with a powerful frame, square chin and grey eyes.

Arthur Marshall on *Tell England* by Ernest Raymond,
in *Girls will be Girls*, 1974

Wednesday was a half-holiday at Crichton House, and so, soon after dinner, Paul found himself marshalled with the rest in a procession bound for the football field. They marched two and two, Chawner and three of the other elder boys leading with the ball and four goal-posts ornamented with coloured calico flags, and Mr Blinkhorn and Mr Tinkler bringing up the rear.

Mr Bultitude was paired with Tom Grimstone, who, after eyeing him askance for some time, could control his curiosity no longer.

'I say, Dick,' he began, 'what's the matter with you this term?'

'My name is not Dick,' said Paul stiffly.

'Oh, if you're so particular then,' said Tom: 'but, without humbug, what is the matter?'

'You see a change then,' said Paul, 'you do see a difference, eh?'

'Rather!' said Tom expressively. 'You've come back what I call a beastly sneak, you know, this term. The other fellows don't like it; they'll send you to Coventry unless you take care.'

'I wish they would,' said Paul.

'You don't talk like the same fellow either,' continued Tom; 'you use such fine language, and you're always in a bait, and yet you don't stick up for yourself as you used to. Look here, tell me (we were always chums), is it one of your larks?'

'Larks!' said Paul, 'I'm in a fine mood for larks. No, it's not one of my larks.'

F. ANSTEY, *Vice Versa*, 1882

The other girls were beginning to notice the dispute, and they came crowding round to hear what it was all about. Most of them were in time to see Jean Murray walk off with her head in the air, just as the little new girl clenched her fists and crouched down as if to make a spring. Then the storm broke, and the Babe's fury was let loose among the fifty-five occupants of the junior playroom.

It was an easy matter, in that spring forward, to send some half dozen or so spinning out of her way, but Barbara did not stop to see what happened to them. All she wanted to do was to reach the arch offender of them all, the one who had dared to slight her father, and to hold him up to the ridicule of fifty-five girls.

Nobody quite knew what did happen on this unexampled occasion in the annals of Wootton Beeches; and certainly nobody stirred a finger to put a stop to it. All that the girls in the senior playroom could tell about it afterwards was that a sudden scuffle and several screams broke the hush and hum of voices on the other side of the curtain; and then Angela Wilkins dashed through the archway with a terrified look on her face, and seized Margaret by the arm.

'Oh come! do come!' she sobbed out in her fright. 'Barbara Berkeley has got Jean Murray down on the floor, and she's *killing* her!'

EVELYN SHARP, *The Youngest Girl in the School*, 1902

Trouble began on the very second day of term. Adah, in her new capacity of head girl, had pinned a paper on the notice board announcing a general meeting of the Dramatic Society for 4.15 in the studio. The old members turned up at the time named, to find a group of Hawthorners already in possession of the room. Adah, after waiting a minute, glanced at the clock and coughed significantly; then, as this produced no result, she remarked:

'Won't you be rather late if you're not getting home soon?'

'We don't much mind,' returned Annie Broadside easily.

'Well, the fact is, we want to use this room,' continued Adah. 'We're going to have a meeting.'

'I know. That's why we've come.'

Adah's eyebrows elevated themselves to an astonishing angle.

'You've come to our meeting?' she exclaimed incredulously.

'Certainly we have. Why not?'

Annie asked the question aggressively.

'Because you're not members of the Dramatic.'

'But we want to join.'

Adah turned to her friends, who stood looking scornfully at the intruders.

'Did you hear that?' she remarked. 'They actually want to join the Dramatic!'

'Cheek!' murmured Consie, and the others giggled.

'And why shouldn't we join?' flamed Gladys Wilks.

'Why? Because you're day girls, and the Dramatic's only for boarders. That's the reason.'

ANGELA BRAZIL, For the School Colours, 1918

'Ferguson, the House is getting jolly slack; something's got to be done.'

Ferguson sat up in his chair. Clarke had been quiet nearly the whole of hall; there was obviously something up.

'Oh, I don't know. Why, only a quarter of an hour ago I came across Collins and Brown playing stump cricket in the cloisters instead of studying Thucydides. That's what I call keenness.'

'What did you say to them?'

'Oh, I've forgotten now, but it was something rather brilliant. I know it was quite lost on them. The Shell can't appreciate epigram. They ought to read more Wilde. Great book *Intentions*. Ever read it, Clarke?'

'Oh, confound your Wildes and Shaws; that's just what I object to. Here are these kids, who ought to be working, simply wasting their time, thinking of nothing but games. Why, I was up in the House tutor's room last night and was glancing down the list of form orders. Over half the House was in double figures.'

'But, my good man, why worry? As long as the lads keep quiet in hall, and leave us in peace, what does it matter? Peace at any price, that's what I say; we get so little of it in this world, let us hang on to the little we have got.'

'But look what a name the House will get.'

'The House will get much the same reputation in the school as England has in Europe. The English as a whole are pleasure-loving and slack. They worship games; and, after all, the Englishman is a jolly sight better fellow than the average German or Frenchman.'

'Yes, of course he's a better fellow, but the rotten thing is that he might be a much better fellow still. If as a country we had only ourselves to think about, let us put up a god of sport. But we have not. We have to compete with the other nations of the world. And late cuts are precious little use in commerce. This athleticism is ruining the country. At any rate, I am not going to have it in the House. In hall they've got to work; and if their places in form aren't better next week there's going to be trouble.'

ALEC WAUGH, The Loom of Youth, 1917

Stalky curled gracefully round the stair-rail. 'Head in a drain-pipe. Full confession in the left boot. Bad for the honour of the house— very.'

'Shut up,' said Harrison. 'You chaps always behave as if you were jawin' us when we come to jaw you.'

'You're a lot too cheeky,' said Craye.

'I don't quite see where the cheek comes in, except on your part, in interferin' with a private matter between me an' Beetle after it has been settled by Prout.' Stalky winked cheerfully at the others.

'That's the worst of clever little swots,' said M'Turk, addressing the gas. 'They get made prefects before they have any tact, and then they annoy chaps who could really help 'em to look after the honour of the house.'

'We won't trouble you to do that!' said Craye hotly.

'Then what are you badgerin' us for?' said Beetle. 'On your own showing, you've been so beastly slack, looking after the house, that Prout believes it's a nest of money-lenders. I've told him that I've lent money to Stalky, and no one else. I don't know whether he believes me, but that finishes my case. The rest is *your* business.'

'Now we find out'—Stalky's voice rose—'that there is apparently an organised conspiracy throughout the house. For aught we know, the fags may be lendin' and borrowin' far beyond their means. *We* aren't responsible for it. We're only the rank and file.'

'Are you surprised we don't wish to associate with the house?' said M'Turk, with dignity. 'We've kept ourselves to ourselves in our

274

study till we were turned out, and now we find ourselves let in for—for this sort of thing. It's simply disgraceful.'

'Then you hector and bullyrag us on the stairs,' said Stalky, 'about matters that are your business entirely. You know we aren't prefects.'

'You threatened us with a prefect's lickin' just now,' said Beetle, boldly inventing as he saw the bewilderment in the faces of the enemy.

'And if you expect you'll gain anything from us by your way of approachin' us, you're jolly well mistaken. That's all. Good-night.'

They clattered upstairs, injured virtue on every inch of their backs.

RUDYARD KIPLING, *Stalky & Co.*, 1899

'Why the blazes didn't you wash the cups?' he said. 'I told you to do Pearson's work.'

Martin trembled. 'I forgot,' he said. 'I couldn't think of all the things Pearson did.'

'I should have thought that the washing of cups might have struck you as a fairly obvious thing to do.'

'Yes; I'm sorry.'

'The fact of the matter is, you're getting a bit above yourself. Just because you're clever you think you're everyone. Now you're too good to wash cups.'

'It wasn't that really, Leopard. I forgot.'

'Well you damned well mustn't forget. You're too good to keep awake. That's just as bad. Now get out, you little beast, and come to me after prayers.'

Martin went back to his Keats in misery. He could guess what was in store for him, but he could not be certain, because Spots might have recovered from his wrath by the appointed time and then he might treat the matter as a joke. But if Spots didn't recover . . . well, then he would be swiped. Martin had never been caned at his private school and this would be his first experience; he wondered how much it would hurt. Then fear came surging over him, not the dread of anything definite, but the hideous fear of the unknown. He was not so much afraid that he would be hurt as that he would show that he had been hurt: that was the deadly, the unpardonable, sin. He wished to heaven he had been swiped before so that he might know his own capacity for endurance. Keats became intolerable. House tea was a long-drawn agony. Discussion centred on the match and the brilliant play of Raikes.

'What did old Spots want?' asked Caruth. 'He seemed to be in the deuce of a hair.'

'Only about cleaning cups,' said Martin gloomily.

'Thank the Lord I'm not a study-slut. Was he very ratty?'

'Oh, not very. Flannery, you hog, pass the bread.'

The conversation had at any cost to be changed, and Martin was pleased when the general attention was directed to the colossal hoggishness of Flannery, who was mixing jam, sardines, and potted meat.

IVOR BROWN, *Years of Plenty*, 1915

The girls at Mellyfield developed very early a feeling for character. They were interested in their own personalities, which they displayed, discussed, and altered. They were very much aware of each other and studied each other's profiles in chapel or during concerts. They read psychology to each other on Sunday afternoons. Everyone knew, for instance, that Jenna's insincerity arose from a nervous opposition to circumstance; that Marise to live at all would have to break down her overpowering sense of order, that Hester since she was six had ruined all her friendships by her intolerance and that Ludmilla must be ignored when she squeaked at games because of a bad heredity.

So that Jenna (notoriously over-anxious to put herself in the right) resumed later to Marise: 'If we all can't bear Theodora it must be because she's aggressive, mustn't it? I mean it isn't as if she looked so awful, or smelled or anything, or were at all common. Now I do wonder *why* she—'

'She certainly is aggressive. She can't even do her hair without banging the things on her dressing-table about as though she were cooking.'

'Perhaps she's unhappy.'

'I don't suppose she's more unhappy than we are,' said Marise with some annoyance.

'But we at least do *know* we're unhappy.'

Marise, who saw where this was leading, said: 'Well, I don't think she need be asked about it her first term.'

'I do think she's got a good deal of personality,' said Jenna wistfully.

'Well, you try. You just have her in *your* dormitory. And besides, she snores.'

June was kind that year and Mellyfield beautiful. Classes gathered under the trees; girls, stepping in and out of the windows, crossed the lawns from shadow to shadow in fluttering red tunics; lime-flowers dropped on one's book in French. Theodora warmed a little to the spectacle. She distinguished herself as a young man in one of the Saturday night plays—these improvised, unrehearsed, in the manner of *commedie dell'arte*.

'You make a marvellous man,' said Jane and Ludmilla.

ELIZABETH BOWEN, *Friends and Relations*, 1931

I look back nostalgically upon those summer months spent either in the School Library discussing books with that dear man, Mr Bendel the librarian, listening to Tom Mitford play Bach in the Music School, reading poetry with Basil Ava and Rupert Hart-Davis, or leisurely sculling in a whiff up the Thames to Queen's Eyot and getting drunk on draught cider with Desmond Parsons in the long grass beside the river under a golden sun which never set. The last week was spent in exchanging photographs with my intimates, and succinctly writing over them To Tom, or Desmond, from Jim, for it was only in our last year that we addressed each other by christian names. What depths of promise, what bonds of affection lay in the discreet superscriptions! I suspect that these few simple pledges meant more to the givers and receivers than those expensively calf-bound and for the most part unreadable tomes perfunctorily distributed by previous generations. I still possess as many as thirty—with titles like 'Inside Sebastopol' (anonymous) and Wharton's 'Wits and Beaux'—given to my grandfather on his leaving Eton in 1863, and all uniformly signed 'from his affectionate friend'—who was probably nothing of the kind—followed by the initialled surname.

JAMES LEES-MILNE, *Another Self,* 1970

A playground, partly cobbled, partly cindered, lay in the L formed by the school buildings, where the letter writing had taken place, and the House, which contained the common room, the studies, the dining room and dormitories. The boys ran or drifted across it in twos and threes. 'Come and have a Jimmy Riddle, Bracher,' said a plump boy with two protruding front teeth to a tall dark boy standing hesitantly under the marble war memorial tablet in the lobby. Bracher assented, and the two went inside the urinals at the cobbled end of the playground. The urinals, smelling of a unique disinfectant, had been converted from the House's stabling and were surmounted by a now inappropriate cupola which had led them to be popularly known as the One Valve Receiver.

'What's up, Bracher?' said the plump boy, as they stood side by side. 'You look a bit putrid.'

ROY FULLER, *The Ruined Boys,* 1959

Not even the horrors of *North and Hilliard* could significantly diminish the peculiar sensation of being happy at school. I set off unnecessarily early each morning after impatiently consuming the cooked (but by some strange alchemy usually cold) breakfast that my mother insisted upon frying as the proper preparation for the day. I looked forward to seven out of the day's eight lesson periods. And I thought of the staff—Etchells and Walker as well as Goodfellow, Potter and Hodge—as my senior friends to be treated with a fraternal respect. If one cloud darkened my horizon it was not the prospect of the impending examinations nor the scramble to find a place in a university. It was the realisation that, as I was growing up, reality must now take the place of fantasy. I had become a far greater success in lessons than I had ever been on the playing field, and I had to adjust my life accordingly.

ROY HATTERSLEY, *A Yorkshire Boyhood*, 1983

Of course, I always claimed to be Irish, but an Irish boy who had been in the house about a year and a half longer than myself resented this claim. He went out of his way to hurt me, not only by physical acts of spite like throwing ink over my school-books, hiding my games-clothes, attacking me suddenly from behind corners, pouring water over my bed at night, but by continually forcing his bawdy humour on my prudishness, and inviting everybody to laugh at my disgust. He also built up a humorous legend of my hypocrisy and concealed depravity. I came near a nervous breakdown. School ethics prevented me from informing the housemaster of my troubles. The house-monitors, though supposed to keep order and preserve the moral tone of the house, never interfered in any case of bullying among the juniors. I tried violent resistance, but as the odds were always heavily against me this merely encouraged the ragging. Complete passive resistance would probably have been wiser. I got accustomed to bawdy-talk only during my last two years at the school, and had been a soldier for some little time before I got hardened and could reply in kind to insults.

G. H. Rendall, the then Headmaster at Charterhouse, is reported to have innocently said at a Headmasters' Conference: 'My boys are amorous, but seldom erotic.' Few cases of eroticism, indeed, came to his notice; I remember no more than five or six big rows during my time at Charterhouse, and expulsions were rare. The housemasters knew little about what went on in their houses, their living quarters being removed from the boys'. Yet I agree with Rendall's distinction between 'amorousness' (by which he meant a sentimental falling in love with younger boys) and eroticism, or adolescent lust. The intimacy that frequently took place was very seldom between an elder boy and the object of his affection—that would have spoiled the romantic illusion—but almost always between boys of the same age who were not in love, and used each other as convenient sex-instruments. So the atmosphere was always heavy with romance of a conventional early-Victorian type, complicated by cynicism and foulness.

ROBERT GRAVES, *Goodbye to all that*, 1929

The remarkable thing about Orwell was that alone among the boys he was an intellectual and not a parrot for he thought for himself, read Shaw and Samuel Butler and rejected not only St Wulfric's, but the war, the Empire, Kipling, Sussex, and Character. I remember a moment under a fig-tree in one of the inland boulevards of the seaside town, Orwell striding beside me and saying in his flat, ageless voice: 'You know, Connolly, there's only one remedy for all diseases.' I felt the usual guilty tremor when sex was mentioned and hazarded, 'You mean going to the lavatory?' 'No—I mean Death!' He was not a romantic, he had neither use for the blandishments of the drill sergeant who made us feel character was identical with boxing nor for the threats of the chaplain with his grizzled cheektufts and his gospel of a Jesus of character who detested immorality and swearing as much as he loved the Allies. 'Of course, you realize, Connolly,' said Orwell, 'that, whoever wins this war, we shall emerge a second-rate nation.'

Orwell proved to me that there existed an alternative to character, Intelligence. Beaton showed me another, Sensibility. He had a charming, dreamy face, enormous blue eyes with long lashes and wore his hair in a fringe. His voice was slow, affected and creamy. He was not good at games or work but he escaped persecution through good manners, and a baffling independence. We used to mow the lawn together behind an old pony, sit eating the gooseberries in the kitchen garden, or pretend to polish brass in the chapel; from Orwell I learnt about literature, from Cecil I learnt about art. He occupied his spare time drawing and painting and his holidays in going to the theatre.

On Saturday nights, when the school was entertained in the big schoolroom by such talent as the place could offer, when Mr Potter had shown lantern slides of *Scrooge* or Mr Smedley, dressed up like a pirate at a P. & O. gala, had mouthed out what he called 'Poethry'—there would be a hush, and Cecil would step forward and sing, 'If you were the only girl in the World and I was the only boy.' His voice was small but true, and when he sang these sentimental songs, imitating Violet Loraine or Beatrice Lillie, the eighty-odd Wulfricians felt there could be no other boy in the world for them, the beetling chaplain forgot hell-fire and masturbation, the Irish drill-sergeant his bayonet practice, the staff refrained from disapproving, and for a moment the whole structure of character and duty tottered and even the principles of hanging on, muddling through, and building empires were called into question.

CYRIL CONNOLLY, Enemies of Promise, 1938

Percival Mandeville, the perfect boy,
Was all a schoolmaster could wish to see—
Upright and honourable, good at games,
Well-built, blue-eyed; a sense of leadership
Lifted him head and shoulders from the crowd.
His work was good. His written answers, made
In a round, tidy and decided hand,
Pleased the examiners. His open smile
Enchanted others. He could also frown
On anything unsporting, mean or base,
Unworthy of the spirit of the school
And what it stood for. Oh the dreadful hour
When once upon a time he frowned on me!

Friends and Enemies

Just what had happened I cannot recall—
Maybe some bullying in the dormitory;
But well I recollect his warning words:
'I'll fight you, Betjeman, you swine, for that,
Behind the bike shed before morning school.'
So all the previous night I spewed with fear.
I could not box: I greatly dreaded pain.
A recollection of the winding punch
Jack Drayton once delivered, blows and boots
Upon the bum at Highgate Junior School,
All multiplied by X from Mandeville,
Emptied my bladder. Silent in the dorm
I cleaned my teeth and clambered into bed.
Thin seemed pyjamas and inadequate
The regulation blankets once so warm.
'What's up?' 'Oh, nothing.' I expect they knew . . .

And, in the morning, cornflakes, bread and tea,
Cook's Farm Eggs and a spoon of marmalade,
Which heralded the North and Hilliard hours
Of Latin composition, brought the post.
Breakfast and letters! Then it was a flash
Of hope, escape and inspiration came:
Invent a letter of bad news from home.
I hung my head and tried to look as though,
By keeping such a brave stiff upper lip
And just not blubbing, I was noble too.
I sought out Mandeville. 'I say,' I said,
'I'm frightfully sorry I can't fight today.
I've just received some rotten news from home:
My mater's very ill.' No need for more—
His arm was round my shoulder comforting:
'All right, old chap. Of course I understand.'

JOHN BETJEMAN, *Summoned by Bells*, 1960

I was standing at the end of the lower playground and annoying Mr Samuels, who lived in the house just below the high railings. Mr Samuels complained once a week that boys from the school threw apples and stones and balls through his bedroom window. He sat in a deck chair in a small square of trim garden and tried to read the newspaper. I was only a few yards from him. I was staring him out. He pretended not to notice me, but I knew he knew I was standing there rudely and quietly. Every now and then he peeped at me from behind his newspaper, saw me still and serious and alone, with my eyes on his. As soon as he lost his temper I was going to go home. Already I was late for dinner. I had almost beaten him, the newspaper was trembling, he was breathing heavily, when a strange boy, whom I had not heard approach, pushed me down the bank.

I threw a stone at his face. He took off his spectacles, put them in his coat pocket, took off his coat, hung it neatly on the railings, and attacked. Turning round as we wrestled on the top of the bank, I saw that Mr Samuels had folded his newspaper on the deck chair and was standing up to watch us. It was a mistake to turn round. The strange boy rabbit-punched me twice. Mr Samuels hopped with excitement as I fell against the railings. I was down in the dust, hot and scratched and biting, then up and dancing, and I butted the boy in the belly and we tumbled in a heap. I saw through a closing eye that his nose was bleeding. I hit his nose. He tore at my collar and spun me round by the hair.

'Come on! come on!' I heard Mr Samuels cry.

We both turned towards him. He was shaking his fists and dodging about in the garden. He stopped then, and coughed, and set his panama straight, and avoided our eyes, and turned his back and walked slowly to the deck chair.

We both threw gravel at him.

'I'll give him "Come on!" ' the boy said, as we ran along the playground away from the shouts of Mr Samuels and down the steps on to the hill.

We walked home together. I admired his bloody nose. He said that my eye was like a poached egg, only black.

'I've never seen such a lot of blood,' I said.

He said I had the best black eye in Wales, perhaps it was the best black eye in Europe; he bet Tunney never had a black eye like that.

'And there's blood all over your shirt.'

'Sometimes I bleed in dollops,' he said.

On Walter's Road we passed a group of high school girls, and I cocked my cap and hoped my eye was as big as a bluebag, and he walked with his coat flung open to show the bloodstains.

DYLAN THOMAS, *A Portrait of the Artist as a Young Dog*, 1940

Tony was always being pulled up with a shock by Freeman's limitations. It meant that you couldn't talk to him about anything that mattered. To be sure, there were other things: football, white mice, Lowson minor's form at cricket, the eccentricities of Monsieur Poupart, the French master, Tony's bull terrier pup, Peter, what you were going to do in the holidays, how long it took to walk from Jack Straw's Castle to the Spaniards, the best sort of chocolates, sailing Freeman's model yacht on the White Stone pond, and whether you liked lemonade or ginger-beer best. Oh, a lot of things.

It was awful Freeman's not liking Homer, but Tony had chosen Freeman for his friend and he was going to stick to him, Homer or no Homer.

MAY SINCLAIR, *History of Anthony Waring*, 1927

Sunday was the most civilized day of all. In the afternoon I would generally go for a walk with Geoffrey Forbes. If we were going towards Milton, we would knock on the door of a grim-looking cottage near the stream, and buy large pieces of cake from the woman who lived there. The passage was so dark and stale-smelling that I often wondered about the cake, but I would soon be hungry enough to break large lumps off and eat them with Geoffrey.

As we had both been at school for two years we were allowed to carry umbrellas. I never had one, but Geoffrey always flourished his.

He would wave it and recite to me as we walked along. Suddenly he would stop in the middle of the road and ask me if I had enjoyed Hamlet's speech. If I showed no pleasure he would begin to shout, 'You little sissy, you can't think about anything but yourself.' He would poke me with the umbrella, and once he tried to tie me to a tree with my scarf.

When he was tired of trying to punish my vanity he would say, 'I'll sing to you.' He set his face very carefully, then began, 'Hark, hark, the lark at Heaven's Gate sings,' or 'Who is Sylvia, what is she?' It always seemed to be Schubert.

DENTON WELCH, Maiden Voyage, 1943

Outside the whistled gang-call, *Twelfth Street Rag*,
then a Tarzan yodel for the kid who's bored,
whose hand's on his liana . . . no, back
to Labienus and his flaming sword.
Off laikin', then to t'fish' oil all the boys,
off tartin', off to t'flicks but on, on, on,
the foldaway card table, the green baize,
De Bello Gallico and lexicon.

It's only his jaw muscles that he's tensed
into an enraged *shit* that he can't go;
down with polysyllables, he's against
all pale-face Caesars, *for* Geronimo.

He shoves the frosted attic skylight, shouts:

Ah bloody can't ah've gorra Latin prose.

His bodiless head that's poking out's
like patriarchal Cissy-bleeding-ro's.

TONY HARRISON, 'Me Tarzan', in The School of Eloquence, 1978

Good cloth makes good divided skirts with pleats. They swing as the younger children run. Until the Second World War there were purple knee socks for the younger children and green wool stockings for the older girls, but in wartime wool came in beige or fawn. The Founder in her later years, although embracing socialism in spite of its threats to her and her institution, was heard to say, 'I do hope that nice Mr Attlee will reintroduce some colour somewhere in our lives. The children's socks are so lack-lustre.'

The weakening elastic of the knicker and the knee sock. Girls in wartime and post-war stopped twice as often to hitch up at waist or knee. And shoes were worse. Good children's shoes for girls of sizes over four were unavailable, and Erica and Mousey in Remove both had strong boys'-type walking shoes.

They were not friends as yet, however. Here was Erica, flanked by Judy and by Penny. Cordelia was with them too. And Mousey wandered on her own because she could not feel exactly easy with Anne Browne. She'd slipped away from her at tea. The polished floor, still lavender-fresh because the Easter term was only one week old and the smell of chalk and wellingtons and disinfectant had not yet taken hold.

There was Erica ahead along the corridor towards the exit from the Founder's End to the cloisters. She was holding above her head a bag of peardrops and swinging it. And Mousey, seeing this, hung back and bent to hitch one knee sock up. 'You're always hanging around,' said Judy once.

I must not hang around, thought Mousey now, rubbing the toe of her new heavy shoes, size six for still growing feet. There are some snapshots of her on her mother's desk about this age. They've faded and you cannot see the face too well, but you can see the shine on her new shoes. Mousey here is standing leaning on a trellis just outside her father's Wiltshire vicarage. The trellis leans as well. It must be summer since she's wearing a check gingham frock. But the light is grey.

To tell the truth she really quite liked wearing a uniform. Her own clothes were cast-offs mostly, from a cousin five years older than herself. Shoes and uniform were the only brand-new things she had.

Erica stood with the bag of peardrops, calling out, as was her wont: 'Those who don't ask don't get. Those who ask don't get.'

Mousey stood and looked along the corridor. Once on her way she must not hesitate. Walk past them or go back the way she came and take a different route down to the form room? She did the first, walked past them on her heavy clumping shoes and did not look in their direction once. You had to not look as though you wanted people, then you might get people interested. That was the way to get on in a world which had no artifice. Knack and charm were not admired: you had to find them on your own in later life.

ELIZABETH NORTH, *Dames*, 1981

What endless discussions of tactics and strategy we used to hold after supper! I still think I gave very good advice to those love-lorn maidens on how to deal with each other. But whenever the advice happened to be 'Hold off for a bit', like many wiser and older they couldn't take it. One of my afflicted friends I think bound all raves into a nutshell when she said to me:

'It's so heartless to like Patsy better than me, when you think how I filled her hot-water-bottle for her every night of the winter term. I don't think Patsy would have filled her hot-water-bottle for her every night—at least I'm sure she wouldn't have done it in quite the same way.'

THEODORA BENSON, in Graham Greene (ed.), *The Old School*, 1934

I entered the house, encountering in the hall its familiar exhalation of carbolic soap, airing blankets, and cold Irish stew—almost welcoming after the fog outside—and mounted the staircase towards tea. A thick black stripe of paint divided the upper, and yellow, half of the wall from the magenta dado beneath. Above this black line was another, mottled and undulating, where passers-by, up and down the stairs, rested arm or shoulder, discolouring the distemper in a slanting band of grey. Two or three boys were as usual standing in front of the notice-board on the first floor, their eyes fixed on the half-sheets of paper attached by drawing-pins to the green baize, gazing at the scrawled lists and regulations as if intent on a tape-machine liable at any moment to announce the winner. There was nothing more recent than one of the recurrent injunctions emanating from Le Bas, our housemaster, requiring that all boots should be scraped on the scraper, and then once more scoured on the door-mat on entering the hall, to avoid dispersion of mud throughout the house. On the corner of this grubby fiat Stringham, some days before, had drawn a face in red pencil. Several pairs of eyes were now resting glassily on that outward protest against the voice of authority.

Since the beginning of the term I had messed with Stringham and Templer; and I was already learning a lot from them. Both were a shade older than myself, Stringham by about a year. The arrangement was in part a matter of convenience, dictated by the domestic economy of the house: in this case the distribution of teas. I liked and admired Stringham: Templer I was not yet sure about. The latter's boast that he had never read a book for pleasure in his life did not predispose me in his favour: though he knew far more than I of the things about which books are written. He was also an adept at breaking rules, or diverting them to ends not intended by those who had framed them. Having obtained permission, ostensibly at his parents' request, to consult an oculist, Templer was spending that day in London. It was unlikely that he would cut this visit short enough to enable him to be back in time for tea, a meal taken in Stringham's room.

When I came in, Stringham was kneeling in front of the fire, employing a paper-knife shaped like a scimitar as a toasting-fork. Without looking up, he said: 'There is a jam crisis.'

ANTHONY POWELL, *A Question of Upbringing*, 1951

'David, old chap,' he said, 'I don't believe two fellows ever had such a good time as we've had, and it would be rot to pretend not to be sorry that this bit of it has come to an end. I dare say we shall have splendid times together again, but there's no doubt that this is over. On the other hand, it would be equal rot not to feel jolly thankful for it. The chances were millions to one against our ever coming across each other at all. So buck up, as I said.'

David had rolled over on to his face, but at this he sat up, picking bits of dry grass out of his hair.

'Yes, that's so,' he said. 'But it will be pretty beastly without you. I shan't find another friend like you———'

'You'd jolly well better not,' interrupted Frank.

David could not help laughing.

'I suppose we're rather idiots about each other,' he said.

'I dare say. But it's too late to remedy that now. Oh, David, it's a good old place this. Look at the pitch there! What a lot of ripping hours it's given to generations of fellows, me among them. There's the roof of house through the trees, do you see? You can just see the end window of our dormitory. I wonder if happiness soaks into a place, so that if the famous Professor Pepper———'

'Oh, mammalian blood?' said David.

'What's that? Oh yes, the crime at Naseby. Same one. I wonder if he would find a lot of happiness-germs all over the shop.'

'I could do with a few,' said David, with a sudden return to melancholy.

'No, you couldn't. You've got plenty of them, as it is. . . . Lord, there's that rotten speech I have to make at house-supper. What am I to say?'

'Oh, usual thing. Say Adams is a good fellow, and we're all good fellows, and it's a good house, and a good school, and a good everything—hurrah.'

'That's about it,' said Frank. 'Oh, there's one other thing, David. Look after Jevons a bit, will you? He's turning into rather a jolly little kid.'

E. F. BENSON, *David Blaize*, 1916

NOT CRICKET

In the course of my three years at school both the ilex and mulberry trees took on an emotional significance; under the mulberry a friend whose brother at that time captained the Winchester eleven, and who was herself our only overhand bowler, criticized my behaviour on an occasion, saying I had done something that was not cricket.

ELIZABETH BOWEN, 'The Mulberry Tree',
in Graham Greene (ed.), *The Old School*, 1934

Girls! although I am a woman
I always try to appear human

Unlike Miss So-and-So whose greatest pride
Is to remain always in the VI Form and not let down the side

Do not sell the pass dear, don't let down the side,
That is what this woman said and a lot of balsy stuff beside
(Oh the awful balsy nonsense that this woman cried.)

Girls! I will let down the side if I get a chance
And I will sell the pass for a couple of pence.

STEVIE SMITH, 'Girls!', in *Collected Poems*, 1975

Girls' games, so far as *schools* of about the same time were concerned, were Hockey, Lacrosse, Net-ball, and, bearing some resemblance to a primitive form of cricket, Stool-ball: all played in whatever length of skirt was normal wear. A form of short gym tunic, worn over knickers, was in being by something like the 1890s. Boys had Squash and Fives; and the ancient art of Fencing, not denied to girls, was at least available if one wanted it. Ringoal, a hybrid form of Quoits playable by both sexes, enjoyed a burst of popularity in the later 1880s when the 'risks' attendant on this 'New and Charming Game' evoked a sardonic comment in *Punch* from George du Maurier (1888). Hockey (for either sex) was, like the already mentioned Badminton a '70s version of an older game, Badminton being called after the Duke of Beaufort's Gloucestershire seat where it was first played by J. L. Baldwin. Though a late arrival in England, the game they renamed Lacrosse was being taken over by Canadian settlers from the Red Indians in Early Victorian days.

F. GORDON ROE, *The Victorian Child*, 1959

If I were to try to describe more particularly the different things we were induced to do at school I am afraid that many of them would nowadays seem quite trivial. Nevertheless, at the time we found them interesting and diverting, and if their purpose was no more than to relieve the monotony of our education they were entirely successful. I doubt if that was their only purpose, or, indeed, their real purpose. I believe that they were intended by our teachers as a means of encouraging us to remain eager and curious. Our teachers knew, just as well as our parents, the kind of adult world into which we would enter in the first year of our teens. If we followed the most common pattern we would become 'factorified' in a matter of months, old before our time, anxious to give the impression that we too were as morose, taciturn, and matter-of-fact as our elder work-mates appeared to be.

When I left school I had no particular regret at the parting. By that time the first World War was half-way through, there was a shortage of labour, and life in the mill had become easier. But, like my parents, I too soon began to think of my schooldays, not as days on which we had to swot, but as those tingling frosty mornings on which, with the other lads, I set out for school babbling about football with not a care in the world.

George Woodcock, in Brian Inglis (ed.), *John Bull's Schooldays*, 1961

In deadly silence the School watched the flight of the ball. It sailed high and straight towards the goal. 'It's over,' murmured the Chief excitedly. But as the ball neared the posts it travelled slower, a slight breeze caught it, blew it over to the right. It hit the right post and fell back into play. As the full-back returned it to mid-field the whistle blew for no-side.

'School, three cheers for the House!' shouted Livingstone.

'House, three cheers for the School!' responded Richards.

And then everyone poured over the ropes on to the field.

'Never mind, you men,' said Simonds; 'it was a damned fine show and better than fifty wins.'

The House was proud of its side. As the fifteen trooped across the courts on the way to the changing-room the House lined up by the chains of the Sixth Form green, and cheered them.

'Well played, Caruthers!' shouted someone.

It was Gordon's first taste of real success.

That night there was a big feed in No. 19. They were all out of training for three days; and they made the most of it. During the last fortnight they had been allowed only fruit between meals.

'It's the finest performance since I've been in the House,' Mansell declared. 'Meredith's Two Cock wasn't in it. Their side was twice as strong on paper, and my Lord, we gave it them.'

'Yes,' said Lovelace, 'and you wait till this side is the Three Cock; there'll be a bit of a change then.'

'You're right there,' shouted Mansell. 'We shan't pull it off this year, nor the year after that; but you wait and see what'll happen in 1915. That's the year when the House will revive the great days of Trench. My lads, we shan't regret the lean years when the years of plenty come and the Three Cock Cup is back on the old oak sideboard. Our day will come.'

ALEC WAUGH, *The Loom of Youth*, 1917

All recreations and sports of scholars would be meet for gentlemen. Clownish sports, or perilous, or yet playing for money are no way to be admitted. The creations of the studious are as well to be looked unto, as the study of the rest: that none take hurt by his study, either for mind or body, or any way else.

Yet here of the other side, very great care is to be had in the moderating of their recreation. For schools, generally, do not take more hindrance by any one thing, than by over-often leave to play. Experience teacheth, that this draweth their minds utterly away from their books, that they cannot take pains, for longing after play and talking of it; as also devising means to procure others to get leave to play: so that ordinarily when they are but in hope thereof, they will do things very negligently; and after the most play they are evermore far the worst.

JOHN BRINSLEY, *Ludus Literarius; or the Grammar Schoole*, 1621

He was as useless and ill at ease with cricket as with football, nor in spite of all his efforts could he ever throw a ball or a stone. It soon became plain, therefore, to everyone, that Pontifex was a young muff, a molly-coddle, not to be tortured, but still not to be rated highly. He was not, however, actively unpopular, for it was seen that he was quite square *inter pares*, not at all vindictive, easily pleased, perfectly free with whatever little money he had, no greater lover of his school work than of the games, and generally more inclinable to moderate vice than to immoderate virtue.

These qualities will prevent any boy from sinking very low in the opinion of his school-fellows; but Ernest thought he had fallen lower than he probably had, and hated and despised himself for what he,

as much as anyone else, believed to be his cowardice. He did not like
the boys whom he thought like himself. His heroes were strong and
vigorous, and the less they inclined towards him the more he worshipped them. All this made him very unhappy, for it never occurred
to him that the instinct which made him keep out of games for
which he was ill-adapted, was more reasonable than the reason which
would have driven him into them. Nevertheless he followed his
instinct for the most part, rather than his reason. *Sapiens suam si
sapientiam nôrit.*

SAMUEL BUTLER, The Way of All Flesh, 1903

Those cross-country runs!—how hateful
They were. One finished the course—
It was the only way home.

Jumping too. Light and long of leg, I
Could jump considerable heights if necessary.
They supposed that I liked it.

I told the head I couldn't jump this year,
It was my last year, my ankles were weak.
He sent me to a doctor, a rude man,
Who diagnosed a different weakness.

So off to the field. At the first jump
I sprained my ankles. The head was silent.
But thereafter, three times a week, I cycled
To the hospital, where a pretty nurse
Massaged my ankles. How content I was.

When summer came, I gave the master in charge
Of cricket to believe I had opted for tennis,
The master in charge of tennis I permitted
To assume I was playing cricket.

Thirty years later, in error, I attend
The Old Boys' Dinner as a distinguished guest.
Says the Chairman, 'The School will always remember
Dennis Enright as—'
(Oh, I think, perhaps I've underestimated them)
'As a fine sportsman.'

D. J. ENRIGHT, 'Sports', in *The Terrible Shears*, 1973

The lesson which experience usually teaches to the temper of a schoolboy is, that strength, and power, and cunning, will inevitably govern in society; as to reason, it is out of the question, it would be hissed or laughed out of company. With respect to social virtues, they are commonly amongst school-boys so much mixed with party spirit, that they mislead even the best dispositions. A boy at home, whose pleasures are all immediately connected with the idea of self, will not feel a sudden enlargement of mind from entering a public school.

MARIA and R. L. EDGEWORTH, *Essays on Practical Education*,
new edn. 1822

1724.

He discovered a great ambition to excel, which roused him to counteract his indolence. He was uncommonly inquisitive; and his memory was so tenacious, that he never forgot any thing that he either heard or read. Mr Hector remembers having recited to him eighteen verses, which, after a little pause, he repeated *verbatim*, varying only one epithet, by which he improved the line.

He never joined with the other boys in their ordinary diversions: his only amusement was in winter, when he took a pleasure in being drawn upon the ice by a boy barefooted, who pulled him along by a garter fixed round him; no very easy operation, as his size was remarkably large. His defective sight, indeed, prevented him from enjoying the common sports; and he once pleasantly remarked to me, 'how wonderfully well he had contrived to be idle without them.'

BOSWELL, *Life of Johnson*, 1791

We were *obsessed* with games—team-games, lacrosse one term, hockey in the next, cricket in the third, standing in highest repute, though one could also obtain half-colours (I had almost written 'a half-Blue') for swimming, gym, dancing, etc. We all played the team-games, compulsorily, every school-day afternoon, the whole school being divided by the games mistresses into about eighteen elevens which played one another on three days in the week, and house elevens which played on the two others. The full list of elevens, written in pencil, hung in the long corridor between No. III and No. IV Houses, and at intervals the sight of the senior games mistress advancing upon it, india-rubber in hand, collected a crowd eager for first news of promotions. There were at least four elevens which played outside matches; there were also four to each house, competing for house cups. 'Fielding practice' or its equivalent, between breakfast and morning school, was compulsory; 'watching matches' on a Saturday afternoon all but compulsory until the Girl Guide Movement (Heaven bless it!) was introduced and provided alternative recognised occupation with the additional chance of getting outside the place; when we beat Wycombe Abbey in the great match of the year we had a school holiday. It was all like the Boy's School Story raised to the *nth*. I have no personal objection to games as such; in after years I enjoyed both playing lacrosse and watching cricket, when I was not forced to; and only mildly regretted the fact that, as there were only three tennis courts for a school of three hundred, I had gained no proficiency in a game much more socially useful than those which require twenty or more other participants. But I do feel that the games-worship at Roedean gives some support to the complaints of anti-feminists that women ought not to be allowed to do the things that men do, because they have no sense of proportion and drive everything to death.

MARGARET COLE, *Growing Up Into Revolution*, 1949

Jennifer had been in the First for four years, first as wing half and for the last two seasons as centre. She had been a person of consequence ever since the two had played hockey at all. They had never done more than address shy smiles to her. Now, Captain and a Senior Prefect, she seemed more above them than ever. They waited for her, wondering. She smiled and joined them, and did not begin to speak until they had walked a few steps and were out of earshot of the rest of the crowd.

'I want you two to pull up your socks,' she said. 'I want you in the First, because I know I can depend on you. But you mustn't think it's going to be quite easy. It must have seemed like it, last year, when you knew who was leaving'—she nodded and her eyes twinkled at the beginning of their confused protests.—'Naturally. But there's Amabel. I'm not a bit sure about Amabel, she's so erratic. But she's so good sometimes that she's got to be tried. Then there's that new kid. She comes from Roedean—her people want her at home or something—so she's sure to be good. She was in their Second. And there's Joyce—it's a question of either her or Amabel as half. That's all. I thought it was only fair to tell you. But I'd like you two to get in—'

She left them, with a friendly little wave as she rode off in the opposite direction. They stood looking after her, and Elizabeth drew a long breath of amazement.

'That was jolly decent of her!' she said.

Throughout that year, nothing made them feel so grown up as that sudden confidence of Jennifer's, which treated them almost as equals. Binkie had entrusted them with a certain responsibility, but this made them see that they were on the way to becoming person-ages. They were too busy and, up to the present, too matter-of-fact, to indulge in 'raves' as did some of their weaker sisters, but they had a very healthy respect for Captains and Prefects and people who were outstanding at games, or who had reputations as leaders. They caught the glance of some of the crowd on them as Jennifer threw them that friendly wave, and, seeing no surprise in it, felt dimly some of Jennifer's glory reflected on themselves. It was a pleasant feeling. But Evelyn realized with a shock that they would have to get into the First if they wanted to keep it. She happened to catch sight of her own legs as she mounted her bicycle. Why, they were quite big legs. Elizabeth's were simply enormous, and most extraordinarily muscular. They were not skinny, kids' legs. Their owners were not kids any more, they were in the Upper Fifth. She grinned as she sped after Elizabeth. It was fun to grow up and be talked to as equals by Jennifer.

JOSEPHINE ELDER, *Evelyn Finds Herself*, 1929

'Are you ready?' 'Yes.' And away comes the ball kicked high in the air, to give the School time to rush on and catch it as it falls. And here they are amongst us. Meet them like Englishmen, you School-house boys, and charge them home. Now is the time to show what mettle is in you—and there shall be a warm seat by the hall fire, and honour, and lots of bottled beer to-night, for him who does his duty in the next half-hour. And they are well met. Again and again the cloud of their players-up gathers before our goal and comes threatening on, and Warner or Hedge, with young Brooke and the relics of the bull-dogs, break through and carry the ball back; and old Brooke ranges the field like Job's war-horse, the thickest scrummage parts asunder before his rush, like the waves before a clipper's bows; his cheery voice rings over the field, and his eye is everywhere. And if these miss the ball, and it rolls dangerously in front of our goal, Crab Jones and his men have seized it and sent it away towards the sides with the unerring drop-kick. This is worth living for; the whole sum of school-boy existence gathered up into one straining, struggling half-hour, a half-hour worth a year of common life.

The quarter to five has struck, and the play slackens for a minute before goal; but there is Crew, the artful dodger, driving the ball in behind our goal, on the island side, where our quarters are weakest. Is there no one to meet him? Yes! look at little East! the ball is just at equal distances between the two, and they rush together, the young man of seventeen and the boy of twelve, and kick it at the same moment. Crew passes on without a stagger; East is hurled forward by the shock, and plunges on his shoulder, as if he would bury himself in the ground; but the ball rises straight into the air, and falls behind Crew's back while the 'bravos' of the School-house attest the pluckiest charge of all that hard-fought day. Warner picks East up, lame and half stunned, and he hobbles back into goal, conscious of having played the man.

And now the last minutes are come, and the School gather for their last rush every boy of the hundred and twenty who has a run left in him. Reckless of the defence of their own goal, on they come across the level big-side ground, the ball well down amongst them, straight for our goal, like the column of the Old Guard up the slope at Waterloo. All former charges have been child's play to this. Warner and Hedge have met them, but still on they come. The bull-dogs rush in for the last time; they are hurled over or carried back, striving hand, foot, and eyelids. Old Brooke comes sweeping round the skirts of the play, and turning short round, picks out the very heart of the scrummage, and plunges in. It wavers for a moment— he has the ball! No, it has passed him, and his voice rings out clear over the advancing tide, 'Look out in goal.' Crab Jones catches it for a moment; but before he can kick, the rush is upon him and passes over him; and he picks himself up behind them with his straw in his mouth, a little dirtier, but as cool as ever.

The ball rolls slowly in behind the School-house goal, not three yards in front of a dozen of the biggest School players-up.

There stand the School-house praepostor, safest of goal-keepers, and Tom Brown by his side, who has learned his trade by this time. Now is your time, Tom. The blood of all the Browns is up, and the two rush in together, and throw themselves on the ball, under the very feet of the advancing column; the præpostor on his hands and knees arching his back, and Tom all along on his face. Over them topple the leaders of the rush, shooting over the back of the praepostor, but falling flat on Tom, and knocking all the wind out of his small carcase. 'Our ball,' says the præpostor, rising with his prize, 'but get up there, there's a little fellow under you.' They are hauled and roll off him, and Tom is discovered a motionless body.

Old Brooke picks him up. 'Stand back, give him air,' he says; and then feeling his limbs, adds, 'No bones broken. How do feel, young 'un?'

'Hah-hah,' gasps Tom as his wind comes back, 'pretty well, thank you—all right.'

'Who is he?' says Brooke. 'Oh, it's Brown, he's a new boy; I know him,' says East, coming up.

'Well, he is a plucky youngster, and will make a player,' says Brooke.

And five o'clock strikes. 'No side' is called, and the first day of the School-house match is over.

THOMAS HUGHES, *Tom Brown's Schooldays*, 1857

In true Magnet style I came in to bat at No. 11, thirty-five needed to win against the holders, Lawrence. Pitts-Tucker and I made all but three of them together in the highest partnership of the match. Since I had taken two wickets in the few overs I was allotted in the Lawrence innings I returned walking on air and to much applause, not least from members of the DC, dragooned on this occasion into watching. I became aware of Mitchell and various other 'bloods' looking at me as if they had never seen me before despite my presence at their elbows for every meal over the last three months.

ALAN ROSS, *Blindfold Games*, 1986

Boldly, I refused to change into icy football clothes and run round the frozen sports ground. Instead, wearing an overcoat and scarf to keep warm in the equally cold indoors, I hid myself from view. Bored, I wandered from corridor to corridor, migrating towards the improvised theatre built over the swimming pool for our forthcoming production of *Pinafore*. As luck would have it, Mr Vaughan-Wilkes was showing some prospective parents round the school. He spotted me looking out of a window at the wintry scene. By slow, appalling degrees he tracked me down. Oh horror, the party entered the theatre! I crept to the back of the stage. They followed closer. There was nothing to do but squeeze under the platform. Footsteps echoed overhead. My place of refuge in the darkness was discovered by a large torchlight playing on my doubled-up form. The victim was dragged out from under the stage, covered with shavings and sawdust and doubly shamed in view of the prospective parents. Weakly, I said I'd been helping the carpenter. This immediate disgrace proved bad enough, but when Flip returned from London I came to realise the full horror of what I had done.

CECIL BEATON, The Wandering Years, 1961

I had a harassed life and got many a black eye and had many outbursts of grief and rage. Once a boy, the son of a great Bohemian glass-maker, who was older than the rest of us, and had been sent out of his country because of a love affair, beat a boy for me because we were 'both foreigners'. And a boy, who grew to be the school athlete and my chief friend, beat a great many. His are the face and name that I remember—his name was of Huguenot origin and his face like his gaunt and lithe body had something of the American Indian in colour and lineament. . . . I was very much afraid of physical pain, and one day when I had made some noise in class, my friend the athlete was accused and I allowed him to get two strokes of the cane before I gave myself up. He had held out his hands without flinching and had not rubbed them on his sides afterwards. I was not caned, but was made to stand up for the rest of the lesson. I suffered very much afterwards when the thought came to me, but he did not reproach me.

Not Cricket

I had been some years at school before I had my last fight. My friend, the athlete, had given me many months of peace, but at last refused to beat any more and said I must learn to box, and not go near the other boys till I knew how. I went home with him every day and boxed in his room, and the bouts had always the same ending. My excitability gave me an advantage at first and I would drive him across the room, and then he would drive me across and it would end very commonly with my nose bleeding. One day his father, an elderly banker, brought us out into the garden and tried to make us box in a cold-blooded, courteous way, but it was no use. At last he said I might go near the boys again and I was no sooner inside the gate of the playing field than a boy flung a handful of mud and cried out, 'Mad Irishman'. I hit him several times on the face without being hit, till the boys round said we should make friends. I held out my hand in fear; for I knew if we went on I should be beaten, and he took it sullenly. I had so poor a reputation as a fighter that it was a great disgrace to him, and even the masters made fun of his swollen face; and though some little boys came in a deputation to ask me to lick a boy they named, I had never another fight with a school-fellow. We had a great many fights with the street boys and the boys of a neighbouring charity school. We had always the better because we were not allowed to fling stones, and that compelled us to close or do our best to close. The monitors had been told to report any boy who fought in the street, but they only reported those who flung stones. I always ran at the athlete's heels, but I never hit any one. My father considered these fights absurd, and even that they were an English absurdity, and so I could not get angry enough to like hitting and being hit; and then too my friend drove the enemy before him. He had no doubts or speculations to lighten his fist upon an enemy, that, being of low behaviour, should be beaten as often as possible, and there were real wrongs to avenge: one of our boys had been killed by the blow of a stone hid in a snowball.

W. B. YEATS, *Reveries over Childhood and Youth*, 1914

Lessons must have occupied a good deal of our time, but I remember very little of this. What I learnt seems to have been absorbed into my system, which shows how well taught I was. I used to sit riveting, or trying to rivet, the mistress's eye, but must otherwise have been pretty passive. I spent an inordinate amount of time over the preparation for some lessons; the rest of my preparation time went by in reading poetry or the Bible or looking up more about the facts of life in the *Encyclopaedia Britannica*. We were morbidly honourable girls and never spoke to each other at preparation or in our bedrooms after the lights were out. I often wonder whether in after life one has not suffered from an overstrained honour from having been too constantly put upon it in youth, and whether the espionage one hears of in foreign schools might not have kept one's sense of delinquency more enduringly active. In these ways, we were almost too good to last. We did not pass notes either, though one of my friends, just back from a day in London, once wrote on the margin of her rough note book, and pushed across to me, that Kitchener had been drowned. Perhaps the occasion may have excused the breach. I simply thought, however, that she was pulling my leg. Games were compulsory and took up the afternoon: it did not matter being bad at them so long as you showed energy. At lacrosse, girls who could run would pound up and down the field; those who could not gripped their crosses fiercely and stalked about. Lacrosse is such a fierce game that I wonder we all lived through it. Hockey, though ungainly, is not nearly so perilous. The only real farce was cricket, a humiliating performance for almost all. I never thought worse of anyone for being good at games so long as she was not unattractive in other ways; one or two of the games committee had, however, an air of having no nonsense about them that was depressing. We were anything but apathetic about matches: when a match was played away the returning team would, if victorious, begin to cheer at a given turn of the road; we all sat with straining ears; if the charabanc rolled up in silence we knew the worst. Our team so often won that I should like to think we had given them moral support.

ELIZABETH BOWEN, in Graham Greene (ed.), *The Old School,* 1934

Not Cricket

Games were voluntary. I have practically never played football or cricket, for which I am profoundly thankful. Even to watch these games is for me an anguish of boredom. The first conversational exchange I had at a *Punch* lunch occurred when one of the staff asked me whether I was interested in cricket. I replied briefly: 'No.' This total absence of a games *mystique* eliminated hero-worship. There was no Steerforth at my school. My days have not been haunted by any lingering adoration of some god-like athlete, compared with which adult fleshly love seems coarse and demeaning. Plato did not come into our lives. Our adolescent sensuality was directed exclusively towards girls, whose persons, as we grew older, we ventured to explore, in scented cinema darkness, or beside blackberry bushes under the August sun. I had never even heard of homosexuality until I went to Cambridge. The idea of embracing, or being embraced by, persons of one's own sex when females were available seemed to me highly bizarre.

School, to us, was a place to get away from as soon as possible and for as long as possible. Everything exciting, mysterious, adventurous happened outside its confines, not within them. We were poorly taught, admittedly, and lacked utterly the team spirit. Our South London Cockney grated sharply on the ear. No group photographs of us were taken. We had no blazers or gilded caps. We were urchins of the suburbs. Looking back, I feel grateful that it should have been so. On the whole, the more boring and flat education is, the better. Glamorizing it constitutes a kind of brain-washing.

MALCOLM MUGGERIDGE, in Brian Inglis (ed.),
John Bull's Schooldays, 1961

'I shall only have to endure her dullness in the geography lessons,' laughed Basheen.

The 'classical scholars' groaned loudly.

'I shall ask to change. What is the lesson in Latin time?' demanded Gretta, glancing in the direction of a printed time-table which hung on the wall.

304

The girl nearest it looked down the columns till she came to the hour for Latin. 'Physiology, otherwise bones. You know you took Latin to get out of it—said you didn't want to know about your internal mechanism,' she observed.

Gretta groaned again. 'Nor do I. Miss Frost's explanations made me shiver all down my spine. I shall have to stick to Latin after all. As a matter of fact, I couldn't have changed; my dad was so bucked about my being able to read an old Latin inscription that he gave me a new watch, so I couldn't very well let the dear old boy down,' she remarked.

'That's a bore. If we could all of us in the Latin class have given it up, it might have been the first step towards ridding ourselves of this nuisance.—By the way, Basheen, what's her name?'

'Her name, like herself, is prehistoric—Tregathwick. A nice mouthful for an insignificant undermistress,' replied Basheen.

'Tregathwick? Not any relation to Lord Avon, I suppose—that's their family name?' remarked Gwenda.

The others laughed.

'Not very likely; or is she an aristocrat down on her luck, Basheen?' inquired Hilda.

'She's nothing particular. Wears glasses, and has her hair parted in the middle and done up in a kind of bun behind—rather like an old print we have of Queen Victoria as a girl,' explained Basheen.

'I'm rather keen to see her, she must be a freak by all accounts. Anyway, she's bound to be only a "temporary", so.don't let's get the blues over her. I've brought a hundred cigs to cheer us up first night, and a lot of chocs. We'll have them after our skating,' said Hilda.

'Good girl! We'll have to wait till lights are out and Mousie or— oh, bother it all!—it will be this Miss—what's her name?— Tregathwick has been her rounds.—Now, Gretta, mind you blow your match out before you throw it away.—And get out your ash-trays, girls,' commanded Basheen.

'You're never going to smoke in dorm, after the fuss there was last term,' protested Maureen.

'Where else should we smoke? We should be certain to be seen if we smoked on our walks, and that would be a scandal. Can't I see

Priorytown Chronicle with a letter from "Outraged Citizen" on the subject of those disgraceful girls of Priory School?' said Gretta.

'Yes, and a leader on the modern girl and the bad influence of this "school for the upper classes",' added Hilda.

'Anyway, you can't smoke in our dormitory, it will smell of it; and there'll be a row first go off, and Mrs Welbeck will pat herself on the back for having engaged this watch-dog. If you want to smoke, do it in recreation; you can hide among the trees if you are ashamed of it,' said Maureen.

'Hark at her,' cried Gretta, while the other girls all turned to look at Maureen.

'You're very superior, because you don't happen to smoke; but you're not going to dictate to us, you know. We've always had a jollification first night, and we're not going to stop for you or the new Trick—or whatever her name is,' cried another girl, called Joan.

Her companions clapped their hands. 'The new Trick. Good for you, Joan! The new Trick she shall be,' they cried.

'And as for the dorm—which I notice Maureen now pedantically calls dormitory—we each have a window in our cubicles, and all we have to do is to open them and, hey presto! the air is purified at once.'

'Oh, is it? It hangs about curtains and clothes for days, and weeks even,' objected Maureen.

'Somebody sit upon Maureen, she's a regular wet blanket this term. It's her illness. She must be converted, or something,' jeered Basheen.

Maureen flushed up. 'I'm simply talking common-sense. One doesn't need to be ill to learn that, I should think. However, go your own way, and learn by bitter experience, you silly things,' she cried angrily.

MAY BALDWIN, *High Jinks at the Priory School,* 1929

At most schools in the 'twenties there was never any question of being let off cricket. The thought of asking not to play it never entered anybody's head. If it had, the consequences, at a public school anyhow, were clearly foreseeable. Suppose, let us say, a poetically-minded boy had announced that he wished to spend the afternoon writing an ode, he would have been immediately beaten (four strokes) by the Head of the House. Poetry was unhealthy stuff. Look at Byron. If the poet had been more specific and had said that he wanted to write an Ode to the Matron ('Oh Matron, when with grizzled head half bent with care, sweet ministrant of salve and unguent, breasting thy way defiant bust worn high . . .'), he would have been beaten (six strokes) by the Housemaster, and the poor (certainly) innocent (probably) Matron would have found herself writing to the scholastic agents, Chitty and Gale, for a new situation ('. . . said to have pleasant personality . . . prepared take sole charge . . . excellent "mixer" . . .'). If the embryo Shelley had said that he wished to write an Ode to the Captain of Cricket ('Oh Dennis, when with auburn head half bent with care . . .'), expulsion would have been considered, this extreme measure being subsequently watered down, after an infinity of scowls and threats, to a beating (eight strokes) by the Headmaster. These ceremonies used to take place at 9 p.m., the Headmaster sporting a dinner-jacket and being freshly vitamin-charged. The beatings were done, as usual, in the spirit of this hurts me more than you, which was said to be plenty.

When blessed rain had made the cricket pitches too sodden for activity, the obvious alternative, inactivity, was not permitted. We were herded together in the gymnasium. Sometimes there was boxing, that hideous and useless invention. Sometimes there was a pastime called Figure Marching. In Indian file we followed each other round strange geometrical figures, crossing and criss-crossing as instructed and forming patterns which would, no doubt, have looked pretty and interesting from a helicopter hovering above. It was before the days of helicopters.

More often than not, Physical Jerks were our lot, an unfortunate name implying as it does fits and starts and jolts and dislocations. The brochures which dealt with this form of exercise were copiously and incomprehensibly diagrammed. Dotted and arrowed lines and Fig. 6 seemed to prescribe patently absurd contortions. The instructors who steered us through them had chests like pouter-pigeons, crimson-veined faces and army connections. At the end of the lesson, it wasn't the done thing to invite the class quietly to stow away the medicine balls and falling mats that we had been using. Even this simple action had to have a military aura—'Mats away, *GO*! Balls away, *GO*!'

ARTHUR MARSHALL, 'The Crooked Bat', in *Girls will be Girls*, 1974

'To get off cricket,' said Psmith, dusting his right trouser-leg, 'was the dream of my youth and the aspiration of my riper years. A noble game, but a bit too thick for me. At Eton I used to have to field out at the nets till the soles of my boots wore through. I suppose you are a blood at the game? Play for the school against Loamshire, and so on.'

'I'm not going to play here, at any rate,' said Mike.

He had made up his mind on this point in the train. There is a certain fascination about making the very worst of a bad job. Achilles knew his business when he sat in his tent. The determination not to play cricket for Sedleigh as he could not play for Wrykyn gave Mike a sort of pleasure.

P. G. WODEHOUSE, *Mike and Psmith*, 1909

I had a strong preference for school stories and above all for the penny weeklies, the *Gem* and the *Magnet*. Their appeal for me was that the characters in them were getting a really good education, and that some of it was bound to brush off on me. All the same, a really good education like that demanded a great many things I did not have, like an old fellow who didn't drink and an old one who didn't work, an uncle with a racing car who would give me a tip of five pounds to blow on a feed in the dormitory after lights out, long trousers, a short jacket and a top hat, bicycles, footballs, and cricket bats. For this I should need a rich relative in the States, and we were short of relatives in the States. . . .

So I adored education from afar, and strove to be worthy of it, as later I adored beautiful girls and strove to be worthy of them, and with similar results. I played cricket with a raggy ball and an old board hacked into shape for a bat before a wicket chalked on some dead wall. I kept in training by shadow boxing before the mirror in the kitchen, and practised the deadly straight left with which the hero knocked out the bully of the school. I even adopted the public-school code for my own, and did not tell lies, or inform on other boys, or yell when I was beaten. It wasn't easy, because the other fellows did tell lies, and told on one another in the most shameless way, and, when they were beaten, yelled that their wrists were broken and even boasted later of their own cleverness, and when I behaved in the simple, manly way recommended in the school stories, they said I was mad or that I was 'shaping' (the Cork word for swanking), and even the teachers seemed to regard it as an impertinence.

FRANK O'CONNOR, *An Only Child*, 1961

I was sent to a small private school; an excellent one in its way no doubt; but it was not my way. The emphasis was all on Young-ladyhood, slightly tinged with Christianity (C. of E. variety), and I should never have felt comfortable there if I had stayed there for a million years. When, a little later, I went to the Slade School, I felt perfectly happy there at once; and I was at ease with the students, though many of them came from backgrounds which were quite unfamiliar to me. But that seemed like my own country. At boarding-school I was always a foreigner.

Not that I wanted to leave school; I wanted to stay on, if only I could manage to bear it; for I was very curious about the extraordinary habits of the girls. For instance, that first day, they were all singing: 'I am the Honeysuckle, You are the Bee.' Why? What on earth was it? (I had never heard a popular song in my life.) And they were all busy making hat-pin knobs out of coloured sealing-wax. Now why in the world did they like doing that? Nearly everything they did mystified me.

It took me some time to realize that it was considered queer to be interested in anything whatever except horses, or things like hatpin-knobbing; or, of course, games or gossip. However, presently I began to enjoy hockey myself, and I even got into the team, and felt very grand with my red cap (like a boy's cap) pinned on to my hair. We played in white blouses and blue skirts, which had to clear the ground by six inches; and our waist-belts were very neat and trim over our tight stays. And when we came in from a game—and our play was most ferocious—all covered with mud and streaming hot, we had to go straight into school, without having time to change, or wash, or comb our hair, at all.

Gwen Raverat (b. 1885), *Period Piece*, 1952

'I'll play you for sixpence if you like, next game, and give you eight and two hands . . . No? Prudent fellow. I wish the rain wouldn't get into my eyes, though it's sweat as well, I expect. Lord, I am hot! Isn't it ripping?'

David paused a moment both from talk and athletics, a truce gladly accepted by the panting Bags, and pushed his dripping hair out of his eyes. He was a completely dishevelled and yet a very jolly object, and was quite altogether wet, his knickerbockers clinging like tights to his thighs, the skin of which showed pink through them, while the water trickled steadily down his bare calves into the dejected socks that lay limply round the tops of his shoes. They and his legs were stained with splashes of watery gravel, his shirt, open at the neck and slightly torn across the shoulder, lay like a wet bag glued to his back, and his hair was a mere yellow plaster from which the water could have been wrung in pints. Bags was in similar plight, except that he wore a thick woollen jersey over his shirt, which gave him a slightly less drowned aspect.

The game, and with it David's running comments, were resumed after a minute or two, and neither of the two saw a figure with trousers much turned up and a large golfing umbrella who had paused on his way to the gate, just behind them.

'Yes, I'm going to play racquets for the school some time next century,' David was saying, 'and squash is jolly good practice. Nine, six: that's rather a sell, Bags! Oh, I say, look at that for a half-volley. Just a shade Maddoxy, I don't think.'

The half-volley in question, that clung close to the left wall of the court, finished the rally, and David turned to run to pick it up, and found that Maddox was the spectator.

'David, you juggins, why haven't you got a sweater on?' asked he.

E. F. BENSON, *David Blaize*, 1916

The football field was a large one, bounded on two sides by tall wooden palings, and on the other two by a hedge and a new shingled road, separated from the field by a post and rails.

Two of the younger boys, proud of their office, raced down to the further end to set up the goal-posts. The rest lounged idly about without attempting to begin operations, except the new boy Kiffin, who was seen walking apart from the rest, diligently studying the 'rules of the game of football', as laid down in a small 'Boy's Own Pocket Book and Manual of Outdoor Sports', with which he had been careful to provide himself.

At last Tipping suggested that they had better begin, and proposed that Mr Blinkhorn and himself should toss up for the choice of sides, and this being done, Mr Bultitude presently, to his great dismay, heard his name mentioned. 'I'll have young Bultitude,' said Tipping; 'he used to play up decently. Look here, you young beggar, you're on my side, and if you don't play up it will be the worse for you!'

It was not worth while however to protest, since he would so soon be rid of the whole crew for ever, and so Paul followed Tipping and his train with dutiful submission, and the game began.

It was not a spirited performance. Mr Tinkler, who was not an athlete, retired at once to the post and rails, on which he settled himself to enjoy a railway novel with a highly stimulating cover. Mr Blinkhorn, who had more conscientious views of his office, charged about vigorously, performing all kinds of wonders with the ball, though evidently more from a sense of duty than with any idea of enjoyment.

Tipping occasionally took the trouble to oppose him, but as a concession merely, and with a parade of being under no necessity to do so; and these two, with a very small following of enthusiasts on either side, waged a private and confidential kind of warfare in different parts of the field, while the others made no pretence of playing for the present, but strolled about in knots, exchanging and bartering the treasures valuable in the sight of schoolboys, and gossiping generally.

As for Paul, he did not clearly understand what 'playing up' might mean. He had not indulged in football since he was a genuine boy, and then only in a rudimentary and primitive form, and without any particular fondness for the exercise. But being now, in spirit at all events, a precise old gentleman, with a decided notion of taking care of himself, he was resolved that not even Tipping should compel him to trust his person within range of that dirty brown globe, which whistled past his ear or seemed spinning towards his stomach with such a hideous suggestion of a cannon-ball about it.

All the ghastly instances, too, of accidents to life and limb in the football field came unpleasantly into his memory, and he saw the inadvisability of mingling with the crowd and allowing himself to be kicked violently on the shins.

F. Anstey, *Vice Versa*, 1882

Mrs Roberts brought them their beer. Grimes took a long draught and sighed happily.

'This looks like being the first end of term I've seen for two years,' he said dreamily. 'Funny thing, I can always get on all right for about six weeks, and then I land in the soup. I don't believe I was ever meant by Nature to be a schoolmaster. Temperament,' said Grimes, with a far-away look in his eyes—'that's been my trouble, temperament and sex.'

'Is it quite easy to get another job after—after you've been in the soup?' asked Paul.

'Not at first, it isn't, but there're ways. Besides, you see, I'm a public-school man. That means everything. There's a blessed equity in the English social system,' said Grimes, 'that ensures the public-school man against starvation. One goes through four or five years of perfect hell at an age when life is bound to be hell, anyway, and after that the social system never lets one down.

'Not that I stood four or five years of it, mind; I got the push soon after my sixteenth birthday. But my housemaster was a public-school man. He knew the system. "Grimes," he said, "I can't keep you in the House after what has happened. I have the other boys to consider. But I don't want to be too hard on you. I want you to start again." So he sat down there and then and wrote me a letter of recommendation to any future employer, a corking good letter, too. I've got it still. It's been very useful at one time or another. That's the public-school system all over. They may kick you out, but they never let you down.

'I subscribed a guinea to the War Memorial Fund. I felt I owed it to them. I was really sorry,' said Grimes, 'that that cheque never got through.

'After that I went into business. Uncle of mine had a brush factory at Edmonton. Doing pretty well before the war. That put the lid on the brush trade for me. You're too young to have been in the war, I suppose? Those were days, old boy. We shan't see the like of them again. I don't suppose I was really sober for more than a few hours for the whole of that war. Then I got into the soup again, pretty badly that time. Happened over in France. They said, "Now, Grimes, you've got to behave like a gentleman. We don't want a court-martial in this regiment. We're going to leave you alone for half an hour. There's your revolver. You know what to do. Goodbye, old man," they said quite affectionately.

'Well, I sat there for some time looking at that revolver. I put it up to my head twice, but each time I brought it down again. "Public-school men don't end like this," I said to myself. It was a long half hour, but luckily they had left a decanter of whisky in there with me. They'd all had a few, I think. That's what made them all so solemn. There wasn't much whisky left when they came back, and, what with that and the strain of the situation, I could only laugh when they came in. Silly thing to do, but they looked so surprised, seeing me there alive and drunk.

' "The man's a cad," said the colonel, but even then I couldn't stop laughing, so they put me under arrest and called a court-martial.

'I must say I felt pretty low next day. A major came over from another battalion to try my case. He came to see me first, and bless me if it wasn't a cove I'd known at school.

' "God bless my soul," he said, "if it isn't Grimes of Podger's! What's all this nonsense about a court-martial?" So I told him. "H'm," he said, "pretty bad. Still, it's out of the question to shoot an old Harrovian. I'll see what I can do about it." And next day I was sent to Ireland on a pretty cushy job connected with postal service.'

EVELYN WAUGH, *Decline and Fall*, 1928

His courage was tremendous, to play football under his captaincy, on a losing side, was a sensation. For an hour and a quarter he blamed, praised, and appealed to our feelings, leading rush after rush against boys bigger than himself, poaching any kicks he could get and limping off the field with his arm round my neck. 'My God, you went badly today, Nolly—haven't you any guts—to think we lost to those bastards by three to one' and tears of rage would roll down his cheeks. 'Next time we've got to win—we've just got to—understand, Flinchface?'

His personality dominated us because it was the strongest and because it was the incarnation of schoolboyness; the five hundred years of Eton life had gone to make it, the Gothic windows, the huge open fireplace, the table in the middle of Chamber round which our life centred, had been brought into being for him. He was emotional and as Captain of Chamber would 'beat' me for untidiness, half miserable at having to flog his best friend, half pleased at fulfilling a Roman duty, only to suffer remorse at the condition of his own belongings. 'God knows what I'm to do—I can't let you beat *me*— I haven't the authority—if I ask you to hit me as hard as you can I might lose my temper and knock you down. We'll have to make Wayne and Buckley tidy our stalls for us in future.'

Godfrey's relaxation was reading Homer; he adored the Odyssey, for the Homeric world was one in which he was at home and the proverbs of 'the wily Odysseus', to the disgust of the able but Philistine Highworth, were never off his lips. 'Oh, babababarbaba bababababarbaba,' he would storm; 'for God's sake stop spouting Greek—I can't understand a fellow with guts like you Godfrey wanting to quote that filthy Greek all the time—and as for you, Cyril, you're worse—nine bloody beanrows will I have there and a hive for the honey bloody bee—my God it makes me crap.'

CYRIL CONNOLLY, *Enemies of Promise*, 1938

Where are the girls of yesteryear? How strange
To think they're scattered East, South, West, and North—
Those pale Medusas of the Upper Fourth,
Those Marihuanas of the Moated Grange.

No more the shrieks of victims, and no more
The fiendish chuckle borne along the breeze!
Gone are the basilisk eyes, the bony knees.
Mice, and not blood, run down each corridor.

Now poison ivy twines the dorm where casks
Were broached and music mistresses were flayed,
While on the sports ground where the pupils played
The relatively harmless adder basks.

Toll for St Trinian's, nurse of frightful girls!
St Trinian's, mother of the far too free!
No age to come (thank God) will ever see
Such an academy as Dr Searle's.

C. DAY LEWIS, 'A Short Dirge for St Trinian's', in Kaye Webb
(compiler), *The St Trinian's Story*, 1959

I must return to Holt and its education of our morals.

That side was run on what was called the honour system, and for the benefit of those who do not know the school, some explanation of this is necessary.

About a week after arrival every new boy was interviewed separately by his housemaster and the headmaster—half watt hypnotism we used to call it—and was asked—I need hardly say how difficult it would have been to refuse—to promise on his honour three things.

(1) Not to swear.

(2) Not to smoke.

(3) Not to say or do anything indecent.

Having done so, two consequences followed:

(1) If you broke any of these promises you should report the breakage to your housemaster.

(2) If you saw anyone else break them, you should endeavour to persuade him to report and if he refused you should report him yourself.

Before I say anything in criticism, I must add that the system worked, in public at any rate. One almost never saw anyone smoking, heard anyone swear, or came across any smut. From the point of view of master and parent it would seem ideal. Here at last was the clean and healthy school they had been looking for.

From the boy's point of view on the other hand, I feel compelled to say that I believe no more potent engine for turning them into neurotic innocents, for perpetuating those very faults of character which it was intended to cure, was ever devised.

Everyone knows that the only emotion that is fully developed in a boy of fourteen is the emotion of loyalty and honour. For that very reason it is so dangerous. By appealing to it, you can do almost anything you choose, you can suppress the expression of all those emotions, particularly the sexual, which are still undeveloped; like a modern dictator you can defeat almost any opposition from other parts of the psyche, but if you do, if you deny these other emotions their expression and development, however silly or shocking they may seem to you, they will not only never grow up, but they will go backward, for human nature cannot stay still; they will, like all things that are shut up, go bad on you.

Of the two consequences of our promises, the second, the obligation to interfere with one's neighbour, is of course much the more serious. It meant that the whole of our moral life was based on fear, on fear of the community, not to mention the temptation it offered to the natural informer, and fear is not a healthy basis. It makes one furtive and dishonest and unadventurous. The best reason I have for opposing Fascism is that at school I lived in a Fascist state. Of the effect of the system on the boys after they left school I have little direct experience outside my own and those whom I knew personally, but all those with whom I have spoken, whether old boys or others who have come into contact with old boys, have borne out my conclusion that the effect is a serious one in many cases. I am fully aware that the first five years of life are more important than any others and that those cases I am thinking of would have had a difficult time anyway, but I am convinced that their difficulties were enormously and unnecessarily increased by the honour system. Though the system was a peculiarity of Holt, it is only an extreme example of a tendency which can be seen in the running of every school; the tendency to identify the welfare of the school with the welfare of the boys in it, to judge school life not by its own peculiar standards as a stage in the development towards maturity, but as an end in itself by adult standards. Every headmaster is inclined to think that so long as all's fair in his own little garden he has succeeded.

Not Cricket

When later he sees what some of his old boys have turned into he seldom realizes that the very apparent perfection he was so proud of is partly responsible.

W. H. AUDEN, 'Honour' (Gresham's School), in Graham Greene (ed.), *The Old School*, 1934

When I was twelve Mary left school and I went in her place, I hated it and cant bear to think of it even now. Those awful bells and all the discomforts, tepid bath water foul stoves, we didn't see an open fire for months on end, then there was the disgusting food, slimy boiled suet puddings with big lumps of fat in them, burnt porrage, bread and margerene and all the other boiled watery messes we had, how I longed for fresh fruit and to see a really beautiful face. The mistresses were all plain with lumpy figures and blotchy faces, the girls were not so bad but they looked a bit like the food we eat and we had to wear hideous gym frocks and rather dirty flannel blouses, you were considered vain if you took the slightest interest in your appearance, my shoulder leangth curly hair had to be dragged back by a black ribbon and a beastly little fussy tail stuck out behind. You were thought frightful if you said you would like to get married when you were grown up, you had to say you would like to be a games mistress or something dull like that, for a time I said I was going to nurse lepers because that sounded more interesting and no one could say I was looking for a husband in a leper colony, then I got rather frit I might be taken seriously and would find myself in a leper colony before I knew quite where I was.

To my family games were a nightmare too, none of us were any good at them, I never scored a goal at hockey all the time I was at school, even in the practice on the lawn, usually during hockey I would shut my eyes and count sixty slowly, when I had repeated this sixty times an hour had passed and the beastly game was over for the afternoon. Tennis wasn't quite so bad but the grown-ups supplied us with enormouse flat ended racquets weighing about twenty six oz.

left over from Daddies youth, we were awfully ashamed of them and they were so heavy to lift it more than spoilt our game.

We were surprised to find the girls quite liked us although they said we were a bit mad, on the whole they were fairly nice to us and we always had partners for our crocidile walks and were not teased too much, some of the girls had a pretty foul time, schools seem to be very snobish places, the ones who had rich or titled parents had a much better time than the ones who were shabby or came from small suburban homes, very plain girls too were treated like dirt, fortunately for us we were presumably wealthy as we took all the extras and had a fairly large country home, all the same we never dar'd to ask anyone home for the holidays, they might have thought us madder than they did already if we had, there were other reasons too.

BARBARA COMYNS, *Sisters by a River*, 1947

Abigail thought: snow is filling the hockey nets and glittering on the yellow mud, freezing the drive and filling the hedges. Mounting in desolation on the windowsills, wailing at the pane, drifting under doors. Soon it will cover the desks and the algebra books, fill the crucible and the belljar and thoroughly obliterate the blackboard. Blue glaciers will form in the inkwells. Perhaps Benthall's car will skid on the drive and hurtle in frozen flames through the hollyhedge. Supposing they all broke their legs on the hockey pitch. 'Bully off!' and they charged, and their legs broke like hockeysticks, their faces like netballs sank into the snow.

SHENA MACKAY, *Dust Falls on Eugene Schlumburger*, 1964

I must admit that I was most precocious
    (Precocious children rarely grow up good).
My aunts and uncles thought me quite atrocious

For using words more adult than I should;
  My first remark at school did all it could
To shake a matron's monumental poise;
  'I like to see the various types of boys.'

The Great War had begun: but masters' scrutiny
  And fists of big boys were the war to us;
It was as harmless as the Indian Mutiny,
  A beating from the Head was dangerous.
  But once when half the form put down *Bellus.*
We were accused of that most deadly sin,
Wanting the Kaiser and the Huns to win.

The way in which we really were affected
  Was having such a varied lot to teach us.
The best were fighting, as the King expected,
  The remnant either elderly grey creatures,
  Or characters with most peculiar features.
Many were raggable, a few were waxy,
One had to leave abruptly in a taxi.

Surnames I must not write—O Reginald,
  You at least taught us that which fadeth not,
Our earliest visions of the great wide world;
  The beer and biscuits that your favourites got,
  Your tales revealing you a first-class shot,
Your riding breeks, your drama called *The Waves,*
A few of us will carry to our graves.

'Half a lunatic, half a knave'. No doubt
  A holy terror to the staff at tea;
A good headmaster must have soon found out
  Your moral character was all at sea;
  I question if you'd got a pass degree:
But little children bless your kind that knocks
Away the edifying stumbling blocks.

Not Cricket

How can I thank you? For it only shows
   (Let me ride just this once my hobby-horse),
There're things a good headmaster never knows.
   There must be sober schoolmasters, of course,
   But what a prep school really puts across
Is knowledge of the world we'll soon be lost in:
To-day it's more like Dickens than Jane Austen.

I hate the modern trick, to tell the truth,
   Of straightening out the kinks in the young mind,
Our passion for the tender plant of youth,
   Our hatred for all weeds of any kind.
   Slogans are bad: the best that I can find
Is this: 'Let each child have that's in our care
As much neurosis as the child can bear.'

In this respect, at least, my bad old Adam is
   Pigheadedly against the general trend;
And has no use for all these new academies
   Where readers of the better weeklies send
   The child they probably did not intend,
To paint a lampshade, marry, or keep pigeons,
Or make a study of the world religions.

Goddess of bossy underlings, Normality!
   What murders are committed in thy name!
Totalitarian is thy state Reality,
   Reeking of antiseptics and the shame
   Of faces that all look and feel the same.
Thy Muse is one unknown to classic histories,
The topping figure of the hockey mistress.

From thy dread Empire not a soul's exempted:
   More than the nursemaids pushing prams in parks,
By thee the intellectuals are tempted,
   O, to commit the treason of the clerks,

Bewitched by thee to literary sharks.
But I must leave thee to thy office stool,
I must get on now to my public school.

Men had stopped throwing stones at one another,
   Butter and Father had come back again;
Gone were the holidays we spent with Mother
   In furnished rooms on mountain, moor, and fen;
   And gone those summer Sunday evenings, when
Along the seafronts fled a curious noise,
'Eternal Father', sung by three young boys.

Nation spoke Peace, or said she did, with nation;
   The sexes tried their best to look the same;
Morals lost value during the inflation,
   The great Victorians kindly took the blame;
   Visions of Dada to the Post-War came,
Sitting in cafés, nostrils stuffed with bread,
Above the recent and the straight-laced dead.

I've said my say on public schools elsewhere:
   Romantic friendship, prefects, bullying,
I shall not deal with, c'est une autre affaire.
   Those who expect them, will get no such thing,
   It is the strictly relevant I sing.
Why should they grumble? They've the Greek Anthology,
And all the spicier bits of Anthropology.

We all grow up the same way, more or less;
   Life is not known to give away her presents;
She only swops. The unself-consciousness
   That children share with animals and peasants
   Sinks in the 'stürm und drang' of Adolescence.
Like other boys I lost my taste for sweets,
Discovered sunsets, passion, God, and Keats.

Not Cricket

I shall recall a single incident
  No more. I spoke of mining engineering
As the career on which my mind was bent,
  But for some time my fancies had been veering;
  Mirages of the future kept appearing;
Crazes had come and gone in short, sharp gales,
For motor-bikes, photography, and whales.

But indecision broke off with a clean-cut end
  One afternoon in March at half-past three
When walking in a ploughed field with a friend;
  Kicking a little stone, he turned to me
  And said, 'Tell me, do you write poetry?'
I never had, and said so, but I knew
That very moment what I wished to do.

W. H. AUDEN, 'Letter to Lord Byron', in Auden and MacNeice,
Letters from Iceland, 1938

IN THE CLASSROOM

Now my mind's off again. No tears
Of Catullus move me. Though I know in turn
We too will praise these years
Of watching clouds through windows, fluttering pages;
Usefully sometimes, though the beckoning scents
Rise always, wafted from summer grasses:
Hearing the loud bees mumble at the glass,
And sound of sunlight behind the scratching pens.

'Distraction', in *Complete Poems of Keith Douglas*, 1978 (? 1936)

━━━━━━━━━

A quarter of an hour passed before lessons again began, during which the schoolroom was in a glorious tumult; for that space of time, it seemed to be permitted to talk loud and more freely, and they used their privilege. The whole conversation ran on the breakfast, which one and all abused roundly. Poor things! it was the sole consolation they had. Miss Miller was now the only teacher in the room; a group of great girls standing about her spoke with serious and sullen gestures. I heard the name of Mr Brocklehurst pronounced by some lips, at which Miss Miller shook her head disapprovingly; but she made no great effort to check the general wrath; doubtless she shared in it.

A clock in the schoolroom struck nine; Miss Miller left her circle, and standing in the middle of the room, cried,—'Silence! To your seats!'

Discipline prevailed. In five minutes the confused throng was resolved into order, and comparative silence quelled the Babel clamor of tongues. The upper teachers now punctually resumed their posts; but still, all seemed to wait. Ranged on benches down the sides of the room, the eighty girls sat motionless and erect. A quaint assemblage they appeared, all with plain locks combed from their faces, not a curl visible; in brown dresses, made high and surrounded by a narrow tucker about the throat, with little pockets of holland, shaped something like a Highlander's purse, tied in front of their frocks, and destined to serve the purpose of a work-bag; all too wearing woollen stockings and country-made shoes, fastened with brass buckles. Above twenty of those clad in this costume were full-grown girls, or rather young women; it suited them ill, and gave an air of oddity even to the prettiest.

CHARLOTTE BRONTË, *Jane Eyre*, 1847

Martin Rattler was a very bad boy. At least his aunt, Mrs Dorothy Grumbit, said so; and certainly she ought to have known, if anybody should, for Martin lived with her, and was, as she herself expressed it 'the bane of her existence, the very torment of her life'. No doubt of it whatever, according to Aunt Dorothy Grumbit's showing, Martin Rattler was 'a remarkably bad boy'.

Fire was the cause of Martin's getting into disgrace at school for the first time; and this is how it happened.

'Go and poke the fire, Martin Rattler,' said the schoolmaster, 'and put on a bit of coal; and see that you don't send the sparks flying about the floor.'

Martin sprang with alacrity to obey, for he was standing up with the class at the time, and was glad of the temporary relaxation. He stirred the fire with great care, and put on several pieces of coal very slowly, and rearranged them two or three times; after which he stirred the fire a little more, and examined it carefully to see that it was all right. But he did not seem quite satisfied, and was proceeding to readjust the coals, when Bob Croaker, one of the big boys, who was a bullying, ill-tempered fellow, and had a spite against Martin, called out:

'Please, sir, Rattler's playin' at the fire.'

'Come back to your place, sir!' cried the master, sternly.

Martin returned in haste, and resumed his position in the class. As he did so, he observed that his fore-finger was covered with soot. Immediately a smile of glee overspread his features, and while the master was busy with one of the boys, he drew his black finger gently down the forehead and nose of the boy next to him.

'What part of the earth was peopled by the descendants of Ham?' cried the master, pointing to the dux.

'Shem,' shrieked a small boy near the foot of the class.

'Silence!' thundered the master, with a frown that caused the small boy to quake down to the points of his toes.

'Asia,' answered the dux.

'Next?'

'Turkey.'

'Next, next, next? Hallo! John Ward,' cried the master, starting up in anger from his seat, 'what do you mean by that, sir?'

'What, sir?' said John Ward, tremulously, while a suppressed titter ran round the class.

'Your face, sir! Who blacked your face, eh?'

'I—I—don't know,' said the boy, drawing his sleeve across his face, which had the effect of covering it with sooty streaks.

An uncontrollable shout of laughter burst from the whole school, which was instantly followed by a silence so awful and profound, that a pin might have been heard to fall.

R. M. BALLANTYNE, *Martin Rattler*, 1858

Two Bad Things in Infant School

Learning bad grammar, then getting blamed for it:
Learning Our Father which art in Heaven.

Bowing our heads to a hurried nurse, and
Hearing the nits rattle down on the paper.

In the Classroom

And Two Good Things

Listening to Miss Anthony, our lovely Miss,
Charming us dumb with *The Wind in the Willows*.
Dancing Sellinger's Round, and dancing and
Dancing it, and getting it perfect forever.

D. J. ENRIGHT, from *The Terrible Shears*, 1973

He could not but observe how silent and sad the boys all seemed to be. There was none of the noise and clamour of a school-room, none of its boisterous play or hearty mirth. The children sat crouching and shivering together, and seemed to lack the spirit to move about. The only pupil who evinced the slightest tendency towards locomotion or playfulness was Master Squeers, and as his chief amusement was to tread upon the other boys' toes in his new boots, his flow of spirits was rather disagreeable than otherwise.

After some half-hour's delay Mr Squeers reappeared, and the boys took their places and their books, of which latter commodity the average might be about one to eight learners. A few minutes having elapsed, during which Mr Squeers looked very profound, as if he had a perfect apprehension of what was inside all the books, and could say every word of their contents by heart if he only chose to take the trouble, that gentleman called up the first class.

Obedient to this summons there ranged themselves in front of the schoolmaster's desk, half a dozen scarecrows, out at knees and elbows, one of whom placed a torn and filthy book beneath his learned eye.

'This is the first class in English spelling and philosophy, Nickleby,' said Squeers, beckoning Nicholas to stand beside him. 'We'll get up a Latin one, and hand that over to you. Now, then, where's the first boy?'

'Please, Sir, he's cleaning the back parlour window,' said the temporary head of the philosophical class.

'So he is, to be sure,' rejoined Squeers. 'We go upon the practical mode of teaching, Nickleby; the regular education system. C-l-e-a-n, clean, verb active, to make bright, to scour. W-i-n, win, d-e-r, der, winder, a casement. When the boy knows this out of book, he goes and does it. It's just the same principle as the use of the globes. Where's the second boy?'

'Please, Sir, he's weeding the garden,' replied a small voice.

'To be sure,' said Squeers, by no means disconcerted. 'So he is. B-o-t, bot, t-i-n, bottin, n-e-y, bottinney, noun substantive, a knowledge of plants. When he has learned that bottinney means a knowledge of plants, he goes and knows 'em. That's our system, Nickleby; what do you think of it?'

'It's a very useful one, at any rate,' answered Nicholas significantly.

DICKENS, Nicholas Nickleby, 1838–9

It was in the Latin work that I felt the greatest advantage from my move. In the Upper Fifth the teacher had kept a crib on her lap for even the syntax sentences, and we were not allowed any variety of rendering. A fair copy placed boldly on the desk would have been respectable, but a crib on the lap, hidden (supposedly) by the desk, was quite another thing. Now in the Sixth we encountered a Classics mistress who was a mental aristocrat. She seemed not only superior socially to the bulk of the staff, but she knew her subject, and, more remarkable still, she knew the business of teaching. She might have stepped straight out of a public school or a tutor's room at the university. When we made a howler she just stopped in her tracks and looked bewildered: 'Surely, Mary, you would not use the indicative there? Of course . . . Have you any precedent for it?' Slips in gender and such trifles she treated with the polite disregard one would mete out to a coffee-spill at table—quick remedy with no fuss. She certainly, more than any one else, gave the Collegiate touch that justified the title of the school. She was the daughter of the RA, who had executed the medallion of the Princess of Wales, and no doubt her artistic upbringing had heightened the effect of her natural good looks and vivacity. Meeting an old schoolfellow the other day I asked what she remembered of the school. 'Nothing,' was her reply. 'I can recall nothing except my admiration for Miss Armstead; we used to watch what she had on, because she dressed in such good style.'

M. V. HUGHES, *A London Girl of the 80s*, 1936

'Go to your class-room,' said the Doctor, sternly, eyeing the culprits one by one, 'and wait there for me.'

They slunk off meekly in obedience to this order, and waited the hour of vengeance in blank dismay.

Dr Senior did not keep them long in suspense, however. His slow, firm step sounded presently down the corridor, and at the sound each wretched culprit quaked with horror.

Mr Rastle was in the room, and rose as usual to greet his chief; the boys also, as by custom bound, rose in their places. 'Good morning, Mr Rastle,' said the Doctor. 'Are your boys all here?'

'Yes, sir, we have just called over.'

'Ah! And what class comes on first?'

'English literature, sir.'

'Well, Mr Rastle, I will take the class this morning, please— instead of you.'

A groan of horror passed through the ranks of the unhappy Guinea-pigs and Tadpoles at these words. Bramble looked wildly about him, if haply he might escape by a window or lie hid in a desk; while Stephen, Paul, Padger, and the other ringleaders, gave themselves up for lost, and mentally bade farewell to joy for ever.

'What have the boys been reading?' inquired Dr Senior of Mr Rastle.

'Gray's *Elegy*, sir. We have just got through it.'

'Oh! Gray's *Elegy*,' said the Doctor; and then, as if forgetting where he was, he began repeating to himself:

In the Classroom

The curfew tolls the knell of parting day,
The lowing herds wind slowly o'er the lea.

'The first boy—what can you tell me about the curfew?'
The first boy was well up in the curfew, and rattled off a 'full, true, and particular account' of that fine old English institution, much to everybody's satisfaction.

The Doctor went on repeating two or three verses till he came to the line:

The rude Forefathers of the hamlet sleep.

'What does that line mean?' he asked of a boy on the second desk.
The boy scarcely knew what it meant; but the boy below him did, and was quite eager for the question to be passed on. It was passed on, and the genius answered promptly:
'Four old men.'
'Four rude old men,' shouted the next, seeing a chance.
'Four rude old men who used to sleep in church,' cried another, ready to cap all the rest.

The Doctor passed the question on no further; but gravely explained the meaning of the line, and then proceeded with his repetition in rather a sadder voice.

Now and again he stopped short and demanded an explanation of some obscure phrase, the answers to which were now correct, now hazy, now brilliantly original. On the whole it was not satisfactory; and when for a change the Doctor gave up reciting, and made the boys read, the effect was still worse. One boy, quite a master of elocution, spoilt the whole beauty of the lines:

Nor Grandeur hear with a disdainful smile
The short and simple annals of the Poor,

by reading 'animals' instead of 'annals'; while another, of an equally zoological turn of mind, announced that:

On some fond *beast* the parting soul relies,

instead of 'breast'.

But the climax of this 'animal mania' was reached when the wretched Bramble, finally pitched upon to go on, in spite of all his efforts to hide, rendered the passage:

> Haply some hoary-headed swain may say,
> Oft have we seen him at the peep of dawn, etc.

as:

'Happy some hairy-headed swine may say.'

This was a little too much.

'That will do, sir,' said the Doctor, sternly. 'That will do. What is your name, sir?'

'Bramble, please, sir.'

'Well, Bramble, how long have you been in this class?'

'Two years, sir.'

'And have you been all the while on the bottom desk?'

'Yes, please, sir.'

'Sir, it *dis*pleases me. You are a dunce, sir.'

TALBOT BAINES REED, The Fifth Form at St Dominic's, 1887

The door opened quietly and closed. A quick whisper ran through the class: the prefect of studies. There was an instant of dead silence and then the loud crack of a pandybat on the last desk. Stephen's heart leapt up in fear.

—Any boys want flogging here, Father Arnall? cried the prefect of studies. Any lazy idle loafers that want flogging in this class?

He came to the middle of the class and saw Fleming on his knees.

—Hoho! he cried. Who is this boy? Why is he on his knees? What is your name, boy?

—Fleming, sir.

—Hoho, Fleming! An idler of course. I can see it in your eye. Why is he on his knees, Father Arnall?

—He wrote a bad Latin theme, Father Arnall said, and he missed all the questions in grammar.

—Of course he did! cried the prefect of studies, of course he did! A born idler! I can see it in the corner of his eye.

He banged his pandybat down on the desk and cried:

—Up, Fleming! Up, my boy!

Fleming stood up slowly.

—Hold out! cried the prefect of studies.

Fleming held out his hand. The pandybat came down on it with a loud smacking sound: one, two, three, four, five, six.

JAMES JOYCE, *A Portrait of the Artist as a Young Man,* 1916

Back to school! There is not much that I remember about my elementary school education anyway. What do I remember? Episodes like the Inspector calling in Standard II and asking what change you would have from £1 if you had spent so much and so much adding up to 14s. $6^1/_2$d.—or some awkward figure like that. Several got the amounts added up all right, and then failed at the last hurdle to do the subtraction right in their heads. Only one horrible little boy got the answer right—perhaps practice in the shop enabled me to do sums then which I am sure I couldn't do now. I remember that uproarious, unruly standard, forty children or so, because of the charming habit of the young woman-teacher who couldn't keep us in order and used to retire behind the blackboard to have a good cry, and then come out to face the mob again. In the meantime Bedlam broke loose; children are, in such circumstances, fiends. Then there was the one occasion when I was 'kept in' after school. This was for whistling in the class. I was very ashamed and covered with confusion sitting all alone on the long bench in the vast empty room. (That room held about seventy children in two classes: think of teaching anybody anything in such circumstances!) When I was asked what I had done it for, I confessed, what was the truth, that I didn't know how to whistle and that I thought I would try just to see if I could—and then this unexpectedly piercing note was the result. The teacher couldn't refrain from laughing at this innocent explanation, and I was let off, inexpressibly happy and relieved.

A. L. ROWSE, *A Cornish Childhood*, 1942

I was a backward child, good at nothing but singing; and the examiner who visited the school at the end of my first summer term was so disappointed with my answers that he said in a more formidable voice than I had ever heard in my life before, 'This must be a particularly stupid boy.' He was a tall, big-faced man in a brown tweed suit smelling of peat, and his large hands were terribly scrubbed and clean.

I disliked school from the start. The classroom which had to serve us all, with its smell of ink, chalk, slate pencils, corduroy, and varnish, made me feel as if my head were stuffed with hot cotton-wool, and I realized quite clearly that I was caught and there was no escape. A map of the world covered one of the walls, a small, drab world, smaller even than the classroom; the light brown benches with the inkpots let into them seemed too hard and new; the windows showed nothing but the high clouds floating past. Time moved by minute degrees there; I would sit for a long time invisibly pushing the hands of the clock on with my will, and waken to realize that they had scarcely moved. I was afraid of the other boys at first, who seemed to have grown up in a different world from mine. Gradually I made friends with the younger ones on an uneasy footing which might crumble at any moment without my knowing why. Some of my dread and dislike of school was certainly due to bad health.

EDWIN MUIR, *An Autobiography*, 1940

When will the bell ring, and end this weariness?
How long have they tugged the leash, and strained apart,
My pack of unruly hounds! I cannot start

Them again on a quarry of knowledge they hate to hunt,
I can haul them and urge them no more.

No longer now can I endure the brunt
Of the books that lie out on the desks; a full threescore
Of several insults of blotted pages, and scrawl
Of slovenly work that they have offered me.
I am sick, and what on earth is the good of it all?
What good to them or me, I cannot see!

                      So, shall I take
My last dear fuel of life to heap on my soul
And kindle my will to a flame that shall consume
Their dross of indifference; and take the toll
Of their insults in punishment?—I will not!—

I will not waste my soul and my strength for this.
What do I care for all that they do amiss!
What is the point of this teaching of mine, and of this
Learning of theirs? It all goes down the same abyss.

What does it matter to me, if they can write
A description of a dog, or if they can't?
What is the point? To us both, it is all my aunt!
And yet I'm supposed to care, with all my might.

I do not, and will not; they won't and they don't; and that's all!
I shall keep my strength for myself; they can keep theirs as well.
Why should we beat our heads against the wall
Of each other? I shall sit and wait for the bell.

D. H. LAWRENCE, 'Last Lesson of the Afternoon',
in *Complete Poems*, 1957

I remember the bright, windy morning when I set forth for the first
time, holding my stepfather's hand, wearing my little tasselled cap,

like Punch's. I remember the date, March 19th, 1894; Monday, washing day; two months after my fifth birthday. I remember we had had finnan haddock for breakfast. The school building, grim and square and immensely high, rose like a towering prison amid the slums.

Our class-teacher, Miss South, took a dislike to me from the first—I think because I took a dislike to her, her cold blue eyes and pointed nose and thin lips—and told the class I was a nasty little wretch. She made me, and other children she had no fancy for, take turns in wearing the dunce's cap of mockery, a cone of white paper, grotesquely tall, that she fashioned before us with pleasure. With pleasure, too, she resoundingly struck our cheeks with the flat of a large ruler. The lessons I can recall were writing—at first pothooks and such, and later on copperplate maxims in copybooks—at which I was very bad, smudging my way to a daily allowance of abuse and knuckle-rapping and the cruel ruler on the face; and reading, at which I was very good, though Miss South sought to belittle my achievement and sneered at my un-Yorkshire accent. I was bold, as never later in life, and answered her back, cheeking even the headmaster, to whom she sent me for a public caning in the big hall; though once only, no second time after that caning, which hurt. . . .

The children were mostly very poor. I was sorry for them, therefore; I was sorry for myself also, in that I did not attend a school from which they were absent.

G. P. DENNIS, *Bloody Mary's*, 1934

The arts in general were somewhat marginal and things like drawing and painting taught in such a way as to put one off for life. Shading, right to left—or was it left to right?—on cones or cylinders, no nonsense about drawing out of one's head. No lovely poster colours, only unsatisfactory pale water colours and if we put it on too thick that was wasteful. But of course the margins of all one's school books were copiously decorated, especially the Latin grammar (though I never drew on or knowingly messed up a proper book). It was mostly pen or pencil, though we did sometimes have crayons which melted dramatically when put onto the radiators. All schools must have been a lot messier in the good old days of inkwells in the desks, not to speak of ink-soaked paper pellets used as missiles. Inkwells in desks came in handy. I had a share in a grass snake once (as well as a share in an unsatisfactory dormouse that died before it woke); there was quite a sensation in class when the grass snake put its head out of the ink hole. The desks of course were copiously carved with initials and the soft wood gouged out for railways. Some were good enough to run small marbles along. There is a story which seems well authenticated, though I don't actually remember it, to the effect that my brother and I, in VI B, had both broken silence with the same remark: 'Please, sir, the ink has gone and spilt itself.'

NAOMI MITCHISON, *Small Talk*, 1973

The worst thing, somehow more noticeable than at The Downs, was the total lack of privacy. I had a desk in the big schoolroom and literally nowhere else in the world. I had to keep all my possessions in my desk and sit at it from morning to night except when I was out on the playground—a diversion I did not enjoy. I had no difficulty with my work which was more interesting than anything I had done at The Downs. I was always cold. The only heating came from radiators and the only way to get warm was to sit on one—a practice that is said to cause piles, though it did not in my case. There was no heating at all in the bedrooms and of course no hot water. We washed in cold water, took a cold bath every morning and were allowed a hot bath once a week. There were hot showers after games, but as the other boys flicked the bottoms of the smaller ones with a towel I never stopped in the shower for long.

A. J. P. TAYLOR, *A Personal History*, 1983

The least departure from routine was welcome. It was Dictation, say, but outside the day had darkened for dirty weather. Perhaps there was old snow on the window-sills, shrunk and salt-like stuff pitted with soot-specks like a sort of poor man's ermine. The long panes above it began to picture a pervasion of yellow wreaths upon a slate sky. We were interested, of course. Perhaps somebody's chimney was a-fire? No, it was fog. Good—in fact, better still. If it got worse over the dinner break, mebbe we wouldn't be able to see our way back to school. We watched it until our eyes when re-called by the teacher saw a very dim class-room indeed. 'Please, miss, I can't see,' somebody would say hopefully. But he was premature. Teacher could see. Dictation resumed its dreary way. All the same, it *was* getting darker. Several lads had to be reprimanded for lowering their cheeks to desk-level as they poked their pens along. And the windows showed a dingy yellow backed on purple, the colour of bruises going off. In the end, Teacher had to send someone to fetch the caretaker in order to have the gas-lamps lit. Dictation was off pro tem.

When the caretaker came, that same moustached bloke in the aggressively blue work-jacket, we focused a tremendous interest on his every movement. He lit a long wax taper, moved a boy or a girl off a desk under the first gas-bracket and carefully ascended bearing the taper and its wonderful single petal of flame aloft with him. He raised it, topped it into the dim white globe; there was a pop, and the fruit of the gas-tree swelled with a creamy light. It took some time to get them all a-glowing; it might have stopped being Dictation; it might even be near on dinner-time. Ah!

JACK COMMON (b. 1903), *Kiddar's Luck*, 1951

White is the January, and schoolboys' scuffed
Footprints in the snow lead to the sound of a bell.
It is Scotland and I attend the dead dominies.
A hand is spinning the globe, saying 'Galileo'
In a cold classroom, in a puff of chalk-dust.
Dominies, dead now, forgive these gauche lines,
My compromised parsings. Boyhood's grammarians
Set down the long examination, 'ink exercises'

At moments of mania, running riot through
The iron language like a trill of angry Rs.
'What sorts of men were the Caesars? Did you heave an axe,
At the wall, against them? Did you stand for your country?
Keep up with the translation. It is good for you.
Horace. Livy. Ballantyne. I am already historical.'

Douglas Dunn, 'Dominies', in Selected Poems, 1986

My serious schooling really began when I went up to the boys' school at the age of five. Serious, but, as it proved, not strenuous. None of the boys of my year, including myself, ever showed any signs of talent, yet few of us had difficulty in satisfying the teachers at the end of each year that we were fit to move up to the next higher standard. We had no scholarly ambitions, no external examinations and no homework and, consequently, our education made no great demands on our intellects or on our emotions. The teachers were neither tyrants nor bullies. There wasn't one that I could even describe as a 'character'. I think that our natural instinct to stick by each other would have enabled us to resist a bully among the boys if there had been one. In short, in my time and in my school the only possible threat to our contentment was boredom.

In fact we were seldom bored and never for long. This I attribute not so much to our personal qualities as to the efforts of the teachers and particularly of the Headmaster. My school memories are very largely centred around the Headmaster—a short and tubby, straight-backed and dapper little man. Except in his sterner moments his eyes danced with what in anyone other than my Headmaster I would have diagnosed immediately as devilment. His was the main influence in my school life, for, apart from being the Headmaster, he taught the fifth and sixth standards himself, and since I reached the fifth standard at the age of nine my last four years were spent directly under him.

His method of preventing the school from lapsing into boredom was occasionally to inject an unorthodox item into a half-hour scheduled to be spent on a routine lesson. His timing was perfect and his choice of an item to arouse interest never fell flat. I can still recall the afternoons of dull, wet days when the Headmaster revived our flagging interest by unexpectedly discarding a lesson in English or in arithmetic and substituting a talk which soon became an animated discussion on proverbs, parables, quotations, miracles, ghosts, Lloyd George's ninepence for fourpence, Home Rule for Ireland or even the interpretation of the laws of football. On one occasion he challenged each of us in standards five and six to write a poem—we who spoke the flat dialect of Lancashire and who spurned elegant speech as 'sissy'. Surprisingly we found the effort absorbing and, for good measure, the results provided us with a half-hour's hilarity for another day.

His one and only attempt to improve our accents also turned out hilarious—to the school and to the rest of the teachers, but not, I think, to the Headmaster himself. He asked us to repeat after him the phrase: 'Her hair of gold, her hair of gold, the lustre of her hair of gold.' The response he got was something like this:

> Ur ur of go-ald
> Ur ur of go-ald
> The lus-ther of
> Ur ur of go-ald.

He stuck it grimly for a while in growing distress, seeking to make some headway by infiltration and inviting some of us to try it solo. When at last he literally threw up his hands in despair the whole room rocked with laughter. We were sorry for him all the same, for we would have liked to be able to please him.

GEORGE WOODCOCK, in Brian Inglis (ed.), *John Bull's Schooldays*, 1961

'Bunter's making history!' remarked Bob Cherry, at the breakfast table.

He was!

He had been first up of the Form that morning. Now he was last into breakfast! Two records had been broken in one morning!

Not only was Bunter last in to brekker; but he was very late indeed.

Strange to relate, his fat face was bright and cheery when he rolled in late.

If getting up early and being late for meals made Bunter feel merry and bright, he was a changed Bunter!

Fisher T. Fish glared at him. So did Skinner. Already Fishy was spreading the news of the true nature of Bunter's great expectations. The effect on Bunter's friends was to deflate their friendship like a punctured tyre.

But Bunter did not heed.

He was evidently bucked about something, and seemed to have forgotten even the vigorous way in which Fisher T. Fish had handled him before prayers.

Harry Wharton smiled at Frank Nugent, who chuckled. They thought they knew why Bunter was late, and why he came in so cheery and bright. Had he nipped into Quelch's study for those lost coupons instead of coming in when the bell rang for brekker? It looked as if he had!

When the juniors went out after breakfast, the satisfied, happy grin was still on Bunter's fat face.

But it disappeared suddenly, as Bolsover major came across to him in the quad and kicked him.

Bolsover did not speak. He did not condescend to explain why he kicked Bunter. But he did kick him—hard!

Bunter roared.

The bully of the Remove, having kicked him a second time, walked away, leaving the fat Owl wriggling and yelling.

Why Bolsover major had done it, Bunter did not know. He did not, as yet, connect Bolsover's action with what he had told Fisher T. Fish that morning. It was quite a mystery to Bunter—a painful mystery.

Even after that kicking, Bunter was still looking very cheery when he went into class with the Remove.

Had he not cause for satisfaction?

In his pocket reposed, at long last, the set of coupons issued by Ginker's Golden Football Pools!

It had occurred to Bunter's fat brain that during breakfast there would be a last chance of retrieving that treasure.

Quelch was at breakfast in Common-room; and there was a maid in his study with a broom. That did not matter. Bunter was in time.

Naturally, he had not thought of this idea at first. It involved being late for a meal—a thing not likely to occur to Bunter in a hurry!

Still, it did occur to him, and he heroically resolved to postpone brekker while he tried it on. It was worth it, for the enormous sums he was going to win from Ginker's.

The maid with the broom stared at him when he rolled into the study and scouted in the wastepaper-basket. That basket, luckily, had not yet been dealt with.

There, among other wastepaper, was the crumpled envelope and the crumpled sheet of coupons, just where Quelch had thrown them the previous day.

Bunter grabbed them.

The astonished maid watched him, but did nothing but stare. Bunter rolled off with his prize. Fortune at last had favoured him, and it was no wonder that he grinned happily at the breakfast table, no wonder that he recovered from Bolsover's kicking, no wonder that he smirked a fat and fatuous smirk as he rolled into the Form-room with the Remove.

That sheet of coupons in his pocket was worth—what? Hundreds of pounds, Bunter hoped! He had a hopeful nature!

There was a general grin along the ranks of the Remove. Most of the fellows had heard by that time.

It was no longer necessary for Wharton and Nugent to keep Bunter's extraordinary secret. That secret was out. Fisher T. Fish, breathing wrath and indignation, was telling the world.

It seemed no end of a joke to most of the Remove. It did not seem much of a joke to the fellows who had been buttering Bunter in the belief that a big remittance had arrived for him.

Only the fact that Bunter was short-sighted prevented him from noticing the changed looks of his friends in class. They looked at Bunter as if they could have bitten him.

The rest of the fellows grinned. Mr Quelch noticed signs of unusual hilarity in his Form that morning, and frowned. He did not know what was amusing the Remove—rather fortunately for Bunter!

Billy Bunter had never been keen on class. But he found it more boring than ever that morning. He was anxious to get going on his football coupons! Lessons seemed a very irritating waste of time in the circumstances. The fat Owl simply could not give Quelch any attention.

Second lesson was history, and Quelch asked his Form questions. He addressed Bunter twice without receiving an answer. Bunter was deep in thought—not on historical subjects!

'Bunter!' said Mr Quelch, for the third time, in a deep, rumbling voice.

Bob Cherry kicked Bunter under the desk.

'Wow!' gasped Bunter. 'I say—Oh! Yes, sir! Did you speak, sir? I heard what you said, sir!'

'Indeed!' snapped Mr Quelch. 'If you heard what I said, Bunter, kindly answer my question at once!'

'Oh!' gasped Bunter, wondering what on earth question Quelch had asked.

Mr Quelch gave him a grim look. Quelch did not approve of fellows allowing their thoughts to wander during class.

'Bunter, who was defeated at the battle of Bosworth?'

'Manchester United, sir!'

'What?' roared Mr Quelch.

'I—I mean, Sheffield Wednesday, sir!' gasped Bunter.

'Ha, ha, ha!' roared the Remove.

Evidently Bunter's fat mind was running on League teams which he was selecting for his football coupons.

'Bunter! How dare you make such absurd answers!' hooted Mr Quelch. 'You will write out "Richard the Third was defeated at the battle of Bosworth"—a hundred times!'

'W-w-was he, sir?' gasped Bunter.

'Do you not know that he was, Bunter?'

'I—I thought he was defeated once, sir—'

'What?'

'I—I never knew that he was defeated a hundred times, sir—'

'Ha, ha, ha!' shrieked the Remove.

'Upon my word!' ejaculated Mr Quelch. 'This boy's stupidity is beyond belief! Bunter, you will write out a hundred times that Richard the Third was defeated and slain at the battle of Bosworth.'

'Oh! Yes, sir! I—I see! Yes, sir!' gasped Bunter.

'And if you do not give attention to the lesson, Bunter, I shall cane you!'

'Oh, lor'! I mean, certainly, sir.'

After which Bunter tried hard to dismiss more important matters from his fat mind, and give Quelch some attention.

'Frank Richards' [Charles Hamilton], *Magnet*, 1936

One morning just after breakfast Gordon discovered that he had done the wrong maths for Jenks. He rushed in search of help.

'I say, Fletcher, look here, be a sport. I have done the wrong stuff for that ass Jenks. Let's have a look at yours.'

In ten minutes four tremendous howlers in as many sums had been reproduced on Gordon's paper. The work was collected that morning, and nothing more was heard of it till the next day. Gordon thought himself quite safe and had ceased to take any interest in the matter. The form was working out some riders more or less quietly. Suddenly a quick voice interrupted him.

'Caruthers, did you copy your algebra off Fletcher?'

'No, sir.'

Jenks, a fiery little man, was rather fond of asking such leading questions.

Caruthers had got rather tired of it. The man was a fool; he must know by this time that he was bound to get the same answer.

'Fletcher, did you copy off Caruthers?'

'No, sir.'

'Caruthers, did you see Fletcher's paper?'

How insistent the ass was getting.

'Fletcher, did you see Caruthers's paper?'

'No, sir.'

'Oh, you silly fellows. Then I shall have to put both your papers before the Headmaster. I'm afraid you will both be expelled.'

Jenks had a strange notion of the offences that merited expulsion. Every time he reported a boy he expected to see him marching sadly to the station to catch the afternoon train. Once Collins had stuck a pin into a wonderful mercury apparatus and entirely ruined it.

'Oh, Collins, you stupid boy. I shall have to report you to the Headmaster, and you know what that means. We shan't see you here any more.'

Gordon had, of course, not the slightest fear of getting 'bunked'. But still it was a nuisance. He would have to be more careful next time.

'Now look here, you two,' Jenks went on, after a bit. 'If either of you cares to own up, I won't report you at all. I will deal with you myself.'

Slowly Gordon rose. It was obviously an occasion where it paid to own up.

'I did, sir.'

'Oh, I thought as much. You see yours was in pencil, and if possible a little worse than Fletcher's. Sit down.'

ALEC WAUGH, *The Loom of Youth*, 1917

'*Cigars*,' said Mr Prendergast in a stage whisper.

'Ah yes, cigars. Boys, I have been deeply distressed to learn that several cigar ends have been found—where have they been found?'

'*Boiler-room.*'

'In the boiler-room. I regard this as reprehensible. What boy has been smoking cigars in the boiler-room?'

There was a prolonged silence, during which the Doctor's eye travelled down the line of boys.

'I will give the culprit until luncheon to give himself up. If I do not hear from him by then the whole school will be heavily punished.'

'Damn!' said Grimes. 'I gave those cigars to Clutterbuck. I hope the little beast has the sense to keep quiet.'

'Go to your classes,' said the Doctor.

The boys filed out.

'I should think, by the look of them, they were exceedingly cheap cigars,' added Mr Prendergast sadly. 'They were a pale yellow colour.'

'That makes it worse,' said the Doctor. 'To think of any boy under my charge smoking pale yellow cigars in a boiler-room! It is *not* a gentlemanly fault.'

The masters went upstairs.

'That's your little mob in there,' said Grimes; 'you let them out at eleven.'

'But what am I to teach them?' said Paul in sudden panic.

'Oh, I shouldn't try to *teach* them anything, not just yet, anyway. Just keep them quiet.'

'Now that's a thing I've never learned to do,' sighed Mr Prendergast.

Paul watched him amble into his classroom at the end of the passage, where a burst of applause greeted his arrival. Dumb with terror he went into his own classroom.

Ten boys sat before him, their hands folded, their eyes bright with expectation.

'Good morning, sir,' said the one nearest him.

'Good morning,' said Paul.

'Good morning, sir,' said the next.

'Good morning,' said Paul.

'Good morning, sir,' said the next.

'Oh, shut up,' said Paul.

At this the boy took out a handkerchief and began to cry quietly.

'Oh, sir,' came a chorus of reproach, 'you've hurt his feelings. He's very sensitive; it's his Welsh blood, you know; it makes people very emotional. Say "Good morning" to him, sir, or he won't be happy all day. After all, it is a good morning, isn't it, sir?'

'Silence!' shouted Paul above the uproar, and for a few moments things were quieter.

'Please, sir,' said a small voice—Paul turned and saw a grave-looking youth holding up his hand—'please, sir, perhaps he's been smoking cigars and doesn't feel well.'

'Silence!' said Paul again.

The ten boys stopped talking and sat perfectly still staring at him. He felt himself getting hot and red under their scrutiny.

EVELYN WAUGH, *Decline and Fall*, 1928

Most of the class had by now settled down to their own devices—quiet or otherwise. William was the only one who seemed to be taking any interest in the lecture or the lecturer. William, on the strength of his play and story, considered himself a literary character, and was quite willing to give a hearing to a brother artist.

'Well,' said Mr Welbecker, assuming his lecturer's manner, gazing round at his audience, and returning at last reluctantly to William, 'I repeat that I incline to the theory that the plays of Shakespeare were written by Bacon.'

'How could they be?' said William.

'I've already said that I wished you wouldn't keep interrupting,' snapped the lecturer.

'That *was* a question,' said William triumphantly. 'You can't say that wasn't a question, and you said we could ask questions. How could that other man Ham—'

'I said Bacon.'

'Well, it's nearly the same,' said William. 'Well, how could this man Bacon write them if Shakespeare wrote them?'

'Ah, but you see I don't believe that Shakespeare did write them,' said Mr Welbecker mysteriously.

'Well, why's he got his name printed on all the books then?' said William. 'He must've told the printers he did, or they wouldn't put his name on, an' he ought to know. An' if this other man Eggs—'

'I said Bacon,' snapped Mr Welbecker again.

'Well, Bacon then,' said William, 'well, if this man Bacon wrote them, they wouldn't put this man Shakespeare's name on the books. They wouldn't be allowed to. They'd get put in prison for it. The only way he could have done it was by poisoning this man Shakespeare and then stealing his plays. That's what I'd have done, anyway, if I'd been him, and I'd wanted to say I'd written them.'

'That's all nonsense,' said Mr Welbecker sharply. 'Of course I'm willing to admit that it's an open question.' Then, returning to his breezy manner and making an unsuccessful attempt to enlarge his audience: 'Now, boys, I want you all please to listen to me—'

No one responded. Those who were playing noughts and crosses continued to play noughts and crosses. Those who were engaged in mimic battles, the ammunition of which consisted in pellets of blotting-paper soaked in ink, continued to be so engaged. Those who were playing that game of cricket in which a rubber represents the ball and a ruler the bat remained engrossed in it. The boy who was drawing low-pitched but irritating sounds from a whistle continued to draw low-pitched but irritating sounds from a whistle. Dejectedly Mr Welbecker returned to his sole auditor.

'I want first to tell you the story of the play of which you are all going to act a scene for the shield that I am presenting,' he said. 'There was a man called Hamlet—'

'You just said he was called Bacon,' said William.

'I did *not* say he was called Bacon,' snapped Mr Welbecker.

'Yes, 'scuse me, you did,' said William politely. 'When I called him Ham you said it was Bacon, and now you're calling him Ham yourself.'

'This was a different man,' said Mr Welbecker. '*Listen!* This man was called Hamlet and his uncle had killed his father because he wanted to marry his mother.'

'What did he want to marry his mother for?' said William. 'I've never heard of anyone wanting to marry their mother.'

'It was *Hamlet*'s mother he wanted to marry.'

'Oh, that man that you think wrote the plays.'

'No, that was Bacon.'

'You said it was Ham a minute ago. Whenever I say it's Bacon you say it's Ham, and whenever I say it's Ham you say it's Bacon. I don't think you know *which* his name was.'

'Will you *listen*!' said the distraught lecturer. 'This man Hamlet decided to kill his uncle.'

'Why?'

'I've told you. Because his uncle had killed his father.'

'Whose father?'

'*Hamlet*'s. There's a beautiful girl in the play called Ophelia, and Hamlet had once wanted to marry her.'

'You just said he wanted to marry his mother.'

'I did *not*. I wish you'd listen. Then he went mad, and this girl fell into the river. It was supposed to be an accident, but probably—'

'He pushed her in,' supplied William.

'*Who* pushed her?' demanded Mr Welbecker irritably.

'I thought you were going to say that that man Bacon pushed her in.'

'*Hamlet*, you mean.'

'I tell you what,' said William confidingly, 'let's say Eggs for both of them. Then we shan't get so muddled. Eggs means whichever of them it was.'

RICHMAL CROMPTON, *William the Pirate*, 1932

'Good morning, Miss Brodie. Good morning, sit down, girls,' said the headmistress who had entered in a hurry, leaving the door wide open.

Miss Brodie passed behind her with her head up, up, and shut the door with the utmost meaning.

'I have only just looked in,' said Miss Mackay, 'and I have to be off. Well, girls, this is the first day of the new session. Are we downhearted? No. You girls must work hard this year at every subject and pass your qualifying examination with flying colours. Next year you will be in the Senior school, remember. I hope you've all had a nice summer holiday, you all look nice and brown. I hope in due course of time to read your essays on how you spent them.'

When she had gone Miss Brodie looked hard at the door for a long time. A girl, not of her set, called Judith, giggled. Miss Brodie said to Judith, 'That will do.' She turned to the blackboard and rubbed out with her duster the long division sum she always kept on the blackboard in case of intrusions from outside during any arithmetic period when Miss Brodie should happen not to be teaching arithmetic. When she had done this she turned back to the class and said, 'Are we downhearted no, are we downhearted no. As I was saying, Mussolini has performed feats of magnitude and unemployment is even farther abolished under him than it was last year. I shall be able to tell you a great deal this term. As you know, I don't believe in talking down to children, you are capable of grasping more than is generally appreciated by your elders. Education means a leading out, from *e*, out and *duco*, I lead. Qualifying examination or no qualifying examination, you will have the benefit of my experiences in Italy. In Rome I saw the Forum and I saw the Colosseum where the gladiators died and the slaves were thrown to the lions. A vulgar American remarked to me, "It looks like a mighty fine quarry." They talk nasally. Mary, what does to talk nasally mean?'

Mary did not know.

'Stupid as ever,' said Miss Brodie. 'Eunice?'

'Through your nose,' said Eunice.

'Answer in a complete sentence, please,' said Miss Brodie. 'This year I think you should all start answering in complete sentences, I must try to remember this rule. Your correct answer is "To talk nasally means to talk through one's nose". The American said, "It looks like a mighty fine quarry." Ah! It was there the gladiators fought. "Hail Caesar!" they cried. "These about to die salute thee!" '

Miss Brodie stood in her brown dress like a gladiator with raised arm and eyes flashing like a sword. 'Hail Caesar!' she cried again, turning radiantly to the window light, as if Caesar sat there. 'Who opened the window?' said Miss Brodie dropping her arm.

Nobody answered.

'Whoever has opened the window has opened it too wide,' said Miss Brodie. 'Six inches is perfectly adequate. More is vulgar. One should have an innate sense of these things.'

MURIEL SPARK, *The Prime of Miss Jean Brodie*, 1961

Think of it. Twenty girls or so—were there so many?—in the A level French class, and in front of each a similar, if not identical small, slim greenish book, more or less used, more or less stained. When they riffled through the pages, the text did not look attractive. It proceeded in strict, soldierly columns of rhymed couplets, a form disliked by both the poetry-lovers and the indifferent amongst them. Nothing seemed to be happening, it all seemed to be the same. The speeches were very long. There appeared to be no interchange, no battle of dialogue, no action. *Phèdre.* The French teacher told them that the play was based on the *Hippolytus* of Euripides, and that Racine had altered the plot by adding a character, a young girl, Aricie, whom Hippolytus should fall in love with. She neglected to describe the original play, which they did not know. They wrote down, Hippolytus, Euripides, Aricie. She told them that the play kept the unities of classical drama, and told them what these unities were, and they wrote them down. The Unity of Time = One Day. The Unity of Space = One Place. The Unity of Action = One Plot. She neglected to say what kind of effect these constrictions might have on an imagined world: she offered a half-hearted rationale she clearly despised a little herself, as though the Greeks and the French were children who made unnecessary rules for themselves, did not see wider horizons. The girls were embarrassed by having to read this passionate sing-song verse aloud in French. Emily shared their initial reluctance, their near-apathy. She was later to believe that only she became a secret addict of Racine's convoluted world, tortuously lucid, savage and controlled. As I said, the imagination of the other girls' thoughts was not Emily's strength. In Racine's world, all the inmates were gripped wholly by incompatible passions which

350

swelled uncontrollably to fill their whole universe, brimming over
and drowning its horizons. They were all creatures of excess, their
secret blood burned and boiled and an unimaginably hot bright sun
glared down in judgment.

A. S. Byatt, 'Racine and the Tablecloth',
in *Sugar and Other Stories*, 1987

Sir, you were a credit to whatever
Ungrateful slate-blue skies west of the Severn
Hounded you out to us. With white, cropped head,
Small and composed, and clean as a Descartes
From as it might be Dowlais, 'Fiery' Evans
We knew you as. You drilled and tightly lipped
Le futur parfait dans le passé like
The Welsh Guards in St James's, your pretence
Of smouldering rage an able sergeant-major's.

We jumped to it all right whenever each
Taut smiling question fixed us. Then it came:
Crash! The ferrule smashed down on the first
Desk of the file. You whispered: *Quelle bêtise!*
Ecoutez, s'il vous plait, de quelle bêtise
on est capable!
    Yet you never spoke
To us of poetry; it was purely language,
The lovely logic of its tenses and
Its accidence that, mutilated, moved you
To rage or outrage that I think was not
At all times simulated. It would never
Do in our days, dominie, to lose
Or seem to lose your temper. And besides
Grammarians are a dying kind, the day
Of histrionic pedagogy's over.

You never taught me Ronsard, no one did,
But you gave me his language. He addressed
The man who taught him Greek as *Toi qui dores*
(His name was Jean Dorat) *la France de l'or.*
I couldn't turn a phrase like that on 'Evans';
And yet you gild or burnish something as,
At fifty in the humidity of Touraine,
Time and again I profit by your angers.

DONALD DAVIE, 'To a Teacher of French',
in *Collected Poems*, 1990

Well, off we went—there were twelve of us—into the Hamlet class.
We were what was called Set B and few of us had done more than
read bits out of Hamlet before. Not one of us had seen it except for
a very terrible film that had been brought to the school in a bag and
showed Hamlet looking pretty ancient in a gold wig wailing about
some battlements in clouds of what looked like steam.

Before this lesson Bex had had them all reading round the class,
but it was so dreadful that now she had us up in the front like twelve-
year-olds acting it from our books. As usual there were not enough
books to go round so Rosencrantz and Guildenstern were sharing
and chucking the book over to the Queen when needed. Polonius
was bobbing about reading over the shoulder of the first Player and
I remember that a very weird girl called Penelope Dabbs was dragging herself, stomach downwards, across the floor, being Hamlet,
and gazing with great intensity at the King to see if he was going to
have a funny turn. Her eyes stuck out on stalks as she directed them
at the King (played by Bex) and she also held the book high in the
air off the floor. As chief chap she at least had been allowed a book
to herself, but as she waved it around, rolled her eyes, dragged her
stomach over the splinters crying out and carrying on as Hamlet
does, it did occur to me as odd that this was what was necessary to
get me into Cambridge.

I wasn't in it of course.

In the Classroom

Since the time when I couldn't read I haven't been asked to take part in things and I just sat there at my desk. Outside it was raining. The classroom had grown very dark. The desks were all at untidy angles, pushed back, and the dirty blackboard behind and the awful flowers in vile vases on the ledges were especially depressing. Flowers in classrooms are as depressing as flowers in hospitals—they just emphasise the fact that you can't get out and see them growing. Classrooms break your heart.

'No!' bellowed Bex at Penelope Dabbs. 'Not—oh, you are a stupid year! A *stupid* year!'

'Blaa blaa blaa,' droned somebody else.

JANE GARDAM, *Bilgewater*, 1976

I went to the local Catholic school, St Peter's, a building with three rooms and three teachers: Mr Clancy, Mr Crawford, and Miss McDonald. Mr Clancy was the principal. Every morning, half an hour after class started, he left his room and walked down to the Liverpool Hotel, where he drank till he was well drunk, then came back to school to assault Miss McDonald. Miss McDonald, who taught the youngest children, hearing Mr Clancy coming, jammed a wedge of wood under her door, turned the key shut, and put her shoulder to the door. Mr Clancy crashed against the door, but, as he was drunk, his movements were sluggish, no match for a wedge, a lock, and Miss McDonald. After a joyless bout of shoving and crashing, Mr Clancy went back to his own class, muttering under his sodden breath. He had a nervous tic. He kept twitching the point of his nose with his thumb and seemed to keep his nails long for that purpose. His room contained the chemistry laboratory, a glass case with three or four bottles of acids, a Bunsen burner, a pipette, and a scales. These were never used, except on one afternoon, while the class was on lunch break, Mr Clancy took one of the bottles containing sulphuric acid, drank it, and killed himself. I don't remember if he was replaced, or who got the principal's job, because soon after I went to school in Newry.

My teacher at St Peter's was Mr Crawford, a man who lived for music and stories. When he heard Mr Clancy leaving for the Liverpool Hotel, Mr Crawford climbed upon a desk at the back of the room to verify Mr Clancy's departure, and then, satisfied, settled down to tell us stories and to talk about music. He had strange hands. His nails were bitten down to the quick, and the palms of his hands were as soft as butter. He played the organ in the church, and I was in the choir. His hands were always lower than the keyboard, and his fingers seemed to climb to the notes as if slithering over a wall. When he pressed the keys, the skin of his fingers spread itself wide and flat, as if it wanted to adhere to the notes. Years later, I came across a passage in Ralph Cusack's autobiography, *Cadenza*, where he describes an old man, in a café somewhere in Provence, playing silent piano on the surface of the table and bending his head to hear the sounds. After a while Cusack discovered, by following the old man's fingers, that he was playing Beethoven's *Moonlight Sonata*. Mr Crawford never looked at the keyboard while he was playing. His head kept darting and straining from side to side, as if the music came from some secret place and he had to find it.

He was a terrible teacher, except for stories and the talk of music. He, too, left the room as often as the coast was clear and Mr Clancy gone, but Mr Crawford only went for a walk. He had a peculiar manner of walking, always on the bias. If you walked along the street with him, he kept cutting across your path and crowding you off the pavement, as if he hated a straight line. His body was in some acute or oblique relation to his soul. Even if he intended to walk from his house at the west corner of the square to go up Church Street, he always left the pavement and walked as if he were going to the school or the church, and then he would wheel back, tacking his way till he got to where he was going. When he absented himself from the classroom, we resumed the only entertainment available. The room had a high wooden ceiling, and we wrote with Waverley pens, which had wooden stems and long, pointed steel nibs. If you flung the pen hard and true, you could get it to lodge in the ceiling. If it fell down, it had a good chance of hitting someone on the head. Either way, it was worth trying. During the school year the ceiling acquired an impressive array of Waverley pens. At the end of the year, they were removed, and we started afresh.

DENIS DONOGHUE, *Warrenpoint*, 1991

One morning there was some speculation in Gerald's form as to who would take the English period in the sudden absence of their English master with a carbuncle on the neck.

Gerald, lolling in his desk, said: 'They've obviously forgotten us.' He felt a pleasurable aura of anarchy and freedom tinging the dull, regimented weekday.

'Perhaps they'll rope in Miss Pemberton,' said a feeble boarder called Naylor, quite seriously. 'I've heard she's a BA.'

'I've heard you're a b.f.,' said Howarth.

'She could give us a talk on the facts of life,' said Gerald, essaying a prurience which he realized immediately was of a cowardly feebleness.

'Down in a forest that nobody knows Stands Evie Pemberton without any clothes. Along came—' began Howarth, but his voice died as the Headmaster swept through the door. There was utter silence and Gerald unostentatiously assumed a straight back and an alert air. Mr Pemberton took the chair from behind the master's desk, which in this room stood on a dais, and brought it forward close to the front row of desks. As he sat down he said: 'What is Mr Marsh reading with you, boys?'

'*Modern English Lyrics*, sir,' said one or two voices.

'Take out your books.' The Headmaster crossed his legs. 'Thompson, what is your greatest ambition in life?'

Thompson looked alarmed, but after a moment said: 'To play for the first eleven, sir.' Gerald could not help admiring this foolish answer for he was forced to admit to himself that he could have given no kind of answer at all.

'*My* greatest ambition,' Mr Pemberton said and then tantalizingly paused. 'Can you guess, Bracher?'

'No, sir,' replied Gerald faintly.

In the Classroom

'You know, boys,' said the Headmaster, 'the true aim of education is to make good men and women. Not clever men and women or men and women capable of earning a thousand a year or becoming Prime Minister. We all know what is good and what is bad, but we have to learn to choose what is good. You will hear some parents say: "I want my son to become a doctor" or "I want my son to go into the family business". But to train a boy for those things is not the primary concern of school. The primary concern of school is morals. When I see a boy go through the school quite clean in mind and deed, then I know that the school has done its job. To me it is only a secondary consideration that the boy may be brilliant or mediocre in class or on the sports field—though perhaps you wouldn't guess that when you read my comment on a boy's report, would you, Naylor?'

The joke got its laugh.

ROY FULLER, *The Ruined Boys*, 1959

This morning I was in the middle of a rather important demonstration (tangents) on the board when Hillman asked for a new nib. I told him that he did not need a nib in order to listen to a demonstration, and he replied that he would need one as soon as they started on the Riders. 'Then ask for it then,' I said. He objected that this would mean he would lose time while the others were working and would get behindhand. I saw the justice of this, but pointed out that it would have been better for everybody if he had asked for his nib at the beginning of the period instead of interrupting the lesson half-way through. He said he had only just noticed that his nib was broken; it must have got caught in the hinge of his desk while he was looking for a ruler. I might well have asked him what business he had to be looking for a ruler when he was supposed to be following my explanation on the board, but to save time I gave him a nib from the box in my desk and told him to be more careful in future.

Three more boys then came up in quick succession and asked for nibs, and as I had given one to Hillman I could not in fairness refuse them to the others. All this delay was maddening enough, but worse was to follow, for while the third boy was standing by my desk I heard a sharp cry and looked up to see Sapoulos with his head wedged in one of the lockers, while Atkins and Mason were trying to pull him out by the arms. This at any rate was the explanation given me by Mason, and I was forced to accept it, for as I stepped down from the dais I tripped somehow over my gown and fell to the floor, though not heavily, so that I was unable to see whether Sapoulos was really incapable of freeing himself or not. By the time I had recovered my feet and assured the boys who ran to my aid that I was unhurt, the incident was over and the three boys back at their desks.

Naturally I asked Sapoulos why he had gone to his locker without permission, but he was sobbing and unable to speak, so Atkins volunteered the information that Sapoulos was looking, he believed, for a pen.

I threw up my hands.

'*Where* is the boy's pen?' I demanded.

'It is in the tool-house of my gardener's aunt,' said Mason.

I never overlook impertinence, and I gave Mason a talking-to which he will, I think, remember as long as he lives. I told him that he had come to Burgrove not to be a public buffoon nor to practise the art of being rude to those who were a good deal older and perhaps even a little wiser than himself, but to learn. Presumably, I said, it was the wish of his parents who were spending their money on his education that he should fit himself for a Public School and afterwards for some useful career. At present I could see no prospect of either wish being fulfilled. He would have to pull himself together and take up a very different attitude towards his school-work if he was to have the slightest chance of getting through Common Entrance; and as for a career, unless there was an unexpected demand for third-rate comedians, I could not see any way in which the world would be likely to make use of his services. 'There will have to be a big change, Mason,' I told him, 'or you and I will find ourselves at loggerheads.'

H. F. ELLIS, *The World of A. J. Wentworth, B. A.*, 1949

You sat at your desk by the window, and heard about anguish and guilt, passion and grief, Macbeth, Heathcliff, Cathy. And beyond the door the dinner bell rang and people clattered down the stairs to play hockey in North Oxford. Wars were chalked up on the blackboard, and the death of kings, and disposed of in a shower of chalk dust, whole populations wiped out to make way for the declension of a Latin verb. Somewhere, there was a place where these things happened, a place of decision and disaster, but it could be contained between the pages of books and tidied away to make room for the real world of piano lessons and dinner tickets and home at ten to four.

The products of Australia, says Miss Hammond, are meat, and fruit, and grain. The climate is arid, the deserts waterless. Sydney exports tinned peaches. The aborigines eat frogs and lizards, believe that men can be killed by means of magic. 'In New Guinea,' says Clare, 'people think their ancestors are spirits. They talk to them, just like they talk to each other.'

Miss Hammond smiles. She likes people to show an interest. Yes, she says, the customs of primitive tribes are interesting. How did you know that, she says? 'I read a book.' And there's this thing in my attic, I don't quite know what it is, what it means, something my great-grandfather brought here. Liz and Maureen think it's creepy. I don't really. Beautiful, in a funny way. Sad, somehow, but I don't know why.

Outside, the white skies press down on the city. It snows.

PENELOPE LIVELY, *The House in Norham Gardens*, 1974

We were real good
and got to share a desk
that smelt like the head's Bible
when I lifted up its lid
and nicked a sharp HB
from Eileen's leather pouch,
knowing that she knew

but would never tell on me.
There wasn't a single hair
between our sleeping legs
that I could ever see—
only that spiky *différance*
waiting on history.
Hers was a little plum,
mine a scaldy that could pee
yella as the tartan skirt
she slid one tiny bit
to let me touch her pumice-silk,
chalky like my glans might be.

TOM PAULIN, 'Rosetta Stone', in *Fivemiletown*, 1987

He stood by his desk and called: Saepire circumdare?
Silence.
He nodded. He glanced at Catriona.
Is it to do with fencing in?
It is precisely to do with that. Now, all of yous, all you wee first-yearers, cause that's what you are, wee first-yearers. You are here being fenced in by us the teachers at the behest of the government in explicit simulation of your parents viz. the suppressed poor. Repeat after me: We are being fenced in by the teachers
We are being fenced in by the teachers
at the behest of a dictatorship government
at the behest of a dictatorship government
in explicit simulation of our fucking parents the silly bastards
in explicit simulation of our fucking parents the silly bastards
Laughter.
Good, good, but cut out that laughing. You're here to be treated as young would-be adults under terms that are constant to us all; constant to us all. Okay then that last bit: viz. the suppressed poor!
viz. the suppressed poor!
Cheering.

But that was okay. Patrick nodded. What time is it somebody? And he checked the time given with that of his watch, and he gazed at the book on his desk. He reached to close its pages. There wasnt long to go now. And the weans were watching the weans were watching.

I'm reading about the Pythagoreans, he said, I've had the book open on my desk. They were great believers in harmony. Does anybody know what harmony is? And dont answer because it's fucking impossible. By the time you've reached third year you'll just burst out laughing when somebody asks that kind of thing. Okay. What time is it now? Patrick looked at his watch. He wanted to get out and away. He needed to think things out. He opened the pages of the book and closed them at once. He smiled at the class: they were that fucking wee! I'm so much bigger than you, he said, these are my terms. My terms are the ones that enclose yous. Yous are all enclosed. But yous all know that already! I can tell it just by looking at your faces; your faces, telling these things to me. It's quite straight-forward when you come to think about it. Here you have me. Here you have you. Two sentences. One sentence is needed for you and one sentence is needed for me and you can wrap them all up together if you want to so that what you have in this one sentence is both you and me, us being in it the gether.

Please sir!

Yes sir?

Do you think that we shouldnt be here?

Aye and naw. Sometimes I do and sometimes I dont. I think your question's fine. I think for example in Pythagoras you'll find ways of looking at things, at flitting from one thing to the other. And oddly enough it really does have to do with transmigration and maybe even with certain taboos. It makes things fucking really interesting.

Patrick glanced at his watch. The weans didnt notice him doing it thank god. But he had taken great care for just that reason.

When the bell rang he was sitting on his stool with his elbows on the edge of the desk. He didnt look at the kids as they headed toward the door. He didnt feel like a terrible hypocrite. But nor did his stomach feel in as great a condition as it could be. A couple of the kids looked as if they considered lingering. Sometimes they did that in order to ask a question. There was nothing wrong with this in first-year classes. Patrick inclined his head in the direction opposite them and they soon departed.

JAMES KELMAN, *A Disaffection*, 1989

A LITTLE LEARNING

The word parse always struck me as sounding slightly ridiculous: even now it makes me smile when I look at it; but it conjures up for me a very clear picture of that quiet schoolroom: myself in a brown woollen jersey with my elbows on the table, and my tutor in his shabby tail-coat, chalking up on the blackboard for my exclusive benefit the first proposition of Euclid.

SIEGFRIED SASSOON, *Memoirs of a Fox-Hunting Man*, 1929

The Harrow custom of calling the roll is different from that of Eton. At Eton the boys stand in a cluster and lift their hats when their names are called. At Harrow they file past a Master in the school yard and answer one by one. My position was therefore revealed in its somewhat invidious humility. It was the year 1887. Lord Randolph Churchill had only just resigned his position as Leader of the House of Commons and Chancellor of the Exchequer, and he still towered in the forefront of politics. In consequence large numbers of visitors of both sexes used to wait on the school steps, in order to see me march by; and I frequently heard the irreverent comment, 'Why, he's last of all!'

I continued in this unpretentious situation for nearly a year. However, by being so long in the lowest form I gained an immense advantage over the cleverer boys. They all went on to learn Latin and Greek and splendid things like that. But I was taught English. We were considered such dunces that we could learn only English. Mr Somervell—a most delightful man, to whom my debt is great—was charged with the duty of teaching the stupidest boys the most disregarded thing—namely, to write mere English. He knew how to do it. He taught it as no one else has ever taught it. Not only did we learn English parsing thoroughly, but we also practised continually English analysis. Mr Somervell had a system of his own. He took a fairly long sentence and broke it up into its components by means of black, red, blue and green inks. Subject, verb, object: Relative Clauses, Conditional Clauses, Conjunctive and Disjunctive Clauses! Each had its colour and its bracket. It was a kind of drill. We did it almost daily. As I remained in the Third Fourth (β) three times as long as anyone else, I had three times as much of it. I learned it thoroughly. Thus I got into my bones the essential structure of the ordinary British sentence—which is a noble thing. And when in after years my schoolfellows who had won prizes and distinction for writing such beautiful Latin poetry and pithy Greek epigrams had to come down again to common English, to earn their living or make their way, I did not feel myself at any disadvantage. Naturally I am biassed in favour of boys learning English. I would make them all learn English: and then I would let the clever ones learn Latin as an honour, and Greek as a treat. But the only thing I would whip them for is not knowing English. I would whip them hard for that.

WINSTON CHURCHILL, My Early Life, 1930

The head-master was a clergyman, a good-humoured, easy-going man, as temperate, one had no doubt, in his religious life as in all else, and if he ever lost sleep on our account, it was from a very proper anxiety as to our gentility. I was in disgrace once because I went to school in some brilliant blue homespun serge my mother had bought in Devonshire, and I was told I must never wear it again. He had tried several times, though he must have known it was hopeless, to persuade our parents to put us into Eton clothes, and on certain days we were compelled to wear gloves. After my first year, we were forbidden to play marbles because it was a form of gambling and was played by nasty little boys, and a few months later told not to cross our legs in class. It was a school for the sons of professional men who had failed or were at the outset of their career, and the boys held an indignation meeting when they discovered that a new boy was an apothecary's son (I think at first I was his only friend), and we all pretended that our parents were richer than they were. I told a little boy who had often seen my mother knitting or mending my clothes that she only mended or knitted because she liked it, though I knew it was necessity.

It was like, I suppose, most schools of its type, an obscene, bullying place, where a big boy would hit a small boy in the wind to see him double up, and where certain boys, too young for any emotion of sex, would sing the dirty songs of the street, but I daresay it suited me better than a better school. I have heard the head-master say, 'How has so-and-so done in his Greek?' and the classmaster reply, 'Very badly, but he is doing well in his cricket,' and the head-master reply to that, 'Oh, leave him alone.' I was unfitted for school work, and though I would often work well for weeks together, I had to give the whole evening to one lesson if I was to know it. My thoughts were a great excitement, but when I tried to do anything with them, it was like trying to pack a balloon into a shed in a high wind. I was always near the bottom of my class, and always making excuses that but added to my timidity; but no master was rough with me. I was known to collect moths and butterflies and to get into no worse mischief than hiding now and again an old tailless white rat in my coat-pocket or my desk.

There was but one interruption of our quiet habits, the brief engagement of an Irish master, a fine Greek scholar and vehement teacher, but of fantastic speech. He would open the class by saying, 'There he goes, there he goes', or some like words as the head-master passed by at the end of the hall. 'Of course this school is no good. How could it be with a clergyman for head-master?' And then perhaps his eye would light on me, and he would make me stand up and tell me it was a scandal I was so idle when all the world knew that any Irish boy was cleverer than a whole class-room of English boys, a description I had to pay for afterwards. Sometimes he would call up a little boy who had a girl's face and kiss him upon both cheeks and talk of taking him to Greece in the holidays, and presently we heard he had written to the boy's parents about it, but long before the holidays he was dismissed.

W. B. YEATS, *Reveries over Childhood and Youth*, 1914

The modern schoolmaster is expected to know a little of everything, because his pupil is required not to be entirely ignorant of anything. He must be superficially, if I may so say, omniscient. He is to know something of pneumatics; of chemistry; of whatever is curious, or proper to excite the attention of the youthful mind; an insight into mechanics is desirable, with a touch of statistics; the quality of soils, &c., botany, the constitution of his country, *cum multis aliis*. You may get a notion of some part of his expected duties by consulting the famous tractate on education addressed to Mr Hartlib.

All these things—these, or the desire of them—he is expected to instil, not by set lessons from professors, which he may charge in the bill, but at school intervals, as he walks the streets, or saunters through green fields (those natural instructors), with his pupils. The least part of what is expected from him is to be done in school-hours. He must insinuate knowledge at the *mollia tempora fandi*. He must seize every occasion—the season of the year—the time of the day— a passing cloud—a rainbow—a waggon of hay—a regiment of soldiers going by—to inculcate something useful. He can receive no pleasure from a casual glimpse of Nature, but must catch at it as an object of instruction. He must interpret beauty into the picturesque. He cannot relish a beggar-man or a gipsy for thinking of the suitable improvement. Nothing comes to him not spoiled by the sophisticating medium of moral uses. The Universe—that Great Book, as it has been called—is to him indeed, to all intents and purposes, a book, out of which he is doomed to read tedious homilies to distasting schoolboys. Vacations themselves are none to him; he is only rather worse off than before; for commonly he has some intrusive upper-boy fastened upon him at such times, some cadet of a great family, some neglected lump of nobility or gentry, that he must drag after him to the play, to the panorama, to Mr Bartley's orrery, to the Panopticon, or into the country, to a friend's house, or his favourite watering-place. Wherever he goes, this uneasy shadow attends him. A boy is at his board, and in his path, and in all his movements. He is boy-rid, sick of perpetual boy.

CHARLES LAMB, *Essays of Elia*, 1823

She was fond of all boys' plays, and greatly preferred cricket, not merely to dolls, but to the more heroic enjoyments of infancy, nursing a dormouse, feeding a canary-bird, or watering a rose-bush. Indeed, she had no taste for a garden: and if she gathered flowers at all, it was chiefly for the pleasure of mischief—at least so it was conjectured from her always preferring those which she was forbidden to take.—Such were her propensities—her abilities were quite as extraordinary. She never could learn or understand any thing before she was taught; and sometimes not even then, for she was often inattentive, and occasionally stupid. Her mother was three months in teaching her only to repeat the 'Beggar's Petition'; and after all, her next sister, Sally, could say it better than she did. Not that Catherine was always stupid,—by no means; she learnt the fable of 'The Hare and many Friends', as quickly as any girl in England. Her mother wished her to learn music; and Catherine was sure she should like it, for she was very fond of tinkling the keys of the old forlorn spinnet; so, at eight years old, she began. She learnt a year and could not bear it; and Mrs Morland, who did not insist on her daughters being accomplished in spite of incapacity or distaste, allowed her to leave off. The day which dismissed the music-master was one of the happiest of Catherine's life. Her taste for drawing was not superior; though whenever she could obtain the outside of a letter from her mother, or seize upon any other odd piece of paper, she did what she could in that way, by drawing houses and trees, hens and chickens, all very much like one another.—Writing and accounts she was taught by her father; French by her mother: her proficiency in either was not remarkable, and she shirked her lessons in both whenever she could. What a strange, unaccountable character!—for with all these symptoms of profligacy at ten years old, she had neither a bad heart nor a bad temper; was seldom stubborn, scarcely ever quarrelsome, and very kind to the little ones, with few interruptions of tyranny; she was moreover noisy and wild, hated confinement and cleanliness, and loved nothing so well in the world as rolling down the green slope at the back of the house.

JANE AUSTEN, *Northanger Abbey*, 1818

I must confess I have very often, with much sorrow, bewailed the misfortune of the children of Great Britain, when I consider the ignorance and undiscerning of the generality of schoolmasters. The boasted liberty we talk of, is but a mean reward for the long servitude, the many heartaches and terrors, to which our childhood is exposed in going through a grammar-school. Many of these stupid tyrants exercise their cruelty without any manner of distinction of the capacities of children, or the intention of parents in their behalf. There are many excellent tempers which are worthy to be nourished and cultivated with all possible diligence and care, that were never designed to be acquainted with Aristotle, Tully, or Virgil; and there are as many who have capacities for understanding every word those great persons have writ, and yet were not born to have any relish of their writings. For want of this common and obvious discerning in those who have the care of youth, we have so many hundred unaccountable creatures every age whipped up into great scholars, that are for ever near a right understanding and will never arrive at it. These are the scandal of letters, and these are generally the men who are to teach others. The sense of shame and honour is enough to keep the world itself in order without corporal punishment, much more to train the minds of uncorrupted and innocent children. It happens, I doubt not, more than once in a year, that a lad is chastised for a blockhead, when it is good apprehension that makes him incapable of knowing what his teacher means. A brisk imagination very often may suggest an error, which a lad could not have fallen into, if he had been as heavy in conjecturing as his master in explaining. But there is no mercy even towards a wrong interpretation of his meaning; the sufferings of the scholar's body are to rectify the mistakes of his mind.

I am confident that no boy, who will not be allured to letters without blows, will ever be brought to anything with them. A great or good mind must necessarily be the worse for such indignities; and it is a sad change, to lose of its virtue for the improvement of its knowledge. No one who has gone through what they call a great school, but must remember to have seen children of excellent and ingenuous natures (as has afterwards appeared in their manhood): I say no man has passed through this way of education but must have seen an ingenuous creature, expiring with shame—with pale looks, beseeching sorrow, and silent tears, throw up its honest eyes, and kneel on its tender knees to an inexorable blockhead to be forgiven the false quantity of a word in making a Latin verse.

RICHARD STEELE (1672–1725), 'On Flogging Schoolboys'

Where Henley House was most defective from a modern point of view was in its failure to establish any social and political outlook. But there J. V. suffered not only from the limitations of a poorly financed private adventurer who had to make his school 'pay', but also from the lax and aimless mentality of the period in which he was living. The old European order . . . was far gone in decay, and had lost sight of any conception of an object in life. The new order had still to discover itself and its objectives. In the eighteenth century, a school in Protestant England pointed every life in it, either towards hell-fire or eternal bliss; its intellectual and moral training was all more or less relevant to and tested by the requirements of that pilgrimage; for that in the long run you were being prepared. That double glow of gold and red had faded out almost completely from the school perspectives of 1890, but nothing had taken its place. The idea of the modern world-state must ultimately determine the curriculum and disciplines of every school on earth, but even to-day

only a few teachers apprehend that, and in my Henley House days
the idea of that social and political necessity had hardly dawned. The
schools and universities just went on teaching things in what was
called the 'general education'—because they had always been taught.
'Why do we learn Latin, Sir?' asked our bright boys. 'What is the
good of this chemistry, Sir, if I am to go into a bank?' Or, 'Does it
really matter, Sir, now, *how* Henry VII was related to Henry IV?'

We were teaching some 'subjects', as the times went, fairly well,
we were getting more than average results in outside examinations.
But collectively, comprehensively we were teaching nothing at all.
We were completely ignoring the primary function of the school in
human society, which is to correlate the intelligence, will, and conscience of the individual to the social process. We were unaware of
a social process. Not only were Henley House, and the private
schools generally, imparting this nothingness of outlook, but except
for a certain gangster esprit-de-corps in various of the other public
schools and military seminaries, 'governing class' sentiment and the
like, the same blankness pervaded the whole educational organiza-
tion of the community. We taught no history of human origins,
nothing about the structure of civilization, nothing of social or
political life. We did not make, we did not even attempt to make
participating citizens. We launched our boys, with, or more commonly without, a university 'local' or matriculation certificate, as
mere irresponsible adventurers into an uncharted scramble for life.

H. G. WELLS, *Experiment in Autobiography*, 1934

It is very improbable, that out of the numbers of parents who send
their children to large schools, many should suddenly be much
moved, by any thing that we can say, to persuade them to take
serious trouble in their previous instruction. But much may be
effected by gradual attempts: ten well-educated boys, sent to a public
seminary at nine or ten years old, would, probably, far surpass their
competitors in every respect; they would inspire others with so much
emulation, would do their parents and preceptors so much credit,

that numbers would eagerly inquire into the causes of their superiority: and these boys would, perhaps, do more good by their example, than by their actual acquirements. We do not mean to promise that a boy judiciously educated shall appear at ten years old a prodigy of learning; far from it; we should not even estimate his capacity, or the chance of his future progress, by the quantity of knowledge stored in his memory, by the number of Latin lines he had got by rote, by his expertness in repeating the rules of his grammar, by his pointing out a number of places readily in a map, or even by his knowing the latitude and longitude of all the capital cities in Europe; these are all useful articles of knowledge, but they are not the tests of a good education. We should rather, if we were to examine a boy of ten years old, for the credit of his parents, produce proofs of his being able to reason accurately; of his quickness in invention, of his habits of industry and application, of his having learned to generalise his ideas, and to apply his observations and his principles; if we found that he had learned all, or any of these things, we should be in little pain about grammar, or geography, or even Latin; we should be tolerably certain that he would not long remain deficient in any of these.

MARIA and R. L. EDGEWORTH, *Essays on Practical Education*,
in 3 vols.; vol. ii, 1822

Latin I look upon as absolutely necessary to a Gentleman; and indeed Custom, which prevails over every thing, has made it so much a Part of Education, that even those Children are whipp'd to it, and made spend many Hours of their precious Time uneasily in *Latin*, who, after they are once gone from School, are never to have more to do with it as long as they live. Can there be any thing more ridiculous, than that a Father should waste his own Money and his Son's Time in setting him to learn the *Roman Language*, when at the same Time he designs him for a Trade, wherein he having no use of *Latin*, fails not to forget that little which he brought from School, and which 'tis ten to one he abhors for the ill Usage it procured him?

A Little Learning

Could it be believed, unless we had every where amongst us Examples of it, that a Child should be forced to learn the Rudiments of a Language which he is never to use in the Course of Life that he is designed to, and neglect all the while the writing a good Hand and casting Accounts, which are of great Advantage in all Conditions of Life, and to most Trades indispensably necessary? But though these Qualifications, requisite to Trade and Commerce and the Business of the World, are seldom or never to be had at Grammar-Schools, yet thither not only Gentlemen send their younger Sons, intended for Trades, but even Tradesmen and Farmers fail not to send their Children, though they have neither Intention nor Ability to make them Scholars. If you ask them why they do this, they think it as strange a Question as if you should ask them, Why they go to Church. Custom serves for Reason, and has, to those who take it for Reason, so consecrated this Method, that it is almost religiously observed by them, and they stick to it, as if their Children had scarce an orthodox Education unless they learned *Lilly's* Grammar.

JOHN LOCKE, 'Some Thoughts Concerning Education', 1693

As soon as I was clear of the door, I looked up into Ben's face, and said, 'Father, where are we going?'

'Well', replied he, 'I'm going to take you to school.'

'School! What am I going to school for?' replied I.

'For biting your grandmother, I expect, in the first place, and to get a little learning, and a good deal of flogging, if what they say is true; I never was at school myself.'

'What do you learn, and why are you flogged?'

'You learn to read, and to write, and to count; I can't do either—more's the pity; and you are flogged, because without flogging little boys can't learn any thing.' This was not a very satisfactory explanation. I made no further inquiries, and we continued our way in silence until we arrived at the school door; there was a terrible buz inside. Ben tapped, the door opened, and a volume of hot air burst forth, all the fresh air having been consumed in repeating the fresh lessons for the day. Ben walked up between the forms, and introduced me to the schoolmaster, whose name was Mr Thadeus O'Gallagher, a poor scholar from Ireland, who had set up an establishment at half-a-guinea a quarter for day scholars; he was reckoned a very severe master, and the children were kept in better order in his school than in any other establishment of the kind in the town; and I presume that my granny had made inquiries to that effect, as there were one or two schools of the same kind much nearer to my mother's house. Ben, who probably had a great respect for learning in consequence of his having none himself, gave a military salute to Mr O'Gallagher, saying, with his hand still to his hat, 'A new boy, Sir, come to school.'

'Oh, by the powers! don't I know him?' cried Mr O'Gallagher; 'it's the young gentleman who bit a hole in his grandmother; Master Keene, as they call him. Keen teeth, at all events. Lave him with me; and that's his dinner in the basket, I presume; lave that too. He'll soon be a good boy, or it will end in a blow-up.'

CAPTAIN MARRYAT, *Percival Keene*, 1842

My father certainly had the knack of drawing out his pupils. Long before modern methods in teaching geography, he kept telling them to ask why . . . why is Glasgow where it is? Why London? Why is there more rain on the west coast of Scotland than on the east? In geography he had no way of knowing how foreign names were pronounced. For him, the capital of Iceland was *Reeky-a-veek*, Bucarest was *Boo-carest*, Arkansas was pronounced with the final 's'. He had his own pronunciation; pencil was *pincil*, a lantern was a *lantren*, a physician was a *physeecian*. Yet he always knew the meanings of even the most uncommon words. If crosswords had existed in his day he would have been adept at them.

He used to have a class which he called Intelligence. We formed a half-circle and if the boy or girl at the top did not know the answer the one who did went up top. On one occasion I reached the top. The word was 'evident', and I said 'easily seen', but I had a very bad conscience later, for I had just learned the word from a saying of my brother Willie:

'That's quite evident, as the monkey said when he shat on the table cloth.'

I had a vague, frightening idea that the word was associated with shit and that my father knew it.

His method certainly gave us a vocabulary. And my father gave us a sound training in grammar, so that, even today, I have a mild shock when someone says: 'He spoke to Jim and I' or 'These sort of things are useless.' In teaching us Latin he showed us how it helped spelling; we knew that committee had two 'm's' because it came from con (with) and mitto (I send). That was all I ever got from Latin. I had just got to an appreciation of the lines of Virgil when I passed an examination and never opened a Latin book again.

That is the absurd feature about learning the Classics. One spends dreary years over the grammar and unless one takes Classics at the university the whole subject disappears from memory.

My father's teaching of geography consisted mainly of lists of names. I knew all the rivers of Britain, the cotton, the pottery, the iron towns. Snippets remain . . . Hexham famous for hats and gloves, Redditch for needles, Axminster for carpets. Yet, as I say, he asked us to ask why. To this day I feel that if I motor to Scotland I am going uphill; it was uphill on the hanging map.

I cannot recall having drawing classes in Kingsmuir. We had few books to write in; we had slates with wooden frames that did not last long. I can still hear the clatter of them on the floor, when we piled them to see who got the answer to a sum first. Later they were condemned as being unhygienic because we licked them clean, but I cannot recall that any of us caught germs from them.

My father had little humour but some imagination. He made history live for us. His selection of poetry, however, may have had some bearing on my later inability to appreciate poetry. Sentimental ballads . . . 'Little Jim', 'Lucy Gray', 'Mary, go and call the cattle home . . .', they all seemed to deal with early death and family grief.

But he did give us 'The Deserted Village' and no doubt we identified
him with the schoolmaster in it; 'He was a man stern to view.'

A. S. NEILL (b. 1883), *Neill! Neill! Orange Peel,* 1973

Like caterpillars, dangling under trees
By slender threads, and swinging in the breeze,
Which filthily bewray and sore disgrace
The boughs in which are bred th' unseemly race;
While ev'ry worm industriously weaves
And winds his web about the rivell'd leaves;
So num'rous are the follies, that annoy
The mind and heart of ev'ry sprightly boy;
Imaginations noxious and perverse,
Which admonition can alone disperse.
Th' encroaching nuisance asks a faithful hand,
Patient, affectionate, of high command,
To check the procreation of a breed
Sure to exhaust the plant on which they feed.
'Tis not enough, that Greek or Roman page,
At stated hours, his freakish thoughts engage;
Ev'n in his pastimes he requires a friend,
To warn, and teach him safely to unbend;
O'er all his pleasures gently to preside,
Watch his emotions, and control their tide;
And levying thus, and with an easy sway,
A tax of profit from his very play,
T'impress a value, not to be eras'd,
On moments squander'd else, and running all to waste.
And seems it nothing in a father's eye,
That unimprov'd those many moments fly?
And is he well content his son should find
No nourishment to feed his growing mind,
But conjugated verbs, and nouns declin'd?
For such is all the mental food purvey'd

By public hacknies in the schooling trade;
Who feed a pupil's intellect with store
Of syntax, truly, but with little more;
Dismiss their cares, when they dismiss their flock,
Machines themselves, and govern'd by a clock.

WILLIAM COWPER (1731–1800), 'Tirocinium; or,
A Review of Schools'

It was not my happiness to be bred up at the university, but all the learning I had was in the free grammar school, called Christ's school in the city of Gloucester; yet even there it pleased God to give me an extraordinary help by a new schoolmaster brought thither, one Master Gregory Downhale of Pembroke Hall in Cambridge, after I had lost some time under his predecessor. This Master Downhale having very convenient lodgings over the school, took such liking to me, as he made me his bedfellow (my father's house being next of all to the school). This bedfellowship begat in him familiarity and gentleness towards me; and in me towards him reverence and love; which made me also love my book, love being the most prevalent affection in nature to further our studies and endeavours in any profession. He came thither but bachelor of arts, a good scholar, and who wrote both the secretary and the Italian hands exquisitely well. But after a few years that he had proceeded master of arts, finding the school's entertainment not worthy of him, he left it, and betook himself to another course of being secretary to some nobleman, and at last became secretary to the worthy Lord Chancellor Ellesmere, and in that service (as I think) died. And myself, his scholar, following his steps, as near as I could (though furnished with no more learning than he taught me in that grammar school) came at last to be secretary to the Lord Brooke, Chancellor of the Exchequer; and after that to my much honoured Lord, the Earl of Middlesex, Lord high Treasurer of England; and lastly to the most worthy, my most noble Lord, the Lord Coventry, Lord-keeper of the great seal, in whose service I expect to end my days. And this I note, that though I were

A Little Learning

no graduate of the university, yet (by God's blessing) I had so much learning as fitted me for the places whereunto the Lord advanced me, and (which I think to be very rare) had one that was after a Lord Chancellor's secretary to be my schoolmaster, whom (by God's blessing) I followed so close, that I became a successor to his successors in the like place of eminent service and employment.

R. WILLIS (b.1564), *Mount Tabor*, 1639

My career at Temple Grove was quite undistinguished either in work or play. Indeed, it was rather worse than undistinguished. In going over my father's papers after his death, I found that he had preserved all my early school reports. They must have been most disappointing reading for him, for the last of them summed up my character with an incisiveness which must have been satisfactory to Mr Waterfield, if not to my father. At the end of a very inferior list of marks in various subjects, Mr Waterfield wrote: 'Hannay is incurably lazy.'

GEORGE A. BIRMINGHAM [J. O. Hannay], *Pleasant Places*, 1934

In mediæval England a poor boy's chances of picking up some crumbs of learning were rather unequal. Until the Statute of the Apprentices, which became the law of the land in 1406, a villein could be fined for sending his child to school instead of keeping him labouring in the fields, and this cruel decree may have robbed many intelligent boys of their one hope in life. On the other hand, it does not seem that the fines were imposed very freely or very frequently; otherwise why should William Langland, the grim contemporary of cheerful Chaucer, have complained so bitterly that 'every cobbler's son and beggar's brat goes to school nowadays'?

D. M. STUART, *The Boy Through the Ages*, 1938

The Church of England school which served our area (built in 1839) housed about 450 scholars and had a staff of eight, for the most part

376

highly unqualified. When I was twelve one lady assistant, teaching English, gave me a tap on the skull, scornfully crossed out the word 'masticated' from my composition and substituted 'massicated'. 'Chewing food to a mass,' she said, 'not a mast!' The sycophants about us sniggered. Back home with a dictionary I found myself gleefully right, though of course dared not mention it; but my respect for her scholarship plummeted.

ROBERT ROBERTS, *The Classic Slum*, 1971

At Barnfield I became my mother's son: I kept myself to myself and would not be beholden to anyone. I made no friends, partly no doubt because a great part of schoolboy friendships springs from the boys walking the same way home, and none of my classmates lived anywhere near Fussell Street. But perhaps I did make one friend, of a sort. He was a boy named Whipple, the son of a draper in a small way of business. He wooed me in his own currency, which was doughnuts. His wooing was not disinterested. He was fat and stupid but he had the grace to know it, and he fed me with doughnuts in return for tuition with his algebra and Latin. He must have told his parents about me, for, to my surprise, he came one day armed with messages inviting me to visit them on Saturday afternoon to help him with his work. I did so, and after that went every Saturday afternoon. The Whipples lived in what seemed to me enormous opulence: when we worked together on Saturday afternoons the two of us had nothing less than a room to ourselves, a room in which you could have put the whole ground floor of our house. I realise now that they had only just come into this opulence and that they were impressed by it almost as much as I was; for every Saturday, before lessons began, young Whipple would take me upstairs to see the bathroom, a thing which, needless to say, I had never seen before, and solemnly point out to me its grandeur, turning on the taps, both hot and cold, of the wash-hand basin and the bath and flushing the closet to prove to me that it worked.

After our lessons I was regaled with tea, such a tea as I never had at home. A kind of ceremony was made of it, with the parents, who were both fat and red, hovering over me and plying me with good things: steaming pork sausages, muffins, fruit cake, scones and strawberry jam. They obviously believed I did not get enough to eat at home; and always, when the meal was ended and it was time for me to go home, Mr Whipple would say, as though striking a fair balance of qualities, 'You may be poor but you're clever!' and then give me a sixpenny bit.

I am bound to say that I took easily to this patronage. Alas, it was not to last: when I had been at the school four terms I had suddenly to leave: my parents could no longer afford to keep me there. There was a new baby, and it was time I worked for my living.

This seemed to me so reasonable that though I left the school with sadness I did so without repining. Indeed, it was not until comparatively recently, that is within the past thirty years, that I suddenly realised how odd it was that the masters themselves should have made no effort to keep me there. I had after all been consistently at the head of my class. It was my son Phil who pointed out the strangeness of this. I can only think it was not strange then. Yet it was a wonderful experience for me, going to the Grammar School, one that changed my life. Or so I feel, for I cannot prove it. It opened my eyes to horizons I would not have glimpsed from Fussell Street alone. It was rich and strange. Those masters in their gowns were transfigured men, built, or so it seemed to me, on a vaster scale than ordinary humanity. They were Gothic like the building they inhabited, and their ferocity and eccentricity matched the gargoyles that looked down on us as we entered and left the school. I remember the headmaster, The Revd Mr Simmons, MA (Cantab.). How formidable I found him. I believe now that all schoolmasters cultivate some pet foible, some special branch of knowledge to which they attach transcendent importance. Mr Simmons's was mental arithmetic; but the problems he propounded were based on curious knowledge in which each boy, as he came to the school, had to be instructed. This was the length of the human intestines. I can see him now, at prayers in Big School, a giant in his black gown and black beard that completely hid his clerical collar. He reads the

General Confession with enormous dignity, in organ tones, we repeating the words with him, and then the Prayer for the Founder and the Lord's Prayer. And no sooner is the last amen said than, in one prodigious leap it seems, he has come from behind the lectern, is at the edge of the dais pointing an enormous hairy hand at a small boy and shouting, 'You, boy! The price of your tripes at threepence three-farthings a foot? Quick! Next. Next. Next.' And so, if the sum was at all difficult, in the end, 'Ashted!' I am afraid I was never wrong. 'Humph!' he would say, and then, 'Dismiss!'

I was there for fifteen months. There wasn't time for me to learn much more than that in any right-angle triangle the square on the hypotenuse is equal to the sum of the squares on the other two sides, *mensa mensam mensae mensae mensa mensae mensas mensarum mensis mensis* and *amo amas amat amamus amatis amant*. Yet even that was something, and indeed I found even so small an amount of Latin as I have invaluable in my work. As an engraver and die-sinker I was always having to cut Latin mottoes on medals and cups. Our customers were often men of much better education than ourselves, but that did not prevent me on numerous occasions from being able to correct their Latin grammar by inserting the correct case ending or the proper form of the verb. Indeed, on my smattering of Latin I have been regarded as a prodigy of learning in every workshop where I was employed.

WALTER ALLEN, *All in A Lifetime*, 1959; a novel based on the life of Walter Allen's father—called Billy Ashted in the book—who was born in working-class Birmingham in 1875

1624. I was not initiated into any rudiments till I was four years of age, and then one Frier taught us at the church porch of Wotton; and I perfectly remember the great talk and stir about il Conde Gundamar, Ambassador from Spain (for near about this time was the match of our Prince with the Infanta proposed).

1625. I was this year sent by my Father to Lewes, to be with my Grandfather Standsfield, with whom I passed my childhood. This was the year in which the pestilence was so epidemical that there dy'd in London 5,000 a week; and I well remember the strict watches and examinations upon the ways as we passed.

1626. My picture was drawn in oyle by one Chanterell, no ill painter. . . . It was not till the yeare 1628 that I was put to learne my Latine rudiments, and to write of one Citolin, a Frenchman, in Lewes. I was put to schoole to Mr Potts, in the Cliffe at Lewes; and in 1630 from thence to the Free-schole at Southover neere the town, of which one Agnes Morley had been the foundresse, and now Edward Snatt was the master, under whom I remained till I was sent to the University. This yeare my Grandmother (with whom I sojourn'd) being married to one Mr Newton, a learned and most religious gent. We went from the Cliff to dwell at his house in Southover.

1636. This yeare being extreamely dry, the pestilence much increased in London and divers parts of England.

13 Feb. I was admitted into the Middle Temple, London, though absent, and as yet at schoole.

3d April, 1637. I left schoole, where, till about the last yeare, I had been extreamely remisse in my studies, so as I went to the Universitie rather out of shame of abiding longer at schoole, than for any fitnesse, as by sad experience I found, which put me to re-learne all that I had neglected, or but perfunctorily gain'd.

JOHN EVELYN, *Diary*, 1624–37

When I went to a preparatory school in Seaford, of which one of my elder brothers was headmaster, I had received no serious education whatsoever. Strangely, I have never borne any grudge against anyone for this, although I have no doubt that it was the cause of my later failing, despite being a reasonably 'clever' boy, to get any scholarships. Nevertheless, a dislike of the idea of private education—rather than the thing itself—has always been prominent in my Socialist political views; and I suppose that my parents' well-meaning irresponsibility has played a part in forming it. My natural prejudice is to think of the middle classes as rather irresponsible.

Preparatory schools in general do not help to counteract this prejudice. Except for the very largest and most conventional—and these have always struck me as the most desolate and wooden-hearted institutions I have known—the great virtue of preparatory schools is that they are 'individual'. My brother's, being a small school, was peculiarly 'individual'. In the Twenties and Thirties the main thing asked by middle-class parents of preparatory schools was that the boys should be 'happy' and, if possible, excel at games. My brother, perforce as the Depression drew on—but I had left by then—was very insistent that the smaller the school the happier. I enjoyed my days there very much. It was a large and beautiful Georgian house with Victorian extensions, a walled garden, a ha-ha, and so on. The Ben Greet players used to come and give rather hammy but, to me, rapturous performances of Shakespearian comedies in the garden. The official school performances were confined to Gilbert and Sullivan, in which, without any voice, I sang many a role; it was agreed, however, and devoutly believed by me, that I was such a good actor that my singing didn't matter. I think that most of my spare time there was spent in organizing a number of other boys into acting games based on the books which I was then reading. Historical novels were my favourites: I remember organizing a series of Scarlet Pimpernel games in which I played Blakeney, Lady Blakeney, Chauvelin, Fouquier-Tinville with a bell, Robespierre, Marie Antoinette, the Prince Regent, and Madame Elizabeth, leaving only the boring parts of the King and the Dauphin for two other boys; the rest shouted happily under my direction as 'the mob'. Life was certainly never dull.

We had a very nice Captain Grimes sort of master who told us fabulous Philbrick-type stories about his life to illustrate the geography lessons—'Bilbao, a curious spot, in which I had more than one adventure,' 'The Marañon, an upper reach of the Amazon. I hesitate to speak to you boys about the sluggishness of that river.' We half believed him and half laughed with him. He was, I fear, entirely depressed by small losses at racing. My brother, too, could always be looked to for some sudden whim. We climbed the Wilmington Giant in snow before breakfast; we were sent out on to the Downs to find our own way home and returned very late indeed; dinner grew cold while we were made to fall in by the alphabetical order of our mothers' maiden names; once the startled visiting music master found the whole school—masters, boys, elderly matron and all—performing under my brother's directions an improvised 'Indian Dance' on the lawn. We had regular visits from lantern lecturers, readers aloud from Dickens, and 'entertainers', whose unconscious absurdities sent me and one or two sophisticated friends into convulsions of laughter almost before they started speaking.

ANGUS WILSON, in Brian Inglis (ed.), *John Bull's Schooldays*, 1961

We decree and ordain that there shall always be in our cathedral church of Canterbury, elected and nominated by the Dean or in his absence the Sub-dean and Chapter, 50 boys, poor and destitute of the help of their friends, to be maintained out of the possessions of the church, and of native genius as far as may be and apt to learn: whom however we will shall not be admitted as poor boys of our church before they have learnt to read and write and are moderately learned in the first rudiments of grammar, in the judgment of the Dean or in his absence the Sub-dean and the Head Master.

And we will that these boys shall be maintained at the expense of our church until they have obtained a moderate knowledge of Latin grammar and have learnt to speak and to write Latin. The period of four years shall be given to this, or if it shall so seem good to the Dean or in his absence the Sub-dean, and the Head Master, at most five years and not more.

We will also that whenever the Dean of our chapel royal shall signify to the Dean and Chapter of our Church of Canterbury that he is going to send a chorister of our chapel who has served there till he has lost his voice to be taught grammar in our church, the Dean and Chapter shall elect and receive without any fraud or evil craft that chorister so named and certified by the Dean of our chapel into the next place that falls vacant after that signification.

We will further, that none shall be elected a poor pupil of our church who has not completed the ninth year or has passed the fifteenth year of his age, unless he has been a chorister of our chapel royal or of our church of Canterbury.

But if any of the boys is found to be of remarkable slowness and stupidity or of a character to which learning is abhorrent, we will that after a long probation he shall be expelled by the Dean, or in his absence the Sub-dean, and another substituted, lest like a drone he should devour the bees' honey; and here we charge the consciences of the masters that they shall bestow the utmost possible labour and pains in making all the boys progress and become proficient in learning; and that they allow no boy who is remarkable for the slowness of his intellect to remain uselessly too long among the rest, but shall report his name at once to the Dean, or in his absence the Sub-dean, so that he may be removed and another more fit be elected in his place by the Dean, or in his absence the Sub-dean and Chapter.

> Cathedrals of the New Foundation, 1541, 'Grammar Boys and
> their Teachers'; in Leach, *Educational Charters and Documents*
> *1598 to 1909*, 1911

MRS PAGE. Is he at Master Ford's already, thinkest thou?

QUICK. Sure he is by this, or will be presently: but truly, he is very courageous mad about his throwing into the water. Mistress Ford desires you to come suddenly.

MRS PAGE. I'll be with her by and by; I'll but bring my young man here to school. Look, where his master comes; 'tis a playing-day, I see.

Enter SIR HUGH EVANS.

How now, Sir Hugh! no school to-day?

EVA. No; Master Slender is let the boys leave to play.

QUICK. Blessing of his heart!

MRS PAGE. Sir Hugh, my husband says my son profits nothing in the world at his book. I pray you, ask him some questions in his accidence.

EVA. Come hither, William; hold up your head; come.

MRS PAGE. Come on, sirrah; hold up your head; answer your master, be not afraid.

EVA. William, how many numbers is in nouns?

WILL. Two.

QUICK. Truly, I thought there had been one number more, because they say, 'Od's nouns.'

EVA. Peace your tattlings!—What is 'fair', William?

WILL. Pulcher.

QUICK. Polecats! there are fairer things than polecats, sure.

EVA. You are a very simplicity 'oman: I pray you, peace.—What is 'lapis', William?

WILL. A stone.

EVA. And what is 'a stone', William?

WILL. A pebble.

EVA. No, it is 'lapis': I pray you remember in your prain.

WILL. Lapis.

EVA. That is a good William. What is he, William, that does lend articles?

WILL. Articles are borrowed of the pronoun, and be thus declined: Singulariter, nominativo, hic, hæc, hoc.

EVA. Nominativo, hig, hag, hog; pray you, mark: genitivo, hujus. Well, what is your accusative case?

WILL. Accusativo, hinc,—

EVA. I pray you, have your remembrance, child; accusativo, hung, hang, hog.

QUICK. 'Hang-hog' is Latin for bacon, I warrant you.

EVA. Leave your prabbles, 'oman.—What is the focative case, William?

WILL. O—vocativo, O.

EVA. Remember, William, focative is caret.

QUICK. And that's a good root.

EVA. 'Oman, forbear.

MRS PAGE. Peace!

EVA. What is your genitive case plural, William?

WILL. Genitive case?

EVA. Ay.

WILL. Genitive,—horum, harum, horum.

QUICK. Vengeance of Jenny's case! fie on her! never name her, child, if she be a whore.

EVA. For shame, 'oman.

QUICK. You do ill to teach the child such words:—he teaches him to hick and to hack, which they'll do fast enough of themselves, and to call 'horum'.—Fie upon you!

EVA. 'Oman, art thou lunatics? hast thou no understandings for thy cases, and the numbers of the genders? Thou art as foolish Christian creatures as I would desires.

MRS PAGE. Prithee, hold thy peace.

EVA. Show me now, William, some declensions of your pronouns.

WILL. Forsooth, I have forgot.

EVA. It is qui, quæ, quod: if you forget your quies, your quæs, and your quods, you must be preeches. Go your ways, and play; go.

MRS PAGE. He is a better scholar than I thought he was.

EVA. He is a good sprag memory. Farewell, Mistress Page.

MRS PAGE. Adieu, good Sir Hugh. [*Exit Sir Hugh.*
Get you home, boy.—Come, we stay too long.

SHAKESPEARE, *The Merry Wives of Windsor*, IV. ii, 1623

I had scarcely passed my twelfth birthday when I entered the inhospitable regions of examinations, through which for the next seven years I was destined to journey. These examinations were a great trial to me. The subjects which were dearest to the examiners were almost invariably those I fancied least. I would have liked to have been examined in history, poetry and writing essays. The examiners, on the other hand, were partial to Latin and mathematics. And their will prevailed. Moreover, the questions which they asked on both these subjects were almost invariably those to which I was unable to suggest a satisfactory answer. I should have liked to be asked to say what I knew. They always tried to ask what I did not know. When I would have willingly displayed my knowledge, they sought to expose my ignorance. This sort of treatment had only one result: I did not do well in examinations.

This was especially true of my Entrance Examination to Harrow. The Headmaster, Mr Welldon, however, took a broad-minded view of my Latin prose: he showed discernment in judging my general ability. This was the more remarkable, because I was found unable to answer a single question in the Latin paper. I wrote my name at the top of the page. I wrote down the number of the question 'I'. After much reflection I put a bracket round it thus '(I)'. But thereafter I could not think of anything connected with it that was either relevant or true. Incidentally there arrived from nowhere in particular a blot and several smudges. I gazed for two whole hours at this sad spectacle: and then merciful ushers collected my piece of foolscap with all the others and carried it up to the Headmaster's table. It was from these slender indications of scholarship that Mr Welldon drew the conclusion that I was worthy to pass into Harrow. It is very much to his credit. It showed that he was a man capable of looking beneath the surface of things: a man not dependent upon paper manifestations. I have always had the greatest regard for him.

Winston Churchill, *My Early Life*, 1930

Sophie was a teacher. She had no formal qualifications at all, I think, had simply never left school but stayed on to teach the babies the three R's and did so until she retired in the 1950s, qualified eventually by experience, natural aptitude and, probably, strength of character. Besides, by then she had taught several generations of the village to read and write, probably taught most of the education committee to read and write. . . .

I read *The Rainbow* a little while ago, searching for some of the flavour of the lives of my grandmother and her family eighty years ago, ninety years ago, in a village not unlike Eastwood, only a little more gritty, and there was Sophie, teaching school like Ursula Brangwen but making a much better job of it, I'm happy to say, perhaps since nobody sent her to Sheffield High School and taught her to give herself airs. At that, I hear my grandmother speaking in my head.

ANGELA CARTER, 'Family Romances', in *Nothing Sacred*, 1982

When I was young, education for girls of the leisured class was decidedly indifferent. Governesses were chosen for their refinement and high principles, not because they were qualified to teach. Our discipline passed in turn from a small Hanoverian virago to an ignorant English girl who could not even keep order.

'What's the matter with Miss Harcourt?' my elder sister Victoria and I asked Mary one morning. 'She's cross and says we know why,' Mary sniggered. It seems she had crumbled biscuits into Miss Harcourt's bed, who, in consequence, had passed a miserable night. This sort of behaviour was no doubt a reaction from the over-severity of Fräulein Rebentisch. She, I believe, eventually became insane—because of Prussia's annexation of Hanover it was said.

It seems strange that we who were idolised by our parents, and indeed much spoilt by them, should never have told them how unhappy we were with our Fräulein. I suppose we took it for granted that governesses were immovable institutions and fancied that if we complained we should suffer for it afterwards. At any rate we said nothing though once an elder sister Victoria was made to walk for miles with a broken chilblain on her heel, and Mary, learning to read, was often battered and pinched until her poor little arms were pulp. I remember feeling like murder, and clenching my hands with suppressed rage until the nails ran into the palms at this ill-treatment of my sisters. It must have been bad for us to hate as we did then. So miserable were we that Victoria used to pray to die in the night; I used to pray that Fräulein might die!

The casual question of an uncle as to how we liked our governess

A Little Learning

finally brought about our deliverance. Startled by the answer he received, he went straight to our mother about it and she, horrified at his disclosure, sent the lady off to mourn the Hanoverian dynasty at home.

Victoria was eighteen months older than me, yet we were given the same lessons to learn. I remember my difficulty in mastering our daily task of three verses from St Paul's Epistle to the Hebrews, which Victoria repeated with correct precision. I could not understand a word, and no one ever attempted to explain the meaning of what was far too difficult for a child of my age to take in. Even the few verses which remain in my memory, such as: 'God, who at sundry times and in divers manners spake in time past unto the Fathers by the Prophets, hath in these last days spoken unto us by His Son,' I remembered more by the rhythm than the meaning. Further on in the Epistle I was completely lost, and yet our little German tigress expected and exacted a literal recitation of each parrot-learned verse.

We were made to get strings of dates by heart. We quite believed that the world was created in 4004 B.C., while we repeated with conviction the exact dates of Nimrod, the Babylonian captivity, and Alexander the Great. Alaric, King of the Goths, and Attila, King of the Huns, seemed to us a mysterious pair of twins on a par with Romulus and Remus. I cannot believe that a string of supposed facts was of the least use to us, and yet we plodded daily through three new dates, steeple-chasing over centuries, until we finally reached the accession of Queen Victoria.

LOUISA, LADY ANTRIM, 'Some Children in the Sixties', in *Little Innocents*, 1932

In winter, fogs of deep yellow often made dark the midday and it was cold. The windows of the Sixth Form were invariably closed, where thirty-two boys sat in pairs at sixteen varnished desks, grooved with many a knife, pencil, and pen recording initials and devices, while unending thoughts moved without will through heads avoiding the

388

keen blue eyes and pink dome of wisdom, truth, and honour ever-lastingly striving to uplift dull nature to the peaks. The classroom had for me a distressing smell, with hot air arising from pipes under gratings. Ceaselessly the Head, a brilliant scholar named F. W. Lucas, urged us to work harder, to get that mental power, illustrated by clenched fist vibrated like a metronome across his own brows. In his young manhood this exceptionally gifted man had obtained first place in the honours list for English History, Language and Literature at London University, together with first place for his MA Degree in Logic, Philosophy, and Economics; he had also taken a research course in Psychology for his Ph.D. at Freiburg, under Professor Munsterberg.

'Hard at it, boys, hard at it! Get that mental power! I saw your eyes, Williamson! Foxy, sir, foxy! No sugar in your tea for a week? Agreed? Very well. Now concentrate. Quite quiet, boys, quite quiet!' He would leave the room for a few minutes. Immediately the silence would erupt into gusty relief. 'Open the window, for God's sake. I'm stifling!' One unheeded cry among a buzz of voices. Perhaps the study door behind us would open suddenly, catching a figure pointing at the moisture running down the windows.

'Come along, sir! I'll gi'e you that cane! You will have to leave this school, sir, if you are not careful!' etc. Perhaps the offender would be reprieved, owing to the (exaggerated) terror on his face, and sentence be commuted to the Head's favourite charity. 'Do you agree to pay tuppence to the Fresh Air Fund, sir? You do. Put Williamson's name down for tuppence, Latymer. Next time, sir, you will not get off so lightly. You are the worst boy in the school, sir!'

HENRY WILLIAMSON, in Brian Inglis (ed.),
John Bull's Schooldays, 1961

Mr Stelling liked her prattle immensely, and they were on the best terms. She told Tom she should like to go to school to Mr Stelling, as he did, and learn just the same things. She knew she could do

Euclid, for she had looked into it again, and she saw what A B C meant—they were the names of the lines.

'I'm sure you couldn't do it, now,' said Tom; 'and I'll just ask Mr Stelling if you could.'

'I don't mind,' said the little conceited minx. 'I'll ask him myself.'

'Mr Stelling,' she said that same evening when they were in the drawing-room, 'couldn't I do Euclid, and all Tom's lessons, if you were to teach me instead of him?'

'No; you couldn't,' said Tom indignantly. 'Girls can't do Euclid, can they, sir?'

'They can pick up a little of everything, I dare say,' said Mr Stelling. 'They've a great deal of superficial cleverness, but they couldn't go far into anything. They're quick and shallow.'

Tom, delighted with this verdict, telegraphed his triumph by wagging his head at Maggie behind Mr Stelling's chair. As for Maggie, she had hardly ever been so mortified. She had been so proud to be called 'quick' all her little life, and now it appeared that this quickness was the brand of inferiority. It would have been better to be slow, like Tom.

GEORGE ELIOT, *The Mill on the Floss*, 1860

To ask, to guess, to know, as they commence,
As Fancy opens the quick springs of Sense,
We ply the Memory, we load the brain,
Bind rebel Wit, and double chain on chain,
Confine the thought, to exercise the breath;
And keep them in the pale of Words till death.

POPE, *The Dunciad*, 1728, Book II

The parents were gratified at receiving the following letter from their son—

My Dear Mamma,—I am very well. Dr Skinner made me do about the horse free and exulting roaming in the wide fields in Latin verse, but as I had done it with Papa I knew how to do it, and it was nearly all right, and he put me in the fourth form under Mr Templer, and I have to begin a new Latin grammar not like the old, but much harder. I know you wish me to work, and I will try very hard. With best love to Joey and Charlotte, and to Papa, I remain, your affectionate son,

Ernest.

Nothing could be nicer or more proper. It really did seem as though he were inclined to turn over a new leaf. The boys had all come back, the examinations were over, and the routine of the half-year began; Ernest found that his fears about being kicked about and bullied were exaggerated. Nobody did anything very dreadful to him. He had to run errands between certain hours for the elder boys, and to take his turn at greasing the footballs, and so forth, but there was an excellent spirit in the school as regards bullying.

Samuel Butler, *The Way of All Flesh*, 1903

The whole school was pervaded by a tone of slackness. Those who wanted to work, worked, but I was not one of them and there was no compulsion. In this my last year I had arranged my classes so that I had no home preparation at all, nor was the arrangement ever discovered. The principal masters were old, lethargic, drowsy. Nixon, the chief mathematical master, having chalked up a few questions on the blackboard, slumbered quite frankly through the remainder of the hour. All that was asked of you was that you should not disturb his sleep. If you did, he had a cane, and knew how to use it. Doctor Steen, the head, who taught Greek and Latin, was so blind that when a boy was sent to him in disgrace by one of the junior masters, all he had to do was to open the door softly and stand against the coat-rack—the Doctor would drone on without noticing him. Up here, in his room, on the broad window-seat, I sat with one or two others, looking down at the waiting cricket field, watching Henry Hull, the ancient porter, doddering about, listening to the

A Little Learning

subdued murmur from the town beyond, playing such games as could be played without noise. The construe was read openly from an English version: the questions were asked generally, so that two or three of the more industrious were deputed to answer for all. It was very peaceful, and nobody was ever punished. Those days, indeed, come back to me now faintly fragrant with what seems an old-world charm—they are like old letters one finds after long long years hidden in a sachet.

FORREST REID, Apostate, 1926

The method of teaching at Ellerslie was the exact opposite of that to which I had lately been accustomed. At the High School the mistress gave an excellent lesson or lecture, illustrated on the blackboard, at the end of which she would dictate questions, the answers to which we had to write at home in exercise books. There was one flaw in this: if I had not been attending properly during the lecture it was impossible to write the answers, and if, as often happened, I was absent with a cold, there was no means of making up the lessons. . . .

At Ellerslie the classes were small, generally about twelve of us. If they grew larger they were subdivided. We had a great deal of individual superintendence. We used textbooks, and a certain portion would be given us to prepare, not to learn parrot-fashion, as at The Turrets, but merely to get the gist of the thing. Then the mistress would begin her lecture; using the textbook as a basis she would question us on the facts we had learnt from it, and would very much amplify and enlarge the subject herself, adding all kinds of illustrations and explanations, and encouraging us to ask about what we did not understand. . . .

Ellerslie aimed at giving us an all-round education, with very wide and varied interests, but the subject upon which the curriculum concentrated was the teaching of English literature. I have never heard of any other school that spent so much time on this particular study. In every form there were at least three weekly lessons, one on the history of literature, including the lives and main works of all

392

British authors from Anglo-Saxon times to Victorian days, and the rest on selected plays and poems. Chaúcer, Spenser, Shakespeare, Milton, Defoe, Pope, Charles Lamb, and many another literary worthy became as household names. We knew every intimate detail of their biographies. We read extracts from their works and criticisms of their style. We learnt the rules of prosody and scanned their poems. We were taught the intricacies of the construction of a sonnet, and knew the difference between epics, lyrics, and the rest of it. Certain Shakespeare plays we studied exhaustively with notes, also *Lycidas, Il Penseroso, Marmion, The Lady of the Lake*, Bacon's *Essays*, and other classics. We copied voluminous notes, made by our teacher, on the more modern authors, Keats, Shelley, Tennyson, Browning, and Ruskin. We read Dickens aloud.

Every girl who passed up the school would have this tuition every other day for a period of six years, so she would be dense indeed if she did not derive some culture from it.

ANGELA BRAZIL, *My Own Schooldays*, 1925

We were not taught to be loyal: we were born loyal. That is to say, we were born sufficiently egotistical to believe that our own school was the best. I held this firmly myself, and yet, somehow, much as I loved my school I also loved staying away from it. There were few mornings on which I would not rather have stayed in bed than have hurried off after a bolted breakfast to the terrors of a Greek class with no lesson prepared. I doubt, indeed, whether, if it had not been for the wise urgency of my parents, I should have attended school oftener than once a week, or, perhaps, once a fortnight. Yet the love of the school was in my blood. Years before I went to it, I longed to go to it, as I afterwards longed to go to Rome and Florence. If I had been offered my choice among all the schools in the world, I should not have hesitated a second before choosing this one.

I did not at the time realize the labours I was letting myself in for. I saw the school in the golden haze of a dream with great men playing football for it in yellow-and-black jerseys. I had in my dream almost overlooked the endless necessity of preparing lessons. Not that I was hostile or indifferent to learning. I had felt a craving for a knowledge of the Latin tongue ever since I first saw the word *mensa*. I fell in love with Greek, too, at first sight, and, short of working, I would have done almost anything to become a Greek scholar. We human beings are often pulled two different ways, however. We may find the Greek language entrancingly beautiful; and yet at the same time may find the necessity of turning good English into bad Greek, a gross distraction from our amusements. We may worship Greece and nevertheless think the day's portion of Xenophon deadly dull.

The truth is, I never found it easy to sit in a room in the evening and read school-books or write stuff in exercise-books. I always knew that there were several of my fellow-schoolboys roaming about the streets and I could not bear to be wasting time over a grammar while there was better company to be had outside.

Robert Lynd, 'The Old School Tie', in *I Tremble to Think*, 1936

Gerald soon found out why Mr Percy was condemned on Sunday walks to walk alone. He was a man of cold temperament whose lessons were designed for the quick-witted and revealed nothing of his private life and thoughts on other subjects. He dispensed justice with uninterested impartiality, conferred no favours, and his periods were remarkable for absence of indiscipline. He accepted Gerald's arrival with the least possible fuss.

As Gerald accumulated his new form's textbooks in his desk and on the shelf by it, he was seized with a vague but intense excitement, as though within his grasp was some key to happy existence, and he perceived that even in the most unlikely places there resided a mysterious fascination. He saw, for example, that the last chapter of the algebra was on the Binomial Theorem, and the words struck him like the half-familiar words 'Gobi Desert' might strike a traveller who against all expectations is in fact about to start off on an expedition to Central Asia. One of the English books was *Twelfth Night* and in the pencil-scored pages of his copy he came with surprise on the phrase 'Excellent good, i' faith' which all last term he had heard used as a catchword by more senior boys, and observed its precise spelling, punctuation, and meaning (which had been obscured from him by its hitherto wholly oral tradition) with the ineffable pleasure of one who discovers the original setting of what has been corrupted to the song *Land of Hope and Glory*. In spite of the fears that had beset him as he made the change, he soon found that the work of the new form was not beyond his powers, and quite quickly he could look back on last term as the owner of an electric train remembers his clockwork mouse.

ROY FULLER, The Ruined Boys, 1959

Now it chanced that as I used to go along Highbury New Park to my school I had frequently met a girl on her way to the station, carrying books and obviously going to school herself. After a while we used to smile on one another and then came to saying 'good morning', and finally used to stop for a few moments' gossip.

'Where do you go to school?' was of course my first inquiry.

'The North London Collegiate, the biggest school in England, and the finest. You must have heard of it, and of its famous headmistress, Miss Buss?'

No, I hadn't, but I was not to be squashed, and she had to listen to my glowing description of our Prize-day.

'You call that grand!' she exclaimed. 'Why, who do you think gave away *our* prizes? The Princess of Wales!'

I had been duly impressed with this and with later information about the hundreds of girls, the examinations they were going in for, and the great assembly hall. I hadn't given much thought to these glories, but they came to my mind when we were wondering what school would be best for me. So I recounted to mother all I could remember about this big school, whose name, 'The North London Collegiate', had remained in my mind, as well as its locality— Camden Town. I also recalled the name of the head, Miss Buss.

Mother thought that she might venture a note to ask for particulars. A reply came at once to the effect that I might enter the school, provided that I passed the entrance examination, that I obeyed all the regulations, and that my fees were paid in advance.

'Entrance examination?' said I, 'Won't it do if you tell them I've passed the Senior Oxford?'

'Apparently not, dear, for I mentioned it in my note.' I felt that I was indeed up against something big. What would they expect for their entrance examination?

An afternoon was fixed for me to attend, and taking the train from Highbury to Camden Town I found my way to the school—a formidable-looking building. Seeing some steps labelled 'Pupils' Entrance' I went down them, told the first person I saw the reason of my appearance and was ushered into a room in the basement. Here I was provided with paper, pens, and ink, and various sets of questions which I could take in any order.

Keyed up as I was for something stiff, these papers seemed to me pifflingly easy. As for an explanation of the tides, I knew much more about them than men of science do to-day, and drew beautiful diagrams to show how the water was piled up, in Biblical style, with no visible means of support. A blank map of Africa was to be filled in with 'all you know', and I was still busily inserting rivers and mountains, towns and capes, when all the papers were collected. I had floored them all, even the arithmetic, and sat back in a slightly supercilious mood. The very large and motherly official (addressed as Miss Begbie) who swam towards me looked a little surprised as she gathered up my stack of answers, and was almost deferential as she said,

'Now, dear, just make a buttonhole before you go.'

This was a quite unexpected blow. I confessed that I hadn't the faintest idea how to set about it, and thought that buttonholes just 'came'. Up went Miss Begbie's hands in shocked surprise.

'What! A girl of sixteen not know how to make a button-hole!'

'Can't I come to the school then?' I asked in dismay.

'Well, possibly, dear. We shall see. But you must go home, learn to make a buttonhole, and come again this day week to make it.'

Mother was watching at the window for my return, and as she opened the door I exclaimed, 'I've failed.' How heartily she laughed when she heard of my disgrace. 'A buttonhole! Why, I'll teach you to make one in five minutes.' So indeed she did, and I practised the trick so assiduously all the week that even now I can make a button-hole with the best. Meanwhile mother made me a little case to hold needles, cotton, scissors, and thimble, to take with me, 'to look businesslike'. On the appointed day I appeared, was given a piece of calico, made my buttonhole, and went home. It seemed absurd to take the railway journey just for that, but it was a rule of the school that no girl should enter who couldn't make a buttonhole.

M. V. HUGHES, *A London Girl of the 80s*, 1936

In 1893 Bedales was started as a pioneer school for the children of those parents, who, in the words of John Locke, 'were so irregularly bold that they dare venture to consult their own reason in the education of their children, rather than rely on custom.' It was the aim of this new school to give an all-round education in place of the early specialization, which at that date still prevailed in public schools. Aptitude was put before mere knowledge, and to develop harmoniously the body and mind was considered more important than to obtain honours in examinations. Examinations were not, at that date, considered desirable; there was no system of marks or test-papers; versatility was more important than specialization; the young Bedalians were taught to turn their hands to all things, to make beds, clean windows and boots, cultivate gardens, make chairs and tables, milk cows and make butter. There was an emphasis on the dignity of all labour; no task was degrading. To give emphasis to this point, the elder boys cleaned out the earth-privies, under the direction of the head master, who did not on this, or on any other occasion, in the least unbend from his attitude of stern and dignified reserve. They wheeled the barrows into which Mr Badley shovelled the excrement, and very full he would load them for small boys to wheel, for there was no pampering, no thought of weak hearts or of young muscles strained to lift barrows, swimming to the brim.

E. L. GRANT WATSON, in Graham Greene (ed.), *The Old School*, 1934

I must have seemed a clever boy to the teachers, because it was decided that I should be entered for the Victoria Scholarship at 'The Whitgift'—the well-known public school in Croydon where I could have gone (to the preparatory department at first no doubt) as a day-boy. I learned that there was just one Scholarship open for boys like myself, and I can remember thinking about this with—in a childish sense—much misgiving. It was easy to see that I was the top child in my class, but I was not at all the sort of child who thinks that if a distinction exists, it is for him. I didn't in the least see myself as bound for the Victoria Scholarship. Anyway, Croydon for me meant simply the big High Street and the crowds, and wandering about in the toy department at Kennards. At the same time I was vaguely aware that Mr Cartwright the headmaster, and the others too, were being quite business-like and serious about it all. I now see that they thought they were going to get that Victoria Scholarship for their little school. Reviewing it all now, I suppose they were quite possibly right. Not that it matters much. Scholastic ability seems to me to go with car-performance or wealth, not beauty or goodness. It is just a possible means to good things, not a good thing in itself. As such it is rather a bore.

Anyhow, Mr Williams, a young and (as I found him) rather forbidding man, prim and severe, began to coach me in Latin from a slim book with 'Elementa Latina' in red down the spine. My mother tried to help me, but really all she could do was hold the book and hear me say 'to or for a table' and 'with, by or from a table' and 'Caesar kills Balbus' and things like that. 'O table' made us laugh and mystified us a bit: my mother had done some Latin at school, but 'O table' had mystified her then, and the years hadn't changed things. However, in those days the idea that the text book might ask one to learn wrongly, just didn't exist. To learn Latin was to learn

Elementa Latina. I don't think, even now, that there's any harm in this—for the bookish ones. When you're young and quick, it doesn't much matter whether your lessons have been rationalized and streamlined by someone clever and up-to-date, or not. The great thing is to be learning and learning.

Yet I don't believe I did very well with my Latin. A restricted family background—however affectionate, however co-operative— hinders a child's academic success because it leaves him doubting its value and unclear as to its upshot. My slim blue book had to be learned alone, and doing homework while all the others were playing, in order to go I didn't really know where or why. In the end, my Latin and all the rest came to nothing, and I got on by another road in another place.

JOHN HOLLOWAY, *A London Childhood*, 1966;
the period covered is 1920–7

Light was calloused in the leaded panes of the college chapel and shafted into the terrazo rink of the sanctuary. The duty priest tested his diction against pillar and plaster, we tested our elbows on the hard bevel of the benches or split the gold-barred thickness of our missals.

I could make a book of hours of those six years, a Flemish calendar of rite and pastime set on a walled hill. Look: there is a hillside cemetery behind us and across the river the plough going in a field and in between, the gated town. Here, an obedient clerk kissing a bishop's ring, here a frieze of seasonal games, and here the assiduous illuminator himself bowed to his desk in a corner.

In the study hall my hand was cold as a scribe's in winter. The supervisor rustled past, sibilant, vapouring into his breviary, his welted brogues unexpectedly secular under the soutane. Now I bisected the line AB, now found my foothold in a main verb in Livy. From my dormer after lights out I revised the constellations and in the morning broke the ice on an enamelled water-jug with exhilarated self-regard.

A Little Learning

I was champion of the examination halls, scalding with lust inside
my daunting visor.

Seamus Heaney, 'Cloistered', in Stations, 1975

As nothing would persuade Father but that he was a home-loving
body, nothing would persuade me but that I belonged to a class to
which boots and education came natural. I was always very sympa-
thetic with children in the story-books I read who had been kid-
napped by tramps and gipsies, and for a lot of the time I was inclined
to think that something like that must have happened to myself.
Apart from any natural liking I may have had for education, I knew
it was the only way of escaping from the situation in which I found
myself. Everyone admitted that. They said you could get nowhere
without education. They blamed their own failure in life on the lack
of it. They talked of it as Father talked of the valuable bits of
machinery he had stored on top of the wardrobe, as something that
would be bound to come in handy in seven years time.

The difficulty was to get started. It seemed to be extremely hard to
get an education, or even—at the level on which we lived—to
discover what it was. There was a little woman up the road called
Mrs Busteed whose elder son was supposed to be the most brilliant
boy in Ireland, and I watched him enviously on his way to and from
the North Monastery, but his mother had been a stewardess on the
boats and it was always said that 'they made great money on the
boats'. Of course, education implied nice manners instead of coarse
ones—I could see that for myself when I contrasted Mother's manners with those of my father's family—and I was a polite and
considerate boy most of the time, except when the business of
getting an education proved too much for me, and I had to go to
Confession and admit that I had again been disobedient and disre-
spectful to my parents—about the only sin I ever got the chance of
committing till I was fifteen.

So I was drawn to the policemen's sons and the others on the
Ballyhooley Road who produced all those signs of a proper educa-

tion that I had learned to recognize from the boys' weeklies I read. One boy might have a bicycle, another a stamp album; they had a real football instead of the raggy ball that I kicked round or a real cricket bat with wickets; and occasionally I saw one with a copy of the *Boy's Own Paper*, which cost sixpence and had half-tone illustrations instead of the papers that I read, which cost a penny and had only line drawings.

FRANK O'CONNOR, *An Only Child*, 1961

SOCIAL MOBILITY

Ah, the proved advantages of scholarship!
Whereas his dad took cold tea for his snap,
he slaves at nuances, knows at just one sip
Château Lafite from *Château Neuf du Pape.*

Tony Harrison, 'Social Mobility', in *The School of*
Eloquence, 1978

———

I recall the first day at County School For Girls as suffocating. My Burberry coat was so big that two of me could get into it. The sleeves went down to the floor and I couldn't hold anything in my hands because they were well out of reach, suspended where my elbows should have been. My mother had told me I would soon grow into it. My hat was down over my eyes. I couldn't see where I was going unless I put my head right back. I was carrying not only my satchel but my house-shoes bag which had strings so long that it trailed behind me. At least, I did not stand out in my Burberry as there were dozens of other hidden people inside dozens of gigantic macks.

It was a great relief when we were all given a hook in the cloak-room to shed our outdoor clothes. At last, relieved of my hat, I could count how many girls were wearing home-made gymslips. Not many.

Mavis Nicholson, *Martha Jane and Me,* 1991

In these comprehensive days of all-embracing jeans, it is hard to recall the social cachet which was attached to grammar school uniform. Thanks to caps and scarves the difference between 'passing' and 'failing' was visible to every neighbour. Green, maroon and navy blazers were the raiment of success. Second-hand jackets handed down from elder brothers and sweaters hastily knitted by grandma were the apparel of defeat. The lucky parents regarded the weeks of outfitting as a period of public rejoicing. They announced the dates of their visits to the recommended outfitters as if they were events in the social calendar. Close relatives were invited to attend the scene of the actual purchase as if it were a wedding or christening. . . . Aunt Annie accompanied my mother to Cole Brothers and paid for a blazer with crumpled old pound notes. Uncle Ern sent me five shillings wrapped up in a letter of congratulation which referred to me several times as 'the Prof'. The two half crowns were dropped into my National Savings money box and kept safe behind the two rows of teeth that prevented knife-assisted pilfering.

To my profound disappointment I was not allowed to deck myself out in the red and green before the first day of the new term. My mother wanted me to keep the livery free from dirt and stain until the great day actually arrived. And she believed that immediately parading the streets in the manifestation of my new glory would do nothing to encourage the reticent character which she regarded as essential to my future profession. For she had already decided that I should go to university and eventually become a history master at a grammar school—preferably one further up the ladder of parental preference than the one which I was about to attend.

To reinforce her strictures on the need for modesty she held before me the awful example of a boy from nearby Grove Avenue. This unfortunate youth was unlucky enough to possess parents who anticipated his enrolment at King Edward's—the city's most prestigious grammar school—by purchasing and allowing him to wear all the regalia of that institution even before the scholarship results were published. He was actually playing in the street, fully robed, when the postman brought the awful news that, far from passing for King Edward's, he had failed altogether. As a result of his parents' presumption he was required to enrol at some secondary modern dressed in the uniform of his hopes from which the insignia had been cut like chevrons torn from the tunic of a courtmartialled sergeant major. Despite the episode's total irrelevance to my condition, I was remarkably chastened by the story. For I had already begun to suspect that providence punished wrongdoers. And I had a vision of the awful retribution fate might exact from any act of presumption. It would take the form of a note from the Education Office saying that their previous letter was a mistake and I should report in September to Wisewood Secondary.

Roy Hattersley, *A Yorkshire Boyhood*, 1983

Public schools nowadays are, for good or for bad, altogether more informal and relaxed than they were, and even the bleakest and most games-obsessed appear to have been touched by the optimistic, subversive notions initially propagated in places like Bedales and Dartington Hall; with our dislike of organized games, fagging, prefectorial beatings and the sonorous pomposities of Victorian public school life, we were, perhaps, feeble forebears of what was to follow in the 1960s, when masters would shed their gowns and address the boys by their Christian names; when black jackets and boaters and striped trousers, and the minute gradations of privilege in terms of buttons worn undone or hands in pockets or the wearing of coloured socks were jettisoned in favour of sports jackets, anoraks and jeans, and when art rooms and string quartets mysteriously flourished.

Jeremy Lewis, *Playing for Time*, 1987

In the first decade of our troubled century, before Armageddon broke over the world, Dulwich Village was still the rural spot to which Mr Pickwick had retired nearly a century earlier. His villa stood just beyond the village, on the road to Sydenham, opposite a pathway called Lovers' Walk, a retreat arched by gigantic elms and black poplars, with green fields beyond.

In the centre of the village, near the Hamlet School, on a narrow triangle of ground hemmed in by the High Street and Court Lane, stood a Huguenot cemetery, its headstones and monuments awry, many of them yawning to show rough brickwork beneath the sculptured stone. Trees towered over the neglected tombs, and the annual tides of grasses and wild flowers rose above them, broke in spray of seeds, and ebbed again. . . .

Eighteenth-century villas abutted on the cemetery, facing cottages on the opposite side of the High Street that stood back in long gardens of lawn, hollyhocks, and mulberry trees embraced by roses. Towering over both the tall villas and the low cottages stood the ancient trees, so close and abundant that the whole village had the character of being abandoned at the bottom of a canyon green in summer, and brown in winter. Such an exuberance of foliage gave the neighbourhood an air almost of gloom, had it not been so serene; just as the features of a person lost in deep sleep will counterfeit an expression of despair, even though the soul behind them is at rest.

All this was in the immediate surroundings of my new school. The contrast with the environment of Surrey Lane could not have been more emphatic. I had been used to a sinister barrack of sooty brick, crowded by a network of monotonous streets. It was a wonderful experience to come out of school into quietude, to be able to walk under trees immediately I left the school gate, and to find among the boys a temper here and there congenial to my own. Within a few weeks of joining the school I made friends with two boys who remained my companions during the three years I spent there.

RICHARD CHURCH, Over the Bridge, 1955

Their children were indefatigable self-educators, examination-passers, and prize-winners; those shelves were crammed with prizes for good conduct, for aptitude, for general excellence, for overall progress, though my gran fucked it all up for my mother. An intolerably bright girl, my mother won a scholarship to a ladies' grammar school, a big deal, in those days, from a Battersea elementary school. My gran attended prize-days to watch my mother score her loot with a huge Votes For Women badge pinned to her lapel and my mother, my poor mother, was ashamed because my gran was zapping the option her daughter had been given to be a lady just by standing up for her own rights not to be. (My mother used to sing The Internationale to me but only because she liked the tune.)

ANGELA CARTER, 'Family Romances', in *Nothing Sacred*, 1982

How docile the lower orders were
In those days! Having done
Unexpectedly well in the School Cert,
I was advised by the headmaster to leave school
At once and get a job before they found
A mistake in the examination results.

And I almost did.

D. J. ENRIGHT, 'Scholarship Boys', in *The Terrible
Shears*, 1973

Even within our group of scholarship holders, and on the whole we did not distinguish the few fee-payers, there were small differences of grading which made one or two stand out: such as the boy whose doting widowed mother gave her only chick sixpence a day for sweets; we envied him mildly. He could go to the pictures on Saturday evening with a boy similarly privileged; that cost more than going to a matinée, and he could buy a comic as well. He became plump and spotty for a time but was quite generous and amiable . . . Neither he nor the one or two others as well-off for pocket money as he was, in the score or so who had moved up together towards the first big public examination at fifteen or sixteen, showed off or pushed their luck. I can recall no snobbery or bullying in that particular group.

Social Mobility

This was because for the first time in our lives we were in an environment created not by accident but by selection, an environment whose main purpose was to train clever children to make effective use of their brains. There was competition, inevitably; but since we were all being pushed from outside we tended, with a good sense we were not aware of having, not to compete overtly among ourselves. The school thought of itself as training us in more than the use of our brains; it offered diluted versions of some public-school values: a healthy mind in a healthy body, responsibility towards the community and the like. But these values were not urged with any great conviction. Brains plus tenacity were the main things.

RICHARD HOGGART, *A Local Habitation*, 1988

My first impressions of the new school were of new smells: the almost aggressive cleanliness of the buildings that rose up and smote the nostrils with the ubiquitous odour of carbolic soap. Then there was the smell of new paper, stationery, pencils, rubbers, exercise-books, on a much more generous scale than at the elementary school . . .

Unlike the elementary school, the school premises were too large for our numbers. This new secondary school, one of the girdle of schools built about the county as a result of the Education Act of 1902, had so far had rather a chequered, and even contentious, existence. It was by no means a success, nor had the people of the district as yet taken to the idea of secondary education. We were that term 120 in number, in buildings which were built to hold 200. So one had a great sense of space: empty classrooms unused, wide corridors, a staircase which we thought magnificent, an upper story with windows giving on to the football field and looking out across to the bay. (How different the circumstances to-day: the school so much bigger, divided into two, the boys and girls separated, and a large school evacuated there from Plymouth's agony.) It was very grand: one was impressed and happy from the first moment.

There were so many differences that struck the eye at once. You had a desk of your own, with books of your own provided by the County Education Committee for the benefit of minor scholars. You had separate books for different subjects and a sweet little book in which to enter up your homework. You had a hymn-book of your own, a special little school hymn-book, from which you sang at prayers in the morning. The masters and mistresses, no longer plain 'teachers', wore gowns: I think that was what impressed me most. And they changed with each lesson; you didn't have the same person teaching you (or not) all the day; masters and mistresses came and went with their subjects. It was thrilling.

A. L. ROWSE, *A Cornish Childhood,* 1942

Looking back I find it hard to disentangle and arrange in comprehensible order the whole impressions of those years. But I remember the beginning, the first day, well enough. I am not quite sure, but I dare say my mother had bought me a new suit, ready-made, and that I had been made to clean my boots the night before, and to see that my season-ticket was safe in my waistcoat pocket. My parents were decidedly not well off and they were no doubt very pleased and proud when I won a scholarship entitling me to the benefits of higher education. I dare say they may have had vague and happy dreams of my becoming a cashier in a bank or a traveller in leather or perhaps even a school teacher, and I did not tell them that I had already decided to become a farmer, or failing that, a professional footballer. . . .

In truth I was very sick and very nervous when the first day arrived. I had been very happy at an elementary school, where life was crude and exciting and where there was no homework and no punishment except the cane. The school was in the heart of the roughest quarter of a raw industrial town. Almost every day there would be ructions, and those ructions had rules as strict as the laws governing a Greek tragedy. They would begin with the schoolmaster questioning a boy and this would be followed by the boy cheeking the schoolmaster and this by the boy being called to the front of the class. The second act began with the boy refusing to obey and this would be followed by the schoolmaster seizing the boy by the scruff of his neck and dragging him out and producing the cane. After that the boy would be ordered to hold out his hand. He would hold it out, the schoolmaster would raise his cane, the cane would descend, the boy whipping his hand safely behind his back as the stroke fell. At that point the schoolmaster would lose his temper. Up would go the cane and come down again in a mad smash on the boy's shoulders. The boy, whimpering with rage, would kick the master's shins until the bone rang hollow. This sublime and sensational drama would go on until, as though warned by some telegraphic magic, the boy's mother would appear, rolling up her blousesleeves, to avenge her offspring. The fury of the tiger defending its young is a mild emotion beside the fury with which a shoemaker's wife of 1910 would defend her son. And I have never been able to swallow, since that time, the notion that women were altogether the passive and gentler half of humanity.

Life at the elementary school had therefore been very vigorous and sensational. It would, I knew, be very different at the grammar-school. I had not read the school-stories of popular writers for nothing. I knew very well that the masters would wear black gowns and possibly mortar-boards too. The prefects would have studies in which they fried sausages and drank beer on the quiet in the middle of the night and those boys whose parents were a little better off would wear Eton collars and the little black jackets my grandfather called bum-starvers. I should have to learn Latin and French and a new kind of English in which words like cads and rotters, and expressions like bally bounders and beastly fellows, played a large part. Life was going to be on a higher plane altogether. I was prepared for that. What worried me was that a preparatory course in a crude industrial elementary school was hardly the best sort of training for this new educational flight. I was very nervous and my stomach kept turning watery and sick. . . .

The first day was a great shock. In the train a sinister gentleman with a club-foot and very black eyebrows and a dark smear of moustache asked me my name, my mother's name, my father's

name, what my father did, whether I smoked, ordered me to call him
sir, and then proceeded to knock me flat on my back in the carriage
seat, leap on top of me and chastise my behind with a ruler. When
he had finished I stood up and he knocked me down again. It was
rather like the fight with the pale young gentleman in *Great Expectations*. When I recovered I was dusty and dishevelled and the
sandwiches my mother had packed up for my dinner were squashed.
Even so I was the neatest and best dressed boy in the carriage—so
much so that I felt conspicuous. As though thinking this too another
boy proceeded to knock me down, and a great many feet trampled
on me and my behind was belted with a leather strap from the
carriage window.

It was a severe, but not an extreme shock. I clung to my illusions.
Life was going to be higher and different—there was no possible
doubt of that. Horseplay and belting new boys' behinds was all very
well out of school, but I knew that life in the school itself was going
to be extremely serious and high-minded. I believe I hoped it was
going to be aristocratic too.

H. E. BATES, in Graham Greene (ed.), *The Old School*, 1934

Well, as Kavanagh said, we have lived
In important places. The lonely scarp
Of St Columb's College, where I billeted
For six years, overlooked your Bogside.
I gazed into new worlds: the inflamed throat
Of Brandywell, its floodlit dogtrack,
The throttle of the hare. In the first week
I was so homesick I couldn't even eat
The biscuits left to sweeten my exile.
I threw them over the fence one night
In September 1951
When the lights of houses in the Lecky Road
Were amber in the fog. It was an act
Of stealth.

Social Mobility

Then Belfast, and then Berkeley.
Here's two on's are sophisticated,
Dabbling in verses till they have become
A life: from bulky envelopes arriving
In vacation time to slim volumes
Despatched 'with the author's compliments'.
Those poems in longhand, ripped from the wire spine
Of your exercise book, bewildered me—
Vowels and ideas bandied free
As the seed-pods blowing off our sycamores.
I tried to write about the sycamores
And innovated a South Derry rhyme
With *hushed* and *lulled* full chimes for *pushed* and *pulled*.
Those hobnailed boots from beyond the mountain
Were walking, by God, all over the fine
Lawns of elocution.
                  Have our accents
Changed? 'Catholics, in general, don't speak
As well as students from the Protestant schools.'
Remember that stuff? Inferiority
Complexes, stuff that dreams were made on.
'What's your name, Heaney?'
                      'Heaney, Father.'
                         'Fair
Enough.'
        On my first day, the leather strap
Went epileptic in the Big Study,
Its echoes plashing over our bowed heads,
But I still wrote home that a boarder's life
Was not so bad, shying as usual.

SEAMUS HEANEY, 'The Ministry of Fear', for Seamus Deane,
in *North*, 1975

The world of the school and the world of the village didn't meet.
The school was twelve miles away and he travelled by bus every

Social Mobility

morning, returning home in the evening. All the good scholars from the outlying villages attended the big secondary school, standing old and tall and brown-fronted among the trees and leaves on the outskirts of the town. He had friends in the village and some in the school but they never met. When he was at school he could talk about his Highers: when he was in the village he would talk about fish and peats; and football. The only common factor was that he played football in both. Every morning at eight o'clock he would make his way to the bus, climbing an old wall and an old fence on the way, till he came to where the bus would pick him up.

IAIN CRICHTON SMITH, *The Last Summer*, 1969

Today the sharpest feeling is between the grammar schools and the secondary moderns, that is, between those who have gained a scholarship and those who have not in the eleven-plus examination. From the Grammarians it produces such poetry as:

Central School dunces
Sitting on the wall;
Grammar School scholars
Laughing at them all.

Modern School hams
Cannot pass exams,
Makers of mascots
Pushers of prams.

In return the home-work toilers are called 'Grammar grubs', 'Grammar-bugs stinking slugs, dirty little humbugs', 'Grammar School Slops', 'Grammar School Spivs', 'Grammar School Sissies', 'filthy twerps', 'Saps'. One 13-year-old Modern boy almost falls over his pen in his abuse: 'Gramer Swabs with heads like logs, with there nose so flat and eyes aslit the look so daft when the stand on a stick.'

At Caistor, in Lincolnshire, the Moderns chant:

Grammar fleas, mucky knees,
Hang them out to dry.

The grammar school pupils, without great originality, reply:

412

Social Mobility

Modern bugs, mucky lugs,
Hang them out to dry.

Chants are, indeed, frequently turned about so that they make
ammunition for either side, and sometimes the same squib is found
doing service all over Britain. A chant which enjoins respectfulness in
its hearers is current as follows:

Springfield cissies,
Westbourne rats,
When you see White House
Raise your hats.
Ipswich.

Craft School blockheads,
Council School cats,
When they see the Grammar School
Always raise their hats.
Lydney.

High School bulldogs,
Convent cats,
When you see Hinderwell
Raise your hats.
Scarborough.

Come Coronation bugs
Cock up your lugs
While Cockton Hill laddies
    pass yer.
Bishop Auckland.

Bishop Blackall cats,
When you come to our school
Please raise your hats.
Exeter.

Ardwyn school rats,
If you see Dinas School
Please raise your hats.
Aberystwyth.

IONA and PETER OPIE, *Lore and Language of Schoolchildren*, 1959

'Irma! Is it you, old sport? D'you mean to say you haven't heard the
news yet?'

'Only just this minute arrived, and I've flown straight upstairs. I
met Hopscotch in the hall, and asked, "Am I still in the Cowslip
Room?" and she nodded "Yes," so I didn't wait for any more. Has
anything grizzly happened? You're all looking very glum!'

'We may well look glum,' said Laura tragically. 'Something particularly grizzly's happened. You remember that day school at the
other side of the town?'

'The Hawthorns—yes.'

'Well, it's been given up.'

Irma flung her hat on to her bed and her coat after it.

'That doesn't concern us,' she remarked contemptuously.

'Doesn't it? Oh, no, of course—not in the least!' Laura's voice was sarcastic. 'It wouldn't have been any concern of ours—only, as it happens, they've all come on here.'

Irma turned round, the very picture of dismay.

'*What?* Not *here*, surely! Great Minerva, you don't mean it! Hold me up! I feel rocky.'

Laura looked at her, and shook her head in commiseration.

'Yes, that's how it took us all when we heard,' she remarked. 'You'd better sit down on your bed till you get the first shock over. It's enough to make a camel weep. I couldn't believe it myself for a few minutes, but it's only too true, unfortunately for us.'

'The Hawthorns! Those girls whom we never spoke to—wouldn't have touched with a pair of tongs!' gasped Irma.

ANGELA BRAZIL, For the School Colours, 1918

I can't help it, I still get mad
When people say that 'class' doesn't mean
A thing, and to mention one's working-class
Origins is 'inverted snobbery'.

The wife of a teacher at school (she was
Mother of one of my classmates) was
Genuinely enraged when I won a scholarship.
She stopped me in the street, to tell me
(With a loudness I supposed was upper-class)
That Cambridge was not for the likes of me, nor was
Long hair, nor the verse I wrote for the school mag.

Her sentiments were precisely those of the
Working class. Unanimity on basic questions
Accounts for why we never had the revolution.

D. J. ENRIGHT, 'Class', in The Terrible Shears, 1973

Social Mobility

I

αἰαῖ, ay, ay! . . . stutterer Demosthenes
gob full of pebbles outshouting seas—

4 words only of *mi 'art aches* and . . . 'Mine's broken,
you barbarian, T. W.!' *He* was nicely spoken.
'Can't have our glorious heritage done to death!'
I played the Drunken Porter in *Macbeth*.

'Poetry's the speech of kings. You're one of those
Shakespeare gives the comic bits to: prose!
All poetry (even Cockney Keats?) you see
's been dubbed by [ʌs] into RP,
Received Pronunciation, please believe [ʌs]
your speech is in the hands of the Receivers.'

'We say [ʌs] not [uz], T. W.!' That shut my trap.
I doffed my flat a's (as in 'flat cap')
my mouth all stuffed with glottals, great
lumps to hawk up and spit out . . . *E-nun-ci-ate!*

II

So right, yer buggers, then! We'll occupy
your lousy leasehold Poetry.

I chewed up Littererchewer and spat the bones
into the lap of dozing Daniel Jones,
dropped the initials I'd been harried as
and used my *name* and own voice: [uz] [uz] [uz],
ended sentences with by, with, from,
and spoke the language that I spoke at home.
RIP RP, RIP T. W.
I'm *Tony* Harrison no longer you!

You can tell the Receivers where to go
(and not aspirate it) once you know
Wordsworth's *matter/water* are full rhymes,
[uz] can be loving as well as funny.

My first mention in the *Times*
automatically made Tony Anthony!

TONY HARRISON, 'Them & [uz]', for Professors Richard Hoggart &
Leon Cortez, in *The School of Eloquence*, 1978

The school was academically sound but made it a matter of principle not to put much emphasis on these matters, to encourage leadership, community spirit, charity, usefulness and other worthy undertakings. Girls went to university but were not excessively, not even much praised for this. Nevertheless, Emily knew it was there. At the end of the tunnel—which she visualized, since one must never allow a metaphor to lie dead and inert, as some kind of curving, tough, skinny tube in which she was confined and struggling, seeing the outside world dimly and distorted—at the end of the tunnel there was, there must be, light and a rational world full of aspiring Readers. She prepared for the A level with a desperate chastity of effort, as a nun might prepare for her vows. She learned to write neatly, overnight it seemed, so that no one recognized these new, confident, precisely black unblotted lines. She developed a pugnacious tilt to her chin. Someone in her form took her by the ears and banged her head repeatedly on the classroom wall, crying out 'you don't even have to try, you smug little bitch . . .' but this was not true. She struggled secretly for perfection. She read four more of Racine's plays, feverishly sure that she would, when the time came, write something inadequate, ill-informed about his range, his beliefs, his wisdom. . . . On the evening before the first exam, Miss Crichton-Walker addressed to the whole school one of her little homilies. It was summer, and she wore a silvery grey dress, with her small silver brooch. In front of her was a plain silver bowl of flowers—pink roses, blue irises, something white and lacy and delicate surrounding them. The exams, she told the school, were due to begin tomorrow, and she hoped the junior girls would remember to keep quiet and not to shout under the hall windows whilst others were writing. There were girls in the school, she said, who appeared to attach a great deal of importance to exam results. Who seemed to think that there was some kind of exceptional merit in doing well. She hoped she had never allowed the school to suppose that her own values were wrapped up in this kind of achievement. Everything they did mattered, mattered very much, everything was of extreme importance in its own way. She herself, she said, had written books, and she had embroidered tablecloths. She would not say that there was not as much lasting value, as much pleasure for others, in a well-made tablecloth as in a well-written book.

While she talked, her eyes appeared to meet Emily's, steely and intimate. Any good speaker can do this, can appear to single out one or another of the listeners, can give the illusion that all are personally addressed. Miss Crichton-Walker was not a good speaker, normally: her voice was always choked with emotion, which she was not so much sharing as desperately offering to the stony, the uncaring of her imagination. She expected to be misunderstood, even in gaudier moments to be reviled, though persisting. Emily understood this without knowing how she knew it, or even that she knew it. But on this one occasion she knew with equal certainty that Miss Crichton-Walker's words were for her, that they were delivered with a sweet animus, an absolute antagonism into which Miss Crichton-Walker's whole cramped self was momentarily directed. At first she stared back angrily, her little chin grimly up, and thought that Miss Crichton-Walker was exceedingly vulgar, that what mattered was not exam results, God save the mark, but *Racine*. And then, in a spirit of almost academic justice, she tried to think of the virtue of tablecloths, and thought of her own Auntie Florence, in fact a great-aunt. And, after a moment or two, twisted her head, broke the locked gaze, looked down at the parquet.

A. S. BYATT, 'Racine and the Tablecloth', in *Sugar and Other Stories*, 1987

Social Mobility

. . . the Education Act of '44
Was our Great Leveller—the open door
For aspiring children of the industrious poor,

A tunnel from the prison and the pit
To the white collar and the Burton suit:
Examinations were the key to it.

Scholarship boys (some girls, not many) sat in
The Front Room doing Algebra or Latin,

Little Lord Fauntleroys without the satin
Or manners, dripping sweat and brilliantine
On books, a prophylactic medicine
To scour the memory of what had been.

A change of heart? At least a change of vowels,
Slapped on with elocutionary trowels,
Patrician honks for proletarian growls,

French menus, Swedish cars, smoked (not tinned) salmon,
U and non-U *à la* that Mitford woman,
No-one need ever know you started common.

JOHN WHITWORTH, in the *Independent*, 20 November 1992;
ode to Whitbread Poetry Prize Winner, Tony Harrison

School had begun to give me ideas above my station. Some of my rough edges were getting a bit smoother. So I was out to smooth the edges of anyone else who needed treatment, like Richard John Mainwaring, for example. I decided to point out to my father when he was making mistakes in his grammar—'Not *was*, it's *were*. Plural after a plural noun or pronoun.' I also picked him up on his pronunciation of words. If he dropped an 'h' I grimaced. That phase didn't last too long—not because I saw for myself how foul I was being, but because my mother put me right about it.

MAVIS NICHOLSON, *Martha Jane and Me*, 1991

When the Master was calling the roll
At the primary school in Collegelands,
You were meant to call back *Anseo*
And raise your hand
As your name occurred.
Anseo, meaning here, here and now,
All present and correct,
Was the first word of Irish I spoke.
The last name on the ledger
Belonged to Joseph Mary Plunkett Ward
And was followed, as often as not,
By silence, knowing looks,
A nod and a wink, the Master's droll
'And where's our little Ward-of-court?'

I remember the first time he came back
The Master had sent him out
Along the hedges
To weigh up for himself and cut
A stick with which he would be beaten.
After a while, nothing was spoken;
He would arrive as a matter of course
With an ash-plant, a salley-rod.
Or, finally, the hazel-wand
He had whittled down to a whip-lash,
Its twist of red and yellow lacquers
Sanded and polished,
And altogether so delicately wrought
That he had engraved his initials on it.

I last met Joseph Mary Plunkett Ward
In a pub just over the Irish border.
He was living in the open,
In a secret camp
On the other side of the mountain.
He was fighting for Ireland,
Making things happen.
And he told me, Joe Ward,
Of how he had risen through the ranks
To Quartermaster, Commandant:
How every morning at parade
His volunteers would call back *Anseo*
And raise their hands
As their names occurred.

PAUL MULDOON, 'Anseo', in *Why Brownlee Left*,
1980

'State schools are awfully good or can be,' said Trish Conte. 'My cousin went to one and she got into Cambridge—Girton actually.'

'So why should you not all go to state schools, I ask?'

'I don't know really,' said the girl called Xanthe Truelove, who's so happy being married to a rector now and edits *OD News*.

'My father tried to get his rates reduced because of fees,' said Trish. 'He said he saved the county money sending me away and not to any of their schools—to grammar schools and all those other schools, whatever they are called . . .'

'My brother was at the making of the film *The Guinea Pig*,' said Xanthe. 'He was an extra and got twenty-seven and sixpence a day.'

'I don't know what that's got to do with it,' said Harriet.

'*The Guinea Pig* is about a boy who's on a scholarship,' said Xanthe.

Harriet hardly ever went to films. They were not part of life for her.

'I know it seems an awful thing to say,' Oenone said, 'but I have noticed that now Karen has stopped saying "toilet", "pardon", and things like that, it's helped. At least I think it has.'

'She's very quiet and never has been bumptious,' said Trish Conte.

'Oh, well, she wouldn't be that, would she, anyway?' said Harriet.

Miss Bedford smiled the smile that gave her the name for formidably caustic withering wit. Hawklike she swooped on Harriet: 'I rather think you're saying that she knows her place.'

'I didn't mean it quite like that,' said Harriet, casting down her eyes and putting down her cup because her hand was shaking the tiniest bit.

'The boy in the film was played by Richard Attenborough,' said Xanthe.

'The county people said my father had to pay in full. He couldn't get reductions on account of fees he paid for me,' said Trish.

'She knows her place as a new girl, that is what I meant,' said Harriet.

Miss Bedford nodded. 'Suppose there were no private schools?' she said.

'My father says that would be against the freedom of the individual.'

'But what do *you* say?'

'My brother stayed on at school in the holidays to help in the making of the film *The Guinea Pig*. He got Richard Attenborough's autograph.'

ELIZABETH NORTH, *Dames*, 1981

My handsewn leather schoolbag. Forty years.
Poet, you were *nel mezzo del cammin*
When I shouldered it, half-full of blue-lined jotters,
And saw the classroom charts, the displayed bean,

The wallmap with its spray of shipping lanes
Describing arcs across the blue North Channel . . .

Social Mobility

And in the middle of the road to school,
Ox-eye daisies and wild dandelions.

Learning's easy carried! The bag is light,
Scuffed and supple and unemptiable
As an itinerant school conjuror's hat.
So take it, for a word-hoard and a handsel,

As you step out trig and look back all at once
Like a child on his first morning leaving parents.

SEAMUS HEANEY, 'The Schoolbag', in memoriam
John Hewitt, in *Seeing Things*, 1991

ACKNOWLEDGEMENTS

The editor and publisher are grateful for permission to include the following copyright material in this volume.

Ruth Adam, from *I'm Not Complaining* (Virago Press). Reprinted by permission of David Higham Associates Ltd.

Walter Allen, from *All In A Lifetime* (Chatto & Windus). Reprinted by permission of David Higham Associates Ltd.

Kenneth Allsop, quoted in *John Bull's Schooldays*, ed. Brian Inglis (Hutchinson, 1961), © Kenneth Allsop.

Kingsley Amis, from *What Became of Jane Austen?* (Cape, 1970), © Kingsley Amis 1970.

Florence Atherton, quoted in *Edwardian Childhoods*, edited Thea Thompson (Routledge & Kegan Paul, 1981). Reprinted with permission.

W. H. Auden, extract from 'Lord Byron' from Collected Poems, ed. Edward Mendelson; 'Honour' from *The English Auden: Poems, Plays* Repr. by permission of Faber & Faber Ltd.

Gillian Avery, from *The Best Type of Girl* (1991). Repr. by permission of Andre Deutsch Ltd.

H. E. Bates, quoted in *The Old School*, ed. Graham Greene (Cape, 1934).

Cecil Beaton, from *The Wandering Years* (Weidenfeld, 1961).

Theodora Benson, quoted in *The Old School*, ed. Graham Greene (Cape, 1934).

John Betjeman, extracts from *Summoned By Bells*. Reprinted by permission of John Murray (Publishers) Ltd.

Elizabeth Bowen, from *Pictures and Conversations* (Cape, 1974). Reprinted by permission of Random House UK Ltd. From *Friends and Relations* (1931). Reprinted by permission of Constable Publishers.

Jocelyn Brooke, quoted in *John Bull's Schooldays*, ed. Brian Inglis (Hutchinson, 1966). Reprinted by permission of Random House UK Ltd.

A. S. Byatt, from *Sugar and Other Stories* (Chatto, 1982). Reprinted by permission of Random House UK Ltd.

Ciaran Carson, from *The Irish Forno* (1987). Repr. by kind permission of The Gallery Press.

Richard Church, extracts from *Over the Bridge*. Reprinted by permission of Laurence Pollinger. Ltd., on behalf of the Estate of Richard Church.

Winston Churchill, extracts from *My Early Life*. Reprinted by permission of Curtis Brown, London.

John Clare, from *John Clare's Autobiographical Writings*, ed. Eric Robinson (OUP, 1983), © Eric Robinson 1983; 'Evening School Boys' from *Selected Poems and Prose of John Clare*, ed. Eric Robinson and Geoffrey Summerfield (OUP, 1967), © Eric Robinson 1967. Reproduced by permission of Curtis Brown Ltd., London.

C. D. H. Cole and Raymond Postgate, from *The Common People* (Methuen, 1938).

Margaret Cole, from *Growing Up Into Revolution* (Longmans Green, 1949). Reprinted by permission of David Higham Associates Ltd.

Jack Common, from *Kiddar's Luck* (Turnstile Press, 1951). From *The Freedom of the Streets* (Martin Secker & Warburg, 1938). Reprinted by permission of the publisher.

Barbara Comyns, from *Sisters by a River* (Eyre & Spottiswoode, 1947).

Cyril Connolly, from *Enemies of Promise*. Reprinted by permission of Rogers Coleridge & White Ltd.

Richmal Crompton, from 'William Holds the Stage', © Richmal Ashbee 1932, taken from

Acknowledgements

William the Pirate, reproduced with permission from Pan Macmillan Children's Books.

Richard Curtis, from the *Independent*, 31 December 1991. Reprinted by permission of Newspaper Publishing PLC.

David Daiches, from *Two Worlds* (Macmillan, 1957).

Donald Davie, 'To a Teacher of French' from *Collected Poems*. Reprinted by permission of the author.

Anthony C. Deane, extracts from *Time Remembered*. Reprinted by permission of Faber & Faber Ltd.

G. P. Dennis, from *Bloody Mary's* (William Heinemann Ltd., 1934). Reprinted by permission of the publisher.

Denis Donaghue, from *Warrenpoint* (Cape, 1991). Reprinted by permission of Random House UK Ltd.

Keith Douglas, 'Distraction' from *The Complete Poems of Keith Douglas*, ed. Desmond Graham (1978), © Marie J. Douglas 1978. Reprinted by permission of Oxford University Press.

Douglas Dunn, 'Glasgow Schoolboys, Running Backwards' and 'The Student' from *Barbarians*; 'Dominies' from *St Kilda's Parliament*. Reprinted by permission of Faber & Faber Ltd.

Josephine Elder, from *Evelyn Finds Herself* (1929). Reprinted by permission of Oxford University Press.

H. F. Ellis, from *The World Of A. J. Wentworth, B.A.* (1962). © H. F. Ellis 1962.

D. J. Enright, from *The Terrible Shears*. Reprinted by permission of Watson, Little Ltd.

Gavin Ewart, from *The Collected Ewart* (Hutchinson, 1980). Reprinted by permission of Random House UK Ltd.

E. M. Forster, from *The Longest Journey*. Copyright the Provost and Scholars of King's College, Cambridge. Reprinted by permission of The Society of Authors.

Roy Fuller, from *The Ruined Boys* (Deutsch 1959). Reprinted by permission of John Fuller.

John Gale, from *Clean Young Englishman* (Hodder & Stoughton, 1965). © John Gale, 1965.

Jane Gardam, from *Bilgewater* (Hamish Hamilton, 1976). Reprinted by permission of the Penguin Group Ltd.

Robert Graves, extracts from *Goodbye To All That*. Reprinted by permission of A. P. Watt Ltd. on behalf of the Trustees of the Robert Graves Copyright Trust.

Henry Green, from *Pack My Bag* (Hogarth Press, 1940). Reprinted by permission of Random House UK Ltd.

Tony Harrison, from *The School of Eloquence* (Rex Collings, 1978). Reprinted by permission of Peters Fraser & Dunlop Group Ltd.

L. P. Hartley quoted in *The Old School*, ed. Graham Greene (Cape, 1934).

Roy Hattersley, from *A Yorkshire Boyhood*. Reprinted by permission of Chatto & Windus Ltd.

Seamus Heaney, 'Singing School, I: The Ministry of Fear' from *North*; 'The Schoolboy' from *Seeing Things*. Reprinted by permission of Faber & Faber Ltd. 'Cloistered' from *Stations* (Ulsterman Publications, 1975), © Seamus Heaney 1975.

John Hewitt, from *Kites in Spring: A Belfast Boyhood* (1980). Reprinted by permission of the Blackstaff Press.

Richard Hoggart, from *A Local Habitation* (Chatto). Reprinted by permission of Random House UK Ltd.

John Holloway, from *A London Childhood* (Routledge, 1966). Reprinted by permission of the author.

David Hughes, from *But For Bunter* (Heinemann, 1985). Reprinted by permission of Sheil Land Associates Ltd. © David Hughes 1985.

M. V. Hughes, extracts from *A London Girl in the 80s*. Reprinted by permission of Oxford University Press.

L. E. Jones, from *A Victorian Boyhood* (Macmillan, 1955).

James Kelman, from *A Disaffection*, © James Kelman 1989. Reprinted by permission of Martin Secker & Warburg Ltd.

Acknowledgements

Philip Larkin, from *Collected Poems*, ed. Anthony Thwaite. Reprinted by permission of Faber & Faber Ltd.

Laurie Lee, from *Cider With Rosie* (Hogarth Press). Reprinted by permission of Random House UK Ltd.

C. Day Lewis, 'A Short Dirge For St Trinian's'.

C. S. Lewis, from *The Silver Chair* (Geoffrey Bles, 1953); from *Surprised by Joy* (Bles, 1955). Reprinted by permission of HarperCollins Publishers Ltd.

Jeremy Lewis, from *Playing for Time* (Collins, 1987). © Jeremy Lewis 1987. Reprinted by permission of Aitken, Stone & Wylie Ltd.

Penelope Lively, from *The House in Norham Gardens* (Heinemann, 1974). Reprinted by permission of Murray Pollinger, Literary Agent.

Michael Longley, 'Tu'penny Stung', first published in *Poetry Review*, vol. 1974, no. 4, 1985. © Michael Longley 1985.

Eamonn McCann, from *War in an Irish Town* (Penguin, 1974). © Eamonn McCann 1974.

Mary McCarthy, from *A Nineteenth-Century Childhood* (William Heinemann Ltd., 1924).

Sheena Mackay, from *Dust Falls on Eugene Schlumberger* (Gollancz, 1964). © Sheena Mackay 1964.

Louis MacNeice, extract from Autumn Journal (Faber). Reprinted by permission of David Higham Associates Ltd.

Derek Mahon, 'Teaching in Belfast', in *Poems 1962–1978* (1979) © Derek Mahon.

Arthur Marshall, from *Girls Will Be Girls* (1974). Repr. by permission of P. A. Kelland Esq.

James Lees Milne, from *Another Self* (Faber). Reprinted by permission of David Higham Associates Ltd.

Gladys Mitchell, from *Tom Brown's Body* (Michael Joseph, 1949). Reprinted by permission of Edward Cohen, Literary Executor for Gladys Mitchell.

Naomi Mitchison, from *Small Talk* (The Bodley Head). Reprinted by permission of David Higham Associates Ltd.

Malcolm Muggeridge, quoted in *John Bull's Schooldays*, ed. Brian Inglis (Hutchinson, 1961). © The Estate of Malcolm Muggeridge.

Edwin Muir, from *Autobiography* (1939). Reprinted by permission of Chambers Harrap Publishers Ltd.

Paul Muldoon, from *Why Brownlee Left*. Reprinted by permission of Faber & Faber Ltd.

Richard Murphy, from *New Selected Poems*. Reprinted by permission of Faber & Faber Ltd.

A. S. Neill, from *Neill! Neill! Orange Peel* (Weidenfeld, 1973). © A. S. Neill 1973.

Mavis Nicholson, from *Martha Jane and Me* (Chatto, 1991). Reprinted by permission of Random House UK Ltd.

Elizabeth North, from *Dames* (Cape, 1981). © Elizabeth North 1981.

Frank O'Connor, from *An Only Child* (Macmillan, 1961). © Frank O'Connor 1961.

Iona & Peter Opie, from *The Lore and Language of Schoolchildren* (1959). Reprinted by permission of Oxford University Press.

George Orwell, from *Boys' Weeklies* and from *The Road to Wigan Pier*. Reprinted by permission of A. M. Heath on behalf of the estate of the late Sonia Brownell Orwell and Martin Secker & Warburg.

Tom Paulin, 'Rosetta Stone' from *Fivemiletown*, and 'Politic' from *Liberty Tree*. Reprinted by permission of Faber & Faber Ltd.

Anthony Powell, from *A Question of Upbringing* (William Heinemann, 1951). Reprinted by permission of David Higham Associates Ltd. and the publisher.

Alan Pryce-Jones, from *The Bonus of Laughter* (Hamish Hamilton, 1987). © Alan Pryce-Jones 1987.

Sir Arthur Quiller-Couch, from *The Art of Writing* (*Lectures 1913–1914*). Reprinted by permission of Cambridge University Press.

Simon Raven, from *The Old School* (Hamish Hamilton, 1986). © Simon Raven 1986.

Acknowledgements

Gwen Raverat, extracts from *Period Piece*. Reprinted by permission of Faber & Faber Ltd.

Herbert Read, from *The Falcon and the Dove* (Faber, 1940).

Peter Reading, from *Tom O'Bedlam's Beauties*, © Peter Reading 1981. Reprinted by permission of Martin Secker & Warburg Ltd.

Forrest Reid, from *Apostate*. Reprinted by permission of Faber & Faber Ltd.

Robert Roberts, extracts from *A Ragged Schooling* (1976) and *The Classic Slum* (1971). Reprinted by permission of Manchester University Press.

Alan Ross, from *Blindfold Games* (Collins Harvill, 1986). © Alan Ross 1986.

A.L. Rowse, from *A Cornish Childhood*. Reprinted by permission of John Johnson (Authors' Agent) Ltd.

Siegfried Sassoon, from *Memoirs of a Fox-Hunting Man*. Reprinted by permission of Faber & Faber Ltd.

Iain Crichton Smith, from *The Last Summer* (1969). Reprinted by permission of Victor Gollancz Ltd.

Stevie Smith, from *The Collected Poems of Stevie Smith* (Penguin 20th Century Classics). Reprinted by permission of James MacGibbon.

Muriel Spark, from *The Prime of Miss Jean Brodie* (Macmillan). Reprinted by permission of David Higham Associates Ltd.

Stephen Spender, from *Collected Poems*. Reprinted by permission of Peters Fraser & Dunlop Group Ltd.

Geraldine Symons, from *Children in the Close*. Reprinted by permission of the author.

A. J. P. Taylor, from *A Personal History* (Hamish Hamilton). Reprinted by permission of David Higham Associates Ltd.

Dylan Thomas, extracts from *Portrait of the Artist as a Young Dog* (Dent) and *Portrait of the Artist as a Young Boy* (Dent). Reprinted by permission of David Higham Associates Ltd.

Flora Thompson, from *Lark Rise to Candleford* (1945). Reprinted by permission of Oxford University Press.

Thea Thompson, from *Edwardian Childhoods*. Reprinted by permission of Routledge & Kegan Paul.

Alec Waugh, from *The Loom of Youth* (Methuen). Reprinted by permission of Peters Fraser & Dunlop Group Ltd.

Evelyn Waugh, from *A Little Learning* and from *Decline and Fall*. Reprinted by permission of Peters Fraser & Dunlop Group Ltd.

Denton Welch, extracts from *Maiden Voyage* (Routledge, 1943). © Denton Welch 1943.

H. G. Wells, from *Experiment in Autobiography*. Reprinted by permission of A. P. Watt Ltd., on behalf of the Literary Executors of the Estate of H. G. Wells.

Antonia White, in *The Old School*, ed. Graham Greene (Cape, 1934). © the Literary Executors of Antonia White.

John Whitworth, first published in the *Independent*, 20 November 1992. © John Whitworth 1992.

Raymond Williams, from *Border Country* (Chatto, 1960). Reprinted by permission of Random House UK Ltd.

Angus Wilson, quoted in *John Bull's Schooldays*, ed. Brian Inglis (Hutchinson, 1961).

Annie Wilson, quoted in *Edwardian Childhoods*, ed. Thea Thompson (Routledge & Kegan Paul, 1981).

P. G. Wodehouse, extracts from *Mike and Psmith*. Reprinted by permission of A. P. Watt Ltd., on behalf of the Trustees of the Wodehouse Estate.

George Woodcock, quoted in *John Bull's Schooldays*, ed. Brian Inglis (Hutchinson, 1961).

Although every effort has been made to establish copyright and contact copyright holders prior to printing this has not always been possible. We apologise for any apparent negligence.

INDEX

Index

Index